CHRISTOPHER HIBBERT

NAPOLEON

HIS WIVES
AND WOMEN

HarperCollinsPublishers

HarperCollins*Publishers*
77–85 Fulham Palace Road,
Hammersmith, London W6 8JB

The HarperCollins website address is:
www.**fire**and**water**.com

This paperback edition 2003
1 3 5 7 9 8 6 4 2

First published in Great Britain
by HarperCollins*Publishers* 2002

ISBN 0 00 653146 6

Set in PostScript Linotype Minion
with Bodoni and Spectrum display

Printed and bound in Great Britain by
Clays Ltd, St Ives plc

For Peter and Nanette
with love

CONTENTS

CONTENTS

LIST OF ILLUSTRATIONS

Napoleon's birthplace.

Maria Letizia Ramolino Buonaparte, Napoleon's mother. *Painting by François-Pascal-Simon, Baron Gérard.* © *National Gallery of Scotland, Edinburgh/The Bridgeman Art Library, London*

The future Empress Josephine. © *Rex Features*

Viscount Alexandre-François-Marie de Beauharnais. *Painting by Georges Rouget.* © *Château de Versailles, France/The Bridgeman Art Library, London*

Désirée Clary, Princess Royal of Sweden. *Painting by François-Pascal-Simon, Baron Gérard.* © *Musée Marmottan, Paris/ The Bridgeman Art Library, London*

Josephine arriving to visit Bonaparte in Italy on the banks of Lake Garda. *Painting by Hippolyte Lecomte.* © *Château de Malmaison, Paris/ The Bridgeman Art Library, London*

Napoleon on the bridge at Arcola, Italy. © *Mary Evans Picture Library*

Madame Theresa Tallien and the Empress Josephine dancing naked before the Vicomte de Barras in the winter of 1797. *Coloured engraving by James Gillray. Musée de la Révolution Française, Vizille/The Bridgeman Art Library, London*

Napoleon in the Orangery at St Cloud, 1799. © *Rex Features*

Empress Josephine. © *Wallace Collection, London/The Bridgeman Art Library, London*

Pauline Bonaparte, Princess Borghese. *Painting by Robert Lefevre.* © *Château de Malmaison, Paris/The Bridgeman Art Library, London*

Marie Pauline Bonaparte, Princess Borghese. *Painting by Marie Guilhelmine Benoist.* © *Château de Versailles, France/The Bridgeman Art Library, London*

Pauline Borghese. *Sculpture by Antonio Canova.* © *Galleria Borghese, Rome/The Bridgeman Art Library, London*

Elisa Bonaparte, Grand Duchess of Tuscany and her daughter Napoléone-Elisa. *Painting by Pietro Benvenuti.* © *Château de Fontainebleau, Seine-et-Marne/The Bridgeman Art Library, London*

Caroline Murat, Queen of Naples. *Painting by François-Pascal-Simon, Baron Gérard.* © *Christie's London/The Bridgeman Art Library, London*

Joachim Murat. *Painting by François-Pascal-Simon, Baron Gérard.* © *Museo Nazionale di San Martino, Italy/The Bridgeman Art Library, London*

Jérôme Bonaparte, King of Westphalia. *Painting by François Joseph Kinson.* © *Château de Versailles, France/Photo RMN*

Louis Bonaparte, King of Holland. *Painting by Jean-Baptiste Joseph Wicar.* © *Château de Versailles, France/Franck Raux/Photo RMN*

Lucien Bonaparte. *Painting by Robert Lefevre.* © *Château de Malmaison, Paris/Arnaudet/Photo RMN*

Joseph Bonaparte, King of Naples and later King of Spain. *Painting by Jean-Baptiste Joseph Wicar.* © *Château de Versailles, France/Photo RMN*

Napoleon in front of the Château de Malmaison, 1804. *Painting by François-Pascal-Simon, Baron Gérard.* © *Château de Malmaison, Paris/ The Bridgeman Art Library, London*

Charles Maurice de Talleyrand-Périgord. *Painting by Pierre-Paul Prud'hon.* © *Château de Valencay, Paris/The Bridgeman Art Library*

Empress Josephine at Malmaison. *Painting by François-Pascal-Simon, Baron Gérard.* © *Château de Malmaison, Paris/The Bridgeman Art Library, London*

Portrait of the singer Grassini. *Painting by Louise Elizabeth Vigée-Lebrun.* © *Musée des Beaux-Arts, Rouen/Peter Willi/The Bridgeman Art Library, London*

Marie Laczinska, Countess Walewska. *Painting by François-Pascal-Simon, Baron Gérard.* © *Château de Versailles, France/The Bridgeman Art Library, London*

Marie Walewska. *Painting by Robert Lefevre.* © *Hulton Archive*

Marguerite-Joséphine Weimer, the actress Mlle George.

Madame Récamier. *Painting by Jacques-Louis David. © Louvre, Paris/ The Bridgeman Art Library, London*

A detail from the Consecration of the Emperor Napoleon and the Coronation of Empress Josephine by Pope Pius VII, 1804. *Painting by Jacques-Louis David. © Louvre, Paris/The Bridgeman Art Library, London*

Satirical cartoon of Napoleon Bonaparte carving up the world. *© Mansell/Timepix/Rex Features*

A detail from Napoleon Bonaparte receiving Queen Louisa of Prussia at Tilsit, 1807. *Painting by Nicolas Louis François Gosse. © Private Collection/The Bridgeman Art Library, London*

Napoleon Bonaparte with his nephews and nieces on the terrace at St Cloud, 1810. *Painting by Louis Ducis. © Château de Versailles, France/The Bridgeman Art Library, London*

The divorce of Empress Josephine. *Painting by Henri-Frederic Schopin. © Wallace Collection, London/The Bridgeman Art Library, London*

Empress Marie-Louise. *Painting by François-Pascal-Simon, Baron Gérard. © Erich Lessing/AKG, London*

A detail from The Entry of Napoleon and Marie-Louise into the Tuileries Gardens on the day of their wedding, 1810. *Painting by Etienne-Barthelemy Garnier. © Château de Versailles, France/ The Bridgeman Art Library, London*

The marriage of Napoleon and Marie-Louise. *Painting by Georges Rouget. © Château de Versailles, France/Photo RMN*

Napoleon and Marie-Louise disembarking at Antwerp, 1810. *Painting by Louis Philippe Crepin. © Fondation Dosne-Thiers Musée Frederic Masson), Paris/The Bridgeman Art Library, London*

Marie-Louise painting a portrait of Napoleon. *Painting by Alexandre Menjaud, © Château de Versailles, France/The Bridgeman Art Library, London*

Marie-Louise with her baby son, the King of Rome, 1812. *Painting by Joseph Franque. © Château de Versailles, France/Arnaudet/Photo RMN*

Cartoon showing Napoleon and the King of Rome. *Cartoon by George Cruikshank/© Victoria & Albert Museum, London/The Bridgeman Art Library, London*

Napoleon, Marie-Louise and the King of Rome, 1812. *Painting by Alexandre Menjaud. © Château de Versailles, France/The Bridgeman Art Library, London*

Sir Hudson Lowe. *© National Portrait Gallery, London*

Napoleon, St Helena, the last stage. *Painting by James Sant. © Glasgow Museums: Art Gallery & Museum, Kelvingrove*

Longwood Old House. *© Hulton Archive*

ACKNOWLEDGEMENTS

For their help in a variety of ways I want to thank Dr David Chandler, Historical Consultant to La Société Napoléonienne Internationale, Richard Johnson of HarperCollins, Bruce Hunter of David Higham Associates, Frank Giles, Dr Francis Sheppard, Dr Philip Unwin, Captain Gordon Fergusson and Diana Cook. Juliet Davis helped me choose the illustrations for the book and Marian Reid edited it. Hamish Francis has been good enough to read the proofs and my wife has made the comprehensive index.

I am much indebted to Professor T. C. W. Blanning, Professor of Modern History in the University of Cambridge, for having read the book in typescript and for giving me much useful advice for its improvement.

CHRISTOPHER HIBBERT

The Bonaparte Family Tree

Joseph	NAPOLEON I	Louis	Lucien
(1768–1844)	(1769–1821)	(1778–1846)	Prince of Canino
King of Naples	m. (1)	King of Holland	(1775–1840)
King of Spain	Josephine	m.	m. (1)
m.	Tascher de la Pagerie	Hortense	Catherine Boyer
Julie Clary	(1763–1814)	de Beauharnais	(1773–1800)
(1771–1845)	*widow of*	(1783–1837)	
	Alexandre,	*mother of*	m. (2)
	Vicomte	Napoleon III	Alexandrine
	de Beauharnais	Emperor	Jouberthon
	(1760–94)	of the French	(1778–1855)
	and *mother of*	(1808–73)	
	Eugène,		
	Duke		
	of Leuchtenberg		
	(1781–1824)		
	and Hortense		
	(1783–1837)		

NAPOLEON I

m. (2)
Marie-Louise
of Austria
(1791–1847)
mother of
Napoleon II
King of Rome
Duke of Reichstadt
(1811–32)

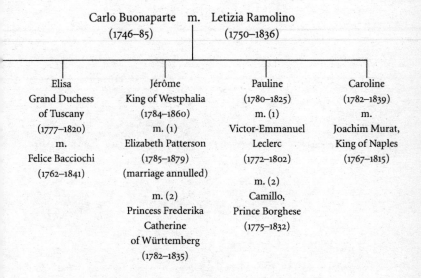

Carlo Buonaparte   m.   Letizia Ramolino
(1746–85)   (1750–1836)

Elisa	Jérôme	Pauline	Caroline
Grand Duchess	King of Westphalia	(1780–1825)	(1782–1839)
of Tuscany	(1784–1860)	m. (1)	m.
(1777–1820)	m. (1)	Victor-Emmanuel	Joachim Murat,
m.	Elizabeth Patterson	Leclerc	King of Naples
Felice Bacciochi	(1785–1879)	(1772–1802)	(1767–1815)
(1762–1841)	(marriage annulled)		
		m. (2)	
	m. (2)	Camillo,	
	Princess Frederika	Prince Borghese	
	Catherine	(1775–1832)	
	of Württemberg		
	(1782–1835)		

Napoleon also tacitly recognized four illegitimate children:
Alexandre Walewski, son of Countess Marie Walewska;
Charles Léon, son of Eléonore Denuelle;
a child of Albine de Montholon;
and a child of Mme de Pellapra.

I

THE CREOLE

'She longs to see Paris and has
a very sweet disposition.'

'CONTRARY TO OUR HOPES, it has pleased God to give us a daughter,'
Rose-Claire Tascher de La Pagerie wrote after the birth of her first
child on 23 June 1763. The baby's father, Joseph Tascher de La Pagerie,
had wished for a son who might, as he himself had done, obtain a post
as a page at court at Versailles – far away from the family's sugar
plantation on the West Indian island of Martinique. The mother had
hoped that the birth of a boy might reconcile her husband to a marriage
which was not a happy one, and which led him to seek such pleasures
as could be found in Fort Royal, the capital of Martinique, where he
was known to spend much of the day playing cards and was believed
to spend the nights in bed with his black mistress.

In his plantation he took scant interest. His father had sailed out
from France in 1726, having high hopes of making his fortune as so
many Creoles – West Indians of European descent – contrived to do.
But he was not a successful planter. Nor was his son and, by the time
his grandchild was born, the plantation's profits had fallen sharply, while
the number of slaves, once as many as 150, summoned to work at
half-past five every morning, had fallen to less than fifty.

These slaves, and the La Pagerie family, had all sought shelter in a
stone-walled wind-house on the night of 13 August 1766 when devastat-
ing gales and a tidal wave tore across the island, killing over four hundred
people, sweeping away the family's mill and slave quarters and all
the other wooden buildings of the plantation, and flattening the sugar

canes, the mangoes, custard apples, tamarisks and bread-fruit trees.

The La Pageries' large wooden house was not rebuilt and the upper floor of the refinery, above the clanking machinery crushing the sugar canes, became the three-year-old Rose's home. Seven years later, after her mother had given birth to three more girls, Rose was sent to a convent school in Fort Royal where she was taught how to behave as a young lady would have been expected to behave in France, how to dance and sing and play the piano, how to use a fan and conduct a polite conversation; but to academic instruction not so much importance was attached.

When she was fourteen, Rose left the school at Fort Royal, and eagerly looked forward to leaving Martinique for a more exciting life in France. The opportunity to do so had been given to her by her aunt, Désirée, the mistress of a *soi-disant* marquis, François de Beauharnais, who had been appointed Governor of Martinique and of several nearby islands. Having, for propriety's sake, married one of François de Beauharnais's aides, Alexis Renaudin – who had thrashed her savagely when he discovered her 'notorious conduct' with the Governor and who had returned home to obtain a legal separation – Désirée followed him to France in order to enter a counter-plea and obtain a share of his money. Soon afterwards, François de Beauharnais and his wife also sailed for France, where Mme de Beauharnais went to live in the country on her family's estate while her husband settled down in Paris with his mistress, Désirée Renaudin.

Désirée now set about arranging a marriage between one of her nieces in Martinique and her lover's son. She accordingly asked her brother Joseph and his wife to send over from Martinique at least one of their daughters as a bride for Alexandre, then sixteen and a half years old. Alexandre thought that the second of the La Pagerie daughters, Catherine, aged twelve, would probably suit him best after a suitable Paris education; but Catherine died of tuberculosis before this could be arranged. Since her sister Rose was considered, at fourteen and a half, too near Alexandre's own age, the youngest daughter, Manette, was then proposed. To be overlooked in this way was too much for Rose to bear. Usually so biddable and languorous, so lazily placid, she burst into frequent floods of tears until her father wrote to Alexandre's family:

The oldest girl, who has often asked me to take her to France will, I fear, be somewhat upset by the preference given to her younger sister. She has a very fine skin, beautiful eyes, beautiful arms and an unusual gift for music. She longs to see Paris and has a very sweet disposition. If it were left to me I would bring the two daughters instead of one, but how can one part a mother from both her remaining daughters when death has just deprived her of a third?

So, in September 1779, Britain having declared war on France the year before, Joseph Tascher de La Pagerie, his daughter Rose, and a freed slave named Euphémie, sailed for Europe in the *Île de France*. After a fearful, three-month-long crossing of the Atlantic in appalling weather, constantly threatened with interception by the English fleet and in danger of capture by pirates, M. de La Pagerie's weary party landed at Brest, where he immediately went to bed to await the arrival of his sister, Désirée, who, accompanied by his future son-in-law, Alexandre de Beauharnais, set out from Paris as soon as she heard that the *Île de France* had docked.

Alexandre was not disappointed by the appearance of his intended bride, shaken though she was by the tossing of the *Île de France* in the Atlantic's rough waters. 'Mademoiselle de La Pagerie may perhaps appear to you less pretty than you had expected,' Alexandre reported to his father, 'but I think I may assure you that her amiability and the sweetness of her nature will surpass even what you have been told about her.' He was not, however, so taken with the girl, now sixteen years old, as this description implied. She seemed good-natured, admittedly, but gauche and rather fat; and he might well have rejected her had it not been for the annoyance his rejection would cause his godmother, Désirée, who had been so kind to him since his mother's death.

As for Alexandre himself, he was certainly a handsome young man, self-assured in his army uniform; proud of the title of viscount and of that of marquis which had by now been officially conferred upon his father; attractive to women, despite a pompous, sanctimonious manner; and already highly satisfied to have been the lover of several ladies of whose names and ranks he made lists to indulge his vanity – one of them, who bore him a son, being the satisfactorily aristocratic comtesse Laure de La Touche de Longpré.

As well as being socially pretentious Alexandre de Beauharnais was also an intellectual snob, inordinately proud of having shared a tutor with the nephews of the duc de La Rochefoucauld, the writer and social reformer, by some of whose views he had been influenced without sharing those which might have damaged his standing in society.

Not long after Rose's arrival in France, on 13 December 1779, she and Alexandre were married. He than returned to his regiment in Brittany, came back to Paris for a few days and, later in the month, left Rose to go back to Brittany again.

2

THE DOOMED MARRIAGE

'Kindly take yourself off to a convent.'

ROSE SEEMED QUITE CONTENT. She was as delighted as she had expected to be with Paris where she lived with her aunt Désirée and Désirée's lover, the marquis, in the ancient part of the city in the rue Thévenot. Admittedly, it was a cold and draughty house, the rooms of which were cast into an unalleviated gloom by the tall houses on the other side of the narrow street, and often rendered noisomely offensive by the stench of the nearby tanneries and the effluent and pieces of skin and streams of blood from the butchers' stalls pouring sluggishly down the kennel. But, in these early days of her marriage, Rose does not appear to have been distressed by the discomfort of the house in the rue Thévenot; and even when her ambition of going to court at Versailles was denied her because of the dubious nature of the title which her husband had assumed, it was he rather than herself who was the more indignant in their shared disappointment.

He was rarely at home; and, when he was, he could not disguise the irritation which his wife's gaucherie and lack of education caused him. He suggested that she should learn the text of contemporary plays, even study Roman history so that she could converse with the kind of people to whom he was ashamed to introduce her. As it was, she was 'an object' who had nothing to say to him.

As time passed, however, and on those rare occasions when he returned from weeks spent away from the rue Thévenot on military duties or, more often, enjoying himself with other women, he did sometimes take his wife on excursions into Parisian society: to fashionable salons, to the receptions held by the duc d'Orléans's attractive if rather precise mistress, Félicité de Genlis, at the Palais Royal, and to the salon at the Swedish Embassy, presided over by Germaine de Staël, daughter of Jacques Necker, the Swiss financier, wife of the Swedish Ambassador, and brilliant woman of letters and conversationalist before whom the Duke of Wellington, in an unaccustomed gesture of obeisance, was to stoop on bended knee, and of whom he was to say, 'She was a most agreeable woman if only you *kept her light* and away from politics. But that was not easy. She was always trying to come to matters of state. I have said to her more than once, "*Je dêteste parler politique*"; and she answered, "*Parler politique pour moi c'est vivre.*"'

In such company, Rose, vicomtesse de Beauharnais, was, at first, a fascinated observer rather than an example of the influence of women over men, irritating her husband by expecting his attention. 'She has become jealous,' he complained, 'and wants to know what I am doing.' Exasperated by what he described as her possessiveness and pettish outbursts, he accepted his godmother's suggestion that he should make a tour by himself of Italy whence he wrote letters home expressing less enjoyment of his travels than envy of those who had been fortunate enough to have been left behind.

When he returned to Paris to a new house near the faubourg St Honoré, he decided he must soon go abroad again – this time to the West Indies, to serve with his regiment in order to gain some experience of active service against the British as a preliminary to a higher command.

Rose – who had borne him a son, Eugène, on 3 September 1781 and was now pregnant with their second child, Hortense – pleaded with him not to leave France again so soon; but he replied in peevish letters complaining of his lot and of a wife who did not, unlike the wives of other officers, write regularly to her husband. To Désirée he wrote to say that the comtesse Laure de La Touche de Longpré, the mother of his illegitimate child, would be sailing in the same ship as himself; so would she keep an eye on their son and the comtesse's other child while they were away and would she also, as the comtesse suggested, send a set of the game of lotto to occupy the idle hours of the long voyage. To his wife he wrote: 'I begin to fear that our marriage is turning out undeniably badly. You have only yourself to blame.'

The letters that subsequently arrived in Paris from the West Indies were almost hysterical in their fury. Her husband told Rose, 'the vilest of creatures', that he had learned that her behaviour at Martinique had been outrageous, and that, on the very eve of her departure for France, she had been discovered in the arms of a lover. 'What am I to think of this second child of yours,' he asked, 'born eight months and a few days after my return from Italy? I swear by heaven that it belongs to someone else. Kindly take yourself off to a convent as soon as you receive this letter. This is my last word on the subject and nothing in the world can move me to change it.'

Other letters from him followed in the same vein, upbraiding his wife and pitying himself, protesting his 'virtuous conduct', even though a man in whose house he had stayed at Fort Royal had locked his own wife up in her room, convinced that the vicomte had seduced her.

Self-righteous and indignant as ever, he returned to Paris, professing fury that Rose had not yet entered a convent as he had required.

His own conduct, he declared, was in striking contrast to his wife's unfaithfulness. His health was badly affected; his legs had become 'extremely weak'; this was due to his fearful state of mind; he was 'greatly to be pitied'. He was not, however, too ill to drive off with his son, Eugène, whom he was obliged to send back to the boy's mother by order of the Provost of Paris. He then demanded the return of both the jewellery which he had given his wife and the furniture in their house.

Since he could produce no proof of the wild accusations he made about his wife's behaviour, he was eventually compelled to retract them, to accept paternity of their daughter, Hortense, and to pay Rose an allowance of five thousand livres a year. With all this settled to her satisfaction, Rose moved into the convent of Penthémont in a fashionable part of Paris, a comfortable establishment which provided rooms for upper-class ladies in need, for one reason or another, of a temporary retreat from the outside world. Here, at the age of twenty-one, she embarked upon her delayed education, watching and listening to the sophisticated young aristocrats in whose company she now found herself, taking note of the subjects and manner of their conversation, assuming their graceful movements and seductive gestures, cultivating a delightful and rather husky tone of voice made all the more alluring by its melodious Caribbean inflexion in which her Rs all but disappeared, contriving even to lose weight and the plumpness in her cheeks, and walking with that slightly swaying gait characteristic of the slaves of Martinique.

After living at Penthémont for just over a year, Rose joined her son Eugène, her daughter Hortense, her aunt Désirée Renaudin, and her aunt's lover, the marquis de Beauharnais, at Fontainebleau, where they were then living in rather straitened circumstances. Rose, extravagant and improvident, was also short of money, although those who met her at this time, and were struck by the elegance of her fashionable dresses, could not suppose that this was the case.

It was generally believed that these dresses were not all bought with her own money. At Fontainebleau, it was rumoured that the alluring, provocative young woman, separated from her husband, was conducting an affair not only with the duc de Lorge, a well-known figure at court in the nearby royal château, but also with the chevalier de Coigny; and it was further supposed that her liaison with one or other, if not both of these men, was the reason why, taking her daughter with her, and leaving Eugène in the care of Mme Renaudin at Fontainebleau, she suddenly left one day in the greatest hurry for Le Havre, where she clambered aboard a merchant ship for the Atlantic crossing to Martinique.

Here she seems to have found other lovers among the officers at the naval base in Fort Royal, among them comte Scipion du Roure. 'Without being exactly pretty,' another naval officer wrote of her, 'she was attractive because of her wit, gaiety and good manners . . . She cared nothing for public opinion . . . And, as her funds were extremely limited, and she was most extravagant, she was often obliged to draw upon her admirers' pockets.'

She remained on the island for two years until, warned that rioting slaves as well as French soldiers, who had mutinied and joined forces with them, were threatening to attack Fort Royal, she and Hortense sought safety aboard comte Scipion du Roure's ship, *La Sensible*, in which, in October 1790, after a voyage of almost two months, they managed to reach Toulon.

3

THE *CITOYENNE*
BEAUHARNAIS

She confessed she was
'too indolent to take sides'.

ROSE AND HER DAUGHTER found France in a mood of expectancy.
The year before, a large crowd of assailants had attacked the Parisian
prison, that symbol of repression known as the Bastille, and had released
its four remaining inmates. Since then the attention of the country had
been directed towards the National Assembly as the people waited for
the next act in the drama to begin.

The President of the Assembly in October 1790, the month of Rose's
return from Martinique, was her former husband, relishing the opportunity now afforded him of making a series of sententious speeches.

Often to be seen listening to the deliberations of the Assembly in
the gallery of the Tuileries Palace riding school, where their meetings
were held, was Rose de Beauharnais, no longer *vicomtesse*, now *citoyenne*,
in accordance with a decision taken by liberal French nobles to disclaim
their titles. She also attended the salons of both Germaine de Staël and
Félicité de Genlis as well as the drawing rooms held in their houses by
the radical German Prince Frederick of Salm-Kyrbourg and his sister,
Princess Amalia.

Forceful as were the opinions expressed in these salons, Rose de
Beauharnais gave no indication that she either approved or disapproved
of them. As she herself confessed, she was 'too indolent to take sides';
and, indeed, as a woman who knew her well was later to observe, her
attention soon 'wandered from any discussion of abstract ideas'. When
it suited her to do so, however, she could readily feign an intelligent

interest in what was said and knew well enough, as Charles Maurice de Talleyrand, the statesman and diplomatist, was to testify, when to keep silent rather than expose her ignorance or *ingénuité*.

As well as in the gallery of the National Assembly, Rose de Beauharnais was also to be seen at the exhibitions of the Academy where, among the portraits on display, was that of her husband, peering proudly from the canvas, his long Roman nose above an undershot chin.

From time to time, Rose came across him during her excursions about the town; and, in a quite friendly way, they discussed their children of whom he was certainly fond. But she could not persuade him to allow her an increased income of which she now stood sorely in need. Even so, she contrived to live well enough in her house in the rue St Dominique which she shared with a friend, Désirée Hosten, maintaining a household which included a valet, a governess for Hortense, and the freed slave, Euphémie, brought over from Martinique.

Adopting the 'language and behaviour of the common people', as one of her contemporaries put it, she cultivated sympathetic friends among the radicals, making use of the name of her former husband, who was twice elected President of the Jacobin Club, and, after his appointment to a military command on France's endangered frontier, ending her letters 'Lapagerie Beauharnais, wife of the *Maréchal de Camp*'.

Like the Abbé Sieyès, a leading member of the States General, who, when asked what he had done in the ensuing months of bloody revolution, replied, 'I remained alive', Rose de Beauharnais also survived. She lived through the attack on the Tuileries in the summer of 1792 and the subsequent September Massacres; she saw the erection of the guillotine in the Place de la Révolution which ended the life of the King on 21 January 1793; and she endured the days of the Terror during which the father of her children was also guillotined in 1794 after failing to prevent the fall of Mainz to the allied army which the excesses of the Revolution had provoked into existence.

When the Law of Suspects imposed the death penalty upon former nobles and their families who had not 'constantly demonstrated their loyalty to the Revolution' or who had been guilty of making remarks 'debasing republican institutions and their elected representatives', Rose thought it as well to leave Paris until she had obtained the Certificate of Good Citizenship for herself and her children which the new law required. Offered a house a few miles outside Paris by her friend Désirée Hosten, she left for Croissy with Hortense, her governess, Marie Lannoy, and Euphémie. Her son, Eugène, who had been sent to school at Strasbourg by his father, joined them there to be apprenticed – in accordance with a revolutionary decree – to a carpenter, while Hortense was apprenticed to 'a dressmaker' who was, in fact, her governess.

Although the blade of the guillotine was still falling and rising on the orders of the implacable Revolutionary Tribune in what Thomas Carlyle was to call relentless systole-diastole, Rose took her household back to Paris when, through her contacts with such influential friends as Jean-Lambert Tallien, a leading member of the Committee of Public Safety, she had managed to acquire Certificates of Good Citizenship.

She had, however, returned to Paris too soon. On the evening of 21 April 1794, three members of a revolutionary committee knocked on the door of her house in the rue St Dominique with an order for the arrest of the 'woman Beauharnais, wife of the *ci-devant* General, and the woman Ostenn'. They searched the house for incriminating papers; but, finding none, they renewed their search the following night when in the attic they discovered various papers which Alexandre had sent to Rose to keep for him. She was arrested and taken to the prison known as Les Carmes where, during the September Massacres, prisoners had been dragged into foetid rooms lit by torches and candles, to face groups of judges wearing red caps and butchers' aprons, sitting round tables littered with papers, prison registers, bottles, pipes and jars of tobacco, their bare arms streaked with blood and tattooed with the symbols of their respective trades. The walls of the prison still bore the marks of the splashed blood of their victims.

Rose was pushed into the prison, already crowded with seven hundred men and women awaiting execution. There were few nobles amongst them: most were tradesmen, a few professional men, a librarian, a musician and an apothecary amongst them. The handsome, dashing General Lazare Hoche was soon to join them.

Hoche, the son of a stableman in royal service, and himself a groom before enlisting in the Gardes Françaises, was one of the talented Revolutionary generals, inexperienced, impromptu and *roturier*, who commanded the *levées en masse* with such success. Hoche himself, then aged twenty-six, had been appointed by the Committee of Public Safety to command the army of the Moselle the year before; but he had been denounced as a traitor by his rival, General Charles Pichegru, a man of peasant stock who had been a sergeant-major in an artillery regiment at the outbreak of the Revolution. Arrested as a consequence of Pichegru's denunciation, Hoche was awaiting his trial by the Revolutionary Tribunal with his customary cheerful demeanour; and, although he had been married for less than a month to a sixteen-year-old wife to whom he was devoted, it was not long before, in the atmosphere of sexual excitement which pervaded the prison, the attractive young general and the promiscuous *citoyenne* became lovers.

They were not to remain so for long. Within a week or two, Hoche was marched out of Les Carmes to face the Revolutionary Tribunal and by the end of November, released on its orders, was in command of the army of Brest.

Rose was left alone with her fear. For much of the time, unlike the other more stoical women in the prison, she was in tears or anxiously setting out her tarot cards in vain attempts to discover her fate.

Beyond the walls of Les Carmes the Revolution was reaching a climax. In the heat of the month known in the new revolutionary calendar as Thermidor, power was slipping from the hands of Maximilien Robespierre who had been elected President by the National Convention in June; and on 28 July 1794, his jaw shattered by a self-inflicted pistol shot, he and twenty-one of his supporters were guillotined before a cheering crowd in the Place de la Révolution. The Revolution was now about to take a sudden lurch to the right.

Rose emerged into startling sunlight, one of the first of the three thousand prisoners to be released by the end of August. Désirée Hosten being still in prison, Rose agreed with another Creole friend, Mme de Krény, to take an apartment in the rue de l'Université. Here she was soon once more deep in debt and borrowing money from anyone who would lend it to her, even from Hortense's governess, who lent her a lifetime's savings, and from General Hoche, who also sent her passionate love letters to which she replied in terms no less ardent, though she was not so exclusively devoted to him that she declined to submit, so it was said, to the rough overtures of one of his grooms.

It was not a time to be short of money in Paris. With the ending of the Terror the city had emerged suddenly from gloomy foreboding into bright and exciting life. Theatres reopened; cafés were thronged; dance halls and brothels sprang up everywhere. Profiteers and speculators, spending money as rapidly as they made it, sped through the streets with their women in ornately painted carriages to expensive restaurants, to gambling dens and to places of entertainment whose private rooms, in the words of a police report, were 'absolute sewers of debauchery and vice'. The *jeunesse dorée*, young men of mostly middle-class and artisan background, marched about the streets carrying short sticks weighted with lead with which to intimidate *sansculottes*, wearing a kind of uniform of square-skirted coats, tight trousers and extremely high cravats, their hair in long locks over their ears and plaited at the back of their heads. Also dandies known as *incroyables*, affecting lisps and dressed in the most outlandish fashions, appeared in the Tuileries gardens and were seen enjoying boating parties on the Seine accompanied by *merveilleuses* whose scanty, revealing clothes were equally exotic and whose wigs were triumphs of the *perruquiers'* art. At *bals des victimes*, entertainments at once riotous and ghoulish, guests whose near relations had perished in the Terror wore hair as though prepared for the blade of the guillotine and thin bands of red silk round their necks. They greeted each other by nodding sharply as though their severed heads were falling into the executioner's basket.

In this society Rose de Beauharnais contrived to survive, even to flourish, borrowing money whenever she could, cultivating new and influential friends and taking care to keep old friendships in good repair. While many Parisians came close to starvation in the fearful winter of 1794 when the Seine froze over from bank to bank, people could be seen in the streets chopping up beds for firewood to cook what little food they could procure, and long queues formed outside the bakers' shops to buy the rationed loaves of so-called bread, a soggy concoction made of bran and beans, which, spurned by Baron de Frénilly's dog, stuck to the wall when his master threw a handful at it.

Rose de Beauharnais did not go hungry. It became customary for guests to bring their own bread and wine and candles when they dined in other people's houses; but it was accepted that Rose was not in a position to do so. Nor was she expected to keep a carriage to carry her about the town, so Jean-Lambert Tallien, who had played a prominent part in Robespierre's overthrow, and Paul Barras, a charming, clever, unscrupulous former army officer of noble birth who had fought bravely before being cashiered, a cousin of the marquis de Sade and Tallien's successor as President of the National Assembly, arranged for her to be provided with both a coach and a pair of horses.

Rose was on the best of terms with Tallien's beautiful young wife, Thérésia, formerly Barras's mistress, and she was often to be seen at the Talliens' house, La Chaumière, where the women guests, adopting the neo-classical fashion of their hostess, appeared in Grecian tunics, scanty and almost as revealing as the dress in which the sensual and heavily scented Fortunée Hamelin paraded lasciviously bare-breasted down the Champs-Élysées.

At La Chaumière, Rose found just the kind of society which she relished, and in which she shone. It was here that she met a man described as 'Barras's little Italian protégé', a twenty-six-year-old brigadier on half-pay, Napoleon Buonaparte.

4

THE CORSICAN BOY

'He is most proud and ambitious.'

EVERY YEAR, on the Feast of the Assumption, High Mass is celebrated in the sixteenth-century cathedral in Ajaccio, the capital of Corsica. On the stiflingly hot day of 15 August 1769, there was an additional cause for celebration: it was the first anniversary of the island's 'reunion' with France after having been a possession of the republic of Genoa for two centuries. In the cathedral's congregation that sultry August day, as, indeed, for at least a short time on every day of the year, was Letizia Buonaparte, the small, nineteen-year-old wife of a lawyer, Carlo Maria di Buonaparte. Suddenly, unexpectedly, she felt the first, urgent pains of labour. She hurried from the cathedral and reached her large stone house in the nearby strada Malerba just in time for the baby, her second son, to be born on a sofa in a downstairs room. Later that day a priest called at her house and it was decided the delicate-looking child should be christened without delay. He was given the name of an uncle who had died recently, Napoleone, the name also of an obscure Egyptian martyr, Neapolus. In the family the boy was called 'Nabulio'.

The mother was a frail-looking young woman, a wife since the age of fourteen, with a pale, eager countenance, dark hair, large dark eyes and a patrician nose, shy but determined and capable and extremely thrifty. One French observer described her as being 'by far the most striking-looking woman in Ajaccio'. She did not often smile, and she spoke Italian in a Corsican dialect.

Her family, the Ramolini, originally came from Lombardy and were proud to number among their ancestors the counts of Coll Alto; but her more recent forebears had been settled in Corsica for some 250 years. Her father was a civil engineer who had died when she was a child. Soon afterwards, her mother had been remarried to a Swiss officer serving in the Genoese marines, Captain Franz Fesch, whose son, Joseph Fesch, was to become a cardinal and French ambassador in Rome.

The Buonapartes were also of old Italian stock, an ancestor, Guglielmo di Buonaparte, having been a distinguished councillor in Florence in the thirteenth century. 'We thought ourselves as good as the Bourbons,' Napoleon was to say, 'and on the island we really were. There are genealogists who date my family from the Flood, and there are people who pretend that I am of plebeian birth. The truth lies between the two. The Buonapartes are a good Corsican family, little known since we have hardly ever left our island, but much better than the coxcombs who take it upon themselves to denigrate us.' His enemy, the diplomatist and Romantic writer, François-René de Chateaubriand, was to comment sardonically that Napoleon was 'so lavish with French blood because he did not have a drop of it in his own veins'.

A sixteenth-century member of their family had sailed for Corsica, when the island was being colonized by the Genoese, in the hope of fortune if not fame. His descendant, Letizia's husband Carlo, was a tall young man, who had studied law at Pisa; charming in manner though vain and frivolous by nature, socially ambitious and compulsively *intrigant*. He was to become well-known for the elegance of his clothes and for the sword he wore as evidence of his noble rank: he was known on the island as 'Buonaparte *il magnifico*'; he himself added to his name the aristocratic *di*. He took to wearing cerise jackets, buckled shoes, embroidered stockings, puce knee breeches and a powdered wig with a black ribbon. It meant much to him *fare bella figura*.

Two years after his marriage, he had taken his wife to meet Pasquale Paoli, the guerrilla leader whose life's work it was to drive the Genoese from Corsica. It had been a long and hard journey on horseback to Paoli's headquarters at Corte, a small town on high ground in the middle of the island. Letizia had clearly been intrigued and impressed by the great patriot who, in turn, had obviously been attracted by the sixteen-year-old girl whom he had asked to sit down to play cards with him and by whom he had been soundly beaten.

Carlo had also created a favourable impression upon Paoli, who had asked him to go to Rome on his behalf to do his best to ensure that, when an attack was made on the Genoese island of Capraia, in order to draw Genoese troops away from the Corsican ports still in their hands, there were no reprisals by the papacy which had given Corsica as well as Capraia to Genoa. The Vatican was disposed to listen sympathetically to Carlo's submissions; but Genoa now offered to sell Corsica to the King of France, ten thousand of whose troops landed to take possession of the island.

Carlo, who had by now returned to Corsica, once more left Ajaccio to join Paoli, taking Letizia with him. In the tangled evergreen shrubs of the maquis, the Corsican guerrillas had defeated the French who retreated from the island with the loss of five hundred prisoners and their commander in disgrace. They came again next year, however, more than twice as many of them, under a more gifted and resolute commander.

Once again, Carlo – accompanied once more by Letizia, pregnant with Napoleone and carrying her first baby, Giuseppe, in her arms – had left Ajaccio for the maquis and had established his family in a cave on Monte Rotondo, the highest ground on the island. Whenever she had emerged from the cave, 'bullets whistled past [her] ears,' she wrote later. 'But I trusted in the protection of the Virgin Mary, to whom I had consecrated my unborn child.' In the middle of May, a French officer had clambered up Monte Rotondo under the protection of a white flag. He had brought a message from his general: following Paoli's defeat at Ponte Nuovo, Corte had fallen to the French; the guns were silent; Paoli himself was sailing into exile in England; all Corsicans under arms were free to return to their homes.

Carlo had accepted the offer and had taken Letizia and Giuseppe back to Ajaccio where, by the time Napoleone was born, the Corsican flag had been replaced by France's fleurs de lys on a blue ground.

Puny as Napoleone had seemed at first – born so suddenly before his time – and worried as his mother had been that he might die, as two of her babies had already done, he soon grew stronger, being fed at his mother's breast as well as by a wet-nurse, a sailor's wife named Camilla Ilari.

In contrast with his quiet, retiring elder brother, Giuseppe, Napoleone grew into a rather rumbustious boy, often provoking Giuseppe into rowdy wrestling matches on the floor until their mother took all the furniture out of one of the rooms and left the children there to be as noisy and rough as Napoleone liked. She was not, however, an over-indulgent mother, insisting on daily baths, regular attendance at Mass, and often giving them a sharp buffet when they were tiresome or naughty. Napoleon himself, so he later confessed, was particularly unruly and stubborn as a child. 'I would hit Giuseppe,' he said, 'and then force him to do my homework. If I was punished and given only plain bread to eat I would swap it for the shepherd's chestnut bread, or I would go to find my nurse who would give me some little squids I quite liked.'

He recalled one particularly severe beating:

> My grandmother was quite old and stooped [he was to tell his natural son, Alexandre Walewski], and she seemed to me and my sister, Pauline [born in 1780], like an old fairy godmother. She walked with a cane; and, although she was fond of us and gave us sweets, that did not stop us walking behind her and imitating her. Unfortunately she caught us doing this and told our mother who, while loving us, would stand no nonsense. Pauline was punished first because skirts are easier to pull up and down than trousers are to unbutton. That evening she tried to catch me also but I escaped. The next morning she pushed me away when I tried to kiss her. Later that day she said, 'Napoleone, you are invited to lunch at the Governor's house. Go and get changed.' I went upstairs and began to get undressed. But my mother was like a cat waiting for a mouse. She suddenly entered the room. I realized, too late, that I had fallen into her trap and I had to submit to her beating.

His mother was, Napoleon said of her, 'both strict and tender'; and he readily acknowledged the influence she had over the development of his character. 'I was very well brought up by my mother,' he was to say. 'I owe her a great deal. She instilled pride.' The children's father sometimes worried that his wife was too strict with them; but she insisted that bringing up the children was her business, not his. She was masterful in her way.

All in all, Napoleone's was a happy childhood, and a very familial one. The big, dark house was large but fully occupied behind its shuttered windows. Napoleone, his parents and siblings lived on the first floor. The ground floor was occupied by Letizia's mother-in-law and an uncle, Luciano, Archdeacon of Ajaccio, who was often incapacitated by gout; while, on the second floor, lived various cousins who were, on occasions, a quarrelsome lot of whom Carlo would have been pleased to be rid had he felt able to turn them out. Relations between the two families went from bad to worse after a tub of slops was thrown out of a second-floor window on to one of Letizia's dresses hanging out to dry below. Although Letizia saw to it that they did not live extravagantly, the Buonapartes did live quite well. Carlo had inherited two good vineyards and both pasture and arable land from his father, while Letizia had brought to the marriage over thirty acres, a mill and a large oven in which bread was baked from corn ground in the family mill. Milk and cheese came from the family's goats, oil from their olives, tunny from the fishermen trawling the Golfe d'Ajaccio. Uncle Luciano was proud to say that the Buonapartes had 'never paid for bread, wine or oil'. Napoleone, however, was not much interested in food – except for cherries, which he consumed with relish. Otherwise, he ate what was put before him without enthusiasm or comment.

When he was five years old, he was sent to a kindergarten kept by nuns at which he would arrive, despite his mother's care, with his clothes awry and his stockings crumpled round his ankles, holding hands with a little girl named Giacominetta. This gave rise to a verse with which the other children would taunt him, deriding him for the stockings that fell down to his ankles and for his love for Giacominetta:

> *Napoleone di mezza calzetta*
> *Fa l'amore a Giacominetta*

Provoked by this, he would throw stones at his tormentors or charge at them with fists flailing.

From the kindergarten he was sent to a school for boys where he learned to read and write both French and Italian and was given lessons in arithmetic which he enjoyed and at which he excelled. In the hot summers of the holidays, his parents took their children to one or other of their farmhouses up in the hills or to a house near the sea, their mother putting them on horseback as soon as they could walk. Napoleone would be taken for rides by his aunt, Galtruda, who told him what she knew about horticulture and agriculture, showed him how to prune a vine, and pointed out to him the damage done to the olive trees by his uncle Luciano's goats. He received a different kind of instruction from his mother, who sent Giuseppe and Napoleone to bed without supper from time to time so that they should 'bear discomfort without protest'. She also told them that although they came of noble stock, they would have to make sacrifices in order to appear before the world as a nobleman was expected to do.

'When you grow up, you'll be poor,' she said to Napoleone one day. 'But it's better, even if you have to live on dry bread, to have a fine room for receiving guests, a fine suit of clothes and a fine horse.' She urged her children to be proud of their ancestry; and while Napoleon was always to bridle when his enemies referred to him derogatorily as 'the Corsican', he was not ashamed of his origins and never attempted to conceal them, though he did once say, 'I'm not a Corsican. I was brought up in France, therefore I am French.'

His mother also persuaded him to believe in destiny and the power of providence and of spirits from another world. Whenever she heard surprising, unexpected news, she would suddenly cross herself and murmur under her breath, '*Gesu!*'

Prospering as a lawyer under French rule and appointed to a seat in the Corsican States-General and to membership of the Council of Twelve Nobles, Carlo was now able to afford a nurse for the children and two maids for his wife. She felt in need of the help: another son, Luciano (Lucien, as he was to be known in France), was born when Napoleone was six years old, and, two years after this, a daughter, Maria Anna, later known as Elisa. Then there was a fourth son, Luigi (Louis), two more daughters, Maria Paula (Pauline) and Maria Annunziata (Caroline) and, lastly, a fifth son, Girolamo (Jérôme), born in 1784.

Repeated pregnancies had not spoiled their mother's good looks which were much admired by the French Governor of Corsica, Charles René, comte de Marbeuf, whose elderly wife had not accompanied him to the island and whose French mistress had returned home. He was said to be much in love with Letizia; but she, deeply religious and mindful of her duty to her husband, seems to have been content to enjoy his admiration without encouraging it, although there were those who believed they were lovers and that Luigi was his child.

Both she and her husband eagerly accepted his offer when the comte undertook not only to find places for Giuseppe and Napoleone at educational establishments in France but also, having no children of his own, to pay the necessary fees. So the brothers were sent to a good school at Autun and from there, so it was planned, Giuseppe should go to the seminary at Aix with a view to entering the church, while Napoleone should train for a career in the army at the military academy at Brienne-le-Château.

When this decision about his future was made, Napoleone was not yet nine years old; and Camilla, his former wet-nurse and still a family friend, wept to see him leave home so early. His mother displayed no such emotion. In accordance with Corsican custom, she took him and his brother Giuseppe to the Lazarists, a congregation of secular priests living under religious vows, to be blessed by the Father Superior, and then accompanied them across the high ground through Corte to the coast at Bastia to see them off on a ship bound for Marseilles. At the quayside, Napoleone seemed apprehensive: his mother bent down to kiss him and to whisper in his ear, '*Coraggio.*' It was to be many months before she saw the boy again.

It seemed that both needed courage again when Napoleon and Joseph, as they were now to be known, had to say goodbye to each other when the time came for Napoleon to leave the school at Autun to go to the military academy at Brienne. Joseph cried bitterly and, although not a single tear was seen to run down Napoleon's cheek, one of the school's masters later attempted to comfort Joseph by saying to him, 'He didn't show it, but he's just as sad as you.'

At Brienne, Napoleon was adept not only at mathematics but also at history and geography. A fellow pupil, however, said that 'he had no taste for the study of languages and the arts'. His dancing and drawing were both described as being 'very poor', while his spelling was 'erratic'. He was no good at German and he spoke inadequate French with a pronounced Corsican accent. He became renowned for a sharp temper, self-sufficiency, pride and arrogance, a rather priggish sense of decorum and a readiness to take offence. On one occasion, when he was about nine years old, having broken one of the school's rules, he was ordered to wear a dunce's cap, to exchange his blue uniform for an old brown coat, and to eat his dinner on his knees by the refectory door. Outraged by this indignity, he was suddenly sick on the floor and then, stamping his foot, he refused to kneel down, crying out, 'I'll eat my dinner standing up. In my family we kneel only to God, only to God! Only to God!'

Such outbursts naturally led to much teasing, but not, it seems, to bullying, since he was only too capable of responding furiously to provocation of that sort. When some boys, frightened by an explosion in a box of gunpowder during a display of fireworks on the King's birthday, rushed headlong into his garden plot, his retreat from the other boys on holidays, knocking down the fence and trampling over his mulberry bushes, he attacked them and drove them off shouting threats and brandishing a hoe. To taunts about his diminutive size or his strange accent he would often react in this violent way, rushing at his tormentors, crying, 'I'll make you French pay for this.' One of his reports described him as being, 'imperious and stubborn'; another adverted to his 'lack of social graces'. His only friend, Louis-Antoine de Bourrienne, who was later to become his secretary, wrote of him:

> Bonaparte and I were eight years old when our friendship began . . . I was the only one of his youthful comrades who could accommodate themselves to his stern character . . . His ardent wish to acquire knowledge was remarkable even then. When he first came to the college he spoke only the Corsican dialect and the vice-principal gave him lessons in French . . . [He was very bad at Latin] but the facility with which he solved mathematical problems absolutely astonished me . . .
>
> His conversation almost always bore the appearance of ill-humour, and he was never very amiable . . . His temper was not improved by the teasing he frequently experienced from the other boys who were fond of ridiculing him because of his odd Christian name and his country . . . He was certainly not much liked and rarely took part in the school's amusements. During play-hours he used to withdraw to work in the library where he read with deep interest books of history. I often went off to play with my friends and left him to read by himself in the library.

One day his parents came to see him. His father, wearing a smart, new wig, was an embarrassing sight, bowing in an extravagantly polite way when he stood aside to allow the headmaster to pass first through a door. But his mother was all that a boy – a Corsican boy in an academy attended by so many French cadets from upper-class families – could hope to have. Her long dark hair was tied back in a chignon and covered by a lace headdress, and her dress was of white silk with a pattern of green flowers. She was not feeling well, however, having recently suffered from puerperal fever. She still had cause to complain of intermittent pain on her left side, an ailment which her husband hoped would be alleviated by a course of the waters at Bourbonne.

She heard with dismay that Napoleon had now set his heart on going into the navy and, as a preparation for life at sea, had taken to sleeping in a hammock in his cubicle. She anxiously pointed out the twin dangers of a life at sea: the chances of being killed on board and of being drowned if thrown into the water. When she returned to Ajaccio she asked the comte de Marbeuf to do all he could to dissuade her son from fulfilling his youthful ambition.

Letizia was also worried by the state of her husband's health: he had lately lost much weight and had little appetite; he looked exhausted and his skin was discoloured by blotchy patches. Carlo was persuaded to go to Aix, then to Montpellier, to seek specialist advice. None of any use was given him: he died of cancer of the stomach in February 1785, a month before his thirty-ninth birthday, seized at the end, so Napoleon was later to say, with a passion for priests: 'There were not enough for him in all Montpellier . . . He ended his life so pious that everyone there thought him a saint.'

Napoleon had by then left Brienne and, no longer set upon a career in the navy, had gone on to the École Militaire in Paris, an establishment which set almost as much store by religious observances as by military training: attendance at Mass was compulsory; so were confirmation and confession.

Napoleon was distressed to hear of his father's death and worried that his mother, a widow with eight children, would find it hard to get by in her straitened circumstances. When someone offered to lend him money, he declined the offer with the words, 'My mother has too many expenses already, I must not add to them.'

He was as proud and as priggish as ever, just as intolerant of criticism and of what he took to be slights to his *amour propre*, furious when he was made to feel foolish – as, for instance, when, never having seen ice before, he demanded to know who was putting glass in his water jug.

Stories were told of his throwing his musket at the head of a senior cadet who, having noticed a mistake in Napoleon's drill, had rapped him over the knuckles, and of his rejecting the overtures of a former friend, Pierre François Laugier, son of a baron, whom he had criticized for associating with young men of homosexual tendencies. 'Your new friends are corrupting you,' he told Laugier. 'So make a choice between them and me.' Later he said, 'You have scorned my advice, and you have renounced my friendship. Never speak to me again.' Laugier's response was to creep up behind him and push him over, upon which Napoleon ran after him and, grabbing him by the collar, threw him to the floor on which he hit his head against a stove.

'I was insulted,' Napoleon told the captain on duty who came up to admonish him. 'I took my revenge. There is nothing more to be said.' He then strode off in a manner which by then had become characteristic, his arms folded, his head bent forwards, taking long steps.

The sexual proclivities of Laugier induced Napoleon to write a paper to be sent to the Minister of War on the subject of the education of the young men of Sparta which, he thought, should be applied in the École Militaire and other French academies. He sent a draft to the headmaster of the school at Brienne who, having read it, advised him not to pursue the matter further.

A report on the Corsican cadet at the École Militaire described him as 'solitary, haughty, egotistical ... Reserved and studious, he prefers study to any kind of amusement ... He enjoys reading good authors and has a sound knowledge of mathematics and geography ... He is most proud and ambitious.'

5

A PROSTITUTE AND A PEST

'A woman who is feared has no charm.'

NAPOLEON WAS NOW SIXTEEN YEARS OLD. His relations with women had, up till now, been largely limited to those with members of his own family and their friends; and he had had little opportunity of coming across girls of his own age. On holiday in Paris, however, he saw something of the two daughters of Panoria Permon, a Corsican of Greek descent, the attractive wife of an army contractor and the mother of two young daughters, Cécile and Laure. When Napoleon was commissioned soon after his sixteenth birthday, he called at the Permons' house in the Place de Conti in his new officer's uniform and long black boots which looked far too big for his painfully thin legs. The girls laughed at the sight of him; and since he was obviously put out by this unwelcome reception and seemed unable then, as always, to tolerate a joke at his own expense, Cécile told him that, now he was entitled to wear an officer's sword, he must use it to protect the ladies and not mind if they teased him.

'It's obvious you're just a little schoolgirl,' Napoleon said grumpily.

'What about you?' the ten-year-old girl replied. 'You're just a puss-in-boots.'

In an attempt to show there was no ill feeling, however, the next time he called at the house, Napoleon brought with him a copy of *Puss-in-Boots* for one of the sisters and, for the other, a model which he had had made, though he could ill afford it, of *Puss*, running in front of the carriage of his master, the marquis de Carabas. Their mockery was not forgotten, however: for years thereafter Laure Permon was known by Napoleon as his 'little pest' and, a whole decade later, when she made some reference to the Puss-in-Boots episode, Laure said she would never forget Napoleon's expression, as he came up to her to pinch her nose so hard that she cried out in pain. 'You're witty, you little pest,' he said, 'but you're malicious. Don't be that. A woman who is feared has no charm.' Napoleon neither then nor later ever forgot a slight. Nor could Laure Permon ever forget the disdainful twist of his mouth when he was angry, nor yet his charm when he chose to exercise it.

Equipped with his sword and his boots, Napoleon had now to decide which regiment he should apply to join. He selected La Fère, a well-regarded artillery regiment stationed at Valence on the Rhône between Marseilles and Lyon, the nearest garrison town to Corsica.

In Valence he lived in a first-floor room in a house belonging to a fifty-year-old woman, Mme Bou. It was a small and by no means quiet room in which could clearly be heard the click of billiard balls in the room next door, the saloon of the Café Cercle. But he liked Mme Bou, who did his washing for him and mended his clothes, and life in Valence was generally pleasant enough: together with his fellow young officers he was invited to the houses of the local gentry. He rarely accepted these invitations, though, feeling he would be out of place, *de trop*. He found the money for a course of dancing lessons. He also scraped together the money to reimburse his mother for the postage of the clothes she sent him. He had little money to spare, however; and he would always borrow a book if he could, rather than buy one.

In the loneliness of his room, he was often desperately unhappy, even suicidal. 'Always alone,' he wrote, 'in the throes of my melancholy my thoughts dwell on death . . . What great rage brings me now to wish for my destruction . . . I see no place for me in this world . . . As I must die sooner or later, why should I not kill myself?'

He read a great deal, mostly history and political theory, the works of Machiavelli, accounts of the religion of the Aztecs, the government of India, of ancient Rome, and books about England, being struck by the ascendancy of Parliament and the decline of the monarchy whose power and the power of whose ministers in France must, he decided, be limited. He also wrote a great deal, papers on the handling and uses of artillery, essays on Plato's *Republic*, on the ancient Greeks and

Persians, on modern England and ancient Greece, on Marigny's *History of the Arabs under the Caliphs*. He wrote hurriedly and far into the night and was often unable to decipher what he had written in the morning.

He made précis of passages that interested him, lists of words hitherto unfamiliar to him and curious facts from books which caught his fancy – such as Jean Gaspard Lavater's *The Art of Judging Character from Men's Faces*. Having read Marigny's *History of the Arabs* he noted, 'Soliman is said to have eaten 100 pounds of meat a day ... Mahomet did not know how to read or write. I find this improbable. He had 17 wives.' From Buffon's *Histoire Naturelle* he copied out, with evident fascination, long passages about castration and about testicles – 'Some men are born with only one, others have three; these men are stronger and more vigorous.' His interest in such matters was at this time largely academic.

At Valence, he made the acquaintance of the family of a Mme Colombier whose daughter was named Caroline; but, as he later commented, 'It will be considered scarcely credible, perhaps: our whole business consisted of our eating cherries together.' On a brief visit to Paris in November 1787, when he was eighteen, he encountered a young prostitute in the Palais Royal one cold evening and took her to bed; but the experience seems to have made no deep impression upon him. He recorded in detail the conversation he had with her, the questions he asked: how could she bear to walk about in the arcades in such bitter weather? Was she not exhausted by such a life as hers? Was there not some other work which would be better suited to her health? She must come from the north to brave such cold as this? How did she lose her virginity? Was she angry with the army officer who took it? How did she come to Paris?

She told him another officer had brought her there. 'He deserted me also,' she said. 'Now I have a third. I have been living with him for three years. He's French, but has business in London. He's there now. Let's go to your place.'

'What will we do when we get there?'

'We'll get warm. Come on. You'll have great pleasure.'

Whether he did or not Napoleon did not say. He did say, however, that 'more than most people', he hated prostitution and always 'felt sullied by a look from women of that sort', but that this young woman's pale cheeks and soft voice 'at once overcame [his] doubts'.

When, in June 1788, Napoleon had been posted from Valence to Auxon, he had, in order to ease the burdens imposed upon his mother, offered to have the eleven-year-old Louis, then his favourite brother, to stay with him; and he did what he could to help Letizia when, following the death of their friend Marbeuf and the establishment in Corsica of a new, stricter authority by officials of the Ministry of Finance, subsidies due to her for improvements carried out on the family's land were withheld. He wrote letters of protest to the new authorities in Corsica; and he went to Paris to press in person his mother's claims.

After the outbreak of revolution in Paris the following year, Napoleon warmly welcomed the decrees of the Constituent Assembly and the formulation of a new constitution. Many of his fellow-officers went abroad in apprehension or disgust; but he remained to become Secretary of the local Society of Friends of the Constitution and to take an oath 'to die rather than allow a foreign power to invade French soil'.

He spent his leaves in Corsica. His mother, who had given birth to thirteen children, five of whom had died in infancy, was unwell, still suffering from the after-effects of puerperal fever and, occasionally, painful stiffness in her left side. He took her to Guagno for a course of the waters there; but she found them of little use. She was still a good-looking woman, though, and was always neatly dressed in her widow's weeds. She had received two offers of marriage, but had declined them both for her children's sake.

When Napoleon went on leave in September 1791, Joseph was by then a lawyer – twenty-three years old, and a rising figure in local government. Lucien was sixteen, Louis three years younger; Jérôme, a rather tiresome, cheeky boy, was nine. Elisa, at fourteen the oldest of the three girls, was still at school at St Cyr; her sister, Pauline, Napoleon's favourite, was eleven, and Caroline was nine.

In caring for them their mother had the help of but one servant now, Severia, who was paid a mere pittance – all that the family could afford, since a contract entered into by Carlo with the French government for a plantation of ten thousand mulberry trees for the manufacture of silk had been cancelled.

Carlo's old uncle, Luciano, the Archdeacon, who now spent most of his time in bed nursing his gout, was known to have concealed in his mattress a large bag of gold, the profits from a number of most un-archdiaconal dealings in land, farm animals and wine; but he was unwilling to part with a single coin. An attempt by the beguiling Pauline, who was sent to his room to see if she could lay her hands on one or two while his attention was distracted, ended in rowdy failure when the whole bag tumbled to the floor. Alarmed by the old man's cries, Letizia rushed downstairs to see what had happened. Uncle Luciano informed her that he was only looking after the gold for a friend. Letizia picked up the coins and handed them to him. He counted them carefully before replacing them in the bag and stuffing the bag back into the mattress.

The old man now had but a short time to enjoy whatever comfort his hoard of gold could give him. In the hope of bringing him some relief from his gout and his other ailments, Napoleon, who still had a lingering affection for him, wrote to a Swiss doctor, Simon Tissot, for his advice. But Tissot, who had written a number of eccentric though celebrated books – in one of which he propounded the view that masturbation led inevitably to insanity – was not prepared to help. He endorsed the letter as of 'little interest' and did not trouble to send a reply.

Soon afterwards, Uncle Luciano died, leaving his gold to his nephew's sons and enabling Napoleon to take part in the expensive business of Corsican politics and to ensure his election to the command of a battalion in the Corsican National Guard at the age of twenty-two.

Back in Paris, he was a witness of the growing violence of the Revolution, of the attack on the Tuileries and the events which led to the prison massacres of 7 September 1792. Three weeks before the massacres, his sister Elisa's convent at St Cyr was closed and Napoleon, concerned for the fifteen-year-old girl's safety, went to fetch her, bringing her back to Paris in her black school uniform and feathered taffeta bonnet.

Elisa had left home soon after her eighth birthday and had received a rigorous education at the school which had been founded by Louis XIV's mistress, Mme de Maintenon. Horace Walpole had seen the girls there marching off to chapel two by two in a most orderly fashion, 'each band headed by a nun . . . to sing the whole service'. There were no signs then of the self-confident woman Elisa was later to become.

On a previous visit, when Napoleon had visited the school with Mme Permon, Elisa had come into the room looking miserable and had burst into tears. When asked what the trouble was, she had said that she had no money to contribute to a farewell party which was being given for one of the other girls. Mme Permon gave her some.

Promoted captain by now, Napoleon took her to the opera, an entertainment which the nuns at St Cyr had warned her to avoid as an indecent spectacle. Her brother noticed that, obedient to their admonitions, she sat at first with her eyes tight shut; but, shortly, unable to resist its allure, she sat in rapt attention.

At Marseilles on her way back to Corsica, her uniform with the cross and fleurs de lys embroidered on the front of the black dress caught the attention of a threatening crowd who, pointing to this and her feathered bonnet, cried, 'Death to the aristocrats!' 'We're no more aristocrats than you are,' Napoleon shouted back at them and, snatching the bonnet from his sister's head, he threw it to them. One of them caught it and they all cheered.

Back once more in Corsica, Napoleon – whom, so his brother Lucien said, no one now cared to oppose – was at loggerheads with the autocratic Paoli, who, having returned to Corsica, was intent upon separating Corsica from revolutionary France with which the Buonapartes were now identified. Napoleon, having decided to make an attempt to seize Ajaccio for France, sent a message to his mother telling her to take the family to a ruined tower at Capitello, east of the gulf of Ajaccio, and to remain there during the forthcoming bombardment of the town. Concerned that they might not be safe at Capitello, he followed them there in a small boat and sent them on to Calvi, a town which was held by the French.

Having failed to take Ajaccio, he joined them at Calvi and with them set sail for Toulon. The family's house was pillaged by the Paolists, and their farmhouses sacked and their mill dismantled. A Paolist congress condemned the Buonapartes to 'perpetual execration and infamy'.

Letizia was not happy living first in Toulon, then in primitive lodgings in the village of La Valette, afterwards in Bandol and later in Marseilles, where the family's gloomy, ill-furnished fourth-floor rooms were in the rue Pavillon, a poor district little better than a slum. However, before long, thanks to Cristoforo Saliceti, a fellow-Corsican, a more comfortable house had been found for them, as well as a post as storekeeper for Lucien and an appointment as assistant to a war commissary for Joseph, while Napoleon continued to do well in the army.

But Letizia missed her homeland. Her halting French, spoken with a strong Corsican accent, was scarcely comprehensible; while malicious stories were already being spread about her daughters who, so it was later alleged, were behaving in a scandalous manner, 'walking the streets in the evening like certain young women who frequent the rue St Honoré and the Palais Royal'.

Even when Napoleon, once he was in a position to help his family financially, had rented the Sallé château, a large country house near Antibes, for them, Letizia still behaved in a Corsican manner, and still insisted on doing her own washing. After all, as she, the most thrifty of women, was often to say in the future, who knew how long the family's present fortune would last?

Her daughters had no such apprehension as they bowled along the country lanes in a barouche provided for them by their brother, Napoleon, who by then was earning fifteen thousand livres a year.

6

THE 'ADORABLE FRIEND'

'How could you think I could cease to love you?'

DEPRESSED AS NAPOLEON HAD BEEN in Valence and frustrated as he had been while in Corsica, soon after his return to France he had begun to make a name for himself in the army. When his superior officer had been wounded during the siege of Toulon in 1793, Napoleon had been given command of the artillery there and, having handled it with exemplary skill, he had been promoted to *général-de-brigade* at the age of twenty-four. He had since been employed in preparing plans for the operations of the army which the government in Paris had sent against the Austrians in Italy; and, in October 1795, he had helped to defeat supporters of a counter-revolution in Paris by ordering his guns to fire upon the mob – the mob he always hated and feared – his famous 'whiff of grapeshot'. 'The enemy attacked us at the Tuileries,' he had reported to his brother, Joseph. 'We killed a great many of them. They killed thirty of our men and wounded another sixty. Now all is quiet. As usual I did not receive a scratch. I could not be happier.' Four hundred men lay dead in the church of St-Roch; and Napoleon's future was made. 'I have lodgings and a carriage at your disposal,' he told Joseph. 'I have already sent sixty thousand livres in gold, silver and paper money to the family, so you need have no worries . . . You know I live only for the pleasure of what I can do for the family.'

Not long afterwards, he was appointed to the command of the Army of the Interior. For this rapid change in his fortunes he was much indebted to the support and patronage of the vicomte Paul de Barras, who had been entrusted with dictatorial powers by the National Convention.

Napoleon was now in a position to marry, and he turned his thoughts seriously to the choice of a bride, preferably a rich one. According to Barras, who wrote long after their friendship had been broken, he was not above dancing attendance, in a most uncharacteristic manner, on wealthy women who, or whose husbands, he thought might be in a position to advance him in his career. One such was the wife of a man of some influence – Mme Louise Turreau de Lignières, with whom, it was improbably suggested, he conducted a brief affair. Another was Mme Ricord upon whom 'he heaped attentions, handing her her gloves and fan and showing her the deepest respect when she mounted her horse, taking her for walks hat in hand, and appearing to be in constant terror lest she should meet with some accident'.

It was Barras who introduced him to another rich woman, Mme Montausier, a woman who was said to be worth over a million francs and who owned a theatre which was also a brothel in the Palais Royal. She was very much older than Napoleon: this in itself did not much concern him; but for one reason or another the relationship did not prosper.

It was not only money and position he was after, as he told his brother Joseph; he 'badly wanted a home'; and if he could find a young woman with a handsome dowry, of course so much the better. In the summer of 1794, while occupying lodgings in the house of the comte de Laurenti near Nice, he thought that he might have found such a bride in the person of the count's sixteen-year-old daughter Emilie whose father, he had good reason to believe, was quite rich. He asked him, evidently without much hope of success, if he might marry Emilie. Her father, polite in his refusal, considered the proposal premature: the young general was about to embark on a campaign in Italy; there would be time enough to consider the matter when his daughter was older and Bonaparte had returned home. In the meantime, the count and his wife thought it as well to send Emilie to stay with cousins at Grasse.

Later on that year in Marseilles, Napoleon was introduced by his brother Joseph to the family of the rich textile-and-soap merchant, François Clary (the husband of one of their mother's friends), who had two daughters, Julie, aged twenty-two, whom Joseph was to marry, and Bernardine Eugénie Désirée, aged sixteen. Julie was a plain young woman with big bulging eyes and a thick flat nose. Short and spotty, she was described in later life as 'a perfectly vulgar little woman, very thin and very ugly', 'hideous' even and 'pimply to the last degree'.

Napoleon expressed the opinion that looks in a wife did not matter. 'It isn't necessary that our wives should be good looking,' he said. 'With a mistress it is different. A plain mistress is a monstrosity. She would fail in her principal, indeed in her only duty.'

It had to be conceded that Julie was extremely unprepossessing in appearance; but she was both good-natured and intelligent.

Her sister was known in the family as Désirée but Napoleon, who was often in future to choose his own names for his women friends, called her Eugénie. She was rather fat and not particularly good-looking with large, slightly protuberant dark eyes; but she was an affectionate girl, kind-hearted like her sister, amenable and shy with a pleasant singing voice, the promise of a generous dowry, and what Napoleon described as 'the most beautiful teeth imaginable' as well as the 'prettiest hands in the world'. A pretty hand and a pretty foot were always features upon which he was likely to comment. His own, so a future valet was to notice, were exceptionally well formed and his fingernails remarkably well cared for.

There could be no doubt that Désirée found him attractive; and he himself was sufficiently taken with her to carry about with him a few strands of her hair in a locket. Her father, however, was not inclined to encourage the friendship: the young Corsican might well have a bright future before him in the army; but he had little money and his character was not appealing. Introspective, unsociable and gloomy, he had been heard to speak of suicide.

Discouraged by her parents, Napoleon wrote to tell his dear Eugénie, after his departure from Marseilles, that, while her sweet nature inspired him with affection, he did not think that, being 'so occupied with work', he ought to allow that affection to 'cut into [his] soul'. As for her, he went on to say, she had a talent for music: she should develop that talent, buy a piano of her own and engage a music teacher. Condescendingly he gave her peculiarly ill-informed advice about her singing technique.

In his next letter, not written until five months later, Napoleon returned to this musical theme: he would subscribe to a music magazine on her behalf and he sent her a list of books which he recommended that she should read. Four more months passed before Napoleon once again appeared in Marseilles and presented himself at the Clarys' house.

Eugénie was now seventeen, less shy and reserved but as sweet-natured as ever. Before long, Napoleon fell in love with her; and now he made it clear that he would like to marry her and he evidently contrived to take her to bed. 'You are always in my thoughts,' he told her. 'How can you think I could cease to love you?' Mme Clary was deeply disturbed by this development: after all, her daughter was by now a most attractive girl with a dowry of one hundred thousand livres, whereas Napoleon was a gauche Corsican with no more to offer than his army pay. She already had one son-in-law who had no money of his own; and, for her, as she is supposed to have said, one Bonaparte in the family was quite enough.

Her mother's reluctance to accept Napoleon into their family did not deter him in his pursuit of her. He wrote to her regularly after his return to Paris. He addressed her as his 'adorable friend'; he was hers for life; he asked her to write to him at least once a day. Yet this ardour did not long survive his absence from her; soon he let days go by before bothering to go to the *poste restante* to fetch the letters, sad and expressive of longing and insecurity, which she wrote to him.

Away from Marseilles, he came across women from a different world. He met Victorine, comtesse de Chastenay, a clever young woman who was intrigued by the pallor of his gaunt cheeks, his long, unwashed hair, his extraordinary taciturnity. After dinner she sang a song in Italian and, when she had finished, she asked him if her pronunciation was correct. He answered her with the one word: 'No.' The next day he was more forthcoming, so much so, indeed, that they talked for four hours during which he elaborated his didactic views on all manner of subjects – from Shakespeare (whose plays were 'pitiful') and the poems of Ossian, exposed as forgeries by Samuel Johnson (and extravagantly admired by Napoleon), to the Parisiennes' use of fans (which, so he said, betrayed their feelings as demonstrated by the actress Mlle Constant at the Comédie Française).

Napoleon also met at this time another interesting young woman, Grace Dalrymple Elliott, a rich physician's flighty divorced Scottish wife whose illegitimate daughter may have been the Prince of Wales's, as she liked it to be supposed, though the child might equally well have been fathered by one of her other lovers. One day she and Napoleon went for a walk together in the Tuileries gardens. It was not a success: he spoke of his dislike and distrust of the English and his wish to see the earth open and swallow up the whole race. She said that it was not very tactful of him to say so in her presence. To this he replied that he had always supposed that the Scots loved France and disliked the English. She said that she herself preferred England to Scotland.

7

CHEZ LES PERMONS

'Napoleon, there are two men in you.'

AN UNCLE OF CÉCILE AND LAURE PERMON, the girls who had teased Napoleon in his absurdly big boots, found him 'pretty morose'. This uncle, Demetrius Comnène, had first caught sight of the fifteen-year-old boy in the Palais Royal as he looked all about him, his 'nose in the air'. He had invited him to dinner; but the occasion was not a success: the boy's conversation was largely limited to condemnation of the extravagance of his fellow students, so much better off, so much more aristocratic than the little Corsican upstart.

Napoleon had created no better impression when subsequently he had gone for dinner and had been put up for the night by the Permons. But some time later, when Laure Permon saw him again, she felt that there was, after all, something peculiarly arresting about him. Through a window she watched him approach across the courtyard:

> He was very careless of his appearance [Laure wrote]; and his hair, which was ill combed and ill powdered, gave him a slovenly look ... He had a shabby round hat drawn over his forehead, and I recollect his hair hanging over the collar of his grey great-coat, which afterwards became as famous as the white plume of Henri IV. He wore no gloves, because, as he used to say, they were a useless luxury. His boots were ill-made and unpolished ... His complexion was yellow and seemingly unhealthy, his features angular and sharp.

He approached the house in a clumsy walk. Yet, when he was inside the house, Laure Permon was struck by 'his face without being able to explain why'. When he smiled his features, which she had earlier thought ugly, were lent an undeniable charm.

He became a regular visitor to the Permons' house; and, when in one of his happier moods, he and Laure, by then eleven years old, would dance together in the middle of the room while Cécile played tunes for them on the piano. Or he would sit by the fire after dinner, stretching his legs out on the hearth, crossing his arms on his chest, and call out to Mme Permon, asking her to come to sit by him to talk about Corsica and his mother. She would do so with reluctance for the smell of his dirty, wet boots drying by the flames was so nauseous that she was compelled to bury her nose in a handkerchief or make some excuse to leave the room until Napoleon, at last realizing what drove her away, would have the maid scrape the mud from his boots before entering the sitting room.

The more he saw of Mme Permon the more he admired her. She was an attractive woman, vivacious, amusing, elegant in her dress and, in Napoleon's words, 'very amiable'. 'She loves her country dearly,' he said, 'and she loves the company of Corsicans.' She claimed to have read only one book in her whole life, Fénelon's didactic romance Télémaque; but she was quick-witted and astute.

In common with most men, Napoleon found her alluring. One day he called at the house holding a bunch of violets and this gallantry, as her daughter Laure said, was 'so unusual' for him that they could not help laughing.

On another occasion, he found Laure and her mother in tears: Monsieur Permon was gravely ill and not expected to survive. He died two days later; and, not long afterwards, Napoleon astonished Mme Permon by proposing that, as soon as her widowhood would conventionally allow it, they should get married. Once again Mme Permon could not help laughing. 'My dear Napoleon,' she said, according to Laure, 'do let us talk seriously. You think you know my age. But really you know nothing about it; and I shan't tell you. That's my secret; though I will tell you that I'm old enough to be your mother. So spare me this kind of joke. It upsets me.' It was 'a ridiculous proposal'.

'I want to get married,' Napoleon persisted with characteristic lack of tact, 'and what I've suggested would suit me in many ways. Think it over.' He had given the matter much careful thought, he said. He was clearly much disgruntled when he took his leave, and was never to forgive her for his rebuff.

Before he left, she reminded him of his undertaking to try to obtain a commission for a cousin of hers. Although he had seemed quite willing to do so when she had first broached the subject, Laure said that 'he did not seem quite as willing' now.

'Napoleon,' Mme Permon said, 'there are two men in you. I beg you always to be the one I love and admire ... Do not allow the other one to gain the upper hand.' He did not reply.

Two days later, he called once more at the house, on this occasion taking with him several aides-de-camp. Mme Permon, so Laure said, once again brought up the subject of her cousin's commission. Napoleon was now non-committal. She accused him of prevarication. He told her she was being unjust to him. He took her hand to kiss it in farewell; but she snatched it away so violently that she hit him in the eye. She did not apologize. Promises were nothing to her, she told him, 'actions everything'.

'These young men are laughing at us,' he said to her quietly, indicating the aides-de-camp, as he tried to take her hand again. 'We are acting like two children.' She made no reply as she folded her arms across her chest so that he could make no further attempt to kiss her hand. He picked up his hat and left.

Some years later at a reception at the Tuileries, Laure Permon, by then married to Napoleon's friend, General Andoche Junot, encountered Napoleon again.

'Well, mam'selle Loulou – you see I don't forget the names of old friends – haven't you got a kind word for me?'

> He had taken my hand [Laure Junot recalled] and, pulling me towards him, he looked at me so closely that it made me lower my eyes ... 'General,' I replied, smiling, 'it's not for me to speak first.'
> He smiled and said, 'Very well parried ... She's got her mother's quickness ... By the way, how is Mme Permon?'
> 'Ill, General. She is very ill.'
> 'Ah! Really, as bad as that. Please give her my kind regards.

She's wrong-headed, damnably wrong-headed. But she has a kind heart and she's very generous.'

A few days later, Mme Permon, by then feeling better, invited General Junot and her daughter to dinner. After the meal, she lay down on a sofa and informed them that she would give a dance to celebrate their recent wedding. Junot offered to make a list of the people who were to be invited. Mme Permon suggested Napoleon. The others expressed their astonishment; but Mme Permon said, 'Why do you sound so surprised? Just because I'm a Corsican, do you think I want to indulge in a vendetta? I can't be bothered with that.'

'All right,' said Junot, 'I'll come to fetch you.'

'Come to fetch me! Why? Where do you want to take me?'

'To go to the Tuileries, of course. To deliver the invitation.'

'My dear Junot, you are completely mad!'

'But how are you going to get him to come otherwise?'

'Well, really! How do you suppose? I shall send him an invitation like everyone else.'

Junot's mouth fell open, as it often did when he was surprised, Laure continued her account. 'He walked about in silence, looking in consternation at my mother . . . who with great gravity took a pinch of snuff.'

The following day, General Junot, Laure and Laure's brother, Albert, went to the Tuileries where Napoleon greeted them 'smiling good-naturedly'. 'Oh!' he said. 'What does this family deputation mean? Only Madame Permon is missing. Do the Tuileries frighten her? Or do I?'

'Madame Permon wanted to come with us,' Junot replied. 'But you know how ill she is and it was impossible for her to leave her room.'

When the invitation was proposed to him, he immediately accepted it, merely asking why they all looked as though they expected him to refuse it.

'Oh! I quite understand Madame Permon is ill,' he added. 'But there is laziness, too, also something else that I don't want to talk about. Isn't that so, Madame Loulou?'

And then he pulled Laure's ear; and, not troubling to control the impulse that so often overcame him, he pulled it so hard that the tears came into her eyes, as they did on another occasion when he pinched her nose so tightly that he made it bleed.

This was rough treatment to which his servants were often to be subjected. 'I can confirm that he used to pinch not merely the tip but the whole of the ear, sometimes catching hold of both of them at once in quite purposeful fashion,' one of his valets was to write. 'Sometimes when I came in to dress him he would rush at me, crying, "Hello, you rascal!" and pinch both my ears at once so hard it made me scream. Quite often he also slapped my face several times, after which I was sure to find him good-tempered for the rest of the day.'

Not only servants but generals, women and children were all subjected to this treatment. General Junot's ear was once pinched so hard that it bled, while ladies at court were reduced to tears. One of his nephews was also once reduced to tears by an exceptionally painful pinch and was then punched hard for making a fuss.

Having altered the proposed date for the dance at the Permons to an evening more convenient to himself, Napoleon arrived at the appointed time in his grey overcoat which he declined to take off even though the house was stiflingly hot. Mme Permon greeted him formally with 'one of her most graceful curtseys'.

'Madame Permon,' he rebuked her, 'is that the way you receive an old friend?' and he held out his hand towards her. He was perfectly agreeable, though his hostess, while remaining polite, was far from friendly towards him. Her daughter, urging her to be more cordial, later persuaded her to go into the room where their guest had established himself.

'He came straight up to my mother,' Laure recalled and said to her '*Eh bien*, Madame Permon, what have you got to say to an old friend? It seems to me you forget them easily.'

She answered him in Italian: 'I cannot forget, dear Napoleon, that you are the son of a friend, brother of my good Giuseppe, of dear Luciano, and of Pauletta.'

'So then,' Napoleon replied, 'if I hold any place in your regard, I owe it to my mother, my brothers and sister.'

He then strode towards the fire while Mme Permon sat on a sofa opposite him, her foot shaking as it was inclined to do when she was annoyed and likely to lose her temper.

'Really,' she said, returning to the contentious matter of Napoleon's prevarication in the granting of a commission to her cousin which had come between them at their previous meeting. 'One may forget something after an interval of some years. Do you mean to tell me that it was difficult for you to remember, after a few days, something that may have affected a young man's whole career?'

'Ah, so that's it,' said Napoleon, walking up and down the room with his hands clasped behind his back. Then, overcoming his annoyance, he took one of Mme Permon's hands as though to kiss it, observing as he pointed to her bitten fingernails, 'It does seem that you don't correct any of your faults.'

'No,' she said. 'They and I have grown old together.'

It was now two o'clock. Napoleon sent for his carriage. Madame Permon asked him if he would not stay for supper. 'Impossible,' he said abruptly but as though with regret. 'However, I will come to see you again.' He never did.

8

PARISIAN SALONS

'I am highly regarded here.
I have friends, pleasures and parties.'

As a protégé of Barras, Buonaparte who, in his own words, 'knew no one else there' was introduced into the salons of Mme Tallien, Mme de Staël, Mme Récamier and of several other hostesses in Paris. Such women, he told his brother Joseph, appeared to 'hold the reins of government', while the men 'made fools of themselves over them' and lived 'only for them'. They were, he told Désirée Clary thoughtlessly, beautiful as the female characters in old romances and 'as learned as scholars'. They were all, indeed, remarkable women.

Thérésia Tallien, wife of Jean-Lambert Tallien, one of the leaders of the Thermidorian reaction after the fall and death of Robespierre, a woman of outstanding beauty and wit, still presided over her salon at the Chaumière from which she would emerge in wigs of astonishingly unnatural colours to act as referee in games of bowls, clothed, so one witness testified, '*à la* Diane, her bosom half naked, sandals on her feet and dressed, if one can use the word, in a tunic above her knees'. Indeed, so Talleyrand was to say of her, Thérésia was usually 'as expensively undressed as it is possible to be'.

Germaine de Staël, the wife of Baron Eric de Staël-Holstein – the Swedish Ambassador in Paris – and mistress of Louis, comte de Narbonne, held Thursday soirées at the Swedish embassy. She greatly admired the young Napoleon, calling him 'Scipio and Tancred, uniting the simple virtues of the one with the brilliant deeds of the other'. It was considered characteristic of her irritatingly fulsome admiration of the general that once, on approaching a drawing-room door, she drew aside to let Colonel Lavalette precede her with the words, 'How could I venture to walk in front of one of Buonaparte's adjutants?' But Napoleon felt no admiration for the woman in return, finding her exasperatingly pretentious and impertinent. She once burst in upon him when he was in his bath with the announcement: 'Genius has no sex.'

Jeanne-Françoise-Julie-Adelaide Récamier, the alluring eighteen-year-old, white-clothed, virginal wife of an extremely rich and elderly banker, an enticing, narcissistic girl who was to give her name to the day bed upon which she so elegantly reclined, held sway in a salon as vivacious as any of her rivals.

Among these rivals was Fortunée Hamelin, a sprightly, amusing young woman of about the same age who, despite an appearance rather too plain to be pronounced *jolie laide*, attracted a succession of lovers, including the high-spirited adventurer, Casimir de Montrond, whom, so she claimed outrageously, she had discovered in a lascivious embrace with Mme Récamier. Mme Hamelin herself was far from averse to such embraces and her appearance in a ballroom, heralded by the heaviest and most liberally applied of scents, was sure to be welcomed by numerous would-be partners eager to be clasped against her inviting breasts. Another of Mme Récamier's rivals was Aimée de Coigny who had been married at fifteen to the duc de Fleury and then to Casimir de Montrond, who had hoped to get his hands on sufficient money to pay his ever-mounting debts and who, while imprisoned with Aimée at St Lazare, contrived to have their names removed every day from the lists of those submitted to the Revolutionary Tribunal by offering extravagant rewards, which he was in no position to pay, to the official whose duty it was to compile them.

In this Thermidorian Paris where women held such sway, Napoleon Bonaparte, as he soon chose to spell his name as appearing less Italian, cut a poor figure. As though in deliberate provocation of his fellow guests in their high fashions and fastidious toilets, he would appear with his hair dirty and uncombed, his face scarred with scabies contracted at Toulon, his body evidently unwashed, and his French as yet so imperfect that other guests sometimes could not, or affected not to, understand him.

At La Chaumière, he was, according to the banker, Gabriel Ouvrard, the least impressive of all the men there. He was at an exceptionally low ebb, once more contemplating suicide. There was only one thing to do in this world, he decided, and that was to acquire money as Paris's *nouveaux riches* speculators were contriving to do; and, having acquired money, to get 'more and more power'. Joseph had money now through his family connections, and Napoleon advised his brother how to invest it; though he himself had neither money nor power. Nor did he attract women. His friend, Andoche Junot, later recalled how, during their rambles around Paris, Napoleon would speak angrily of the *jeunesse dorée*, the Muscadins, who enjoyed 'all the luck' with women, and how, when he saw them promenading in front of him as he and Junot sat in an open-air café, he would petulantly kick the chair in front of him. He was unlucky in love, he declared mournfully, referring, so some thought, to Mme Tallien who rejected a proposal he made to her with what the young banker Gabriel Ouvrard described as 'an incredulous laugh'.

But then his career took a more hopeful turn. Obtaining the requisite medical report, he applied for sick leave so that he would be free to accept a more promising appointment than that of the command of the Army of the West should an alternative be offered him. This caused temporary difficulties: the Committee of Public Safety ruled that the doctor who had supplied the certificate was not qualified to do so and that Bonaparte was to be relieved of his command for insubordination in disobeying orders.

Napoleon turned for help to Barras, who did not disappoint him: he was soon offered an important appointment in an influential department of the Committee of Public Safety in Paris, a useful stepping-stone to the power he craved. 'If I could be happy far from you, I would be now,' he wrote to Désirée in an affectionate letter reflecting his sudden change of mood. 'I am highly regarded here. I have friends, pleasures and parties ... I kiss you a million times and am your loving friend for life.' A new-found friend he did not mention was Paul Barras's *maîtresse en titre*, Marie-Josèphe-Rose de Beauharnais, vicomte de Beauharnais's Creole widow, whom he was to call Josephine.

9

ADVENTURES IN ITALY

'He absolutely worships me. I think he will go mad.'

NOT LONG AFTER that 'whiff of grapeshot' on 5 October 1795 had helped to defeat the supporters of a counter-revolution and had secured his future, Bonaparte received a letter from Josephine de Beauharnais who assured him of her fond attachment to him, gently reprimanding him for neglecting her, and inviting him to lunch on the following day. 'Good night,' she ended her letter, '*mon ami, je vous embrasse.*'

Napoleon answered the letter immediately, begging her to believe that it was only his pressing duties which kept him away from her, that no one desired her friendship as much as he did.

He had often seen this alluring widow at Mme Tallien's house, La Chaumière, at Barras's house and at her small neo-Greek *pavillon* at No 6 rue de Chantereine, the rent of which, so it was widely supposed, as well as the wages of her gatekeeper, her coachman, her groom, her gardener, her chef and her four domestic servants, was paid by her lover, Paul Barras.

She herself gave the impression of being rich, in possession of extensive estates in the West Indies; and this was at least one of her attractions in the eyes of Napoleon who, before becoming too deeply involved with her, went to see her notary to make enquiries about this rumoured wealth – an indiscretion which naturally much annoyed Josephine when she heard about it.

But there was far more to her than her supposed riches. Although six years older than Napoleon and described by the disaffected as 'decaying', as sunk in 'early decrepitude', by no means clever or witty like her young and intimate friend, Thérésia Tallien, she was still a most attractive woman: elegant, beautifully dressed, *simpatica*, voluptuous, languorous, speaking softly in her pleasing voice with its attractive Caribbean inflexion. She had bad teeth; but she had learned to smile without showing them. Napoleon, as he himself admitted, was *gauche* and shy with women, professing a defensive contempt for them as not to be regarded as men's equals, as 'mere machines for making children'. Yet with Josephine he felt at ease: she gave him confidence; she flattered him, paid him, as he said, 'all manner of compliments'. Besides, she was, so he believed, not only rich but a great lady of the *ancien régime*. He soon conceived thoughts of marrying her: she would – as Barras said, advising him to do so – help people to forget his Corsican name and make him 'entirely French'.

She herself regarded a possible marriage to this young and rather uncouth general with misgiving. He was undeniably 'passionate and lively' yet still 'awkward and altogether strange in all his person', though admittedly not so unprepossessing as he had been in the recent past: he now brushed his hair properly and splashed himself liberally with eau de Cologne, and his features were occasionally transformed by a remarkably attractive smile. But, despite his undoubted promise, his future was far from secure, as hers might well be also if she married him. She was evidently concerned that, if she became Bonaparte's wife, she might lose the protection of Barras who had already taken Thérésia Tallien as a supplementary mistress. Moreover, neither his family nor hers was in favour of such a match; nor was her notary, Raguideau, who told her she would do much better marrying an army contractor who would have the means to make her rich. Others proposed Gabriel Ouvrard.

Once he had decided that marriage to Josephine de Beauharnais might well promote his career, Bonaparte for his part had no doubt that he should make her his wife. Having come to that decision, he fell in love with her. After what was evidently their first night together, he wrote to tell his 'sweet and incomparable Josephine' that he drew from her lips and heart a flame that consumed him. He sent her 'a thousand kisses'; and asked her not to send him any in return for they burned his blood. Less romantically, and much later, he told comte Bertrand,

'I really loved Josephine, but I had no respect for her. She had the prettiest little cunt in the world . . . Actually I married her only because I believed her to be rich. She said she was, but it wasn't true.'

It was not until the end of February 1796 that Josephine's reluctance was at length overcome and she agreed to marry Napoleon, telling Grace Dalrymple Elliott that she did not really love him but that she thought he could be of service to her children. He had already written to Désirée, telling her that unless she could obtain her parents' consent to an immediate marriage – consent which, as a minor, it was essential for her to obtain and which he presumed she would not get – he would be compelled to end their relationship. Her answer was contained in a sad little letter, wishing him well and assuring him that she could never love anyone else. He had destroyed her life, she told him, but she was 'weak enough' to forgive him. 'May the woman you have chosen make you as happy as you deserve to be. In the midst of your present happiness do not forget poor Eugénie, and be sorry for her fate.'

Marriage to Josephine de Beauharnais, a civil ceremony, took place on 9 March. For a variety of reasons it was, in fact, invalid: the official who conducted the service was not legally qualified to do so; the young officer who witnessed Napoleon's signature was a minor and, therefore, equally unqualified for this duty; Josephine, claiming that she could not do so because of the British occupation of the Windward Islands, failed to produce her birth certificate and took the opportunity of reducing her age by four years; while Napoleon, also claiming to be unable to produce his own birth certificate, gave his date of birth as Joseph's and place of birth as Paris rather than Ajaccio.

The bride, wearing a white muslin gown with a tricolour sash and an enamelled medallion engraved with the words 'To Destiny' – a present from the bridegroom – waited for the appearance of Napoleon, with the Talliens, Paul Barras and her notary sitting by her side. They waited in the cold room by the light of a tin lantern for an hour, then two hours, then three before Napoleon burst into the room, shook the sleepy official by the shoulder, told him to get on with it, and, within a few minutes, was driving back with his wife to her house.

Four days before, to the annoyance of more senior officers and particularly of Lazare Hoche, under whom he had declined to serve in Vendée,

Napoleon had been appointed commander of the Army of Italy, an appointment described maliciously as 'Barras's dowry'; and, two days after the wedding, he left Paris for the Army's headquarters in Nice. Here he encountered the major-generals who were, with varying degrees of reluctance, to serve under him: Louis Desaix, Pierre Augereau and André Masséna. They were all tall men, powerfully built, towering over Napoleon whom Masséna later described as 'puny and sickly looking', a man who had got his command through the influence of Barras and Barras's women.

Within weeks, their opinion of the pale little Corsican had been transformed. Napoleon found the army under strength, badly equipped and poorly paid. In one of those inspirational addresses which were to exhilarate his soldiers in campaign after campaign, he is said to have promised to lead them into the 'most fertile plains in the world', through rich provinces and great cities where they would find 'honour, glory and riches'. True to his word, he succeeded in splitting the forces of the Austrian Emperor and of the King of Sardinia which outnumbered him. He won a succession of astonishing victories, news of which were sent to the government in Paris, the Directory, by relays of couriers galloping across the plains of Lombardy.

These couriers also took with them not only trophies of victory – flags and standards – but a series of scribbled letters addressed to 6 rue Chantereine for Mme de Beauharnais who had not, as yet, adopted her husband's name. He wrote every day, sometimes twice a day, his pockets stuffed with unfinished, scarcely coherent letters never sent to his 'adorable Josephine', his 'sweet love', the 'pleasure and torment of his life'. Not a day went by, he told her, without his loving her, not a night without his longing to hold her in his arms. He loved her more each day; he longed to kiss her heart and then lower on her body, much, *much* lower, underlining the words with such force that the point of his pen struck through the paper. 'Never has a woman been loved with more devotion, fire and tenderness,' he told her. If she were to leave him he would feel that, in losing her and her 'adorable person', he would have lost everything that made life worthwhile.

Preoccupied with parties, subscription balls, receptions, shopping, fittings at her dressmaker's, visitors who crowded into her boudoir, and relishing the credit she enjoyed at the most expensive shops as the wife of the brilliant young general, the reception accorded to her at the theatre where audiences stood up to applaud her as she entered her box, the shouts of welcome in the streets, and the cheers of fishwives in Les Halles, Josephine did not find time to read all these letters on the days of their arrival. Occasionally, she would pick one up to read an extract or two to a visitor. Once, she read one to the poet and playwright, Antoine Arnault. In this Napoleon had written of his jealousy of other men who could be with her as he could not, and had added, 'Beware of Othello's dagger.' She laughed and commented, '*Qu'il est drôle, Bonaparte.*'

'Josephine, no letter from you,' he complained on 24 May. 'No news from my good friend ... *mi dolce amore* ... Has she forgotten me already?' Couriers arrived from Paris, but brought no letter from her. He was consumed with anxiety and jealousy. He began to think she must have resumed her liaison with Barras, or perhaps found another lover. He could never bear that, he said, sending 'a thousand kisses on your eyes, your lips, your tongue, your cunt'. 'Obviously your pretended love for me was but a caprice.' Then he relented. 'Drowning in my sorrow, I may have written too harshly.'

'I had not believed it was possible to suffer so deeply, so much pain, such awful torment,' he told her in another letter. 'I send you a million kisses. Remember there is nothing so strong as my love for you ... It will last for ever ... The flame that comes from your lips consumes me ... My emotions are never moderate ... I am in an indescribable state ... The ardent love which fills me has, perhaps, unbalanced my mind.'

Frustrated by the few, short letters she sent in reply to his frantic effusions, he sent Andoche Junot to Paris with enemy flags for the Directory and a peremptory order not to return to Italy without his wife. 'You will come, won't you?' he begged her. 'You must return with Junot, do you hear, my adorable one?'

He sent Colonel Joachim Murat with, similar orders and a fateful question: 'There's no one else, is there?' He later heard with great distress that the big, handsome, buccaneering Murat had boasted of a gross intimacy with Mme Bonaparte, giving 'barely decent details, fit only for a hussar officers' mess'. On the day that Murat had arrived in Paris, wearing out numerous post-horses on the way, the glass of the miniature of Josephine which Bonaparte wore on a ribbon around his neck, and which he had shown with such pride to the disapproving major-generals on his arrival in Nice, cracked and shattered. According to his aide-de-camp, Auguste Marmont, Bonaparte had turned deadly pale and, giving way to characteristic superstition, had said, 'Marmont, either my wife is very ill or she is being unfaithful.'

She was being unfaithful.

Captain Hippolyte Charles was a short, lively young man, by no means handsome but attractive, cheerful and amusing, an adept lover, nine years younger than herself. He made her laugh, Josephine said, something quite beyond the ability of Napoleon – whose occasional enforced guffaws were irritating rather than infectious. With his shiny black hair, blue eyes and eager, good-humoured expression, Captain Charles looked very well in his Hussar uniform with its pelisse cast over his shoulder. Men found him a delightful companion; women were entranced by him. Josephine was in love with him.

When Murat delivered Bonaparte's instructions for her to return to Italy, she told him to tell her husband that she could not undertake so trying a journey: she was too ill; she was pregnant.

When Napoleon received this news, he was about to enter Milan, the capital of Lombardy. His military triumph was complete. He felt, he said, as though the earth were flying beneath him, as though he were being 'carried to the sky'. Yet, so he told Josephine, he thought of nothing but her illness night and day, 'without appetite, without sleep, without interest in glory or country'. He 'longed to see her little tummy' which must surely give her a 'wonderfully majestic appearance'.

To Lazare Carnot, the 'Organizer of Victory' who had taken to wearing a miniature of Bonaparte beneath his coat as a badge of loyalty, as well as to his brother Joseph and to Barras, Napoleon revealed his agitated concern. Having received a brief note from Josephine to say that she was still ill and that three doctors were in attendance, he told Joseph, 'I am in despair. Reassure me about my wife's health. You know that Josephine is the first woman I have ever adored . . . I love her to distraction. I cannot stay here any longer without her.' 'I am in despair,' he wrote to Barras. 'My wife won't come. She must have a lover and that keeps her in Paris.'

The days and weeks passed and still Josephine did not write to him and sent no word that she might come to him. His thoughts turned again to suicide: he wrote of lying for just two hours in her arms and then dying with her. If she were to die he would die himself, 'a death of despair'.

He spoke of deserting his post and returning to Paris to be with her. 'My presence,' he said, 'will conquer your illness . . . I have always been able to impose my will upon destiny . . . Without you I cannot be of any use here . . . There has never been a love like mine. It will last as long as my life.'

Their general's threat to abandon his army, just as the Austrians were believed to be preparing a counter-attack, alarmed the Directory to such an extent that Josephine was dispatched forthwith to Milan. She left in tears, so her friend, Antoine Arnault said. 'She looked as though she were going to a torture chamber.' Clutching her dog, Fortuné, in his new leather collar, she was accompanied by Andoche Junot and his aide, Hippolyte Charles. Joseph Bonaparte, Désirée Clary's brother, Nicolas, Josephine's maid and two menservants also went with her.

Josephine, complaining of the heat and troubled by a persistent headache, was loath to leave Turin on the journey to Milan; and it was with evident reluctance that she entered the neo-classical Serbelloni Palace in Milan, which her husband had filled with flowering shrubs to welcome her. That night was only the third they had spent together.

But 'what nights', Napoleon wrote. 'My happiness is being near you, *ma bonne amie* . . . Surely you must have some faults in your character. Tell me.' She could not share his enthusiasm. 'I am dying of boredom here,' she told Thérésia Tallien. 'My husband does not merely love me. He absolutely worships me. I think he will go mad.'

10

THE SERBELLONI PALACE

'They are so regardless of convention as to dress in clothes
revealing legs and thighs in flesh-coloured tights.'

WHEN NAPOLEON DEPARTED from Milan to his army in the field,
his wife evinced no distress. She sent for her friend Fortunée Hamelin
to keep her company in the Serbelloni Palace, having borrowed from
Mme Hamelin's husband, the financier, a large sum of money before
her departure from Paris; a debt, like so many in the past and future,
never to be repaid. Other friends and acquaintances arrived in Milan
where their 'immodest behaviour', as one newspaper put it, caused some
offence. 'Arms, bosoms, shoulders are all uncovered . . . Their hair styles
are scandalous: their heads are crowned with little military helmets from
which tresses of untidy hair escape. They are so regardless of convention
as to dress in clothes revealing legs and thighs in flesh-coloured tights.'

As the days passed, Josephine began to enjoy herself, though she
missed the diversions and pleasures of Paris and the friends she had left
behind there, such as Barras and the Talliens. She was happy to be the
centre of attention as the wife of the brilliant young general. She gave
parties and dances, and graciously accepted the presents of jewellery
and works of art which the heads of great Italian families brought to her
in the hope of being spared the looting which Napoleon had specifically
condoned. This looting led to the plunder and removal to France from
Italian churches, palaces, ransacked cities and towns numerous pictures,
sculptures, manuscripts, silver and all manner of other treasures, including – from the Venetian republic alone – the gilded leather hangings
from the Doge's Palace, Veronese's central panel from the ceiling of the

Hall of the Council of Ten in the Doge's Palace, his *Marriage at Cana* from the monastery of San Giorgio Maggiore, and the four bronze horses from San Marco which were, for a time, to decorate the Arc du Carousel in the Tuileries. As well as the loss of such treasures, Italians also had cause to complain of French soldiers, officers and men alike, taking such opportunities as had been offered them to enrich themselves. Bonaparte's family acquired their share and, on behalf of Bonaparte himself, his secretary, Louis de Bourrienne looked after a large coffer filled with gold and silver coins.

Flattered and indulged in the Serbelloni Palace, Josephine complacently accepted letter after passionate letter from her absent husband who assured her that, much as he had adored her in the past, he loved her now 'a thousand times more than ever'. When he was with her, he wanted 'it always to be night' so that he could take her in his arms; he kept 'remembering her kisses'. Her replies to these effusions were brief but he assured her that they gave him great pleasure, adding what he can scarcely have supposed to be true, that he was certain that she loved writing them.

He was sure that she was better now that her supposed pregnancy had come to nothing; so he hoped that, as soon as she was able to travel, she would join him. So, comforting herself with the thought that Hippolyte Charles was there, she left Milan for Brescia accompanied by Antoine Hamelin. Her journey proved a hazardous undertaking. At Verona, the sudden appearance of Austrian troops obliged them to drive off in great haste for the shores of Lake Garda under an escort of dragoons. Their coach came under fire from a gunboat on the lake; and they had to scramble out to seek the shelter of a ditch along which they crawled towards the carriage which had been driven off to the shelter of a sunken road. For over a week thereafter they drove about Tuscany, eventually arriving in Florence where they found shelter with the Grand Duke Ferdinand III who had signed a treaty with Napoleon. They remained here as guests of the Grand Duke until Pierre Augereau's victory over the Austrians at Castiglione on 5 August 1796 enabled them to leave Florence and, at last, to reach Brescia.

Napoleon, however, was no longer there. He had gone to a newly established headquarters over twenty-five miles away, having left instructions for his wife to join him. Josephine protested that she was too tired to do so: she would go to bed in the rooms that Napoleon had just vacated and have supper there. She invited Hamelin to join her. When he arrived, Hamelin was surprised to see Hippolyte Charles and the table laid for three. They had supper there together and the two men then left. Some time later Hamelin, remembering that he had left his pistols in the room adjoining that in which they had had their meal, returned to fetch them. Outside the door he was stopped by a sentry who denied him entry.

Upon her return to Milan where her husband, who had given himself three weeks' leave, had demanded her presence, Josephine was bored. She missed Captain Charles; she missed her friends in Paris; and she missed her children and the stimulating company of Paul Barras. 'I do love him,' she told her confidante, Mme Tallien. 'I am devoted to him.' It was all very well being fêted by 'all the Italian princes, and even the Grand Duke of Tuscany', she said: she would much rather be a private person in France.

Her husband remained 'all day in admiration' of her; he treated her as though she were 'a divinity'; it would be 'impossible to have a better husband'. There were, however, occasions when it was difficult for her to hide her irritation with his teasing of her, his habit of pinching her so hard it brought the tears to her eyes, his kissing her, fondling her breasts and hugging her so passionately and intimately, even when there were other people in the room, that Hamelin felt constrained to avert his eyes, to walk away and look out of the window as though 'observing the weather'. Comte André Miot de Melito was equally embarrassed when he accompanied Bonaparte and Josephine on a journey by coach to Lake Maggiore during which, as he delicately put it, Bonaparte was 'extremely attentive' to his wife, frequently taking various 'conjugal liberties' with her.

The campaign against the Austrians was going badly, and there was even talk of a French withdrawal from Italy. But then came news of Napoleon's victories, first on 15, 16 and 17 November 1796 at Arcola, then on 14 January 1797 at Rivoli Veronese, which ensured the fall of Mantua after a siege lasting well over six months.

Written in a state of euphoria in the aftermath of these decisive victories, Napoleon's letters to Josephine became more passionate than ever. He wrote of his impatience to give her proofs of his 'ardent love', to be in bed with her, to see again her adorable face, her hair tied up in a scarf *à la créole*, her 'little black forest'. 'I kiss it a thousand times and wait impatiently for the time when I will be in it. To live within Josephine is to live in the Elysian Fields.'

Soon, however, the letters changed their tone. On a visit to Milan, he found that Josephine was not in the Serbelloni Palace. For over a week he waited in vain for her return, writing her a succession of letters by turn angry, self-pitying, mortified and disillusioned. 'I long to hold you in my arms,' he wrote. 'The pain I feel is unbelievable . . . When I ask you to love me as I love you, I am wrong to do so . . . I am not worth it . . . When I am sure that she no longer loves me I will keep silent, wishing only to be useful to her . . . I will submit to all sorrows, all grief, if only the fates will grant Josephine happiness . . . Oh, Josephine, Josephine.'

In his grief and discontent Napoleon pursued a policy in Italy quite at odds with the wishes of the Directory in Paris. Having advanced to within sixty miles of Vienna, he signed a preliminary treaty with the Austrians at Leoben, where onlookers were struck by the brusque demeanour of the little man who spoke in strongly accented French, giving orders, making demands and granting few concessions with supreme confidence. Again ignoring the wishes of the Directory and arousing further annoyance in Paris he deposed the Doge in Venice and destroyed that most ancient republic.

Whilst waiting for the details of his Italian diktat to be settled, in May 1797 Napoleon moved his headquarters from Milan to the huge Baroque palace at Mombello. Josephine, who had again been protesting that her poor health demanded her return to Paris, now announced that she would, after all, remain at Mombello, a decision widely assumed to have been taken because Captain Charles's duties would require his presence there for the whole of that summer.

They were pleasant months for her. She was able to indulge her passion for flowers, which were planted under her direction all over the gardens, as well as her fondness for birds, which fluttered and glided over the waters of the lake and chirruped in cages ordered for her by her husband. By day, Josephine could be seen strolling in her graceful way down the gravelled paths and across the well-mown grass; by night, she presided over the dining-room table in her white muslin dress, with an ivy wreath in her hair, captivating men by the glances of her eyes, 'dark blue,' as one of her admirers described them, 'always half closed under long lids, fringed by the longest eyelashes in the world', sipping coffee after dinner on the terrace, her dog by her side.

This was not Fortuné, who had been so impertinent as to bite Napoleon's leg the first time he shared a bed with the animal's mistress. For this tiresome animal, to whom Josephine had been so unaccountably attached, had been killed by a dog belonging to the Mombello chef, much to the pleasure of Napoleon who expressed the hope that Fortuné's replacement – a puppy secretly given to her by Captain Charles – would meet the same fate.

Content as she was to be under the same roof as Charles, even though the opportunities to be alone with him were not frequent, Josephine did not take kindly to the thought of being thrown into the company of several members of her husband's family whom he now decided to establish at Mombello.

Among the first to arrive on holiday from the Irish college at St Germain, the Dermott Academy, were Josephine's son, Eugène de Beauharnais, now fifteen years old, and Napoleon's brother, Jérôme, aged twelve. Also there was Jérôme's and Napoleon's mother, Letizia: Napoleon had thought it as well not to inform her of his marriage to the widow Beauharnais until after it had taken place, and Letizia did not approve of it or of her. Although Josephine behaved towards her mother-in-law with the utmost courtesy and that charm of manner that others found so beguiling, Letizia never could bring herself to respond to her wayward daughter-in-law's natural warmth. Nor could Laure Junot, who wrote of her: 'Mme Bonaparte was an astonishing woman and must formerly have been very pretty . . . though no longer in the first bloom of youth.' Had she but possessed teeth, 'I do not say pretty teeth but only teeth', she would have been 'more attractive than most of her contemporaries'.

Nor could Letizia's three daughters outgrow their initial wary diffidence in the presence of what seemed to them the assured sophistication of their sister-in-law. Their ill-concealed jealousy soon turned to active dislike.

II

THE FAVOURITE SISTER

'How could my brother be so cruel as to
send me into exile amongst savages and snakes?'

DISTRACTED AS HE WAS by his passion for Josephine, Napoleon was at the same time deeply concerned by the behaviour of his sister Pauline, who at sixteen, was a sensual, wayward, high-spirited girl, 'the prettiest and worst-behaved person imaginable,' in the opinion of the poet, Antoine-Vincent Arnault: 'She had the deportment of a schoolgirl, chattering away without pause, laughing at nothing and everything, contradicting the most eminent personages, sticking out her tongue at her sister-in-law behind her back, nudging my knee when I wasn't paying her sufficient attention, and drawing upon herself from time to time the most terrifying looks of reproof from her brother . . . But, even so, a naturally good-natured child, if without any principle. She was someone capable of doing good from pure caprice.'

Metternich, the Austrian diplomatist and statesman, provided a shorter and less indulgent character sketch. The girl was admittedly 'as pretty as it is possible to be', but she was 'in love with herself and her only occupation was pleasure'.

Pauline had fallen in love with Stanislas Fréron, an unscrupulous, heartless dandy twenty-six years older than herself, a man reputed to be suffering from syphilis and undoubtedly keeping a mistress, an actress, at the Théâtre des Italiens, who had borne two of his children and was shortly to have a third. It had been bad enough, in her mother's opinion, when Pauline's brother Lucien – described by Laure Permon as the 'tall, ill-shaped and very short-sighted Lucien' – married Catherine, the illiterate and distressingly shy daughter of an innkeeper without informing his mother; but, at least, Catherine was gentle and affectionate. This business of Fréron was much worse.

He had been one of the most outspoken deputies in the National Convention and a leading advocate of the September Massacres. He had been sent with Barras to suppress the counter-revolutionary revolt in the south of France where he had ordered the mass execution of hundreds of opponents of the Jacobin regime. Upon his return to Paris, he had been a leading participant in the conspiracy that engineered the downfall and death of Maximilien Robespierre, and had become a prominent supporter of the anti-Jacobin reaction, as well as a vigorous organizer of the gangs of long-haired *jeunesse dorée* who paraded intimidatingly through the streets in their outlandish clothes.

When her mother heard of Pauline's attachment to the devious and dreadful Fréron and of her wish to marry the man – who was admittedly handsome and capable of exercising an undeniably ingratiating charm – Letizia put her foot down: she would not consider it; the girl was a mere child; the proposed marriage was out of the question. Napoleon thought so, too. 'It is not my intention that she should marry Fréron,' he told his brother, Joseph. 'Please arrange the business of Paulette.' He also wrote to Barras, one of Fréron's colleagues, telling him to dissuade Fréron from endeavouring to marry 'a child of sixteen of whom he is old enough to be the father. One does not try to marry when one has two children by a woman still living.'

Her family's opposition to the match inflamed Pauline's passion. '*Ti amo sempre passionatissimamente*,' she wrote to Fréron, '*per sempre ti amo . . . ti amo, amo, amo, si amatissimo amante.*'

Well aware of the consuming fury of his sister's passion, Napoleon decided that the girl, susceptible, passionate and *ingénue*, must be brought to the headquarters of the army in Italy where other more suitable young men would be likely to dampen her burning desire for Fréron, who was later posted to the Army of the North at Napoleon's suggestion and, later, sent as a sub-prefect to the West Indies where he died within a few months.

A few months after Pauline's marriage to Fréron had been prevented, Napoleon, while working in his study in the Villa Crivelli at Mombello, was disturbed by the sounds of some sort of activity in energetic process behind a screen. He got up to see what it was and discovered Pauline, now seventeen, in *flagrante delicto* with one of his young staff officers, Victor-Emmanuel Leclerc. Concerned that his alluring and libidinous sister might well end up in the arms of a man like Fréron, and believing that she might do much worse than settle down with Leclerc, the small but not altogether unpromising twenty-five-year-old son of a well-to-do miller from Pontoise, Napoleon promoted him brigadier-general and, insisting that they get married without delay, arranged for her to be provided with a dowry of forty thousand francs.

Having married Pauline, and proud to have the great General Bonaparte as a brother-in-law, Leclerc took it upon himself to behave as though to the manner born, adopting Napoleon's way of walking with his hands behind his back and standing, as Jérôme Bonaparte also did, with his right hand tucked across his waist beneath his coat. Absurd as these mannerisms were considered to be, Leclerc was not an absurd man; and when Napoleon decided to send out a force of twenty-six thousand men to Saint-Domingue, the West Indian island now comprising the states of Haiti and the Dominican Republic, to suppress a movement for independence led by Toussaint-Louverture, a former slave of remarkable military talent, General Leclerc was chosen to command it. His wife was by then the mother of a boy named Dermide Louis-Napoleon, Dermide being a name taken from the epic poems which were supposedly by the legendary third-century Gaelic warrior and bard, Ossian, whose works had not long since been translated into French and were so extravagantly admired by Napoleon.

Pauline left France with her husband and young son for Saint-Domingue with the utmost regret, complaining to a friend, 'How could my brother be so cruel as to send me into exile amongst savages and snakes?' 'Besides,' she added in her hypochondriacal way without too strict a regard for truth, 'I am very ill. I shall die before I get there.'

She did not die; but she was profoundly unhappy on the island, dabbling in voodooism as a means of relieving her boredom. In the unhealthy tumbledown town of Cap Haïten, she was ill as well as miserable. Her skin turned yellow, she was listless and sick, and her face and beautiful body were covered with sores which had still not cleared up when at length she returned to Paris.

Her husband reported, however, that her behaviour left nothing to be desired: 'Realizing how dreadful it is for her to remain in a country where she has before her eyes only the sight of the dead and dying, I urged her to return to France, but she refused to do so, saying that she must share my fortunes, good or bad.'

These fortunes were bad, indeed. 'Since my arrival I have seen nothing but fires, insurrections, assassinations,' he reported to Napoleon, 'and nothing can expel these fearful images from my mind ... I am fighting here against the blacks, against the whites, even against my army which has lost its courage ... Madame Leclerc is ill, but she is a model of courage and really worthy to be your sister.'

Leclerc was soon seriously ill himself and was nursed devotedly by Pauline who received a letter of encouragement and warning from Napoleon: 'Remember that fatigue and difficulties are nothing when one shares them with one's husband, and is useful to one's country. Make yourself loved by your thoughtfulness, your affability and by conduct which is above reproach and never frivolous. We have some trunks of fashionable clothes packed up for you and the captain of the Syrene will bring them to you. I love you very much.'

Leclerc died – as Fréron had done – of yellow fever in November 1802. His wife cut off some tresses of her hair to place in his coffin and sailed home to France, spending much of the voyage alone in her cabin, mourning her loss, writing to Napoleon on New Year's Day 1803, after an eight weeks' voyage across the Atlantic: 'I have arrived at Toulon after an appalling crossing with my health ruined. This is the least of my sorrows. I have brought back with me the remains of my poor Leclerc. Pity poor Paulette. She is thoroughly miserable.'

Her brother responded by granting her an allowance of sixty thousand francs a year which, together with the surprisingly large sum left by her husband, allowed her to live with satisfactory extravagance. On her return to Paris she stayed for some time convalescing in her brother Joseph's house, before buying a neighbouring house, the Hôtel Charost in the faubourg St Honoré, for four hundred thousand francs. She was now also the owner of a château in the country, bought partly from the money she had persuaded her late husband to acquire, as opportunity offered in Italy, and she could be seen from time to time driving out from its *porte-cochère* in a flamboyant carriage, dressed in costumes as eccentric as her disjointed if amiable conversation. Once again she became the talk of the town: her rumoured venereal disease, her visits to clairvoyants, the interest she shared with her sister-in-law, Josephine, in tarot cards and in the interpretation of the patterns of egg whites dropped into glasses of water, the expensive clothes she bought from the dressmaker, Louis-Hippolyte Leroy, her dislike of Josephine, at whom she could be seen, as in the past, putting out her tongue, and the highly unusual remedies she employed for real, or more often imaginary complaints, including enemas containing the boiled intestines of farm animals – all these were favourite topics of Parisian gossip. So was her notorious reputation for sexual adventures with a variety of lovers who had included, even before her departure for Saint-Domingue, an actor at the Comédie Française, Pierre Lafon, and the marquis de Sémonville, a former Commissioner in Corsica. 'I was one of her lovers,' Sémonville told Baron Mounier, one of Napoleon's secretaries. 'There were five of us sharing her favours in the same house before she left for Saint-Domingue ... She was the greatest hussy you can imagine, but also the most tempting.' Jacques-Étienne Macdonald, an officer of Scottish descent who was to become a marshal and the duc de Tarente, certainly thought so: he spent three whole days with her in the bedroom of a house at Saint-Leu. He and two other officers all had affairs with her at the same time.

12

CAROLINE

'A small claw sometimes showed itself.'

NAPOLEON'S YOUNGEST SISTER, CAROLINE, a girl of fifteen in
1797, was at first prepared to behave in a friendly way towards Josephine,
so much older than herself, and so responsive. At this time Caroline
was a bright and pretty girl who had received a sound education at a
school also attended by Josephine's daughter, Hortense, the Institut
National de St-Germain-en-Laye which had been founded by Mme
Jeanne-Louise-Henriette Campan, an impoverished lady who had been
employed at court as a reader to the daughters of Marie-Antoinette.
The pupils, instructed in a variety of disciplines, skills and accomplish-
ments, wore uniforms the colour of which denoted the forms in which
the girls were placed. The curriculum was more varied than was usual
in such establishments, and included lessons in such subjects as geography and grammar taught by a clergyman, as well as music and dancing,
drawing, deportment and polite behaviour such as that formerly to be
observed at Versailles where ladies had curtseyed when anyone sneezed.

'I must tell you that she knows absolutely nothing,' Napoleon had
told Mme Campan when making arrangements for Caroline to be taken
at the school. 'Try to make her as clever as our dear Hortense.' It was
an exhortation, if repeated to the girls, not likely to ease the relationship
between them. Nor was Mme Campan herself at all pleased when four
grenadiers came clattering up to the school door late one evening with
a message for Mlle Bonaparte from one of her brother's generals. This
general was Joachim Murat, the handsome, swaggering cavalry officer,

thirty-two years old, the man who had seized the cannon at Sablons and brought them to the Tuileries gardens, thus enabling Napoleon to save the Convention.

He had been born on 25 March 1767 in a small village in the province of Guyenne, the youngest of the eleven children of a smallholder who also kept the village inn and posting station. He had been intended for the Church and had been granted a bursary to attend the Collège Saint-Michel. From there he had gone on to a Lazarist seminary at Toulouse, thus being given a far better education than had been available to his brothers. It was not long, however, before he decided that he had no vocation for the priesthood and, resolving to be a soldier, he had enlisted in a cavalry regiment in 1787.

His rise in the army had since been rapid. By May 1793, he was a major in the 16th Chasseurs, and by 1796, Napoleon's aide-de-camp in the Army of Italy with which he served with notable dash and bravery. Wounded by a sabre cut on his arm at Mantua, he was later shot through the mouth, the bullet, as he told his father, going in through one cheek and out of the other without injuring his tongue or breaking a tooth.

Although Napoleon respected Murat as a dashing cavalry leader with an enviable capacity to judge the strength of enemy formations with remarkable accuracy, he was annoyed when he heard that the man, a mere innkeeper's son with a strong provincial accent, wanted to marry his sister Caroline, a girl fifteen years younger than himself. She had been rather plain as a child, thin and pale; but she was now growing into an attractive young woman: there would come a time, he said, when sovereigns 'might vie for her hand'.

'She is a knowing little scatterbrain, with no thought for my position,' her brother complained to Mme Campan. Murat was admittedly a brave man, but that was not enough. Napoleon said as much to Caroline herself. The man had a little learning, he conceded: he had, after all, 'been raised as a priest'. But he had no real intelligence, just as he had no *politesse*. 'One day,' Napoleon told his sister angrily, 'you'll learn what it is to go to bed with a man who can't control himself and find yourself alone with him, without your chemise and the man naked.' He then added, 'In the high position to which fortune has raised me, I simply cannot allow a member of my family to marry into one like that.'

But her eldest brother, Joseph, as head of the family, approved of the marriage. A marriage contract was consequently drawn up and Napoleon was prevailed upon to sign it; but he declined to go to the wedding which took place on 20 January 1800 at Joseph's estate at Mortefontaine.

Once the matter had been settled, however, Napoleon decided to be accommodating; taking with him his two fellow consuls, Emmanuel-Joseph Sieyès, the churchman who drafted the new constitution, and Pierre-Roger Ducos, a compliant protégé of Barras, he attended a ball given at the Ministry of the Interior by Lucien Bonaparte, the Minister, in honour of Caroline and Joachim Murat. Napoleon also provided the bride and bridegroom with a pleasant apartment in the cour des Tuileries at the Hôtel Brionne, while they also acquired an estate in the country at Villiers, overlooking the Seine opposite the Île de la Grand Jatte, and another in the Deux-Sèvres for which they paid almost half a million francs (a sum they could well afford, Caroline having been given a handsome dowry and Murat having acquired a fortune from various dubious activities while serving in Italy).

They were clearly very happy. The comtesse de Chastenay wrote of the pleasant sight of Murat with his 'sunburned face and black hair . . . holding the gloves and fan of the slim, white little creature', his wife. Murat himself described Caroline as 'the most adorable little woman'; yet, although so young, she had a determined will: another observer, Mme Lenormand, wrote of the 'contrast of the rather childish grace of her face with the decisiveness of her character'.

Fond as they were of each other in the early years of their marriage, Murat was not faithful to Caroline, nor she to him. She dutifully bore his children; but it was not long before she embarked upon a series of affairs including, so Hortense de Beauharnais said, one with her husband's aide-de-camp, the comte de Flahaut and, more passionately, with Metternich and also with Laure Permon's husband, Andoche Junot, who came close to murdering his wife when he discovered that she, too, was conducting an affair with Metternich.

Hortense was ambivalent in her feelings for Caroline. She was a mistress, Hortense said, of the 'art of attracting and charming . . . Admittedly a small claw sometimes showed itself . . . She was brave, determined and emotional, the charm which made one long to serve her could not conceal a lust for total domination . . . Nor could she hide her envy of anyone else's success.'

According to Talleyrand, she had the 'mind of Cromwell in the body of a pretty woman. Born with a most forceful character, she was as graceful as she was charming and attractive. But she could not conceal her passion for power.'

Her brother Napoleon recognized this passion as well as her commanding personality; and when, at the age of thirty-nine, Murat was created King of Naples, Napoleon told him, 'With a wife like yours, you can always leave should a war induce me to summon you back to my side. Caroline is perfectly capable of acting as regent.'

The marriage of Caroline's sister Pauline to General Leclerc had taken place in the Mombello oratory on the same day as that of her eldest sister, Elisa, to a thirty-five-year-old Corsican officer, Captain Felice Bacciochi. A man of no discernible personality or talent, he was considered to be the best match that the plain and rather bossy Elisa could hope to make and he was soon shipped off to no very demanding employment on the island of his birth.

While granting Elisa, as he granted Pauline, a generous dowry of forty thousand francs, Napoleon was thankful to be able to dispose of so dull and insignificant a brother-in-law, for his household at Mombello was already assuming the formality and dignity of a royal court.

Officers on Napoleon's staff were now required to make courteous genuflections on encountering his mother or his wife or any of his sisters. Nor did these officers dine at the table of the General who had his meals served separately under the respectful gaze of visitors permitted to watch the meal in progress in the manner of those who had been permitted to watch King Louis XVI at table at Versailles.

On a visit to Mombello in June 1797 the diplomatist, comte André-François Miot de Melito, had expected to find an army headquarters but found instead 'a brilliant court':

> Strict etiquette reigned round him [Miot de Melito said] . . . An invitation was an honour eagerly sought, and obtained only with great difficulty. Bonaparte was not in the least embarrassed by the excessive honours paid to him, but received them as though he had been accustomed to them all his life. His reception rooms

and an immense marquee pitched before the palace were constantly filled with a crowd of guards, administrators, and the most distinguished noblemen of Italy who came to solicit the favour of a momentary glance or the briefest interview. In short, everyone bowed before the glory of his victories and the haughtiness of his demeanour. He was no longer the general of a victorious republic, but a conqueror on his own account, imposing his own laws on the vanquished.

Napoleon's whole manner, indeed, had for some time now been far removed from that of the untidy, gauche young man whom Barras had introduced to Parisian society. His self-confidence, his conviction of a future guided by his 'star', were now complete. Miot de Melito described an encounter with him at Mombello during which Napoleon spoke uninterruptedly for two hours during a walk in the park. The comte described him as 'a man of below average height with hair powdered and cut square and worn in an unusual way below his ears. His coat was buttoned to his chin . . . His brusque and animated gestures revealed both passionate feeling and profound thought. His speech was curt, and in those days very incorrect.'

Even so assertive a man as General Pierre Augereau, the son of a poor Parisian servant, whose rough manner was described as 'loud and vulgar', found him intimidating. 'I don't know why,' he was once heard to murmur on emerging from the room which Napoleon used as a study at Mombello, 'but the little bugger scares me.' Napoleon also frightened General Vandamme who had shown remarkable bravery in the campaign of 1793. 'I, who fear neither God nor the devil,' Vandamme once declared, 'am ready to tremble like a child when I approach him.'

In Josephine's presence he conveyed a far less intimidating impression. Indeed, in the company of his wife, so tactful, so polite, courteous, self-assured and charming, he was capable of exercising, when he chose, a far from spurious charm himself.

13

'PEACE À LA BONAPARTE'

'The Italians may squeal a bit,
but that is of no consequence.'

AS CANNON OPENED FIRE in Paris at three o'clock in the morning of 4 September 1797, General Augereau, who had been sent from the Army of Italy by Napoleon for the purpose, led a force of some two thousand men into the Tuileries and arrested all the deputies who had won seats in the recent elections and had been summoned to an emergency meeting. Augereau then marched off to the Luxembourg, the palace built for Marie de Medici, to take into custody two Directors who were at odds with their radical colleagues – Lazare Carnot, the military engineer and former driving spirit of the Committee of General Defence, and François, marquis de Barthélemy, a former minister plenipotentiary in Switzerland, who had been elected a Director only three months before. Barthélemy was surprised in his bed; Carnot managed to escape in his nightshirt. No fewer than sixty-three citizens were also arrested and deported in iron cages to the penal colony of Guiana, where many died of fever. Several newspapers were closed; laws were passed prescribing the death penalty for royalist émigrés returning to France without permission and for anyone plotting to restore the monarchy; while the recent elections, the results of which had been decisively anti-Jacobin, were annulled.

These results, reflecting the reactionary mood of the country, had persuaded the three radical Directors, Paul Barras, Jean-François Reubell and the lawyer, Louis-Marie de La Révellière-Lépeaux, Reubell's ally and colleague, the fiercely short-tempered anti-Christian proponent of deism, to organize the coup d'état which was so efficiently and ruthlessly carried out by General Augereau. Once Augereau had carried out his task, these three Directors, with the collaboration of Charles Maurice de Talleyrand and Talleyrand's friend, Germaine de Staël, set about planning the next stage of their coup.

The essential requirement for this was a general who commanded the respect of a large number of troops loyal to the republic and who was himself loyal to the Revolution. The most likely candidates were General Hoche and General Bonaparte.

But, at the age of twenty-nine, General Hoche died of what seemed to be pneumonia; so General Bonaparte, who had already given the radical Directors his assurance that he was prepared to support them by sending General Augereau to Paris, remained the man most likely to give the radical Directors and their allies the backing they needed. The day after the coup, he received a letter from Talleyrand, the recently appointed Minister of External Relations: 'Paris is calm, Augereau's conduct was exemplary. It is clear that he has been taught in the right school.'

For the moment, Napoleon was obliged to remain in Italy at Passeriano, the Doge's summer residence outside Venice, impatiently endeavouring to conclude the peace treaty with Austria, biting his nails, uncharacteristically drinking too much, on occasions losing his temper or simulating ungovernable rage against the Austrian negotiator, Graf Ludwig von Cobenzl, threatening to deliver him up to French soldiers, smashing a valuable tea service on the floor, shouting that that was what was in store for the Austrian empire, declaring that it was just like 'an old hag of a servant whom everyone in the house rapes', storming out of the room and generally behaving, so Cobenzl reported, like a madman.

On other occasions, he tried cajoling rather than threats, and for this approach he called upon the ingratiating talents of his wife who had arrived at Passeriano having spent, so it seems, some time alone with Captain Charles before his departure from Milan on leave. Mme Bonaparte was 'amiability personified'. She invited the members of the Austrian delegation to dinner parties; she arranged *déjeuners à l'herbe* in the surrounding countryside; she paid particular attention to Cobenzl, who gained the impression that her husband – exaggerating both the dignity of his own birth as a Corsican nobleman and her own aristocratic connections – regarded her with a certain *Ehrfurcht*. As though he wished to demonstrate that this was not the case, one evening at dinner, in the presence of both French and Austrian delegates, Napoleon began bombarding her with pellets of bread. But her look of reproachful annoyance soon put a stop to the embarrassing cannonade; and Napoleon, so it was observed, 'hung his head and stopped'.

For all her gracious behaviour at the entertainments she provided for the delegates during the six weeks she spent at Passeriano that summer, Josephine was not happy there. She had heard a rumour that her lover, Captain Charles, was conducting an affair with an Italian lady. She had also been distressed to learn of Lazare Hoche's death, and had been desparately worried that the letters which she had written to him might fall into the wrong hands.* Also, she missed Paris and Paul Barras more than ever. 'I can hardly wait to tell you of my affection for you,' she wrote to him. 'Write to Bonaparte to sign the treaty, and then I will soon be with my friends again ... Goodbye ... I love you with all my heart ... Bonaparte sends you warmest greetings. He still adores me.'

At last, in the middle of October 1797, the terms of the treaty with Austria were ratified and peace was signed at Campo Formio, a village near Udine. The treaty preserved most of the French conquests in Italy and confirmed France's possession of Austria's Belgian provinces. It was also agreed that France should annex the territories it occupied on the left bank of the Rhine from Basel to Andernach. Austria, however, was given the Venetian territory east of the Adige River, including Istria, Dalmatia and the city of Venice.

This disposal of Venice, an independent state for over a thousand years, aroused widespread criticism, many believing that the so-called

---

* Hoche had long been asking for the return of the love letters which he had written to her before her marriage to Napoleon. She now endeavoured to obtain the letters she had written to him. For this she sought the help of a friend of Hoche who succeeded in obtaining them from Rousselin de St Albin, the guardian of Hoche's widow whom he had married when she was only sixteen and was still a minor. After Napoleon had divorced Josephine, St Albin wrote to Napoleon to say that he had performed a valuable service for her in the past for which he had never been rewarded. St Albin was promptly banished to some post far away from Paris. As Barras's executor he obtained his revenge by denigrating Josephine in notes appended to Barras's *Memoirs* of which he was the editor.

Peace of Campo Formio was a truce rather than an end to the war. It was, however, warmly welcomed in Paris where Napoleon's prestige rose to new heights; and Talleyrand thought it as well to write the General a fulsome letter: 'Now there is peace, peace *à la* Bonaparte. The Directory is pleased, the public overjoyed. The Italians may squeal a bit, but that is of no consequence. Farewell General and Peacemaker! My regards, admiration, respect, thanks – words fail me, the list could go on for ever.'

Josephine, no longer required in Italy, was now free to go home to France, as Napoleon himself did on 16 November. But first she decided to visit Venice where the news of its fate had not yet become general knowledge.

The Venetians, in the hope of appeasing her husband and in their eagerness to catch a glimpse of the famous General's wife, crowded at the windows overlooking the Grand Canal and filled the swaying gondolas to watch her entry into their city, cheering her loudly as she floated by. For four days the city was *en fête*: a special performance was given for her at the opera; there was a ball at the Doge's Palace; at night fireworks burst and flickered in the sky. Colonel Auguste Marmont, one of Napoleon's aides-de-camp, was with her; so, it seems, was Captain Charles who soon had to leave immediately for Paris on Napoleon's orders.

Evidently Charles accompanied her at least part of the way when she herself returned to Paris. Being in no great hurry to reach the end of her journey, she passed through towns decorated and illuminated in her honour, beneath triumphal arches, and was welcomed by speeches and proclamations, the roar of cannon and the cheers of the National Guard ringing in her ears. 'My husband,' she replied to the congratulations offered her, 'has been so successful because he has had the good fortune to command an army in which every soldier is a hero.'

'Mme Bonaparte is neither young nor pretty,' wrote a cavalry officer who came across her at this time. 'She has beautiful manners and is good-natured . . . She cries frequently, several times a day, for the most trivial of reasons.'

She took home with her not only the good wishes and congratulations of the people, but boxes packed with presents from Italians anxious to ingratiate themselves with the great French general, and with treasures she had herself purchased for her house in Paris, now being lavishly redecorated at great cost – pictures, statuary, Venetian glass, silks, bronzes and antique cameos. And, by her side in the rattling carriage, was a well-filled jewel box.

14

LIFE IN THE RUE DE
LA VICTOIRE

'I fear that one day we may have to implore him
to tear himself away from his studious retreat.'

UPON HIS RETURN TO THE HOUSE in the rue Chantereine, soon
to be renamed the rue de la Victoire, Napoleon was shocked to find
how much money had evidently been spent on his wife's orders in their
absence. The bills awaiting them were enormous: she had employed the
cabinet-makers, Jacob Frères, sons of the celebrated *menuisier*, Georges
Jacob, and had sent them one hundred and twenty thousand francs on
account with instructions to make the place 'supremely elegant'; and
pieces of furniture continued to arrive almost daily.

Astounded as he was by the money that had been spent, Napoleon
had little cause for concern. It has been estimated that he had extorted
fifty million francs in Italy, scarcely ten million of which had been sent
to the Directory; and while the sums spent on the house in the rue
Chantereine were extravagant enough, he was one day to have as many
as forty-four palaces, the furniture in one room of one of the palaces
costing more than the one hundred and twenty thousand francs sent
to the Jacob *frères* for the pieces they now supplied.

Napoleon's first visitor at the house was Paul Barras who remained with
him until long after midnight. Even so, Napoleon rose early the next
morning and sent a message to Talleyrand to say that he would call to
see him at eleven o'clock. Upon his arrival he was pleased to find
that Admiral Bougainville, the celebrated navigator, whom he had long
admired, was also there. So was Germaine de Staël, whom he most

certainly did not admire and to whom he ostentatiously declined to speak. His conversation with Talleyrand, however, at this, their first meeting, was mutually agreeable; and it was Talleyrand who, a few days later, at the Luxembourg Palace, presented General Bonaparte to the toga-clad Directors and other dignitaries as 'the son and hero of the Revolution'.

To those who saw him here for the first time he did not present a particularly heroic figure. Short and pale, wearing a long, plain grey civilian overcoat buttoned under his chin, he appeared to have none of the panache expected of so splendidly victorious a commander. At pains to emphasize apolitical credentials, he was careful not to present himself as a latter-day Alexander. He had arrived at the Palace by way of back streets in a simple carriage in order to avoid the immense crowds which had gathered in the main thoroughfares to welcome him. As though prompted by him to emphasize his modest demeanour and disinterested patriotism, Talleyrand ended his speech by remarking upon Bonaparte's 'contempt for pomp, luxury and display'. 'Far from fearing his ambition,' Talleyrand said, 'I feel that one day we may have to implore him to tear himself away from the calm of his studious retreat.'

Paul Barras, that year's President of the Directory, struck a different note. Referring to the forces assembling on the coast for an invasion of England, he urged General Bonaparte to march to the banks of the Thames to 'purge the world of the monsters' who oppressed and dishonoured it: 'May St James's Palace crumble into dust. Your country wishes it. Humanity requires it. Revenge demands it.'

This was the kind of language which appealed to Napoleon and which he himself had employed in addressing the Army of Italy. Modest as he had contrived to appear since his return to France, he was a great showman at heart and, as showmen will, he greatly resented those who endeavoured to steal his thunder. On this occasion, towards the conclusion of his brief speech in acknowledgement of the words which had been spoken in praise of him, Mme Récamier stood up in her white dress to obtain a better view of him. Her appearance was greeted by 'a long murmur of admiration'. Napoleon turned around to see what had caused it. The look in his eyes induced her to sit down again.

This was on 10 December 1797, five days after Napoleon's return to Paris. Josephine had still not arrived. Nor had she come a fortnight later when five hundred guests had been invited to attend a reception and ball to be held at the Hôtel Gallifet in her honour. Consequently, the ball had to be postponed, entailing what François-Joseph Bellanger, the architect employed to supervise the Hôtel's decorations, described as 'a very large additional expense' which included the cost of rented items that had to be replaced, 'such as 930 trees'. But by 28 December she had still not arrived; and it was not until 3 January 1798 that she came home at last. The ball took place the following evening.

It was a glittering occasion. The guests of honour were deferred to as though they were already the emperor and empress they were to become; but neither appeared to be entirely at ease. Once again, Germaine de Staël – to Talleyrand's intense annoyance – pushed herself forward to ask Bonaparte a series of irritating questions, ending with, 'General, which woman could you love the most?'

'My wife,' he replied.

'Of course, but which woman, alive or dead, do you most admire?'

'The one who gives birth to the most children.'

He then pushed past her, and went into the dining room where the ladies sat at table while the men stood behind their chairs, Talleyrand himself attending to Mme Bonaparte who was less gracious than usual. Her mind, so some observers thought, was unusually distracted.

As he himself wished, Bonaparte and his wife now led a more or less retired life in the house in the rue de la Victoire, in marked contrast to life at the Palazzo Serbelloni in Milan where the poet, Antoine Arnault, had compared Bonaparte's drawing room to the foyer of the Opéra in Paris. 'Never did a military headquarters look more like a court,' Arnault said. 'It was the forerunner of the Tuileries.' Dinner parties were held in the rue de la Victoire; but, apart from Barras and Talleyrand, political and military figures were rarely invited. Guests were more likely to be members of the French Academy of Sciences, which General Bonaparte had been invited to join – men such as Gaspard Monge, the mathematician, Claude-Louis Berthollet, the chemist, François-Joseph Talma, the actor, and the painter, Jacques-Louis David. Women were less in evidence, though Mme de Staël was to be seen there from time to time, clearly irritating Napoleon by her effusive talk.

On more than one occasion, when it was time for their guests to withdraw from the table for coffee and perhaps to listen to Antoine Arnault read one of his latest poems or to Étienne Méhul, the composer, sing one of his recent compositions, Josephine would gently tap her husband on the shoulder. Making one of those rare attempts at humour that would raise false laughter, the General asked his guests to note that his wife was in the habit of beating him.

At these dinner parties Napoleon ate hastily, as though late for some appointment. He rarely commented on the food and often seemed not to notice what was on his plate unless it happened to be runner beans which he would examine closely, once having been disgusted by a stringy one, part of which he had supposed to be a human hair.

He preferred plain food to rich and complicated fare and was particularly fond of a dish invented in Italy by his chef, Dunand, after the battle of Marengo when Napoleon, who never ate until the fight was over, found himself hungry and far from his supply wagons. A scavenging party was sent out and returned with three eggs, four tomatoes, six crayfish, a small hen, some oil, a few cloves of garlic and a saucepan. Dunand then created what became known as chicken Marengo and Napoleon, having relished it, said to him, 'You must feed me like this after every battle.'

He usually had lunch alone at the Tuileries; but Josephine joined him for dinner at half past seven. The food at both meals was simple and the wine, usually a Chambertin, was well watered in Napoleon's glass. Although guests were often invited to dinner with the Bonapartes, the meal lasted scarcely longer than lunch had done, being commonly over within twenty minutes. Eugène de Beauharnais was not the only guest to take the precaution of having a proper meal before being obliged to eat at his stepfather's table.

At eleven or thereabouts the host would say, 'Let's go to bed.' And he would go up to the bedroom he shared with Josephine, in winter giving a few kicks to the fire, a practice which naturally resulted in much damage to his shoes. He undressed speedily, putting on his nightshirt and a knotted handkerchief on his head, ensuring that all candles in the room were extinguished so that it was in total darkness by the time the warming pan had been removed from the bed.

If not awake already he was roused by his valet, Louis Constant, between six and seven o'clock. Having had a cup of tea or orange-flower water, he would look through his letters before having a very hot bath while Constant read extracts from the newspapers to him, occasionally breaking off to swing the door open and shut to let out the steam which was so thick that it obscured the print. After an hour or so Napoleon shaved carefully with an English razor, brushed his teeth with equal care, vainly endeavouring to get them white, discoloured as they were by his passion for liquorice. Then he cleaned his tongue with a scraper as was common practice in France if not elsewhere in Europe. After this the valet would splash eau de Cologne over his back while he himself rubbed it over his chest and stomach before putting on the underclothes which were changed every day. Eau de Cologne was also splashed on to a handkerchief which he placed in his right pocket, his snuff box going into his left.

He would then go to his desk to work, dropping papers for which he had no further use on the floor around him, making notes in his atrocious handwriting which he was often unable to decipher, preferring to dictate to his secretaries who had difficulty in keeping pace with the flow of his words.

Once a week, his librarian would be summoned to attend him with recently published books for him to glance through and he would throw on the ground or even into the fire 'those which did not interest him, or which annoyed him, and putting one or two – rarely three – aside to read with greater attention'.

Constant and Napoleon's other servants soon became aware that they must become accustomed to certain unchanging rituals and eccentricities, as well as to their master's tiresome penchant for practical jokes: his insistence on blazing fires in summer and winter; the careful arrangement of the porcelain figures on his desk which he would pick up and fiddle with, from time to time breaking off an arm or a leg; his involuntary muscular twitching when concentrating on some problem, 'the shrug of his shoulder', as one of his staff described it, 'accompanied by a movement of his mouth from side to side'; his annoyance if doors were left ajar and if servants entering the room did not open them only just enough to allow them to get through; and his persistent, almost life-long habit of pinching cheeks, ears and noses, sometimes so hard that the bruises on the flesh did not disappear for weeks.

15

'LA PUTANA'

*'I would rather die than lead a life
that cannot be devoted to you.'*

A FREQUENT GUEST at the Bonapartes' dinner parties, Barras was closer to Napoleon than ever, far closer than any of the other Directors (all of whom, in varying degrees, were wary of him). Barras was also as intimate as ever with Josephine: one evening, when she had planned to have dinner at his house, her husband returned unexpectedly early from a visit to the Channel ports. 'Bonaparte came back last night,' she wrote to Barras's secretary. 'I beg you, my dear Botot, to tell Barras how much I regret not being able to dine with him tonight. Tell him not to forget me! You know, my dear Botot, my delicate position better than anyone else.'

Josephine also wrote, and in far more intimate terms, to Hippolyte Charles:*

> Joseph [her brother-in-law] had a long conversation yesterday with Bonaparte and afterwards he asked me if I knew Citizen Bodin and if I had procured for him the purveyor's contract with the Army of Italy and if it was true that Charles was living at Citizen Bodin's house at 100 faubourg St Honoré and if I went there every day. I answered that I knew nothing at all of what he

---

* These letters were not burned with the rest of Josephine's letters to Charles, having been filed separately with his financial papers, possibly, as Evangeline Bruce suggested, because they contained references to Charles's connection – after he had surrendered his army commission – with the Bodin company for which Josephine had worked hard to obtain contracts to supply the Army of Italy. The letters were discovered in the 1950s by Louis Hastier, author of *Le grand amour de Joséphine* (Paris, n.d.).

was talking about and that, if he wanted a divorce, he only had to ask me ... Yes, my Hippolyte, I hate all of them [the Bonaparte family]. You alone have my loving tenderness ... They must see my despair at not being able to see you as often as I would like. Hippolyte, I will kill myself. I would rather die than lead a life that cannot be devoted to you. What have I done to these monsters? ... They must see how I abhor them ... I hate them all ... But however much they torment me, they shall never part me from my Hippolyte ... You alone have my love ... Please tell Bodin to say he doesn't know me, and that it wasn't through me that he got the Army contract ...

I will do my very best to see you during the day. I will send Blondin [a trusted manservant] to tell you what time I can get away to see you in the Parc Monceau. Goodbye, my Hippolyte, a thousand kisses as passionate and loving as my heart ... My life is a constant torment. You only can restore me to happiness. Tell me that you love me, that you love only me. Send me 50,000 livres by Blondin out of the funds in hand. Collot [Jean-Pierre Collot, a corrupt banker] is asking me for the money. Adieu, I send you a thousand tender kisses. I am yours, all yours.

Napoleon's brother, Joseph, was not the only member of his family who had come to Paris. His wife, Julie, had come with him from Rome, where he had served for a time as ambassador; so had Julie's sister, Désirée Clary, and so had packing-cases full of treasures and money which enabled Joseph to buy a fine country estate, the Château de Mortefontaine, as well as a splendid house in Paris, designed by Jacques-Ange Gabriel, architect of the Petit Trianon at Versailles.

Joseph's brother, Lucien, a tall, pretentious man equally antagonistic to Josephine, was able to buy an extensive estate in the country from which he wrote long letters to Napoleon detailing Josephine's real and supposed indiscretions. All their three sisters were, and continued to be, equally antagonistic; Elisa and Caroline frequently expressing their dislike and spreading malicious gossip, Pauline displaying similar animosity between visits to Josephine's *couturières* and *bijoutiers*, and the occasional enjoyment of the 'old woman's' former lovers.

Napoleon's mother was now also living in comfort in France, having abandoned the family house in Corsica, which, after returning to the island for a time, she had rebuilt, redecorated and refurnished with money sent to her by her son. She did not speak against Josephine so openly as her daughters did; and, presumably at Napoleon's behest and probably at his dictation, wrote to her to say, 'My son has told me of his happiness, which is enough to secure my approval.' In private, however, she referred to Josephine as '*La putana*', 'the whore'.

The Bonapartes were far from alone in endeavouring to make trouble between Napoleon and Josephine. One day, Louise Compoint, Josephine's maid who had accompanied her from Italy, came to see the General. She had lost her place, she told him, because Mme Bonaparte had objected to her sharing a bed with General Junot when they stopped for the night at inns. This, she said, was most unfair since Mme Bonaparte herself had seen to it that Captain Charles was with her in her carriage and he had spent the nights at the same inns.

Bonaparte questioned his wife about this. In an attempt to get her to confess, he remarked that of course if a man and a woman slept in the same inn it did not necessarily follow that they shared a bed. 'No, no,' Josephine repeated, bursting into tears which, for the moment, ended the questioning. Her husband, who seems to have paid little attention to Joseph's accusations, seems not to have pursued Louise Compoint's either, turning his attention to the next step in his career, an invasion of Egypt, proposed by Talleyrand, as a means of striking at one of the main sources of England's wealth and threatening her route to India.

The time had not yet come, Bonaparte thought, to take steps nearer to power in France. He had attempted to enlist Barras's help in getting himself elected a Director and then mounting a *coup d'état*, but Barras had not been encouraging. At the same time, Bonaparte was beginning to believe that an invasion of England was not practicable, while to remain in Paris, where many of those who had formerly been so ready to praise his achievements were now openly expressing the belief that he wished to make himself a dictator, was not a course to be recommended either.

He had also begun to fear that his life itself was in danger from an assassin's knife in Paris. It was noticed that, as though in readiness for flight, he never took off his spurs, and that at public dinners his own servant kept a careful eye on the food he ate and the wine he drank.

He was depressed by the lack of encouragement received for Talley-rand's proposal for a campaign in Egypt. Of the Directors only Barras supported him and he did so without enthusiasm. There was a risk, it was argued, that it might entail a war with Russia, as well as with the Ottoman Empire of which Egypt was a province. When Bonaparte gave his opinion to the Directors that the French navy was not strong enough for an invasion of England and that the great sum of money needed for it was not available, the Directors promised him more money. Exas-perated by their reluctance to consider an invasion of Egypt, he threat-ened to resign. The Director, Jean-François Reubell, offered him a pen, inviting him to write there and then his letter of resignation. But the Directors well knew that he would not resign and, in the end, they submitted to his demands for the Egyptian adventure which he himself hoped would end in a speedy and decisive victory and enable him to return home with his reputation even further enhanced and the time ripe for the next step towards the fulfilment of his destiny.

While the preparations for the campaign were being made with the secrecy which was essential if Admiral Nelson's fleet were to be kept in the English Channel, and while a Commission of Arts and Sciences, including artists and all manner of scholars from astronomers to car-tographers and geologists, was being formed to accompany the expedition, Napoleon took Josephine to look for a suitable country house to which they could return when the campaign was over.

He could well afford to buy one. He protested publicly that, while commanding the Army of Italy, he had nothing but his general's pay. But in addition to the large dowries he had given his two elder sisters and the money for the purchase of the rented house in the rue de la Victoire, he had found the means for the education of his youngest sister as well as his youngest brother at schools which were among the most expensive in France. Yet, even so, when Josephine was much taken with one of the country houses they saw, the Château de Malmaison – a house built on the bank of the Seine just outside Paris near Bougival in the early seventeenth century on the site of one burned down by the Black Prince, son of King Edward III – Napoleon decided he could not afford the price asked for it.

He had not yet made up his mind whether or not to take Josephine to Egypt with him. There were those who thought she did not want to go, that her professed desire to accompany him was characteristic make-believe. Yet there were also those who supposed that she was beginning to realize what a remarkable man her husband was and what a splendid future lay in front of him, even that, since she had grown to know him better, she was growing fond of him. Certainly, she pressed him to allow her to go with him to Egypt, all the more insistently when she saw how well his flagship, the *Orient*, had been fitted up and supplied (even to the extent of having his bed provided with casters so that he should not be troubled by the *mal de mer* from which he habitually suffered when at sea); and when General Alexandre Dumas called to see Bonaparte one morning while he and his wife, obviously naked beneath the sheet, were still in bed, he found her in tears. Bonaparte explained that she was upset because he had still not made up his mind whether or not to take her with him. In the end, he decided not to do so, at least until the convoy had managed to evade the enemy fleet: in the meantime she was to go to Plombières in Lorraine, to take a course of the waters of the spa which were said to be efficacious in cases of sterility.

Her husband set sail on 19 May 1798. The crossing to Egypt was expected to take about six weeks, allowing for the acquisition of the island of Malta and the treasure of the Knights Hospitallers on the way. For most of that time, Bonaparte rarely left his cabin. He did not suffer from seasickness as badly as he had feared he might; but most of the soldiers cramped below did so, their plight made worse by the stale water and weevil-infested biscuits of their daily fare.

He had brought an extensive library with him, and on most days his friend and secretary, Louis-Antoine de Bourrienne, read to him, generally from books of history, particularly of the history of the Islamic world. One day he asked Eugène de Beauharnais and General Berthier what they themselves were reading and was annoyed to discover they were both enjoying a novel. 'Reading fit for chambermaids!' he told them angrily. 'Men should only read history.' In the evenings, he talked about all manner of other subjects with his senior officers, discussing politics and French foreign policy, warfare and religion, the interpretation of dreams, the age of the world and how it might be destroyed, and whether or not there was life elsewhere in the universe.

When not talking of such matters, reading, or being read to he spoke about Josephine. 'Passionately as he loved glory – both France's and his own,' Bourrienne commented, Josephine was almost constantly in his thoughts. 'His fondness for her was close to idolatry.'

16

A CONVERSATION
WITH JUNOT

'I was astonished to discover, that he was capable
of the most bitter jealousy.'

A FEW DAYS AFTER SETTING SAIL, Bonaparte decided to make
arrangements to send a frigate to fetch Josephine to join him. He was
missing her, and she, so she told Barras, was missing him. 'I am so
distressed at being separated from him,' she wrote to Barras, 'that I
cannot get over my sadness ... You know him and you understand
how upset he would be at not hearing from me regularly. The last letter
I had from him was very affectionate ... He says that I am to rejoin
him as soon as possible and I am making haste to finish the cure [at
Plombières] so that I can be with him again very soon. I am very fond
of him despite his little faults.'

But then the balcony of the *pension* where she was staying at Plombières collapsed into the street and she fell with it, injuring herself badly.
Compresses and leeches were applied; she was given enemas and soaked
in hot baths; but for weeks she remained in severe pain – unable, so
she said, to 'remain standing or sitting for ten minutes' without causing
agony in her kidneys and lower back. She told Barras that all she did
was cry, and that he had no idea how much she suffered.

There was even worse to come. On 19 July 1798, as they walked
together beside an oasis in the desert, General Junot confirmed to Bonaparte that Josephine was having an affair with Hippolyte Charles. Bourrienne, who had overheard Junot's confidences, saw Bonaparte's already
pale face turn almost white. 'If you had cared for me,' Bonaparte said,
striding up to him, 'you would have told me about this before now ...

Josephine! . . . Divorce, yes, divorce. I will have a public and sensational divorce. I will write to Joseph and have it arranged . . . I can't bear to be the laughing-stock of Paris . . . I love that woman so much I would give anything to have what Junot has just told me pronounced untrue.' For years afterwards, thoughts of Josephine's infidelity returned to distress him:

> Napoleon never uttered Monsieur Charles's name [Laure Junot wrote in her *Mémoires*]. And he never allowed anyone else to mention it in his presence. He hated Charles; and I was astonished to discover that he was capable of the most bitter jealousy . . . One day when he was out walking with General Duroc, he squeezed his companion's arm. His face had paled even beyond its usual pallor. Duroc was about to fetch help when Napoleon silenced him: 'There's nothing wrong with me, be quiet!' A carriage had over-taken them and Napoleon had glimpsed Monsieur Charles inside.' It was the first time he had caught sight of him since the Italian campaign.

Soon after learning about Josephine's betrayal, Napoleon wrote to Joseph, asking him to have a country house ready for him to move into upon his return. He intended to be shut away in seclusion there for the winter. He needed to be alone, he said. He was 'tired of grandeur'; he no longer cared about glory. At the age of twenty-nine he had 'exhausted everything'.

This letter was intercepted by a British cruiser in the Mediterranean, together with a letter from her son, Eugène de Beauharnais, to Josephine in which he wrote:

> Bonaparte has been miserable since a conversation with Junot . . . I have heard that Captain Charles travelled in your carriage until you were within three posting stages of Paris, that you have seen him in Paris, and been to the theatre with him, that he gave you your little dog, and that he is with you now. I feel sure this is all gossip, invented by your enemies. Bonaparte loves you as much as ever and is as anxious as ever to embrace you. I hope that when you come here all this will be forgotten.

It was not to be forgotten, though; and while talking incessantly about Josephine's betrayal, Bonaparte was ready to betray her, too.

* * *

Below deck in the French ships that had arrived in Aboukir Bay earlier that month were some three hundred women. Some – laundresses, *cantinières* and the like – were officially authorized to be there. But, although strict orders had been issued against the embarkation of other women, wives and mistresses, several had been smuggled aboard in the uniforms of their husbands' and lovers' regiments: General Verbier, for example, spirited aboard his attractive Italian wife; while Lieutenant Fourès of the 22nd Regiment of *Chasseurs à Cheval* also contrived to take with him his wife, Pauline, an exceptionally pretty, blue-eyed, twenty-year-old young woman who looked most attractive in the uniform of her husband's regiment, blue jacket and tight, white breeches. Her fair hair, gathered tightly under one of her husband's cocked hats, was said, when she was *en déshabillé*, to fall to her waist. She was the illegitimate daughter of a cook named Bellisle and was known to her friends as Bellilotte. Before her recent marriage to Lieutenant Fourès she had been employed as a *vendeuse* in a milliner's shop in Paris.

Bonaparte caught his first glimpse of her on the first day of December 1798 when he and his staff gathered to watch the ascent of a balloon which, so the Egyptian spectators were assured, could fly through the air from one country to another. The display, however, was a disaster: the balloon caught fire and the basket crashed to the earth. 'It was a mere kite,' commented one of the Egyptian spectators whom it was intended to impress. 'If the wind had driven it a little further, the trick would have worked and the French would have claimed that it had travelled to a faraway country.'

Amongst the witnesses to this fiasco was Pauline Fourès who soon caught the attention of one of Bonaparte's aides-de-camp, his stepson, Eugène de Beauharnais, who pointed her out to one of his companions. Overhearing their comments, Bonaparte looked at her, too. That evening he saw her again and spent minutes on end staring at her with that appraising, silent watchfulness which so often disturbed and embarrassed the objects of his attention.

Upon his arrival in Cairo, he had been presented with some becoming young women by the sheiks. There were rumours that he had also been offered young men and that he had accepted one of them and had indulged in a homosexual experience which he did not care to repeat.

He fancied only one of the young women offered to him; the others were either too fat for his taste or their smell displeased him. Napoleon had a very keen sense of smell which, however, did not appear to disgust him on the battlefield. Later in Russia, when he entered Smolensk, the stench of corpses was so nauseating that even the most hardened and experienced soldiers were sick. But Napoleon appeared unmoved. 'Isn't that a fine sight?' he said to Armand-Augustin-Louis, marquis de Caulaincourt, indicating the flickering glare of the burning buildings and the bodies of the Russian soldiers amidst the flames.

'Horrible, sire,' said Caulaincourt.

'You must always remember,' Napoleon told him, 'the saying of one of the Roman emperors, that the corpse of an enemy always smells sweet.'

Yet, Baron Fain, Napoleon's former secretary, said, 'I have seen him move away from more than one servant who was far from suspecting the secret aversion his smell had inspired.' And, in Madrid and on St Helena, he was to turn girls away because he could not stand their smell. In Spain, indeed, the smell of an actress to whom he was introduced so offended him that, so he said, 'I very nearly fainted, I did indeed.' Now in Egypt, however, the evidently odourless or fragrant Zenab, the sixteen-year-old daughter of the sheikh El-Bekri, did appeal to him; and, it being supposed that he took her to his bed, she became known as 'the General's Egyptian'.

Her father, it seems, raised no objection. A man who consumed stupendous quantities of brandy and burgundy every night, who was much occupied with a handsome slave boy, El-Bekri may well have believed that the liaison might be turned to his advantage. It was not, however, to benefit poor Zenab: when the French were about to leave Egypt, religious zealots set about punishing women who had consorted with the infidel foreigners.

> Zenab had been debauched by the French [the chronicler, Abd el-Rahman El-Djabarti recorded]. The Pasha's emissaries presented themselves after sundown. They brought her and her father to court. She was questioned about her conduct, and made reply that she repented of it. Her father's opinion was solicited. He answered that he disavowed his daughter's conduct. The unfortunate girl's head was accordingly cut off.

17

'CLEOPATRA'

'Heavens! It isn't *my* fault.'

IT APPEARS THAT Bonaparte's brief supposed affair with the pitiable Zenab was petering out, or perhaps already over, when his attention was drawn to Pauline Fourès, whom he soon set about separating from her husband. He gave orders for the lieutenant to leave immediately by diligence for the coast at Rosetta. From there he was to take dispatches (all of no importance) to Paris by way of Malta. He was to remain in Paris for ten days and then – Bonaparte might well have tired of Bellilotte by then – Fourès was to return to Egypt 'as quickly as possible'.

As soon as the unwilling Fourès had been dispatched on this assignment, Bonaparte sent General Andoche Junot to Mme Fourès to make his proposition. But Junot delivered his message in such a coarse and clumsy way that she indignantly declared that she would always remain faithful to her husband. Bonaparte thereupon sent a more reliable and tactful emissary in the person of General Geraud-Christophe-Michel Duroc to Mme Fourès with an apology for General Junot's clumsy manner and the present of a valuable bracelet.

Soon afterwards, Bonaparte arranged for General Dupuy, the military commandant of Cairo, to give a dinner party to which Mme Fourès was to be invited with several other ladies. During the course of this party, Bonaparte subjected her to that intense observation with which he had examined her during the balloon fiasco.

Towards the end of the meal, when coffee was served, the officer sitting next to Mme Fourès upset his cup on her dress. Having apologized for the evident mishap, he offered to escort her to a bedroom where she might do her best to clean her skirt before rejoining the party. While she was endeavouring to remove the stain, General Bonaparte walked into the room. It was a long time before either of them reappeared.

The next day, Bellilotte was installed in a house next door to the Commander-in-Chief's in Eskebiya square; and the young woman, by then known as 'Cleopatra', was often to be seen riding about the town in Bonaparte's carriage attended by his aides-de-camp, a duty from which Eugène de Beauharnais was excused only after objecting that he could hardly be expected to perform it for his stepfather's mistress.

No attempt was made to conceal the liaison which Bonaparte flaunted as a retaliation for Josephine's affair with Hippolyte Charles. 'Rumour has it that the young and pretty wife has caught the fancy of the Commander-in-Chief,' wrote Major Detroye in his diary. 'Details of his taking possession of her are openly talked about by everyone.' 'This liaison was soon the talk of headquarters and the subject of nearly every conversation,' Bourrienne confirmed.

Lieutenant Fourès heard about it as soon as he returned to Cairo. This was sooner than anyone expected, since the courier ship, *Le Chasseur*, in which he was sailing was intercepted en route from Alexandria to Malta by H.M.S. *Lion* – whose captain behaved in a manner which seemed to suggest that he knew quite well why Lieutenant Fourès was aboard *Le Chasseur*. The French ship's crew and her passengers were delivered up to the Turks, while Lieutenant Fourès, spared this fate and having given an undertaking not to serve against England for the rest of the war, was sent back to Alexandria where the officer in command, General Marmont, vainly endeavoured to delay his departure for Cairo where he was sure to discover what his wife had been doing in his brief absence.

It was not long before he did discover it and, when he did so, his behaviour was so violent that Bellilotte applied for a divorce which was granted her without delay; and so Mademoiselle Bellisle, as she now called herself, became the Commander-in-Chief's *maîtresse en titre*. He intimated that he himself would obtain a divorce and marry her once she had given birth to his child. Yet, try as they would, pregnancy eluded her. The 'stupid little slut' wouldn't make a child for him, Bonaparte complained to Bourrienne. When told of Bonaparte's annoyance and pressed to consider how well her future would be assured if she did provide him with an heir, she responded, 'Heavens! It isn't *my* fault.'

Within a few weeks, Bonaparte left Cairo to lead an invasion of Syria as a means of preventing a Turkish incursion into Egypt. Mlle Bellisle would have liked to go with him; but neither now nor later did he permit a woman to accompany him in the field.

Bonaparte's progress in the field was far from being as successful as it had been in Italy. The campaign had opened with a victory over the fierce and frantic Mamelukes in – as Bonaparte dramatically called it – the Battle of the Pyramids, and it ended with the defeat of a Turkish force – half the size claimed for it in Bonaparte's report – in Aboukir Bay. Between the two engagements the French expeditionary force had not greatly distinguished itself.

Following the destruction of almost the entire French fleet by the ships of Admiral Nelson in the Battle of the Nile, Bonaparte's troops suffered a series of setbacks – which were nevertheless transformed into victories in his reports to the Directory – and were involved in a succession of disgraceful atrocities. When the fortress of Jaffa surrendered, the place was sacked and looted and the garrison, including women and children, were slaughtered. Promised that their lives would be spared, three thousand Turks capitulated and were then drowned or bayonetted to death on the orders of Bonaparte who made the excuse that he could not spare the ammunition to shoot them, nor the supplies to feed them.

Bonaparte, still enraged no doubt by the knowledge that he had been so humiliatingly cuckolded by his wife, displayed similar ruthlessness at Acre where two thousand French soldiers lay wounded or suffering from plague outside its walls. The British naval commander offered to take the wounded on to his ships, but this offer was refused because Bonaparte declined to have any reason to be grateful to the enemy. 'The heart of our army was pierced by our leaving our plague-stricken men behind,' wrote an officer who was distressed to have to abandon them. 'They pleaded with us not to forsake them . . . Their heads were cut off by the enemy as soon as we left.'

Other wounded men and those suffering from plague, whom Napoleon wished to have poisoned, had to be left behind as the rest of the bedraggled troops marched along the rough and seemingly endless roads back to Cairo. 'I saw officers with amputated limbs thrown from the stretchers by their bearers,' Bourrienne wrote. 'I saw wounded men and those suffering from plague left by the roadside . . . We were entirely surrounded by the dying, by pillagers and arsonists . . . Our march was illuminated by towns and villages set on fire by our angry men . . . The whole countryside was on fire . . . The sun was hidden by palls of smoke . . . We had the sea to our right and, to our left and behind us, the desert we ourselves were laying waste as we advanced.'

The Directory was told none of this. 'We want for nothing here,' General Bonaparte reported in anticipation of his return. 'We are bursting with strength, good health and high spirits.' Any faults that might have been found in the conduct of the campaign were either glossed over or blamed on others. As Bourrienne said:

> The full truth was never to be found in Bonaparte's dispatches when that truth was even slightly unfavourable and when he was in a position to dissimulate. He was adept at disguising, altering, or suppressing it whenever possible. Frequently he even changed the dispatches of others and then had them printed, whenever their view differed from his own or might cast some aspersion on his reputation and actions . . . He never hesitated to disguise the truth when he could make it embellish his own glory. He considered it sheer stupidity not to do so.

Bonaparte's intention to return to France was not divulged to Mme Fourès. Not long before he set sail, he had been in a light-hearted mood as he strolled in the garden of the palace of the Mameluke, Mohammed Bey el-Elfi, talking to his aides-de-camp and leaving them from time to time to give a playful but painful pinch to Mme Fourès who, dressed in the hussar's tunic and tight trousers which so became her, was taking the air in a different part of the garden.

He had still not told her of his intention to leave Egypt when he bade her a brief farewell, gave her a hurried kiss, a pat and another of his sharp pinches and was gone, assuring her he would return in a few days.

General Kléber was left in command of the army. He much disliked Bonaparte and was only too ready to accede to Mme Fourès's request and send her back to France where her presence would, no doubt, embarrass her former lover. She accordingly returned to France in 1800.

Bonaparte declined to see her upon her return, but he did give her several sums of money and a large house just outside Paris. Still a most attractive and enterprising young woman in her early twenties, she soon married a former major serving with the Turkish army, Henri de Ranchoup, with whom, however, she seems never to have been on very close terms. While he served abroad in various consular posts in Spain and Sweden, she remained in France, living at first in the house given to her by Bonaparte, then at Craponne in Haute-Loire. She occupied her time in painting, playing the harp and in writing novels; the first, a romantic historical novel entitled *Lord Wentworth* and then a second, in the same vein – *Une châtelaine du douzième siècle* – caused not the least tremor of excitement in the literary world.

Unsuccessful as a novelist, and having obtained a separation from Major de Ranchoup, she sailed for Brazil in the company of Jean-Auguste Bellard, who had been an officer in the Imperial Guard. She returned alone with a variety of rare woods which she sold at a handsome profit. Encouraged by the success of this venture, she paid several further profitable visits to South America until, at the age of thirty-nine, she settled down permanently in France.

She became increasingly eccentric as the years passed, sitting at the window of her house in Craponne smoking a pipe; taking a dog with her to church on Sundays; frequently walking abroad in men's clothes; and keeping a variety of pets, including parrots and monkeys (as well as dogs) which scampered and flew about her rooms, barking, squawking and screeching, much to the consternation of her friends. One of these was the sculptor and painter, Marie-Rosalie Bonheur, a woman, quite as eccentric as herself, who also wore men's clothes, kept a lioness and exhibited at the Salon where her celebrated painting, *The Horse Fair*, now in the New York Metropolitan Museum of Art, was first shown in 1853 and subsequently acquired by Cornelius Vanderbilt for a sum which had not then been equalled for a similar work.

Her friend, Pauline de Ranchoup, Bonaparte's former mistress, died in 1869 at the age of ninety. She had outlived Napoleon by almost half a century.

While enduring his exile on St Helena, he spoke of having once encountered her, years after her return from Egypt, at a masked ball.

Despite the mask, he recognized her and reminded her that in Egypt she had been known as Cleopatra. She did not recognize him, he claimed improbably; but she spoke affectionately of 'Caesar'.

18

THE GENERAL'S RETURN

'I will never forgive her.'

JOSEPHINE BONAPARTE'S AFFAIR with Hippolyte Charles was by now well known in France and, her dealings with the corrupt Bodin company long since suspected, she was becoming more and more isolated and depressed as she waited anxiously for her husband's return from Egypt. It was noticed, for instance, how distressed she was at a dinner at the Luxembourg, where she was sitting next to Talleyrand who ignored her, devoting himself throughout the meal to her friend, Thérésia Tallien, sitting on his other side. She stood up and left the room in tears before the meal was over.

She was also heavily in debt. This did not, however, prevent her from buying the Château de Malmaison with its farm and three hundred acres of arable and meadow land, vineyard, orchard and woodland for over three hundred and twenty-five thousand francs, a sum either provided by Barras or Gabriel Ouvrard or borrowed elsewhere.

The possession of this estate did little to lighten her mood; nor, apparently, did her renewed affair with Hippolyte Charles who, having returned from Italy, where he had been working for the Bodins, came to stay at Malmaison, disappearing from view when visitors came to the château but not escaping the notice of those informants who reported to the Bonapartes her every move and activity.

She wrote of her 'miserable situation'. She pleaded with Barras not to desert her, for friendship's sake to sacrifice a quarter of an hour to come to see her or to let her come to him, not to refuse this kindness to the wife of his friend. She invited the former abbé, Emmanuel Sieyès, recently appointed a Director and now regaining his former influence, to come to see her at Malmaison; but he made it clear that he had no wish to do so.

As the weeks passed, however, as the fortunes and influence of the Jacobins began to revive, and as French armies were defeated in the field and demands were made by a reconstituted Jacobin Club for the re-erection of the guillotine, there was a growing feeling in the country, now increasingly counter-revolutionary, that only a dictatorship could save it from anarchy.

A *coup d'état* was being planned. Barras and Talleyrand, Sieyès and Lucien Bonaparte, Jérôme Gohier, now President of the Directory, and Joseph Fouché – the unscrupulous Minister of Police who was, like Talleyrand and Sieyès, a defrocked ecclesiastic – were all involved, and were all considering the possibility of calling upon a man who could bring first order, then victory, then peace.

Fouché, like Gohier, believed that Bonaparte was that man. They both visited Madame Bonaparte at Malmaison; and Gohier, a man rather staid in manner who nevertheless kept a private memorandum of the women he had seduced, also went to her house in Paris almost every day when she was there, presumably hoping that he might persuade her to allow him to have occasion to add her name to his list.

But, the nearer the time of her husband's return from Egypt approached, the more nervous and reclusive Josephine appeared to be. 'I have become so shy that I am afraid of the great world,' she told Barras. 'In any case, I have become so unhappy that I don't want to be an object of pity to anyone else ... I need to talk to you, to ask your advice. You owe this to Bonaparte's wife, and to his friendship for you.'

'She lives a very retired life at Malmaison, seeing only Mme Campan and me,' her daughter Hortense wrote in a letter to her brother Eugène. 'She has given only two big dinner parties since you left. The Directors and all the Bonaparte family were invited but the latter always refuse to come ... Maman is, I assure you, very distressed that the family won't live on friendly terms with her, which must upset her husband whom she loves very much. I am sure if Maman could have been sure of reaching him she would have gone, but you know how impossible that would be now.'

This letter never reached Eugène; nor did one written by Josephine to Napoleon who had by then left Egypt and was shortly expected in Paris, having had what he later described to Mme Rémusat, a lady-in-waiting to Josephine, as 'the most delightful time of my life because it was the most ideal'. 'In Egypt,' he said, 'I found myself freed from the obstacles of an irksome civilization. I was filled with dreams. I saw myself founding a new religion, marching into Asia, riding an elephant, a turban on my head and in my hand a new Koran that I would have composed to suit my needs.'

Having left General Kléber in Egypt, in command of an army whose strength its former commander was later to claim was not very much less than it had been at the outset of the campaign but had, in fact, been reduced by half, Bonaparte set sail from Alexandria in the middle of the dark night of 22 August 1799. As well as his cook, his chef and his secretary, he took with him a young Mameluke, Roustam Raza, as bodyguard, valet and procurer, Eugéne de Beauharnais, three other aides-de-camp and Generals Murat, Berthier, Duroc, Lannes and Marmont. Andoche Junot, who had told him about Josephine's affair with Hippolyte Charles, was pointedly left behind.

Contriving to evade the ships of the Royal Navy patrolling the waters of the Mediterranean, the *Muiron* reached the safety of Ajaccio where, for over a week of windless days, Bonaparte paced about the town and harbour in what was almost a frenzy of impatience, fearful that the luck by which he set such store might desert him and that he would arrive in Paris too late to seize the power he was determined to attain.

Once he had landed at Fréjus, however, his confidence returned: his exaggerated account of his victory over the Turkish army had helped to ensure that he would be welcomed as a returning hero; and so he was: his journey north through France was a triumphal progress and the acclamations and blaring bands that greeted him in Paris on 14 October assured him of the continuing power of his name.

When he arrived at his house in the rue de la Victoire, however, and found that Josephine was not there, he flew into a sudden rage as he paced through the empty rooms. That evening he went to see Barras, assuring him that he would divorce the woman. His brothers Joseph and Lucien, who had gone to meet him at Lyons, encouraged him in his determination to be rid of her and extracted from him an under-taking that he would certainly do so, and that he would be deaf to any pleas she might make to him.

'I will never forgive her,' he shouted at the banker, Jean-Pierre Collot, who called at the house to find him throwing logs on to a fire and emphasizing the words with stabs of a poker. He threw open the doors of her cupboards and wardrobes and told a servant to take all their contents down to the *portière*.

Hoping against hope, as she said, to reach him before his brothers had an opportunity to pour fresh poison in his ears, she and Hortense had rushed down to intercept him at Lyons where they were told he had already passed through the town on his way to Paris. Two days later they themselves, worn out by the journey, also arrived in Paris at the house in the rue de la Victoire where the concierge told them that he had orders not to admit them. Ignoring the man, they ran up towards the house where a frightened maid told Josephine that the General was in his dressing room with the door locked. Josephine begged him to let her in: she would explain everything. He took no notice. She continued to plead with him. So did Hortense and her brother Eugène, who had come down from his room on the top floor, until, tired out, Josephine fainted. At last, after what Bourrienne described as 'three days of marital pouting', the door was unlocked. Josephine went in, closing it behind her. Hortense and Eugène could hear their stepfather's angry voice, their mother's tearful interjections. He could never live with her again, he told her. They must live apart for the rest of their lives.

When Lucien called at the house the next morning to give further details of Josephine's misbehaviour, he found her and Napoleon in bed together.

Throughout the next few days, while politicians and generals talked and plotted, while General Bernadotte urged the necessity of court-martialling Bonaparte for his desertion of his post, while Sieyès told Gohier that the 'insolent little man' should be shot, while the Directors made a hesitant attempt to get him out of Paris by asking him which of France's armies he would now like to command, while Barras deeply offended him by proposing that he return to the command of the Army of Italy, and while a succession of politicians and army officers passed in and out of No. 6 rue de la Victoire (where the picturesque and enigmatic Roustam appeared silently from time to time, offering refreshments on a tray) Bonaparte endeavoured to present himself as a man of moderation, a soldier without political ambition, a man who shunned the limelight, a contented husband who could be seen sitting by the fire, playing backgammon with his wife.

Josephine played her part willingly and well in this charade. Her 'at homes' diverted attention from the plots and manipulations conducted clandestinely in her house; her friendship with Gohier, now President of the Directory, who came to see her almost every afternoon and talked to her openly, allowed Bonaparte to discover what other Directors were now proposing to do. Her charm was also exercised – admittedly not so successfully as upon Gohier – upon Jean-Baptiste Bernadotte who, with his wife, one day spent four hours travelling with the Bonapartes to Joseph's country estate.

Not only was Napoleon grateful to his wife for the help she gave him, he was once more happy in her company, going so far as to tell Talleyrand of the delight he felt in it, while she, for her part, found her husband 'more affectionate than ever'.

By 8 November 1799, with her help, all arrangements for the coup had been made. Senior officers were individually told to come to 6 rue de la Victoire at half past six the following morning. Barras, who was expecting Bonaparte at eleven o'clock that night, was told that he had a headache and could not come. 'Tomorrow,' Napoleon said to Bourrienne, 'our business will be done.'

19

THE COUP

'There was a hubbub to deafen one.'

THE BUSINESS WAS NOT DONE EASILY. Bonaparte appeared perfectly calm as he spoke to the officers who began to assemble before dawn in his house where they were greeted by Mme Bonaparte who, however, seemed less at ease than her husband. There were those among them who were reluctant to support him in the coup which was evidently planned. Among these was Jean-Baptiste Bernadotte, who was not in uniform like the others and who declared that he 'would not take part in a rebellion'. He did, however, undertake not to oppose Bonaparte in what he intended to do; and, when he left, Joseph Bonaparte was instructed to go after him and to ensure that he kept his word.

General François Lefebrve, the military governor of Paris, once assured by Bonaparte that Barras was on his side, readily promised support and emerged from Bonaparte's room with characteristic braggadocio. The President of the Directory, Jérôme Gohier, was far more cautious. Josephine had been told by her husband to send Gohier and his wife an urgent invitation to breakfast at eight o'clock that morning, emphasizing its importance. 'Do not fail me,' she had written. 'I must discuss matters of the greatest importance with you.' Concerned by the tone of this letter and worried by the early time specified, Gohier decided not to go, sending his wife on her own, much to Napoleon's annoyance. 'Gohier didn't turn up,' he said to Bourrienne later on that day. 'So much the worse for him.'

Bourrienne was worried by the way in which the coup was

developing, although he did his best to reassure Josephine, who had vainly been endeavouring to find out exactly what was happening. As the day wore on, her husband was clearly on edge, less confident than he had appeared to be earlier, despite his words to Bourrienne before he went to bed: 'Today went well. We shall see about tomorrow.' That night he slept with two pistols beside his bed.

The next day, 10 November, he appeared to be more apprehensive than ever. After he had gone downstairs, Josephine sent a message recalling him to her room. 'I will go up,' he replied. 'But this is not a day for women. It's all far too serious.'

So it proved to be for him. When the deputies, summoned to the palace at St Cloud outside Paris, appeared far less ready to deal with the crisis than he had hoped, he marched furiously into the Gallery of Apollo to deliver a ferocious and, in parts, incoherent harangue, his face white with anger. 'As soon as these dangers are passed, I will hand over all power,' he declared. 'I only want to be the right arm of whatever government you are about to elect.'

His speech was greeted with loud calls of 'Names! Names! Name the conspirators!' As Bonaparte rambled on, stumbling for words, his face bleeding where he had scratched his cheek in his agitation, he threatened to appeal to his 'brave companions in arms'. 'Remember,' he shouted, 'that I march accompanied by the god of victory and the god of fortune.' Outside, he declared, there were men ready to fight for him: he could see their bayonets. 'General,' whispered Bourrienne, tugging at his arm, appalled by the impression he was creating. 'General, you don't know what you are saying.'

Napoleon allowed himself to be led away; but in the courtyard he was given a message from Fouché, the Minister of Police, and Talleyrand, soon to return to the Foreign Ministry, who wrote to say that there was not a moment to lose, that the time for decisive action had come. Surrounded by soldiers, he thereupon marched into the Orangery where the recently established body with the right to initiate laws, the deputies of the Five Hundred, rose to their feet in horror at this illegal intrusion. Some of them left their seats, shaking their fists in his face, punching him in the chest, seizing hold of his collar. 'Outlaw him! Outlaw him!' they shouted. 'Down with the military dictator!' Looking shocked and as though about to faint, he was dragged from the hall by four of his grenadiers.

When the rest of the men heard what had happened to their General, they furiously demanded orders to clear the rabble out of the Orangery. And when shouts of 'Outlaw him! Outlaw him!' continued to reach Bonaparte's ears through the windows of the hall, he realized that he must act if only to save himself. Resolving to make an appeal to the Council of Five hundred's bodyguard, who seemed as yet reluctant to support him, he sent a message to his brother to come out to help him.

Lucien, as President of the Council, had been presiding over the increasingly rowdy session, firmly resisting the demands for a vote to be taken on a motion declaring the General an outlaw. In response to his brother's request he came out of the hall immediately, and went over with him to the Council's guards.

'The President of the Council of Five Hundred declares to you that the great majority of the Council is, at this very moment, terrorized by certain deputies,' Lucien announced to them. 'They are armed with daggers ... and probably in the pay of England.' He added that an attempt had been made to assassinate the General, whose pale face lent force to the suggestion.

The Guards were at first hesitant, but when Lucien, pointing a sword at his brother's chest, cried out, 'I swear to kill my own brother if he ever interferes with the freedom of Frenchmen', they allowed themselves to be persuaded by his lies, and stood while a column of soldiers, led by Joachim Murat, marched upon the Orangery with drums beating and bayonets fixed. At the sight of their approach the deputies fled from the building, several of them jumping out of the windows and running off through the park.

Meanwhile, Mme Letizia had decided to go to the Feydeau Theatre with Mme Permon, Mme Permon's daughter Laure, and Pauline Leclerc. Soon after the curtain was raised, the stage manager ran from the wings to announce that an attempt had been made to assassinate General Bonaparte at St Cloud. 'On hearing these words,' so Laure Permon said, 'Mme Leclerc uttered so piercing a shriek that immediately the attention of all the company was attracted to our box, in spite of the agitation which the news had universally excited. Mme Leclerc still continued crying; and her mother, who was doubtless as much affected as she could be at the intelligence, endeavoured to quieten her, though she herself could hardly hold the glass of water which the box-keeper handed us, so great was her agitation.'

Napoleon's mother, her face 'white as a marble statue', bent over her daughter who had slumped forward in her chair and seemed on the point of fainting. 'Stop it and get up,' she said to her impatiently, pulling her towards the exit. Pushing through the crowds outside, they managed to find a carriage to take them to the rue de la Victoire, where 'the courtyard of the Bonapartes' house and the avenue were filled with horses and with people on foot who jostled and shouted,' Laure Permon continued her account. 'There was a hubbub to deafen one.' From the shouts in the street she gathered that the coup had succeeded: Bonaparte was to become one of three Consuls of the French Republic, the others being Sieyès and the lawyer, Roget Ducos. Bonaparte's name came last of the three; but no one doubted that his was the one that mattered. 'There is a pike,' Mme Permon remarked, 'who will gobble up the other two fish.' Indeed, before long, Napoleon was to become First Consul.

Josephine had been waiting anxiously for news, frightened by rumours that attempts had been made on her husband's life, rumours that Bonaparte chose to confirm in a proclamation he dictated to Bourrienne in which it was stated that 'twenty armed assassins' had fallen on him, 'seeking his heart with their daggers'.

When he arrived home to reassure Josephine and tell her what had happened he asked if that 'devilish fellow' Bernadotte had kept his word not to interfere. If he had not, revenge regrettably was out of the question because, after all, Bernadotte's wife was Joseph's sister-in-law and the whole family would be against him. Oh, how tiresome it was, he lamented, 'to have to consider family ties'.

Soon after breakfast the next morning, Napoleon and Josephine left the rue de la Victoire to occupy apartments in the Luxembourg, where he worked so hard in making new appointments to the government, in preparing a new constitution and in dealing with the manifold problems facing the country at home and abroad that Josephine rarely saw him during the day, except on those occasions when, so agitated with impatience at having to listen to Sieyès elaborating his views on the precise nature of that constitution, he was driven to biting his nails and stabbing the arms of his chair with a penknife, then escaping from the room for a few minutes to run up the stairs to his wife's apartments.

He was clearly happy, though. He went about whistling and singing in that exasperatingly tuneless way of his. Beguiled by Josephine's charm and contrite tears, he was no longer even vaguely considering divorce. He had undertaken never to see 'Bellilotte' again, while Josephine promised to be faithful to him always hereafter.

She was more than a little in awe of him now. Victorine de Chastenay went so far as to say that 'she trembled like a leaf when he appeared'. Certainly, she was submissive to the behaviour he required of her as the new Consul's wife: she was not to associate any more with her disreputable friends who were not to be admitted to Malmaison; she was to become associated with various charities and charitable events; when she went to the theatre she was to be demurely dressed and certainly not to display too many of her jewels; she was to overcome her notorious tendency to extravagance.

When he heard from Talleyrand that people in Paris were talking about her debts, he told Bourrienne to find out how much they were and to show him all those which were outstanding. 'I can't do it, Bourrienne,' she said in the greatest alarm. 'You know how violent he can be. I couldn't face his anger.'

She owed well over a million francs, but surely she need not confess to so much: could Bourrienne tell him that the sum owed was six hundred thousand? Bourrienne objected that Napoleon would be so shocked by being told six hundred thousand francs, that she might just as well acknowledge the true, far higher sum. However, Bourrienne did keep the acknowledged figure down to six hundred thousand, and he and Napoleon went through the bills together, shocked to discover, for instance, that in one summer alone she had bought thirty-eight hats, as well as almost two thousand francs' worth of herons' plumes; and in another year, a thousand pairs of gloves and even more pairs of stockings which she changed three times a day, choosing a new pair every time. Napoleon told Bourrienne to settle the accounts, however; and Bourrienne was able to do so by haggling with the creditors.

20

DAYS AT MALMAISON

'Except on the field of battle I never saw
Bonaparte as happy as he was at Malmaison.'

FIRM AS NAPOLEON COULD BE with Josephine, when he found time to spend a few days with her at Malmaison, he was so content and cheerful that she now had far less need to be wary in his presence. Once, when she found him at a window taking aim at a swan on the lake, she pleaded with him not to shoot, although he was such a bad shot he would probably have missed it anyway. Obediently, he put down the gun. It was, however, reported on another occasion that when he proposed shooting some animals in the park, Josephine tearfully pleaded with him not to do so. 'The animals are 'with young,' she said. 'It is not the season for shooting.' 'It seems,' he commented angrily, 'that everything is prolific here, except Madame.'

He was rarely so pettish at Malmaison. He would listen patiently while she played her harp, even though she did not play it very well and, according to his secretary, Méneval, knew only one piece. While toying with her needlework, she would appear to listen patiently as he gave voice, minute after minute, to his thoughts.

She loved her birds at Malmaison, her swans, her falcons and parrots, her ostriches and the Egyptian gazelles; and she loved the other animals she collected there, the antelopes and zebras, monkeys, merino sheep, kangaroos and flying squirrels. Above all, she loved the gardens through which she would often walk with her husband after dinner. She had greenhouses built and filled them with all manner of exotic plants, often pointing out to visitors her rare hibiscus and tulips, her eucalyptus and double jacinthas, and those flowers which she associated with her husband's victories, the lilies of the Nile, the Parma violets and the Damietta roses. She spent almost as much on plants as she did on pictures and clothes, thinking nothing of spending three thousand francs on a single bulb. She wrote to agents in London to ask them to obtain for her specimens from Kew Gardens and to her mother in Martinique for such exotic plants as the island could offer, tropical bougainvillea, jasmine and orchids.

Plants were also sent to her, or given to her, by French ambassadors and travellers, by botanists who soon learned of her interests, by her husband who was to send her no fewer than eight hundred plants while on campaign in 1809, by the German explorer and naturalist, Alexander von Humboldt, and by the French botanist, Aimé Bonpland, who provided her with six thousand specimens from South America. The distinguished botanist, Charles François Brisseau de Mirbel, became director of the gardens at Malmaison in 1803, the year in which appeared the first volume of Etienne Pierre Ventenat's *Jardins de la Malmaison*; while the Belgian-born artist, Pierre Joseph Redouté, was to provide the colour plates for Bonpland's *Description des plantes rares cultivées á Malmaison*. He was also to engrave pictures of Josephine's two hundred varieties of rose.

Bonaparte seemed as content at Malmaison as never before elsewhere in France. He bought some five thousand acres of surrounding land including vineyards; he improved and extended the farm buildings; he had barracks built for the Consular Guard; he built a rotunda where meals were sometimes served at tables surrounded by flowers and plants in tubs; he had paintings and sculpture brought home from Italy displayed like trophies against the walls; he commissioned Anne-Louis Girodet-Trioson to paint a series of murals depicting scenes from the poems of Ossian which he so much admired. Josephine collected paintings and water-colours also, assembling over the years a fine and extravagant display. She once told Mme de la Tour du Pin that she had works of art which had been presented to her by Antonio Canova, the Pope and the city of Milan. Mme de la Tour du Pin thought to herself, however, that they had been secured for her by means of the point of her husband's sword in Italy.

Josephine was eventually obliged to ask her architects to build a gallery almost a hundred feet long leading out of her music room; and here could be seen an astonishing collection of statues, busts, cameos and medallions, as well as paintings by masters from Michelangelo and da Vinci to Rembrandt, Vermeer and Titian, from Raphael, Veronese and Dürer to Holbein, Claude Lorrain and Poussin.

In the evenings when he had finished work, Napoleon would enjoy playing chess or rowdy games with children and he would take part in theatrical performances and charades, assigning the best parts to himself. When he had not had time to learn them, he watched the others perform, often under the direction of the tragedian, François-Jospeh Talma, and commented, not always approvingly, on the more gifted members of the cast – Eugène de Beauharnais, Bourrienne, Hortense and his aide-de-camp, the marquis de Lauriston.

When there were no theatricals to watch, Napoleon would hold forth to the assembled company on subjects as diverse as science, literature or art, or relate supernatural or dramatic stories, or, in Claire de Rémusat's words, he would 'enjoin complete silence . . . and listen to slow and soft pieces of music . . . He would fall into a reverie, and then, coming out of it, he would describe the sensations he had experienced and analyze his emotions.'

'He loved everything that led him into reverie,' Laure Junot said, 'the twilight hour, melancholy music. I have seen him become passionate at the murmur of the wind, speak with rapture at the soughing of the sea, and speculate that nocturnal apparitions were not altogether beyond belief. He had, indeed, a penchant for superstition.'

'Except on the field of battle,' Bourrienne said, 'I never saw Bonaparte as happy as he was at Malmaison.' Indeed, these days of the Consulate were among the happiest days of his life. His private secretary, Méneval, who greatly admired him, wrote of his 'most beautiful smile', his 'calm, meditative and gently grave expression':

> I could not master my surprise at finding such simplicity of habits in a man like Napoleon. I had expected to find him brusque, and of uncertain temper, instead of which I found him patient, indulgent, easy to please, by no means exacting, merry but with a merriness which was often noisy and raucous . . . His laugh was often loud and mocking . . . and familiarity on his part did not

invite any ideas of reciprocity. Napoleon played with men without mixing with them . . .

He used to have me woken up in the middle of the night when he felt obliged to get up himself; and it sometimes happened when I handed him a document to sign in the evening, he would say, 'I won't sign it now. Be here tonight at one o'clock or at four in the morning and we will work together . . .'

When he got to the study before me, I used to find him walking up and down with his hands behind his back, or helping himself up from his snuff-box . . . When his dictation was finished, and sometimes in the middle of it, he would send for sherbert and ices . . . Then he would go back to bed and straight back to sleep . . . After an hour's sleep, he would get up as wide awake and as clear in his mind as if he had slept quietly the whole night. As soon as he had lain down his wife would place herself at the foot of the bed and begin reading aloud. As she read very well he took pleasure in listening to her.

Not all his servants found him as patient as Méneval claimed to have done. Louis Marchand, who was to succeed Louis Constant as his valet, described his alarming introduction to Napoleon's fits of temper:

The first day of my service with the Emperor [Napoleon] he asked me for some tea. I sent the wardrobe boy to get some in the pantry, and he brought back a tray bearing all that was needed. I took it to the Emperor who poured himself a cup, put sugar in it, and was about to drink it when he asked, 'Where does this cup come from?'

When I told him from the pantry, he hurled the cup against the wall and smashed it. 'In future,' he said, 'use only those things set out for the purpose and no others.' I was taken aback and apologized for my ignorance. This first lesson was harsh. I was not immune to the fear inspired by the Emperor.

This kind of outburst was not, however, a common occurrence at Malmaison. Indeed, like Méneval, Marchand too was to describe his master as being 'easy going and kind', and there was 'always good reason for his anger'. He denied the 'absurd tales' of his harshness, the epileptic seizures which made him unmanageable, the widespread rumours that he wore armour under his uniform.

Admittedly, Napoleon 'was not in the habit of saying he was satisfied. He even seemed to pay little attention to efforts made to please him, or he greeted them with indifference. But if after scolding someone he noticed that he seemed hurt, he would go up to him and either pinch his ear hard or tug at it. This implied all was forgiven.'

In his memoirs, Marchand recounted what he had observed of Napoleon's habits and foibles, his tastes and dislikes. He wrote of the care he took of his 'elegant' hands and nails and of his teeth; his habit of singing tunelessly while repeating the same words over and over again; his fondness of potatoes but dislike of beans; his indifference to fine wines; his pleasure in lingering in hot baths: 'he had a habit of remaining in his bath an hour and a half or sometimes two hours. He would then go to bed for an hour with hot sheets ... Upon emerging from his apartment, the first valet would hand him his three-cornered hat. He would take this in one hand, and in the other a handkerchief sprinkled with eau de Cologne with which he would dab his lips and forehead. He was then handed a snuff box, a spyglass and a box containing liquorice.'

> He loved luxury and magnificence [Marchand continued] but at the same time he insisted upon getting his money's worth ... Once, at a hunting party, he asked one of his sisters who was wearing a charming pink hat shaped like a helmet with white feathers, how much such finery cost. 'Three hundred francs,' she said.
>
> 'You're being robbed, Madame,' he told her. 'I could get ten dragoons equipped as splendidly for that.'

On a visit to Malmaison one day, Talleyrand – stigmatized by Napoleon in a characteristic phrase as 'a shit in silk stockings' – found the host and hostess and their guests sitting on the grass of the bowling green. 'It was nothing to him with his camp habits, his riding boots and his leather breeches,' Talleyrand said, 'but, I in my silk breeches and silk stockings! Can you picture me sitting on that lawn? I'm crippled with rheumatism as it is. What a man! He always thinks he is camping out!'

At Malmaison in these years Josephine seemed to be as happy as her husband. She told her mother so. 'Bonaparte makes your daughter very happy,' she wrote to her. 'He is kind, amiable, in a word a charming man.' She was growing to love him; and, while she could never bring herself to curb her extravagance, she did endeavour to please him in other ways. She had, for instance, abandoned the once fashionable transparent, low-cut dresses which her husband professed so much to dislike. One day, he had rung for a footman to pile logs on to the fire until the room was unbearably hot. 'I wanted,' he said, 'to make sure there was a really good fire as it is an extremely cold evening and these ladies are almost naked.' Thereafter, Josephine's dresses became more modest and their high waists, short, puffed sleeves and generally restrained appearance became fashionable in Parisian society.

Napoleon's behaviour at Malmaison was almost that of a paterfamilias: he invited his nephews and nieces to stay, and played games and leapfrog with them in the gardens, cheating at prisoners' base by refraining to give the warning shout of '*Barre!*' and cheating also at blind man's buff by peeking under the blindfold. He amused the young son of his sister Caroline with what sounds a far more dangerous game which entailed giving Josephine's gazelles doses of snuff and then running away with the boy to escape the animals who charged at them with lowered horns.

Napoleon did not, however, get on so well with the five-year-old daughter of his sister, Elisa, to whom he said one day, in that bantering way which he supposed to be amusing, 'What can you have been up to, Mademoiselle? I hear you've peed in your bed.' 'Uncle', the child replied, 'if you can only say silly things like that I'm not going to stay in the same room with you.'

Accommodating and easygoing as Marchand and Méneval found him, the atmosphere at Malmaison was far more relaxed when Napoleon was not there. 'Alas, it is not at all pleasant living with a great man,' Bourrienne complained. 'Everyone breathed more easily, became more cheerful in the absence of the master . . . All changed immediately when he came back.'

Napoleon himself was aware of this. 'What do you think they would say if I died suddenly?' he asked Louis de Fontanes, the poet and *Grand-Maître* of the University of Paris, one day. 'Well, I'll tell you,' he continued when Fontanes was at a loss to find a suitable answer. 'They would simply say, "Ah, we can breathe again. That's the end of him, thank goodness and good riddance."'

21

ASSASSINS AND VICTIMS

'As soon as he returns, tell him he can have Hortense.'

'IT IS NOT ENOUGH TO BE HERE,' Napoleon remarked to Bourrienne in 1800, having moved from the Luxembourg Palace to apartments in the Tuileries. 'The problem will be to stay.'

Josephine doubted that she could be happy in these new surroundings. Allotted apartments once occupied by Marie Antoinette, she said to Hortense, 'I was not made for such grandeur . . . I can feel the Queen's ghost asking what I am doing in her bed.' Napoleon endeavoured to reassure her. 'Come on, little Creole,' he said on their first night there, carrying her towards the bed they shared as though he were a bridegroom carrying his bride across the threshold of their first home.

With Bourrienne, his mood was less playful. He understood only too well how insecure his new position was. 'My power,' he said, 'rests on my glory, and my glory on my victories.'

The country was still at war not only with the Habsburg monarchy but also with England, Russia and the United States; and, in the hope and need of winning an early victory as First Consul, he set out in the summer of 1800 to relieve the French army which was besieged in Genoa by the Austrians.

On his march south towards Milan, he sent Josephine a succession of letters to his 'sweet little one' in whose arms, he assured her, he longed to be. There was, he believed, some kind of 'magnetic fluid' which passed between them as always between people who truly loved each other. Yet, anxious as she had now become to please her husband, to give way to his moods and satisfy his wishes and desires when they were together, she could not bring herself to overcome her indolence and write to him when they were apart.

'I've had no letter from you,' he reminded her once more in one of his own. Yet she remained his 'sweet little one'.

Then, on 14 June 1800, the Austrians were defeated at Marengo; and Napoleon returned in triumph to Paris where the spontaneous and noisy celebrations and acclamations were 'as sweet to [his] ears,' so he said, 'as the sound of Josephine's voice'.

There was, however, another voice now that greatly appealed to him, that of Giuseppina Grassini, the sensuous soprano of La Scala, who, as it was said of her, 'spoke a kind of mixture of French and Italian all her own which allowed her to say anything and by which she contrived to make the queerest remarks, throwing the blame for what she said on her ignorance of the language whenever she uttered anything likely to hurt or shock'.

Napoleon had first come across her in 1797 but at that time had shown little interest in her, a slight for which she scolded him in a gently sardonic letter three years later when they became lovers:

> I was in the full glory of my beauty and talent. I was the one and only topic of conversation. I blinded all eyes and inflamed all hearts. While the young general remained cold, my every thought was of him and him alone. How strange it seems ... When all Italy was at my feet, when I spurned all homage for just one glance from your eyes, I could not obtain it. And now, now your gaze rests upon me, now when it is not worthwhile, now when I am no longer worthy of you.

Josephine heard that her husband had been discovered in bed with Grassini in Milan by General Berthier when they were on their way back from Marengo. She also heard that Grassini, later known as '*La Chanteuse de l'Empereur*', had been brought to Paris to be established in a house in the rue Caumartin and then in the rue de la Victoire, where Napoleon went to see her regularly, his face concealed by the collar of a very large greatcoat. She did not live there in reclusion. She sang at Malmaison; she sang in the Théâtre de la République and at Les Invalides and in the Champ de Mars; she received fifteen thousand francs a month from her lover who, as well as going to her, asked her to come to him from time to time at the Tuileries. Later, after her return from a series of engagements in London, Napoleon lavished further sums upon her as well as giving her a portrait of himself set in diamonds which was later stolen by four Swiss deserters, two of whom were executed.

'I am so unhappy,' Josephine told her intimate friend and fellow Creole, Mme de Krény, the artist Dominique Vivant Denon's mistress, with whom she had shared an apartment years before. 'Every day there are scenes with Bonaparte, for no apparent reason at all. I tried to guess why, and learned that la Grassini had been in Paris for the past week ... Evidently she is the cause of all my troubles ... Do please try to find out where the woman is living, and whether he goes to her or she comes to him here.'

Josephine had no reason to be so concerned. It was later to be widely supposed in Paris that the sexually alluring Grassini, having had an affair with the young violinist and composer, Pierre Rode, had become the mistress of Lord Wellington, 'ce cher Villainton' as she called him. Certainly, Wellington was to keep a picture of her in his room in Paris, together with portraits of Napoleon's sister Pauline and Pope Pius VII;* and he was so often to be seen in the company of Grassini that Lady Bessborough, who was in Paris at the time, complained not so much of the immorality of the liaison as of 'the want of procédé and the publicity of his attentions'. But, in any case, before long Grassini, notoriously promiscuous, was having an affair with someone else and let it be known that Napoleon, fond of him as she professed to be when displaying a valuable snuffbox which he had given her, had not been a very satisfactory lover.

Josephine remained insecure. She could not forget that Bonaparte had threatened divorce when he had learned about her affair with Hippolyte Charles; nor could she feel other than anxious when he questioned her about her debts which she endeavoured to settle by underhand dealings with army contractors, or, indeed, when anything annoyed or disturbed him.

For most of the time, however, whether at Malmaison or the Tuiler-

---

* The comte d'Artois commented that the portrait of Pope Pius, hanging between those of Pauline and la Grassini, reminded him of Jesus Christ hanging on the cross between the two thieves.

ies, her days were spent pleasantly enough. Her husband still relished her company, still slept in the same bed with her, still joined her for lunch and dinner, was still anxious to dash into their apartments when he could spare the time from his work, from his numerous visitors, and from his plans and directives. When he wished to think, she would sit by him quietly and patiently; and showed but the mildest impatience when he pushed the pots about on her dressing table as she endeavoured to make up her face, when he ruffled her hair or pinched her arms too hard to be playful.

With few women friends other than Mme de Krény, Josephine's life at the Tuileries soon began to pall. There were visits to the theatre with her daughter Hortense, aged seventeen in the year of Marengo; there were games of whist or piquet in the long evenings. But it seems that she no longer saw Hippolyte Charles; nor did she see Paul Barras, who was living in virtual exile on his estate at Chaillot; nor could she contrive to see much of Gabriel Ouvrard who, having declined to lend the government money, was imprisoned and not released until he had agreed to make a large contribution towards the expenses of the Marengo campaign.

Denied the pleasure of her old friends' company, she occupied herself with the seeking of favours from civil servants and ministers for those who appealed to her for help, in particular for returning exiles. Bonaparte, recognizing her usefulness in the pursuit of his policy of what he called 'fusion' in reconciling the new regime to the old aristocracy, brought her out of the seclusion to which he had formerly consigned her, and allowed her to act as hostess at official dinners and receptions, and to appear with him as his consort at the theatre.

It was announced, for instance, in the press that on Christmas Eve 1800, the First Consul would accompany Mme Bonaparte, his sister Caroline and his stepdaughter Hortense, to the Opéra for the opening night of Haydn's *Creation*. When they were dressed for this occasion they went down to find Napoleon sitting by the fire in the drawing room, half asleep after a busy day. He was reluctant to accompany them; but when his wife said that, in that case, she would stay with him, he rose to his feet. He dressed quickly and, since it was already eight o'clock, he hurried downstairs and, leaving the others to follow, he climbed into a carriage which, escorted by a troop of grenadiers, was driven off immediately by César, the rather inebriated coachman. Fast as the carriage was driven, Napoleon dozed off again and had a dreamy recollection of approaching the Tagliamento river in Italy and ordering the driver to take the coach across it, though he had no idea how deep it was (it was, in fact, very deep; the horses stumbled and he had nearly drowned). Awakened from his slumbers as César whipped the horses to pass a cart and mare partially blocking the rue St Niçaise, Napoleon was rattled along into the rue de la Loi.

Meanwhile, Josephine had been delayed at the Tuileries. It was a cold evening and she was wearing a shawl which had recently been sent to her from Turkey. One of her husband's aides-de-camp who had served in the Egyptian campaign, and was to receive no fewer than twenty-one wounds in Russia, admired the shawl but wondered whether it would not be better worn in the Egyptian manner around her head. He took hold of it, folded it, and rearranged it to his satisfaction. He then escorted her, Hortense and Caroline to a waiting coach which left the Tuileries two or three minutes after Napoleon's.

As Josephine's party drove towards the rue de la Loi, there was a shattering explosion. The cart which Napoleon's carriage had just passed was hurtled, disintegrated, into the night sky. A little girl who had been left to hold the mare was killed, so was the mare, so were eight bystanders. A woman standing at a shop door to watch Napoleon drive by had her breasts sliced off; another woman was blinded; over twenty other people were injured. The horses bolted; the fronts of the houses above them were torn off. Hortense's hand was cut; Caroline, who was later to give birth to an epileptic child, was stunned by the shock. Josephine fainted.

Bonaparte, waiting for them in the box at the Opéra, greeted them when they arrived as though nothing untoward had happened, merely sending for a programme. But when the performance was over, he sent for Fouché and, his voice raised in fury, demanded that the Jacobins responsible for the outrage must be arrested and shot. Fouché replied that Jacobins had not been responsible, the culprits were royalist guerrillas, two of whom were shot. This did not prevent Bonaparte seizing the opportunity to have numerous Jacobins deported.

He swore to be avenged. 'For such an atrocious crime we must have vengeance like a thunderbolt,' he told the Council of State. 'Blood must

flow. We must shoot as many guilty men as there have been victims.'
But the Bourbonists who had plotted the assassination attempt were
beyond his reach in England; and only two of their agents were caught
and condemned to death. A third escaped to America and became a
priest.

Soon after this attempt at assassination, when Josephine, accompanied
by her mother-in-law and Hortense, left for Plombières in the hope
that another course of the waters and baths might yet help to make her
fertile, Bonaparte ordered a strong cavalry escort to ride beside her
carriage and two other carriages to follow with several young officers.
No sooner had they left, than Bonaparte sat down to write to Josephine
to assure her, his 'adorable, sweet and lovable' Josephine, that he loved
her now as much as he had ever done. In a subsequent letter, complaining as so often in the past that he had heard nothing from her, he
sent her a 'passionate kiss, endless love'. 'I am sad,' he added, 'and all
alone.'

This was not true. As Josephine had reason to believe, he was taking
the opportunity of her absence to sleep with a young actress.

After her return from Plombières, Josephine became increasingly concerned about her inability to bear her husband a child and the likelihood
that one day, unless she did so, he would demand a divorce. She could
not be in any doubt that this was what his jealous family were hoping
for and working towards. So eager was Josephine to thwart them, to
preserve her marriage and her position, she was even prepared to agree
to sacrifice the happiness of her daughter.

Hortense had by then become an extremely attractive young woman;
generous, kind, intelligent and poised. She had already declined several
offers of marriage when she fell in love with General Duroc, the handsome and highly capable young officer who had gained Bonaparte's
respect in both the Italian and Egyptian campaigns. Despite the confidence that he reposed in him, Bonaparte considered that Hortense could
do better for herself and for himself. So he summoned Bourrienne and
said to him bluntly:

'Where is Duroc?'

'He has gone to the Opéra.'

'As soon as he returns, tell him he can have Hortense. The wedding must take place within two days. I will give him half a million francs and the command of a division at Toulon. They must go there the day after the wedding. I will have no sons-in-law around me. I must know immediately if this suits him.'

As was to be expected, Duroc deeply resented these terms and the peremptory manner in which they were put to him.

'Tell him he can keep his daughter,' he shouted at Bourrienne. 'I am off to the brothel.'

With Duroc out of the way, Napoleon and Josephine decided that Hortense should marry Napoleon's brother, Louis Bonaparte, an unappealing paranoid young man believed to be suffering from gonorrhoea. Hortense accepted her fate with appalled resignation, having broken down and sobbed when she learned what it was to be.

The miserable couple were married on 4 January 1802 by Cardinal Caprara, the Archbishop of Milan, in the house in the rue de la Victoire which Napoleon gave them as a wedding present. Hortense, pale and tense, was clearly struggling not to give way again to the tears which she had been shedding for most of the previous night. While her mother cried throughout the ceremony, Louis did not attempt to hide his reluctance to repeat the words required of him. That night he enumerated all the lovers Josephine had had before her marriage to Napoleon and informed Hortense that she must never spend the night under the same roof as her mother again. Moreover, if she gave birth to a child which he had the least reason to believe was not his, he would have nothing more to do with her for the rest of his life. He was soon to develop a morbidly paranoiac concern about rumours that Hortense was conducting an illicit affair with his brother Napoleon; rumours which were supposedly lent some unwarranted credibility by Napoleon's seeming to be rather in awe of her and, as Laure Junot noticed, by his refraining from using 'indecent expressions' in her presence.

After the ceremony of Hortense's marriage to Louis had taken place, Joachim Murat and Caroline Bonaparte knelt down before Cardinal Caprara to have their own marriage blessed. This double ceremony made a 'most disagreeable impression' on Hortense, so she said. 'The other couple were so happy, so much in love with each other', whereas she felt utterly miserable.

22

MISTRESSES AT COURT

'I am not like other men. The commonly accepted rules
of morality and propriety do not apply to me.'

BENEFITING FROM the increasing prosperity of France, Bonaparte's
popularity grew month by month, inflating his ambition while increasing
Josephine's insecurity. 'Her melancholy presented a striking contrast
to the prevailing gaiety,' noted Bourrienne when, in August 1802, the
announcement of Napoleon's new title – Consul for Life – was greeted
with a grand display of illuminations, fireworks and parades. 'She had
to receive a host of dignitaries and officials on that evening and she did
so with her usual grace, despite the profound depression that weighed
down her spirits. She believed that Bonaparte's every step towards the
throne was a step away from her.'

She felt this ever more deeply when he decided to move from
Malmaison, where she had been so content, to the palace of St Cloud,
where the atmosphere was so infinitely more formal and courtly. Here
her husband – who spent enormous sums on waterfalls and fountains
for the gardens and on frescoes in the palace – took to wearing a red
velvet coat, embroidered in gold, while the officials and footmen of the
household also wore an equally imposing uniform. Josephine was given
precedence over the Second and Third Consuls, and her flattering portrait by François Gérard was hung above the marble staircase beside
Jacques-Louis David's melodramatic picture of Napoleon crossing the
Alps. A long list of rules was drawn up for the behaviour of the household, decreeing, for example, that if the chamberlain of the day had
reason to enter the apartments of the First Consul's wife to take her

orders, he must scratch lightly on her door to seek the permission of one of her ladies – who must always be in attendance – to be introduced into her presence.

The household was, indeed, assuming the formality of the pre-revolutionary court. When Bonaparte and his wife entered the salon where distinguished visitors were received, the First Consul walking a few paces in front of his consort, young ladies were required to curtsey in the manner in which they had done at the Bourbon court at Versailles. When Josephine entered a room they all stood up, and did so again when she left it.

At receptions for foreign ambassadors and their retinues, Josephine, having entered the room, her hand on the back of Talleyrand's, remained seated, half rising from her chair as each person was presented to her, behaving with what Napoleon's valet described as 'perfect grace and both natural and cultivated skill', as though, said Méneval, 'she had been born for the role good fortune had given her'. She had a remarkable memory for names and faces and, as Metternich testified, 'a quite extra-ordinary social tact'.

Her husband never acquired such grace, and his court incurred the derision of those who had known more ancient regimes.

'However splendid it may have seemed from a distance,' commented Countess Potocka, a niece of the last king of Poland, 'Napoleon's court just did not bear close examination. There was an obvious muddle and discord which destroyed the brilliant atmosphere which people expected. It really was quite a ridiculous scene. One might have believed oneself at a rehearsal in a theatre with the actors trying on costumes and practising their parts.'

At receptions in one or other of the extravagantly decorated salons, Napoleon could overawe and intimidate; but he rarely troubled to charm. He would appear, accompanied by two household officials chosen for their comparatively diminutive size, and march from guest to guest, asking a few brusque questions and then – in contrast to the interested demeanour, either real or convincingly assumed, of his wife – stride on, often without troubling to listen to the answers. 'It is difficult to imagine anything more awkward than Napoleon's manner in a draw-ing room,' Metternich commented. 'His efforts to correct the mistakes he made because of his background and education served only to make them more obvious. He had no idea how to conduct a polite conversation. He was always trying tò impress and, aware of his undignified lack of inches, walked on tiptoe.'

Occasionally, he would think it amusing to hint to a lady that he knew of her husband's infidelities or even whisper that he had heard of her own, evidently taking pleasure in her discomfiture. He once asked General Junot's wife if she had heard about the harem which her husband had kept in Egypt; and, on another occasion, burst out in affected astonishment upon a young lady's appearance at court for the first time: 'My God! I heard you were pretty!' 'Madame,' he was also said to have remarked, 'they told me you were ugly. They certainly did not exaggerate.' An aristocratic lady was told that she was well past the age at which she should wear a décolleté dress; and an eighteen-year-old girl was asked how many husbands she had had.

He was equally unpleasantly rude and impertinent on occasions to men. He once attacked the British ambassador, the tall, patrician Lord Whitworth, with what Whitworth described as a 'total want of dignity as well as of decency', storming from the room after insulting him. In his report of the incident, the ambassador declared that he was convinced that 'there was not a single person who did not feel the extreme impropriety of his conduct'.

And when the Crown Prince of Bavaria attended a levee, Napoleon asked him bluntly who his mistress was. When the Prince denied having one, Napoleon said, 'Nonsense, tell me,' before moving on. To his wife's ladies he was often equally rude and coarse. He once profoundly shocked Mme de Rémusat by telling her that she had the reputation of being 'quick and good' in bed.

He also behaved not so much impatiently and impolitely as, at times, insultingly to the women he took as temporary mistresses at this time. One of these was Mlle Duchesnois, an actress at the Comédie Française who had formerly been a maidservant and a sempstress. She was highly talented but far from good-looking; and, as Napoleon once said, a woman must be beautiful to please him. When, on one occasion, Constant came to knock on the door of his study to tell him that Mlle Duchesnois had arrived in the room next door as arranged, he called out to him to tell her to wait. When, an hour later, there was another knock on the door, he said, 'Tell her to get undressed.' Mlle Duchesnois obeyed his instructions; but still Napoleon did not stir from his desk. After a further long wait there was another knock which Napoleon answered by impatiently calling out, 'Tell her to go home.'

This cavalier treatment of a woman was far from an isolated incident. In the room next to his office which was reserved for sexual encounters, women were required to wait undressed until it was convenient for Napoleon to come to them. He would remove his sword but little else; preliminaries, he maintained, were quite unnecessary; the 'matter', he said, 'was all dealt with in three minutes'. It was as though he was making excuses for his own sexual inadequacy. 'Love is not for me,' he once admitted. 'I am not as other men.' And in his memoirs, comte Horace de Viel Castel wrote of a conversation he had had with the comte de Las Cases, Napoleon's companion in exile. 'I often talked about the Emperor with Monsieur de Las Cases,' de Viel Castel said. 'He told me that Napoleon used to speak sometimes of his feebleness in the game of love: it did not amount to much.'

Napoleon's supposed occasional impotence was widely discussed in France; and so was the supposed inadequacy of his semen and the small size of his penis. Josephine was quoted as having once said, in reference to her husband's capacity as a lover, '*Bon-a-parte c'est bon à rien*'; and Giuseppina Grassini observed that Napoleon's 'caresses were on the furtive side and often left his mistresses unsatisfied'.

In the room in which the naked Mlle Duchesnois waited so fruitlessly a bed was prepared every day and fresh flowers were placed on a table. Josephine knew of this, since Napoleon no longer took any trouble to conceal his liaisons from her. Not long before, while on a tour of inspection of the troops on the Channel coast, still threatening an invasion of England, he had written her an affectionate letter to which she had replied with pathetic gratitude, telling him that he could not conceive how much joy his letter had given her. She would always keep it, she wrote, and press it to her heart. 'It will comfort me when you are away and guide me when you are near me ... I want to be always in your eyes as you want me to be ... All I want is to be your sweet and tender Josephine devoted only to your happiness ... I will never forget the last sentence of your letter ... Yes, yes, that is my wish, to please you and to love you – no, to adore you.'

Thankful as she had been to receive Napoleon's letter, she could not overcome her fear that he might fall in love with one of his young mistresses. The prospect of divorce was never far from her mind. Hortense now had a son, who had been given the name of Napoleon-Charles and who might be proposed as the First Consul's heir; but there might equally well come a time when he would insist upon having a legitimate child of his own.

The brief affair with Mlle Duchesnois, preceded by a similarly brief one with another young actress, Louise Rolandeau, was followed by a more serious and, for Josephine, far more disturbing one with a more celebrated and clever actress.

Marguerite-Josephine Weimer, a big, buxom, beautiful and sensuous young woman, whose stage-name was Mlle George and who had given a splendid performance as Clytaemnestra in Racine's *Iphigénie en Aulide* at the outset of her distinguished career in classical tragedy, was barely sixteen years old when she first came to Napoleon's notice and was summoned to St Cloud.

Mlle George confessed to being 'nearly frightened to death' when his valet, Constant, came to fetch her to his master. 'Come now,' Constant said to comfort her. 'Everything will be all right. But go on looking frightened because he'll like that.'

At St Cloud, according to her own colourful account, Mlle George was shown into a large, brightly lit bedroom in which a fierce fire burned in the massive fireplace. Hearing steps approaching from the room she was to discover to be the library, she pulled her veil down over her face.

'I stood up and he came towards me,' she wrote. 'He took me by the hand and made me sit beside him on the enormous divan. Then he took off my veil and threw it carelessly on to the floor. "Your hand is trembling. You're not afraid of me? Do I seem so frightening? I thought you so beautiful last night. I wanted to compliment you on your performance. I'm really much more polite and amiable than you are ... Tell me what your name is."'

She told him it was Marguerite-Josephine. He said that he was very fond of the name Josephine but that he would call her Georgina.

'Come, Georgina,' he said, 'tell me all about yourself ... Tell me everything.' And, as she began to do so, she lost her nervousness in his presence and began to feel at home. They talked, she said, until five o'clock in the morning when he kissed her on the forehead, then arranged her veil over it, and made her promise to come to see him again the following day. Before leaving she mentioned the name of her patron and admirer, Prince Sappiéha; and at this Napoleon snatched the veil from her head, tore it to pieces and, together with her shawl and cornelian necklace, trampled it underfoot.

'Georgina,' he said, 'you must have nothing except what I give you.'

> One could not for long be annoyed with such a man [she commented]. There was such charm and attraction in his voice that one felt obliged to say to oneself, 'Really, he is quite right.' 'You are quite right,' I said. (I swear on my life that all this is true.)

She returned to St Cloud the next night when he made her promise that on the third they would become lovers. When she agreed to this he took from his pocket two fine diamond earrings. 'These are for you, my dear Georgina,' he said. 'I spoilt your jewellery last night so it is only right that I should repair the damage I did.'

It was not long before this new affair of Napoleon's was well known in Paris; and at a performance at the Théâtre Française of one of his favourite plays, *Cinna*, the audience made it clear that they had heard of it. At the words spoken by Mlle George, 'If I have charmed Cinna, I shall charm other men as well', they cheered and clapped, looking up at the Consul's box.

Mlle George was concerned that Napoleon would be angry because she had been indiscreet in telling her friend, the actor, François-Joseph Talma, about her affair with Napoleon. But he did not mention the uproar in the theatre, talking instead about the performance of the play, praising Talma and herself. 'How well he talks about the theatre!' she wrote. 'What good criticisms he gives.'

'He overwhelms me with kindness,' she added. 'Little by little he took off my clothes, and made himself my *femme de chambre* with so much gaiety and tact that it was impossible not to give into him despite oneself . . . I left him at seven in the morning. But, feeling ashamed of the disorder the night had caused, I said, "Please let me tidy everything up." "Yes, dear Georgina, I will help you." And he was kind enough to assist me in straightening out the couch, the scene of so much abandon and affection.'

He was not always so considerate and polite. When she was reluctant to remove her stockings he was induced to make one of those caustic remarks it amused him to address to women: 'You must have hideous feet!' Nor did he prove a patient and skilful lover. He presented her with a special kind of garter made of elastic which he found easier to undo than the usual sort of garter with a buckle. In later years, liking it to be known that she had become the mistress of the Duke of Wellington, she declared that, of the two men, the Duke was '*de beaucoup le plus fort*'.

Napoleon was exceptionally playful with Mlle George, enjoying her company as that of a spirited child. Indulging and sharing his taste for childish humour, she would pretend to be unable to find him when he hid from her and she would laugh helplessly when he took a wreath of roses from her head, placed it on his own, danced around the room with it, stopping from time to time to grimace at his reflection in a looking-glass and make absurd remarks. Once, when she asked him for a lock of his hair as a souvenir, he rushed away from her, pretending to be frightened as Mlle George chased after him, brandishing a pair of scissors; and, on another occasion, so she recalled, Napoleon was 'in a laughing, light-hearted mood, and he made me run after him in his library. So as not to be caught, he climbed up the step-ladder, and, since it was light and stood on wheels, I pushed it the whole length of the room. He laughed and shouted, "You'll hurt yourself. Stop, or I'll be cross."'

One evening, when Claire de Rémusat had come to see Josephine, they were waiting for Napoleon to come down to join them in the Yellow Salon. Time passed and it was after midnight when Josephine suddenly leapt to her feet. 'I can't stand this a moment longer,' she said. 'Mlle George must be up there with him. I am going to surprise them.' She told Mme de Rémusat to come with her as she climbed the stairs. But they had not reached the top when they thought they heard the bodyguard, Roustam, stirring outside his master's door. 'He is quite capable of cutting our throats,' Josephine warned her friend as she dropped her candle in her rush to get back to the salon. 'When she saw my startled face,' Claire de Rémusat continued her account, 'she burst out laughing and this set me laughing too.'

On a later occasion when Mlle George was with him, Josephine was alarmed by the sound of her screams and rushed up to Napoleon's room from which Mlle George fled, clutching her clothes to her naked breast. Napoleon had suffered one of those convulsive seizures resembling epilepsy.

This was, apparently, the last time he made love to Mlle George between whose ample breasts he pushed forty thousand francs by way of a parting present. But he was soon conducting an affair with another actress, Mlle Bourgoin, later a celebrated courtesan and Tsar Alexander's mistress. However, despite a bottom which he found exceptionally alluring, he dismissed her when her taste for coarse jokes repelled him, and began to look out for a more amenable mistress. He found one in the attractive, flighty Anna Roche de Lacoste, one of Josephine's rarely employed readers, and her favours were secured by the present of a piece of very valuable jewellery. Later, in Josephine's presence, Napoleon gave Mlle de Lacoste a ring. Outraged by this indelicacy, Josephine demanded the young woman's dismissal from her household. Her husband agreed to this provided that she was received at a forthcoming court function. Napoleon then took as Mlle de Lacoste's replacement an Italian girl from Genoa, Carlotta Gazzini, 'the most attractive woman,' so Mme de Rémusat said, 'in a court full of attractive women'; she was appointed to her predecessor's place as reader even though she spoke very little French, a disadvantage which Napoleon dismissed as irrelevant in the circumstances.

He was determined that his wife should accept that he needed other women: her obvious jealousy exasperated him. It was not as though he were in love with them: his affections, he insisted, were not engaged. 'I am not like other men,' he declared more than once. 'The commonly accepted rules of morality and propriety do not apply to me.'

'It is your place to submit to all my fancies,' one of Josephine's ladies-in-waiting once overhead him telling his wife impatiently. 'You ought to think it perfectly natural that I should allow myself amusements of this kind. I have a right to answer all your complaints . . . I am a person apart. I will not be dictated to by anyone.'

He insisted that these temporary distractions were essential to him; and when his wife presumed to question such declarations, 'he turned on her with a violence [she] did not choose to record', as, indeed, he did when he embarked on an affair with one of her ladies-in-waiting, Elisabeth de Vaudey.

'Bonaparte,' commented Mme de Vaudey, 'was by turns imperious, hard, defiant to excess. Then, suddenly, he would show some feeling; he would relent and become almost sweet-tempered, endeavouring to repair with a good grace the harm he had done, although he never showed any sign of mending his ways.'

His liaison with Elisabeth de Vaudey was followed or preceded by various other ladies about Josephine's court, including the duchesse de Rovigo, and Félicité Longrois, one of Josephine's Women of the Bedchamber whose duty it was to guard the door of her apartment and to announce visitors.

'As soon as he acquired a new mistress,' Mme de Rémusat wrote, 'Napoleon became hard, violent and pitiless towards his wife. He did not hesitate to tell her about the affair, nor to go into details about the perfections and imperfections of her body ... nor to show an almost ferocious astonishment that she should disapprove of it.'

Evangeline Bruce, in her outstanding dual biography, *Napoleon and Josephine*, draws attention to an example of Bonaparte's cruelly insensitive treatment of his wife.

Although she was suffering from one of those severe migraines which had troubled her intermittently ever since she had been imprisoned in Les Carmes, and although he well knew that she was always frightened when being driven at speed in a carriage, he insisted that she hurried off with him to see a house which he had bought near Malmaison. He and Bourrienne rode ahead leaving Josephine to follow in a carriage with Laure Junot and two other ladies. When they came to a ditch over which Napoleon and Bourrienne had jumped with ease, Josephine asked the postillion to halt the carriage so that she could alight and walk before an attempt was made to get the carriage across. Napoleon told her not to be so childish and hit the positillion with his riding crop, ordering him to take the slope and the ditch at its bottom as fast as he could. The horses cleared the obstacle but, as the carriage crashed into the bank it almost broke in two. Josephine burst into tears. Napoleon told her that crying always made her ugly.

When he was in less bullying moods, Josephine succumbed to the charm which her husband could summon up at will; and she clearly enjoyed the occasions when he took her on tours of inspection, when the crowds cheered them both, bands played in welcome, and towns were decorated and illuminated in their honour. She remembered people's names and she was able to put them at ease with a few kindly spoken words. Napoleon recognized that her popularity was an important factor in the maintenance of his own. He was seen on occasions to kiss her with affection and as though in gratitude for the part she played in the furtherance of his career, the realization of his destiny.

At no time had he more reason to feel gratitude than when, feeling endangered by royalist as well as Jacobin conspiracies, he and Talleyrand plotted the judicial murder of a man who might well have become a royalist pretender to the throne which Napoleon already had thoughts of occupying himself. This was Louis XVI's nephew, the duc d'Enghien.

Orders were given to a group of French soldiers to kidnap the duc one evening in March 1804, when he was taking his dog for a walk, and to bundle him across the Rhine from the duchy of Baden to the prison of Vincennes. When this outrage became known at St Cloud, so Mme de Rémusat said, Josephine knelt down in front of Napoleon and, characteristically in floods of tears, begged him to spare the duke. 'Women shouldn't meddle in affairs of state,' he told her. 'You know nothing about politics.' She was ordered not to mention the subject again. According to Joseph, their mother was also in tears when she reproached him. 'He listened in silence. She told him it was an atrocity from which nothing could ever absolve him. He had yielded to treacherous advice from men . . . who were only too pleased to blacken his name by such a wicked act.'

Enghien's execution had already been ordered and his grave in the prison dug. He was shot through the heart on 21 March.

Three days later, Talleyrand was told to organize a ball. It was not a success: it was as though the murder of the duc d'Enghien had cast a pall over the proceedings. Yet the next week, after the public had read the doctored version of the duc's death which was published in the newspapers, Napoleon decided to make a public appearance at the theatre. He seemed unaccustomedly nervous; and, instead of preceding Josephine into his box, he waited for her arrival so that they might enter it together. As they did so, Napoleon looking even paler than usual, Josephine smiling in that beguiling way of hers, the audience rose to their feet, clapping and cheering.

The house in the strada Malerba, Ajaccio where Napoleon was born on 15 August 1769.

Letizia Buonaparte, née Ramolino, Napoleon's mother, a portrait by François-Pascal-Simon, Baron Gérard.

Marie Josèphe Rose Tascher de La Pagerie, the future Empress Josephine, was born on the family sugar plantation in Martinique on 23 June 1763.

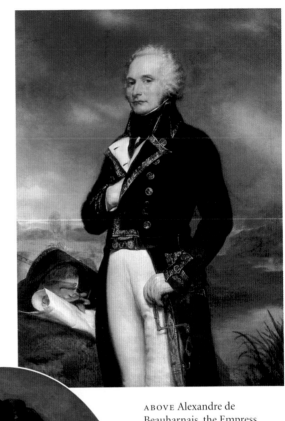

ABOVE Alexandre de Beauharnais, the Empress Josephine's first husband.

LEFT Désirée Clary, a portrait by François-Pascal-Simon, Baron Gérard.

ABOVE Josephine
arriving to visit
Bonaparte in Italy
on the banks of
Lake Garda in 1796:
a painting by
Hippolyte Lecomte.

LEFT Napoleon on
the bridge at Arcola,
15 November 1796:
a painting by Antoine-
Jean Gros.

'Ci-devant occupations – or – Madame Talian and the Empress Josephine Dancing Naked Before Barras in the winter of 1797 – A Fact! Barras (then in power) being tired of Josephine, promised Buonaparte a promotion, on condition that he would take her off his hands; – Barras had, as usual, drunk freely, & placed Buonaparte behind a screen . . . Madame Talian is a beautiful Woman, tall and elegant . . . Josephine is smaller & with bad teeth something like cloves.' Barras lolls tipsily in his chair while Bonaparte lifts the curtain, holding his cocked hat behind his back. (Caricature by James Gillray, BM catalogue, 10369, 20 February 1805)

The scene in the Orangery at Saint-Cloud during the *coup d'état* of *Brumaire*, 9 November 1799.

RIGHT The Empress Josephine, a portrait by Pierre-Paul Prud'hon.

ABOVE Pauline Bonaparte, Princess Borghese, a portrait by Robert Lefevre.

RIGHT A portrait by Marie Guilhelmine of Princess Borghese.

BELOW Antonio Canova's sculpture of Princess Borghese.

Elisa Bonaparte, Grand Duchess of Tuscany, with her daughter, Napoléone Elisa, a portrait by Pietro Benvenuti.

ABOVE Joachim Murat, King of Naples, a portrait by François-Pascal-Simon, Baron Gérard.

LEFT Caroline Murat, Queen of Naples, a portrait by François-Pascal-Simon, Baron Gérard.

Napoleon's brother, Jérôme, King of Westphalia.

Napoleon's brother, Louis, King of Holland.

Napoleon's brother, Lucien.

RIGHT Napoleon's brother, Joseph, King of Naples and later King of Spain.

23

THE IMPERIAL HIGHNESSES
AND MADAME MÈRE

'They were dumbfounded by this distinction between
themselves and their sisters-in-law.'

ON 28 MAY 1804, the day that the Senate proclaimed the First Consul
to be 'Emperor of the French Republic', a state banquet was held at
St Cloud. It was not a happy event. Royalists and old soldiers of the
Revolution alike deplored the contentious new title. Andoche Junot
actually wept; and Mme de Staël thought it a tragedy that a man who
'had risen above every throne' should come down 'willingly to take his
place amongst kings'.

It was further regretted when, at the banquet, it was announced
that both Joseph and Louis Bonaparte were to be created Princes of the
Empire, and their wives, Julie and Hortense, consequently becoming
princesses. According to Claire de Rémusat, the Emperor's sisters, Elisa
and Caroline, were 'dumbfounded by this distinction between themselves and their sisters-in-law'. Caroline, in particular, could scarcely
conceal her resentment. During the dinner, upon hearing her brother
address Hortense as Princess Louis, she was so little in control of herself
that she could not hold back her tears. She drank several glasses of
water in an attempt to recover her composure, and, upon trying to eat
something, she was overcome by sobs. Elisa, older and more self-
possessed, did not cry; 'but she adopted an offhand and cutting manner,
treating the ladies-in-waiting with pointed hauteur'.

Caroline was in tears again the next day when she asked to have a
private talk with her brother in the Empress's boudoir. She 'demanded
to know why she was being condemned to obscurity and public

contempt when strangers were being heaped with honours and titles'. In her agitation she fainted – or contrived to collapse – to the floor. The next day the *Moniteur* announced that the Emperor's sisters would bear the title of Imperial Highness.

Caroline was now twenty-one years old. One of her daughters was later to write of her: 'She was a little plump and of a complexion so dazzlingly white that, in evening dress, her shoulders looked as if they were covered in white satin . . . Her eyes were almond-shaped and . . . her expression soft and sweet . . . Her hands and feet were tiny.'

Her marriage was not an unhappy one, though she was discreetly unfaithful to her husband while he was notoriously unfaithful to her. 'Evidently Murat has to sleep with a woman every night,' Napoleon commented. 'Any woman does for him. Nothing stops him, whether he has the pox or not. When one is so easy to please one finds what one needs anywhere, which is indeed fortunate.'

Since his sisters had now been given grand titles, his mother, so Cardinal Fesch told Napoleon, considered that she should have one, too. She was 'very upset' that 'some people called her "Majesty" or "Empress Mother", while others addressed her, as they addressed her daughters, as "Imperial Highness"'. Having discussed the problem with men presumed to be authorities on the subject, Napoleon proposed that his mother should be known officially as '*Son Altesse Madame, Mère de Sa Majesté l'Empereur*'. She became generally known thereafter as '*Madame Mère*', a title she accepted without enthusiasm.

She was not in the best of moods when she left for Italy where Cardinal Fesch 'presented her to the Pope at the Quirinal, together with her daughter [Pauline] and Mme Clary'. 'She was greeted with full ceremonial,' the Cardinal reported to Napoleon in March 1804. 'The Swiss Guard escorted her to the first ante-chamber, where she was received by the gentlemen-in-waiting . . . The Roman nobility call on her ceaselessly . . . and the Dean of the Sacred College has asked all cardinals to pay their respects to her within twenty-four hours.'

Having stayed for a time in a house near the Spanish Steps which Lucien had bought, she moved to the Palazzo Falconieri, in via Giulia, before going to take a course of the waters at Bagni di Lucca – to which Gabriel Fallopius, the sixteenth-century anatomist, had given credit for curing his deafness – letting it be known that she did not intend to be present at Napoleon's forthcoming coronation as Emperor, determined not to be a witness of a crown being placed upon the head of '*la putana*'.

24

CORONATION

'He resembled the King of Diamonds.'

NAPOLEON SUPERVISED THE ARRANGEMENTS for his coronation, which was to take place on 2 December 1804, with the greatest care. He demanded alterations to the interior of Notre Dame, authorized the demolition of several houses which were considered to be too close to the building, and commissioned a painting of the ceremony, *The Coronation of Napoleon*, from Jacques-Louis David as well as suitably dramatic designs for costumes from Jean-Baptiste Isabey, who was also to produce thirty-two drawings commemorating the event which are now in the Louvre. He even ordered a model of the interior of the cathedral and hundreds of paper figures representing the chief participants in the ceremony.

Whether or not Josephine was to be one of these participants had not yet been decided and, in the meantime, while Napoleon made yet another inspection of the forces assembled on the coast for his projected invasion of England, she was to go to Aachen for the doubtful benefits of its spa water. She was to travel there, Napoleon decreed, in a style suitably imposing for the wife of a prospective emperor, accompanied by a suite consisting of over fifty attendants, including a master of horse, a comptroller, four ladies, two women of the bedchamber, equerries, ushers, footmen, cooks and coachmen. Orders were given for towns along the route to be decorated as though *en fête*, bands were to play, guns to thunder.

Josephine performed her part with her usual charm and tact, keeping her head when handed a relic of the Emperor Charlemagne, whose tomb is in the church of St Mary at Aachen. Unwilling to touch the grisly object, a bone of the great man's arm, she found the perfect excuse for not doing so by declaring that she had for her own support an arm quite as strong as Charlemagne's.

Napoleon, highly gratified by reports of her successful progress, decided to go to meet her at Aachen and to take her on a state visit down the Rhine. She was delighted. He had sent her a succession of affectionate letters – to which, of course, she had not replied – assuring her of his continuing love, that she was 'essential' to his happiness. 'I cover you with kisses,' he wrote. 'I cannot wait to see you . . . A bachelor's life is horrid. I miss my good and beautiful wife . . . I have not heard from you for several days. I would have liked to have news from you.'

He would also have liked to have news of the lady-in-waiting, Elisabeth de Vaudey, to whom Josephine confided how rough and unpleasant Bonaparte became when indulging in one of his affairs, when, in his own typically coarse phrase, he was in his 'rutting season'. At Mainz, Napoleon provided characteristic evidence of this affair when Josephine protested that she felt too tired and ill to go to a ball. Her husband angrily grabbed her arm and, not for the first or last time, pulled her out of bed and ordered her to get dressed immediately.

After his brief liaison with the capricious and extravagant Elisabeth de Vaudey, who was dismissed from Josephine's household by Napoleon after being charged with pilfering, he next began an affair with a young divorced woman named Adèle Duchâtel, a friend of his sister Caroline: 'a lively creature', in the opinion of his stepdaughter, Hortense, 'with black hair, large, appealing dark blue eyes, a long, very pointed nose, the finest teeth in the world and a complexion which was dull in the morning but wonderful at night'.

He was at his most graceless when Adèle Duchâtel first caught his eye one evening at a buffet supper. Leaning over her shoulder, he said, 'You shouldn't eat olives at night. They're bad for you! And you, Madame Junot,' he added, turning to her neighbour, 'you've not eaten olives and you're quite right not to do so, doubly right in not trying to imitate Madame Duchâtel who is beyond imitation.'

Unusually, so his valet, Louis Constant, said, Napoleon endeavoured to prevent his wife learning of this new affair. 'He used to wait until everyone was asleep before joining his mistress, and so great were his precautions that he went from his room to hers in his night attire with neither shoes nor slippers on his feet.'

Josephine was, however, given an inkling of this new affair one evening when she noticed that both Bonaparte and Mme Duchâtel had slipped away from the company assembled in the drawing room at St Cloud before dinner. Josephine followed them, crept up the staircase to the room next to her husband's study, and when she heard his voice and that of Mme Duchâtel behind the locked door, she summoned up the courage to knock on it and demand to be let in.

Bonaparte, half undressed, threw open the door and appeared before her in a terrifying rage. She ran away down the stairs and sought the safety of her own apartments from which the shouts of the furious Bonaparte could clearly be heard in the drawing room below as he raged about, kicking the furniture, demanding that she leave St Cloud immediately – as the frightened Mme Duchâtel had already done – accusing her of spying on him, interfering in his private life, incapable of giving him a child and driving him to marry another woman who could.

When he had stormed off, Josephine begged Mme de Rémusat to go to Hortense and ask her to intercede with her stepfather on her mother's behalf. But Hortense declined to do so. Her husband Louis had forbidden it, she said. 'My mother will only lose a crown,' she told Claire de Rémusat, 'and there are lots of women more to be pitied than she is.' Her only hope of placating Napoleon, Hortense added, was to use her influence over him by relying upon her 'own sweet and gentle nature, and her tears'.

This was sound advice. By relying upon what Mme de Rémusat called her 'complete submissiveness', her 'adroit and tender sweetness', Josephine succeeded in making Napoleon relent. He no longer insisted on a divorce, and while still undecided as to whether or not she should be crowned as he was shortly to be – his family were united in urging that she should not be – he began to consider that it was only right, as he put it, that she should share his grandeur. 'If I had been thrown into prison instead of ascending a throne,' he remarked, 'I know she would have shared my misfortune.'

In the end, a few weeks before the coronation was due to take place, 'harassed and pushed too far by his scheming family,' according to Mme de Rémusat, 'and resentful of their premature air of triumph', Napoleon went to Josephine's room, put his arms around her and comforted her as though she were a child. 'The Pope will be here at the end of the month,' he said. 'He will crown us both. Start to get ready for the ceremony.'

As soon as they learned that Napoleon had at last come to this decision against their known and repeatedly expressed wishes, the family rose up in anger against him. His sisters flatly refused to carry Josephine's train as their brother proposed. After successive almost sleepless nights, he gave way to their heated objections, permitting them to make mere gestures instead and agreeing that their own trains should be carried by attendants.

Then there was trouble with the Pope, Pius VII, who had been reconciled to the French republic by the concordat of 1801, which regulated the relations of Church and State. Josephine confessed to him that her marriage to Bonaparte, because of the troubled times, had been a civil marriage only. In that case, said the Pope, they were not married at all in the eyes of the Church. It would consequently be impossible to anoint either of them with the holy oil which the already mutilated coronation service required. Accordingly, Napoleon told his uncle, Joseph Fesch, who had received his cardinal's hat the year before, to arrange a marriage service that very night. This was done with such haste and secrecy that there were no witnesses to the impromptu ceremony – the validity of which was, therefore, open to question. Even so, Josephine took the precaution of asking Cardinal Fesch for a copy of the marriage certificate.

The procession of carriages began to leave the Tuileries for Notre Dame at nine o'clock on the cold morning of 2 December 1804, many of the ladies in these carriages having been sitting up for hours on end, anxious not to derange the tall, elaborate coiffeurs upon which their hairdressers had been at work for most of the night. Escorted by dragoons, the Pope's carriage splashed through the streets, on which snow followed by rain had fallen in the night. His hands were raised in a gesture of blessing through the window; and several of the spectators knelt down in the slush at sight of it.

There was little evidence of public rejoicing. Napoleon had insisted that it was not to be an event staged for the populace. The congregation was to consist of distinguished people only. The ceremony had not been designed for the entertainment of 'twenty thousand fishwives and the corrupt population'. Carriage after carriage followed, bearing ministers and generals in the exotic costumes designed for them by Jean-Baptiste Isabey, appearing to be ill at ease in their pantaloons and ruffs and their high-heeled shoes decorated with rosettes. The crowds were respectful rather than enthusiastic, such royalists as had been driven by curiosity to turn out to watch being scornful of such a ludicrous spectacle which the Minister of Finance reckoned cost well over eight million francs.

Napoleon, still at the Tuileries, appeared to be not at all embarrassed by his finery and the numerous, glittering jewels which he wore, giving him the appearance, so someone said, of 'a walking looking-glass'. Another observer, the comtesse de Boigne, thought that, while his costume might have looked all right on the drawing board, it looked 'terrible on the short, fat Napoleon'. He 'resembled the King of Diamonds'.

Napoleon seemed in no hurry to leave for Notre Dame and it was almost two hours after the departure of the Pope that the glass and gilt imperial state coach, with four eagles bearing a crown on its roof, was driven out of the courtyard of the Tuileries. In it, facing Napoleon and Josephine, were Joseph and Louis Bonaparte – both dressed in white satin with a liberal complement of diamonds.

When Napoleon, grasping a sceptre, emerged from the robing room next to the cathedral, he appeared more exotic than ever. He was now wearing a purple velvet mantle, lined in ermine and sewn with bees;* and, on his head, was a wreath of gold laurel leaves. His face was remarkable for its pallor. Laure d'Abrantès, whose husband, General Junot, was now the duc d'Abrantès, noticed that, more than once, he was seen to be stifling a yawn.

His wife, smiling that closed-lips smile of hers, seemed quite at ease, though the expressions of her sisters-in-law who were in the end most reluctantly supporting her mantle, made it quite clear that they resented having to do so.

---

* Bees were symbols of assiduity and were used as such by the Emperor Charlemagne, who united by conquest nearly all the Christian lands of Western Europe.

When the imperial procession came into view, the members of the congregation who had been waiting in the bitterly cold cathedral for almost six hours and had staved off their hunger by eating the sausage rolls which enterprising *colporteurs* had surreptitiously offered for sale, rose to their feet to applaud.

The acclamations continued as Cardinal Fesch led the way towards the two thrones at the far end of the nave before the altar. His progress was too slow for Napoleon who was walking behind him, prodding him in the back with his sceptre.

Having at last reached the thrones, the Emperor and Empress knelt on cushions before them to receive anointment on head and hands with holy oil. The Pope, having celebrated High Mass, then placed two crowns on the altar and blessed them. Before he could take them up again, Napoleon forestalled him by marching up the steps to the altar and, picking up the larger of the two, turning round to face the congregation, holding it up towards them, before slowly, very slowly, placing it on his head, his countenance 'irradiated' by an expression which Laure d'Abrantès found it 'impossible to describe'.

> The manner of his crowning Josephine was most remarkable [Mme de Rémusat said]. After picking up her smaller crown, he first put it on his own head and then transferred it to hers ... His manner was almost playful. He took great pains to arrange this little crown, which was set over Josephine's diadem. He put it on, then took it off, and finally put it on again.

Before this, Mme de Rémusat added, he had 'looked with an air of complacency at the Empress ... who knelt down as tears, which she could not repress, fell upon her clasped hands ... Both appeared to enjoy one of those fleeting moments of shared felicity which are unique in a lifetime.'

This moving interlude was followed by an embarrassing scene when the Emperor and Empress began to climb the steps to two larger thrones erected on a dais by the cathedral's west door. As the Empress began to mount the steps, a member of the congregation watched the behaviour and demeanour of her sisters-in-law behind her: 'Nothing was more comical than the way in which they performed the duty' [of supporting the Empress's mantle]. 'One sister sulked, another held smelling salts under her nose and the third let the mantle drop.'

Consequently, Josephine almost fell over; but, even so, lost nothing of her dignity. That night, she and Napoleon had dinner together *à deux*. He asked her to wear her crown: she looked 'so pretty' with it, he told her. 'No one could wear a crown with more grace.'

His discarded mistress, Mlle George, went home 'with a heavy heart'. There were fêtes, illuminations and fireworks, yet she certainly 'had no desire to see any of them'.

25

ADOPTED AND NATURAL SONS

'I win battles; Josephine wins hearts.'

HAVING MADE HIMSELF EMPEROR, Napoleon decided to create himself King of Italy; and, in the spring of 1805, he set out for Milan, taking Josephine with him.

The Emperor was in cheerful and accommodating, even playful mood. After the ceremony of the coronation, he endeavoured to amuse Josephine by imitating some of those officials and ecclesiastics who had taken part in it, then began chasing her round the room, prodding, pinching and tickling her.

They appeared to be as much at ease with each other as they had ever been. When Napoleon left Italy for what was to prove a last inspection of the army assembled on the coast for the invasion of England, he sent for an Italian girl to sleep with him while he was away. But he wrote to Josephine with undiminished affection, sending her 'a thousand kisses everywhere', while she assured her son, Eugène – who had strongly urged her to take no notice of her husband's liaisons – that there were 'no more jealous scenes now' and that they were both much happier in consequence.

She begged Napoleon to take her with him when he returned from the Channel coast with the intention of marching against the Austrians – who were reported to be preparing to join Britain and Russia in alliance against him. The Emperor acceded to her request and, on 24 September 1805, they set out together for the episcopal palace at Strasbourg in his large travelling coach drawn by eight horses.

They parted company a week later and Napoleon was so overcome with emotion, according to Talleyrand, that he suffered an epileptic seizure – after having been sick and reduced to tears.

Marching at great speed in order to reach the Austrian army before it was joined by the Russians, the Grand Army, a force of some 350,000 men under a centralized command, succeeded in doing so. 'I have fulfilled my destiny. I have destroyed the Austrian army,' Napoleon reported to Josephine after the Austrian surrender at Ulm on 20 October: 'This is the briefest, the most successful and brilliant campaign I have ever fought . . . Adieu, my Josephine,' he added, ending his letter with a phrase he so often employed when writing to her: 'a thousand sweet kisses everywhere'.

When Josephine received this letter she was still at Strasbourg, playing the part of Empress and representing her husband as he would have wished, both as disarming imperial hostess at dinners and receptions and as the concerned and sympathetic wife of a general whose wounded men she visited in hospital. And she was still there five weeks later, when, on 2 December 1805, Napoleon again defeated the Austrians, by then joined by the Russians, at Austerlitz. This was, he told her, 'the most beautiful battle' he had ever fought. It was, also, he told Claude Méneval, Bourrienne's successor as his secretary, the happiest day of his life. It more than compensated for the destruction by Lord Nelson of the French fleet at Trafalgar on the day after the battle of Ulm, an event upon which he did not care to elaborate.

By the time Napoleon reached Vienna, Josephine had still not written to congratulate him on his great victory at Austerlitz. He wrote her an only too familiar letter of complaint in that facetious manner which was the nearest he could ever come to humour: 'Mighty Empress, I have not had a word from you . . . Deign to descend from the height of your splendour to take a little notice of your slave.'

The letter went on to inform her that he had told her son, Eugène, to marry Princess Augusta, the daughter of the Elector of Bavaria. Josephine was accordingly to make an imperial progress to Munich, the capital of Bavaria, where she would meet her prospective daughter-in-law for the wedding. He then issued precise instructions as to her route and supererogatory advice as to her behaviour at the courts of the various German rulers through whose states she was to pass. She was, of course, to be polite to all of them, but to accept their homage as respect due to the Empress of the victorious French. The Electress of Württemberg, however, was to be treated with no more than common courtesy: she was the daughter of the English King, George III. As for her enormously fat husband, Napoleon said that God had created him merely to demonstrate how far the human frame could be stretched without bursting.

Throughout the journey, Josephine behaved with exemplary grace and composure and her usual beguiling charm. 'I win battles,' Napoleon commented on being told of this, 'Josephine wins hearts.' He was less pleased, however, to find that his decision as to the future of Josephine's son was not being accepted with the enthusiasm which he had expected. After all, the Princess's father pointed out, Augusta was already engaged to be married to the Crown Prince of Baden. Besides, the Crown Prince of Baden's sister was Augusta's stepmother and had had hopes of marrying the duc d'Enghien, and the less said about that the better.

Napoleon dismissed these objections out of hand: the Crown Prince of Baden could marry a niece of the Empress Josephine; the Elector of Bavaria could become King; and Eugène could be styled Imperial Highness, appointed Viceroy of Italy and officially recognized as the Emperor Napoleon's adopted son. The eighteen-year-old Princess Augusta would make an excellent wife for him and a most suitable Vicereine at Milan – as, indeed, she proved to be.

Josephine, at first distressed by the realization that her son would have to leave France, soon comforted herself with the thought that Eugène, as the Emperor's adopted son, might be recognized as his heir. And if he were not, then her daughter's son, the little Napoleon Charles, might be. In either case, the dreaded prospect of divorce receded.

The Bonaparte family were now, more than ever, concerned that Napoleon would not abandon the idea of divorce altogether; and, in the hope of establishing the fact that he was capable of having children – a capability which they believed was by no means certain – his sister Caroline contrived to introduce him to the tall, attractive and ambitious, eighteen-year-old Eléonore Denuelle de la Plaigne, a former pupil at Mme Campan's school, where she had not distinguished herself as a scholar. She was Caroline's secretary, Caroline's husband's mistress, and, in the valet Constant's opinion, 'a great coquette'. Her own husband was conveniently in prison for forgery.

Napoleon was much taken with her, spent two hours every day with her and, on his return to Paris, took a house for her in the rue de la Victoire. She, however, was not so taken with him and, on at least one occasion, she put the clock forward so that he was led to believe it was half an hour later than it was.

In December 1806 Eléonore Denuelle gave birth to a son of whom he, at first, was persuaded to believe he was the father, although attempts were made to disabuse him of this idea by, among others, the well-informed Fouché who assured him that the child was Murat's. Nevertheless, when Eléonore asked permission to name the child Napoleon, he agreed to 'half the name'. So the boy became Charles Léon Denuelle and certainly grew to bear a marked resemblance to the Emperor.

26

LIFE AT COURT

'What I want is grandeur above all.'

ON HIS RETURN TO PARIS from the Austrian and Bavarian courts, after his decisive victory over the Austrians and their allies on 2 December 1805, Napoleon determined to impose upon his own court a formal routine and etiquette even more imposing than theirs, a ceremonious procedure befitting the victor of Austerlitz.

The size of this court was also considered by him as befitting an emperor possessing so many palaces spread across his European empire. The various departments comprised an astonishing number of people: there were, for example, 630 employed in the stables alone, grooms, coachmen, equerries and footmen who were responsible for well over a thousand horses and almost two hundred carriages. In all, by 1813, it has been calculated that the Emperor's court numbered over four thousand denizens from the Grand Marshal of the Palace – one of Napoleon's very few intimate friends, General Duroc, duc de Frioul – to stableboys and kitchen scullions. When on the move, irrespective of officials and clerks, the Emperor would always be accompanied by a numerous entourage: on a journey to Holland in 1811, he took with him, as well as Duroc, the Grand Equerry and the Grand Huntsman, four ordnance officers, two aides-de-camp, two equerries, four pages, a doctor and carriages full of lower servants.

The Empress's household was almost as large. Beneath her Grand Chamberlain and the Dame d'Honneur, there were twenty ladies-in-waiting, as well as an almoner, a lord-in-waiting, women of the bedchamber, several chamberlains and equerries, doctors, pages and flocks of maidservants.

The Emperor's sisters also had large retinues. Elisa's court was especially extravagant. The five palaces in the small principalities in northern Italy which she had been granted were required to support a host of ladies-in-waiting, equerries, aides and pages, presided over by Grand Masters of the Court and of Ceremonies, a Grand Almoner, a Grand Chamberlain, a Captain of the Bodyguard, and a Grand Equerry, Bartolommeo Cerami, Elisa's lover, whose wife, Olimpia, was one of her ladies-in-waiting.

Later, as Grand Duchess of Tuscany, she had twelve ladies-in-waiting, nine chamberlains, five equerries and nineteen pages.

Princess Pauline's household was smaller and less expensive, but even more imperiously conducted. The rules governing its organization ran to a thousand or so paragraphs, each one signed by herself. Visitors to this court were shocked to see the Princess putting her feet up on the bended form of a lady-in-waiting to use her as a footstool. Prince Eugène's wife, Princess Augusta, was astonished by what she took to be the vulgarity of all the Bonapartes. 'I could never imagine anything so abominable as their ill-breeding,' she wrote to her brother in 1810. 'It is torture to me to associate with such people.' There was one person in Princess Pauline's household to which such strictures could not fairly be ascribed. This was her pretty, soignée lady-in-waiting, Christine de Mathis, who became yet another of Napoleon's mistresses.

At Napoleon's own court there was rarely such louche behaviour as could be encountered in his sister's. And presentations there were regulated by the strictest rules. Charles James Fox's beloved friend and future wife, Mrs Elizabeth Bridget Armistead, was not allowed to dine at the Tuileries because she had not been presented at the Court of St James in London.

Precise rules governed the procedure to be adopted at the imperial court in Paris: 'When Their Majesties eat in public, the Grand Chamberlain proffers a basin for the Emperor to wash his hands; the Grand Equerry offers him his armchair; the Grand Master of the Palace takes a napkin and presents it to His Majesty. The Empress's First Prefect, the First Equerry and the First Chamberlain perform the same functions for Her Majesty. The Grand Almoner goes to the front of the table, blesses the meal and retires. During the meal the Colonel-General-in-waiting stands behind the Emperor's chair with the Grand Chamberlain on his right and the Grand Equerry on his left.'

At all times and upon all occasions, guests were required to keep a 'reasonable distance' from the Emperor; and he alone of any monarchs who happened to be present was allowed to wear a hat, often a most elaborate concoction surmounted by a spray of white plumes. In a similar way, determined never to be outdone, at the congress at Erfurt, when he met Tsar Alexander I in 1808, he insisted that he must have the largest palace because he had brought the largest suite.

Upon entering the room, ladies being presented at court were required to curtsey to the Emperor and Empress who sat on gilt chairs surrounded by members of the Emperor's family and by court officials, chamberlains, lords and ladies-in-waiting, equerries, pages, marshals and ministers. Ladies had then to make a second curtsey, having advanced a little way into the room, then to take a few more paces before curtseying a third time. They then had to withdraw, walking backwards and making three more curtseys before reaching the door. The Emperor ordered that this ceremony should be rehearsed in his presence, but became so restless with impatience that he was with difficulty dissuaded from leaving his chair before it was over.

He displayed the same exasperated impatience when being dressed in the morning, so his valet, Louis Constant, said, hitting his attendants, pushing them away, cursing their incompetence, kicking them and kicking the logs in the fireplace as he threw into the flames garments that felt uncomfortable.

He was more impatient than ever now at meal times, which, despite the prescribed etiquette, rarely lasted more than a quarter of an hour, bolting his food and helping himself, sometimes with his fingers and in any order, to the several dishes which were placed on the table in front of him, taking little interest in what was in them. Indeed, he ate so fast that frequently he suffered from indigestion or was sick, and Constant recalled occasions when he came upon the Emperor lying down on the carpet – 'which he often did when he felt ill' – Josephine seated at his side with his head in her lap. He found liquorice a comfort when suffering from indigestion and continued throughout his life to carry strips of it in his pocket, together with his snuff box and handkerchief.

Except at meal times and at night, Josephine now saw little of her husband. He spent most of the morning dictating to Méneval, or to another secretary, dealing for hours on end with all manner of business from affairs of state, military and civil concerns, to relatively trivial household matters. Nothing was too mundane for him to consider, from the details of the kitchen accounts at the Tuileries, Malmaison and St Cloud to the decoration and furnishing of these imperial residences which, 'too bare and too simple' in the Emperor's opinion, were now transformed into magnificence by the architects and interior decorators, Pierre-François-Léonard Fontaine and Charles Percier, who were mainly responsible for creating the Empire style, and by the cabinet makers, the Jacob Frères. 'What I want,' the Emperor declared, 'is grandeur above all. Whatever is grand is always beautiful.'

While these palaces were being transformed so were parts of Paris itself. The Arc de Triomphe, commemorating the military triumphs of the Revolutionary and Napoleonic troops, was taking shape at the junction of the avenue de la Grande Armée and the avenue des Champs-Élysées. In the Place Vendôme there arose a tall column made of the melted-down bronze from one thousand, two hundred captured cannon which was surmounted by a statue of the Emperor. The four bronze horses from the façade of San Marco were displayed on columns in the Tuileries Gardens. The arcades of the rue de Rivoli were being raised on the foundations of the old riding school.

From time to time, Napoleon would drive out to watch the progress of these various works. But he did not linger in contemplation of them. There was so much work to do – so much, in fact, that even more frequently than in the past, he would call for Méneval in the middle of the night so that he could dictate to him through the steam of a very hot bath.

He found it difficult to relax. In the evenings, after sipping the sugared coffee which Josephine handed to him, having first taken a sip herself to ensure that it was to his taste, he might play a game of chess or billiards, cheating quite openly when playing with Josephine who usually beat him easily nonetheless. Sometimes, before going to bed he would, as in the past, ask Josephine to read to him, but never for very long.

She never read for her own pleasure or instruction, according to Mme de Rémusat; but she spent many hours at her writing table, dealing with a voluminous correspondence with her children, friends, those for whom she tirelessly endeavoured to obtain pensions and posts, with nurserymen about plants for her garden at Malmaison, and with dealers in exotic animals and birds for her miniature zoo and aviaries.

She was still wildly extravagant, distributing large sums to charities, supporting numerous poor relations and former servants, never asking the price of anything, constantly adding to her enormous collection of jewels and precious stones, buying furniture, commissioning portraits, spending a fortune on clothes. It was calculated that she had bought no fewer than nine hundred dresses in a single year as Empress, not to mention the eight hundred francs she spent on scent.

She was always dressed with the greatest care. Every day, after her dogs and her maids had entered her room, after she had had her morning bath, after her face had been made up and her hairdresser had treated and arranged her hair, her ladies carried in baskets of clothes and boxes of hats and shoes, so that she could choose what to wear that day, being careful to please her husband who took much interest in what she wore and once threw a bottle of ink over a dress which he disliked so that she could not wear it again. Far from now insisting that she should be modest in her dress, he liked her to be heavily made up and extremely décolleté and, if he considered her over-modest, he would snatch off the offending shawl and throw it away.

He never complained that she spent too much with her dressmaker. Indeed, he expected her ladies to be extravagant also, considering that a display of prodigality at court was a manifestation of power. He required all the Empress's ladies to wear a dress at court but once. Some of the Empress's own dresses could, indeed, not be worn twice, one being entirely covered with thousands of fresh rose petals. One day he said to the duchesse d'Abrantès, 'Madame, you have worn that dress several times. It is a pretty dress, but we have seen it before.' On another occasion, he upbraided her for having worn a black dress at his coronation: 'Was it in mourning? Tell me, why did you choose that sombre, I might almost say sinister, colour?'

'Your Majesty did not observe that the front of my dress was richly embroidered with gold, and that I wore diamonds. Many others were wearing dark dresses. I am not a court lady, and therefore not obliged to wear court dress.'

'Is that remark intended to convey an indirect reproach? Are you like certain other women who sulk because they have not been appointed *dames du palais*? I don't like sulkiness and ill-humour.'

When Josephine appeared one day in a white muslin dress which Napoleon found particularly pleasing, he made a show of his approval. 'The Emperor was clearly struck by this charming dress,' Laure d'Abrantès observed. 'He went up to her, kissed her on the shoulder and on her forehead and led her to a looking-glass so that he could see her from all sides at the same time. "I think I should be jealous, Josephine," he said. "You must have some conquest in mind. Why are you so beautiful today?" "I know that you like to see me in white. So I put on a white gown, that's all." "Very well then," he replied. "If it was to please me, you have succeeded." He then kissed her again.'

Josephine endeavoured not to be jealous of his attentions to other women, although there were occasions when she was still unable to contain her anger, even though these rare outbursts inevitably roused Napoleon to fury and brutal response. She knew very well when Napoleon was beginning or ending an affair. Indeed, he went so far as to seek her help in getting rid of women of whom he had tired, and took little or no care to ensure that she was kept in ignorance of affairs he was still conducting. His valet, Constant, would have orders to let no one into the room next to his master's office when the Emperor was there with an actress or with one of the court ladies who had caught his fancy. But, in conversation with officials of the household and with Josephine herself, he made no secret as to who had been there with him.

According to Mlle Avrillon, who looked after the Empress's jewels, he commented quite openly on the physique, sensuality and experience of these temporary mistresses; and, so Claire de Rémusat said, he readily gave accounts of his love-making with 'the most indecent frankness'. Mme de Rémusat added that his emotions were never involved in these affairs: such affection as he was capable of feeling, he felt for his wife.

Constant described how, between seven and eight o'clock in the morning he would go into the bedroom the Emperor and Empress shared to take their orders for tea or an infusion of orange flowers. He rarely found them asleep; and, when the Emperor got up, the Empress would say, 'Oh, must you get up already? Do stay a bit longer.' The

Emperor would reply, 'Oh, you're not still asleep then', and he would 'roll her up in a blanket, give her little taps on her cheek and shoulders, laughing and kissing her'.

It was supposed at court, so Claire de Rémusat said, that the Emperor was so much enjoying life there that when the King of Prussia entered into a treaty with the Tsar and mobilized his army, Napoleon marched for the Rhineland to attack the Prussians before the Russians joined them, with the greatest reluctance to return to camp life. He left in the early hours of 24 September 1806; and when the Empress heard that he was on the point of leaving, she rushed downstairs and jumped into his campaign coach to go with him.

At Mainz they parted company, he to lead his army against the Prussians, she to remain in Mainz in apartments at the archbishop's palace. Mme de Rémusat, a witness to their parting, described it as a highly emotional scene: 'The Emperor held his wife in his arms as though reluctant to release her ... Eventually he did so in tears, then gave way to a nervous spasm and convulsions which induced severe vomiting.'

Josephine too was deeply distressed after his departure, often in tears as she examined the tarot cards spread out on the table in front of her, studying them, so it was supposed, to divine what they might be able to tell her about the possibility even now of her bearing a child. This, she knew, was never far from his mind, just as it was never far from her own. Whenever they quarrelled, it became a subject of contention. She would draw his attention to her two Beauharnais children; and he would say they were born a long time ago. Once he was heard to repeat what he had been told by her doctor: 'But your menses have stopped.' She herself was now persuaded that she could not have another child: perhaps the abortions she had had in the past and the crude measures she had taken to avoid conception had made it impossible.

A fortnight after leaving Josephine at Mainz, Napoleon sent her news of the defeat of the Prussian army at Jena and Auerstädt on 14 October 1806. His letters to Josephine thereafter were exceptionally affectionate: he assured her of his devotion, his continuing desire for her; he told her that, while everything in this world must come to an end, his happiness in having found his good, sweet Josephine would not; when she made some comment about his rough treatment of the Prussian Queen Louise, he replied, 'I detest scheming women. I am accustomed to ones who are gentle, sweet-natured and captivating. It is your fault: you have spoiled me for the others.'

When he heard that she was reported to be unhappy in Mainz, that she was 'always in tears', he comforted her by suggesting that she might join him in Poland 'as soon as a place had been fixed for quarters'. But the days passed and he did not send for her. She began to imagine that he had found another mistress. She told him that she had dreamed that he had done so. He replied that 'in these frozen Polish wastes one is not likely to think of beautiful women', that there was only one woman for him. 'Do you know her?' he asked archly. 'I could paint her portrait for you but it would make you conceited ... The winter nights are long, all alone.'

She wrote again, expressing her concern about the attractiveness of Polish women. 'Your letter made me laugh,' he replied. 'You overestimate the fascination of Polish ladies.'

Three days later, he was no longer prevaricating about her coming from Mainz to join him but suggesting that she should return to Paris where her presence was needed; and on 7 January 1807, he wrote to say that the roads were very rough and unsafe: he could not expose her to such dangers; it was his wish that she should go home. The next day he wrote to say that he would have liked to share the long winter nights with her, but Paris claimed her.

'Believe me,' he wrote in subsequent letters from Warsaw, 'it is harder for me than for you to delay the happiness of our meeting ... I am sometimes bored with these long nights ... Go back to Paris now, it is my wish ... One must submit to circumstances ... I have a lot to deal with here ... You should return to Paris, where you are needed ... I am keeping well ... The weather is bad ... Be worthy of me. Show more strength of character, I don't like cowards ... The trouble is,' he added with extraordinary incongruity, 'you have no religion.'

At last she obeyed him. She went back to Paris with a heavy heart, becoming by now convinced that the Polish lady of whom she had dreamed was a reality.

27

MARIE WALEWSKA

'He treats me like a prostitute.'

ON NEW YEAR'S EVE 1806, Napoleon's coach, which was taking him to Warsaw, had drawn up at Bronie, the last relay post before the city. It was snowing hard, but a large crowd of Poles soon gathered around the carriage to welcome him. Among them was an exceptionally good-looking fair-haired young woman in a fur hat, whom he took to be a peasant girl until she spoke in good French to General Duroc and asked to be presented to the man who had promised to liberate Poland from her foreign masters and had defeated Austria, Prussia and Russia, her country's oppressors.

Napoleon offered her one of the bunches of flowers which had been thrown into the carriage when he opened the window. She took the flowers from him and, as the coach drove away, withdrew into the crowd from which she had suddenly appeared.

Intrigued by her, Napoleon asked Duroc to find out who she was. This did not prove difficult. She was soon identified as the eighteen-year-old third wife of an elderly and rich Polish nationalist, Count Anaste Colonna de Walewice Walewski, and the mother of his child. She had been brought up and educated under the supervision of a French tutor, Nicolas Chopin (father of Frédéric, the future pianist and composer). She was said to be kind, intelligent, demure and as firm a patriot as her husband.

As with Pauline Fourès in Egypt, Napoleon arranged for this enticing young countess to be invited to a party at which Napoleon was to be the guest of honour. She declined the invitation, upon which he said that he would not attend the function either. Count Walewski was approached: the countess must be persuaded to change her mind; much might depend upon it; the interests of Poland were at stake; it would be of inestimable value to have a Polish patriot in the French camp; Poland needed France to obtain her freedom from her Prussian and Russian enemies.

Count Walewski was naturally reluctant to give up the wife he had married when she was only sixteen to this French adventurer. But he was urged by the heroic general, Prince Joseph Poniatowsky, and others to believe that, as a patriot, it was his duty to do so. When, therefore, a delegation of other nationalists came to his house and assembled outside Marie's bedroom door, her husband admitted them and allowed them to harangue her in their endeavours to persuade her that her duty to Poland demanded this sacrifice.

Countess Walewska gave way: she attended the ball, but she made no attempt to attract the guest of honour who was observed kissing her hand and dancing extremely badly as usual. She wore a dowdy white dress with an excessively modest bodice upon which Napoleon, who always prided himself on being 'a connoisseur of costume', commented with rude disapproval, 'White on white is no way to dress, Madame.' She did not answer him and declined invitations to dance, whereupon two French officers paid her marked and flirtatious attention and were consequently sent abroad, as Lieutenant Fourès had been from Egypt.

In the days following the ball, the Emperor was relentlessly persistent in pursuing his quarry. He wrote letter after letter, determined to break down her reserve and resistance: 'I saw only you at the ball. I desired only you, I admired only you,' ran one of these letters delivered to her with a huge bunch of flowers by Géraud Duroc. 'I want to force you to love me ... Yes, force you. I have revived your country's name. I shall do much for you.' He implied that her submission was the price to be paid for her country's peaceful future. 'Come to me. All your hopes will be fulfilled. Your country will be dearer to me when you take pity on my poor heart ... Whenever I have thought a thing impossible to obtain, I have wanted it all the more. Nothing discourages me ... I am accustomed to having my wishes met ... I have brought back to life your country's name. I will do much more ... Send an immediate answer to calm the impatient passion of N.' She sent no answer. She refused invitations to dinner with the Emperor; she threw a jewel box which he sent her, without opening it, to the floor with the comment, 'He treats me like a prostitute.'

> The Emperor was in a state of unusual agitation [commented his valet, Constant] ... He could not remain still for a moment ... He got up, walked about, sat down, got up again ... He did not say a word to me, though he usually talked in an easy way while dressing ... He still had had no answer to his letters and could not understand it. He considered himself irresistible to women.

At last, under the combined pressure of the Emperor, the Polish nationalists and eventually of Talleyrand, she gave way and went to him one night to offer herself to him. But, when once in his presence, his arms round her, his lips on hers, she suddenly resisted him, frightened by his impatient ardour. According to her own account, he then lost his temper. He threatened the destruction of her country and, as though in demonstration of his intention, he hurled his watch at her feet and stamped it to pieces beneath his heel. She then fainted and when she came to and found that Napoleon had 'abused her', she burst into tears.

Napoleon himself later told General Gourgaud that she did not struggle too much and that, when he had made love to her, he wiped the tears from her eyes and promised to do all that he could for her country. Nights now passed in her submissive company. He showed that he could be patient and caressing as well as crude, impatient and selfish. She fell in love with him and, in time, became as enthusiastic a mistress as he had ever had.

To Josephine, who was pressing him to be allowed to join him in Poland, he made excuses for dissuading her:

> *Mon amie*, I am touched by all that you tell me; but this is no time of year to travel. It is cold and the roads are bad and unsafe, so I cannot allow you to undertake so many trials and dangers. Go back to Paris [from Mainz] and spend the rest of the winter there ... This is my wish. Believe me, it is more painful for me than for you, to have to postpone for several weeks my happiness in seeing you.

While Josephine was denied permission to join him, he saw Marie Walewska as often as it could be arranged. The contrast between the two women could scarcely have been greater: Josephine was wildly extravagant, Marie was carefully sparing, declining to accept Napoleon's extravagant presents. Josephine was headstrong, Marie cautious, Josephine flirtatious, Marie reserved and, as a model pupil of Nicolas Chopin, as intellectually inclined as the Empress was certainly not.

After the indecisive and appallingly bloody battle of Eylau fought on 8 February 1807 between France and the combined Russo-Prussian army – a 'memorable' victory as it was described in a letter to Josephine – Marie Walewska moved into the Schloss Finkenstein where Napoleon had established his headquarters. She appeared to be more deeply in love with him than ever; and the Emperor was entranced by her, as it was plain to see: she did not play cards but, as Anna Potocka noticed, when he was playing 'he always wanted her in the room within his sight'. He kept her at the Schloss for five weeks from 1 April, while assuring Josephine – to whom he addressed five letters in less than a week after the dreadful slaughter at Eylau – that the rumours of his involvement with the Countess which reached France were quite without foundation.

'I don't know what you mean by ladies I am supposed to be involved with. I love only my dear little Josephine who is so good, though sulky and capricious . . . and lovable except when she is jealous and becomes a little devil . . . As for these ladies, if I needed to occupy my time with one of them I assure you I would want her to have pretty rosebud nipples. Is this so with the ladies you write to me about?'

28

PRELIMINARIES OF DIVORCE

'Why the devil can't the man
make up his mind?'

IN MAY 1807, Napoleon received the news that Napoleon-Charles, the four-year-old son of his stepdaughter, Hortense, had died at the Hague. Hortense was heartbroken; and Napoleon – although he had been very fond of the child, had evidently enjoyed going down on all fours to play with him, making faces for his amusement, and had considered establishing him as his heir – grew impatient with what he took to be Hortense's excessive grief. He was also impatient with Josephine, who, saddened by her daughter's loss, was also distressed by the spectre of divorce once more rising up to haunt her. 'I wish you'd be reasonable,' he wrote to her. 'Do you want to make me sadder than ever? Grief has its limits. Do be more reasonable in yours . . . Try to be calm . . . Don't add to my sorrow.' 'I have myself,' he was reputed to have added, 'no time to feel regret like other men.'

There was always so much else to occupy his mind. In the space of a few weeks before and after the death of Hortense's child, he had, for instance, to upbraid his brother Louis for being like a 'docile, timorous monk' as Napoleon's nominee as King of Holland; give detailed instructions to the Minister of the Interior about the enlargement and organization of the Collège de France and the establishment of new chairs there; occupy himself with the details of the curriculum and out-of-school activities of a recently established school for young ladies; be in communication with the Minister of Police about that 'foolish woman' Mme de Staël, who was making trouble for him in England and on the continent; with his brother Joseph, King of Naples, about his plan to have the whole of Europe using one single currency; and with his other brother, Jérôme, about the best treatment for piles.

Even in his carriage, Napoleon kept busily at work:

> The Emperor always sat in the back on the right with Duroc on his left [according to a Polish officer in his escort]. The whole of the front seat was piled high with reports and documents. As they bowled along at great speed, Duroc opened the sealed envelopes and threw them out of the window, handing over the contents to the Emperor, who often just glanced at a paper, shrugged his shoulders and promptly discarded it also. They drove along in a positive blizzard of paper flying out from both sides of the carriage.

Having so much to do, Napoleon was exasperated by Hortense's prolonged grief. 'She doesn't deserve our love,' he told Josephine in a later unfeeling letter. 'She loved only her child . . . I am very displeased with her.' And to Hortense herself he wrote: 'I wish you were braver . . . Your mother and I had hoped to occupy a greater place in your heart.'

He had, he added, won a great victory over a combined Russian and Prussian force on 14 June 1807 near Friedland in East Prussia (now Pravdinsk in Russia) where, for the loss of some 8,000 casualties, he had inflicted 20,000 on the enemy and taken 80 guns.

He was annoyed that Hortense had not written 'a single line' to him on this triumph. Nor, for that matter, had Josephine, to whom he wrote: 'I have received your letter of June 25 and I am hurt to see that you are completely egotistical and appear to be quite uninterested in my military success . . . I, too, am eager for our reunion, but that must depend on the will of destiny.'

When he wrote this letter, he was on his way to Tilsit where, on 7 July, in a pavilion erected on a raft in the middle of the river Niemen, he was to confer with the King of Prussia, Frederick William III, and with the Tsar Alexander whom he found so agreeable and so physically attractive that, as he later told Josephine, had Alexander been a woman, he would have made him his mistress. Their affection for each other was undisguised: onlookers were astonished by the unaffected manner in which they hugged each other, by their holding hands as they walked upstairs, by the Tsar's suddenly standing up and kissing the Emperor fondly when an actor in a play had declared, 'The friendship of a great man is a blessing of the gods.'

At Tilsit (now Sovetsk) it was agreed that both Russia and Prussia should join the Continental Blockade intended to ruin Britain's commerce, and that the free Polish state, which Napoleon had undertaken to create, should not be established. Prussia, harshly and with open contempt, was obliged to give up territories for the creation of both the Grand Duchy of Warsaw for Napoleon's ally, the King of Saxony, and the Kingdom of Westphalia for his brother, Jérôme. In addition, Prussia was required to pay an enormous war indemnity.

The King of Prussia's queen, the much-loved Louise, daughter of Prince Charles of Mecklenburg-Strelitz, was so distressed by the harsh terms imposed upon her country that she knelt before Napoleon begging for concessions. But he, annoyed by her popularity in Prussia, distrustful of her friendship with the Tsar, and irritated by a woman's interfering in matters of such importance, merely and insultingly asked her of what material her dress was made. 'The Queen of Prussia is really charming,' he reported to Josephine. 'She is very flirtatious with me. But there's no need to be jealous. It's like water off a duck's back with me. I can't be bothered to play the gallant with her.'

Napoleon returned home from Tilsit having established France's hegemony in western and central Europe. He was by now 'intoxicated by himself', in Talleyrand's phrase. He gave orders for the rebuilding of parts of Paris, including the construction of a new bridge, the Pont d'Iéna, named after his defeat of the Prussians the year before; he gave orders for the censorship of books and plays as well as newspapers; and he showed himself to be determined to make his own court more formal than even the most stately of the royal and ducal courts which he had seen during the months he had been away, despite the scornful amusement of the aristocrats of the Faubourg St Germain. The leading ministers and generals had already been given, or were now to be given, grandiose titles rivalling those of the *ancien régime*: Charles-Maurice de Talleyrand, for example, became his Serene Highness, prince de Bénévent and Vice Grand Elector; Joseph Fouché, duc d'Otranto; Andoche Junot, a farmer's son, was already duc d'Abrantès; Joachim Murat, duc de Berg et Clèves; Masséna, a poor wine merchant's son who had been a cabin boy, duc de Rivoli; Jean Lannes, the son of a livery stables keeper, duc de Montebello; Ney, the ill-educated son of a cooper, duc d'Elchingen; Augereau, the son of a footman, duc de Castiglione; and Lefebrve, a former sergeant in the Gardes, whose wife had been a *blanchisseuse* attached to her husband's regiment, became duc de Danzig: when a footman addressed the *duchesse* by her title at the Tuileries she winked at him and said, 'What about that, *mon vieux*?'

Having acquired great riches, these men and their like were also required to purchase grand houses and live in awesome splendour. The Emperor himself lived in even more magnificent state, indulging what Méneval called 'a penchant for the old noblesse', with whose members he surrounded himself, and occupying himself for hours on end with the details of protocol, etiquette and ceremonial.

As Stendhal said, he had 'the weakness of all parvenus, that of having too great an opinion of the class into which he had risen'. Murat had made the same point earlier in a letter to Napoleon:

> When France raised you to the throne it was because she expected you would be a people's leader, a plebeian given a title which placed you above and apart from every other European sovereign, not because she wanted to recreate Louis XIV's monarchy with all the old court's pretensions. Yet you surround yourself with members of the old nobility and fill your drawing rooms with them so that they have grounds for believing that they've recovered all their former privileges. The old nobility regards all your soldier comrades, and perhaps you also, as mere parvenus ... By allying yourself with the Bavarian royal house through the marriage of Eugène, you're showing all Europe how much you value what each one of us lacks – blue blood! You pay homage to great titles which weren't created by you, which make nonsense of ours, and you're showing France all too plainly that you simply want to carry on the old regime, although you're reigning just because France doesn't want an *ancien régime* dynasty. Well, I can tell you that your dynasty is always going to look parvenu to other monarchs.

To this homily, Napoleon merely observed, 'So this marriage of Eugène's doesn't please you. Well, it pleases me and I consider it a great success.'

At Fontainebleau, the splendid château built for François I, which had been redecorated and refurnished under the supervision of Percier and Fontaine while Napoleon had been away, there was to be a ball every night. At these balls the Empress, having dined alone with the Emperor, would appear, gracious and charming, and take her seat as the company fell into silence, awaiting the appearance of the Emperor who would arrive simply dressed in marked contrast to the splendour of the others. Everyone stood up upon his entrance and, so Mme de Rémusat said, they appeared to be apprehensive if his expression was forbidding, as, indeed, it often was.

Since returning from Tilsit, he had become increasingly arrogant and impatient, flying into rages, real and assumed, exhausting the members of the Council of State with seemingly endless speeches, chiding various ladies about the court for wearing unsuitable clothes, telling one of them to go and rouge her face since she 'looked like a corpse', complaining to others that their hairstyles were absurd or ugly, speaking roughly to Hortense, who was still mourning: 'Do stop this absurd childishness. You have wept enough now over the death of your son. It's becoming ridiculous ... Enjoy yourself ... Don't let me see any more of these tears.'

Napoleon's attitude to women is reflected in the Code Napoléon, the reformed legal system of France, which gave legal expression to his belief that 'women these days require restraint. They go where they like, do what they like. It is not French to give women the upper hand. They have too much of it already.'

Towards his own wife, so Metternich thought, Napoleon behaved 'in a cold and often embarrassed manner'. He was certainly more than ever convinced that he would have to divorce her so that he could have a son by a new wife for the sake of the dynasty.

One day at Fontainebleau, Fouché broached the subject with Josephine. She asked him if the Emperor had instructed him to do so; and when Fouché told her that he had not, she said that she would never discuss the matter with anyone else. She later asked Napoleon if he had told Fouché to talk to her. He said he hadn't, and added, 'You know very well that I couldn't live without you.'

It was obvious, so Claire de Rémusat said, that he felt a real affection for Josephine and was uncomfortable when he upset her. This did not, however, prevent him from still taking various other mistresses, at least two of whom came to his room at this time; nor did he refrain from telling Josephine of these new liaisons and of the attributes and imperfections of the young women involved. In her memoirs, Laure Junot, the duchesse d'Abrantès, provided several instances of Napoleon's offhand treatment of women, his rudeness towards them, his misogyny. His old friend Bourrienne also wrote of his unpleasant and sometimes shocking manner with women, particularly with fat women and tall women whom he particularly disliked, just as he disliked tall men such as the British Ambassador, Lord Whitworth, in whose company he had been seen to stand on tiptoe to lessen the difference in height between them.

'He seldom said anything agreeable to women,' Bourrienne said, 'and frequently made the rudest and most extraordinary remarks. To one he would say, "Good heavens, how red your arms are", or to another, "What an ugly hat!" Or he might say "Your dress is rather dirty. Don't you ever change your clothes? I've seen you in that at least a dozen times."' He once observed to Germaine de Staël, who was in the habit of wearing extremely low-cut dresses, revealing an ample proportion of her imposing bosom: 'You evidently nursed all your children yourself, Madame.' For once, she was lost for words. This was not, however, the case with Aimée de Coigny to whom Napoleon addressed the rude question, 'Do you still fancy men as much as ever, Madame?' 'Yes,' she replied, quite unabashed, 'when they are polite.'

Soon after her marriage, when Laure Junot was seventeen years old and staying at Malmaison, while her husband was in Paris as commandant of the city and Josephine was taking the waters at Plombières, Napoleon burst into her bedroom before five o'clock in the morning, woke her up, drew up a chair by her bed and began to open a bundle of letters he had brought with him. After reading the last of them, he burst into laughter, told her it was from a beautiful woman who had loved him for years and wished to arrange a meeting, then, pinching her foot beneath the bedclothes, he left the room as abruptly as he had entered it, singing tunelessly.

The next morning, Napoleon came into her room at the same time, read his letters by her bed, tweaked her foot once more as he left, singing as before. When he had gone, Laure told her maid not to open the outer door to anyone so early in the morning. But Napoleon had a master key and, using that, he stormed towards her bed, asking furiously,

'Are you afraid of being assassinated then? You are not among a horde of tartars.' He then turned on his heel and left.

That day, Junot returned from Paris and was persuaded by Laure to stay the night at Malmaison, so that when Napoleon burst into the room as early as usual, he found them in bed together. Napoleon suppressed his anger but later, as they all set off for a hunting party, it was clear that he was furious. He made Laure sit next to him in his phaeton and upbraided her for persuading her husband to stay the night with her, neglecting his duties in Paris. They quarrelled bitterly; Napoleon repeatedly struck the side of the phaeton with his fist. 'You may dispose of my room,' Laure said at length. 'I shall never occupy it again.'

'As you will. You are right to go. You and I cannot meet with any pleasure for the time being.' He jumped down from the carriage, called for his horse, and, without another word, rode off.

'Why the devil can't the man make up his mind?' exclaimed Talleyrand, exasperated by Napoleon's indecision about a divorce. One minute, he seemed to have come to a firm decision to remarry; the next, he told Talleyrand that he could not bring himself to leave Josephine who understood him so well, who was so pleasant a presence in his private life. It would be showing the basest ingratitude after all she had done for him.

She herself was determined to be patient. She told Eugène that there were to be 'no more scenes, no jealousy'. When Napoleon left for Milan in November 1807, she did not ask to go with him, resisting the opportunity of seeing Eugène. She told her son that she would henceforth do all that was required of her and lead a blameless life. 'I have no pleasures,' she said. 'People are amazed that I can endure such an existence ... I can't go out any more.' She was often in tears, and whenever she had indigestion, so her husband told Lucien, 'she suspected that she was being poisoned by the people who wanted her husband to remarry'.

Napoleon went to see a possible bride, Eugène's sister-in-law, Princess Charlotte of Bavaria; but he returned, having struck her off his list as unsuitable; and soon afterwards, while guests were awaiting his appearance at a reception at the Tuileries, he called for Josephine, complaining that he was ill. She found him lying on his bed, fully dressed, in pain and in tears. He asked her to get into bed with him, telling her that he could never bear to leave her. There followed a night of love, so she told Mme de Rémusat, with intervals of restless sleep.

Later that year, Napoleon sent French troops into Spain, planning to depose the King and place a Bonaparte on the throne in his place. He summoned the Spanish King and Queen, the Crown Prince and Godoy, the Prime Minister, to Bayonne, telling Josephine to join him there, to help entertain them in what, to all intents and purposes, was to be confinement. As usual, she was the perfect hostess, attentive, agreeable, accommodating; and, when an uprising in Madrid against the French occupying forces had given Napoleon the opportunity to bring about the Spanish King's abdication and the exile of his family to France, he and Josephine celebrated with a display of high spirits as though they were on a seaside holiday. Running barefoot along the beach, Napoleon pushed her over on to the sand and threw her shoes into the sea.

After their return to Paris, there was another display of *enjouement* described by Louis Constant: 'The Emperor and Empress and some of their friends played a game of prisoner's base ... It was at night. Two footmen carried torches ... The Emperor fell once as he ran after the Empress, and when he had had enough of the game, he went away with her in spite of the protests of the others. This was the last time I saw the Emperor play.'

'For the last six months,' Josephine wrote to her son, 'the Emperor has shown his attachment to me by so much concern [when she was suffering from intermittent excruciating headaches], sometimes getting up as often as four times a night to come and see how I was feeling ... He has been simply perfect to me ... When I saw him off this morning it was with sadness at the parting, but with no disquiet about our relationship.'

She had need to feel concern, though. After the French army's defeat at Bailen in Spain on 19 July 1808, Napoleon had decided that he must go to the Peninsula himself to avenge this humiliation, but first he must meet the Tsar to ensure that, should Austria march against him he could rely upon having an ally in his rear whilst engaged so far to the west. The Tsar agreed to meet him in October at Erfurt where Napoleon hoped not only to satisfy himself about Russia's military cooperation but also to broach the possibility of his marrying one of the Tsar's sisters.

Having failed to arrange this Russian marriage, because of the Tsar's reluctance to sacrifice his sister to the French Emperor, Napoleon returned to France where he found the people increasingly restless, resentful of the demands made upon young men to fill the ranks of his army, and highly critical of the behaviour and extravagance of his family. Aware of the unrest in the country, Napoleon once again backed away from the idea of a divorce, telling Fouché that the time was not opportune to 'shock public opinion by repudiating the popular Empress'. 'I am not loved,' he acknowledged. 'She is a link between me and the people. And she reconciles a part of Parisian society to me which would abandon me if I abandoned her.'

Fearful of losing him even so, Josephine clung to him with an almost wild intensity. She had begged him to allow her to accompany him to Spain. 'Will you never stop making war?' she had asked him after he had refused to take her with him.

'It is not I who direct the course of events,' he said with a characteristic reference to his 'star', 'I only obey them.'

When, in April 1809, the Austrians invaded France's ally, Bavaria, and he hurriedly left for Strasbourg, she did not allow him the opportunity of forbidding her to go with him. 'On hearing the sounds of departure,' Louis Constant wrote, 'she jumped out of bed and, without stockings or bedroom slippers, ran down the stairs into the courtyard ... Crying like a child, she threw herself into the carriage.' Napoleon spread the sable-lined coat, which the Tsar had given him, over her and 'gave orders for her luggage to be sent after her'.

While Napoleon rushed off to lead his army against the Austrians, Josephine remained behind in Strasbourg at the Rohan Palace where Hortense joined her with her two surviving sons.

The scanty messages that reached the Rohan Palace from the army were not encouraging. After a savage and indecisive battle at Aspern-Essling, where Napoleon lost over twenty thousand men, he lost a further twenty-three thousand soldiers killed and wounded at Wagram, eleven miles north-east of Vienna, on 5 and 6 July. Then, following hard upon this butchery, came reports that Countess Walewska had arrived in Vienna to join Napoleon at the Schönbrunn Palace.

Feeling by now, as she told a friend, that she was 'really married to him', she had written to ask him if she might come to be with him there. 'Marie, I have read your letter with the pleasure your memory always inspires in me,' he had replied without marked enthusiasm. 'Yes, do come to Vienna. I would like to give you further proof of the tender regard I have for you.'

Upon receipt of this letter, Marie had set out for Vienna immediately; and there, every day after his long day's work, Napoleon found time to be with her. But his passion for her had begun to cool; and, having gone into the city from the Palace for a few days in August to consult the physician, Professor Lanefranque, about what he considered to be his failing health, he encountered a pretty Viennese girl, Eva Kraus, nineteen years old, with whom he had a brief affair. It was rumoured that she bore him a son. Certainly at this time Marie Walewska became pregnant, and there could be no doubt on this occasion – as there had been doubt in the case of Eléonore Denuelle – who the father was.

Napoleon was clearly delighted and Marie was equally happy. 'I belong to him now,' she told Constant, so the valet said. 'My thoughts, my inspiration all come from him and return to him . . . always.'

He gave the impression that he was as much taken with her as ever, going with her for rides in the park when he could spare the time from his work and for drives along the banks of the Danube in an unmarked carriage.

29

SISTERS AND SISTERS-IN-LAW

'My family did much more harm to me
than the good I did for them.'

NAPOLEON'S POTENCY now confirmed beyond doubt, there was no reason to hesitate any longer about the divorce. As he put it to his brother Lucien, he must lose no time in allying himself with sovereigns; and he was more than ever ready to deprecate his brothers' and sisters' propensity for choosing to marry for love.

As it had been with his sister Caroline, who had married an inn-keeper's son, and with his brother Lucien, whose wife was an innkeeper's illiterate sister, so it was with his brother Jérôme, who, having abandoned the ship in which he was serving as a lieutenant, made his way to the United States and there, on 24 December 1803, at the age of nineteen, had contracted a marriage which had annoyed Napoleon quite as much as Caroline's to Joachim Murat and Lucien's to Catherine Boyer.

Elizabeth Patterson, Jérôme's American wife, was neither poor nor socially undesirable. Extremely good-looking and with a pleasing personality, she was the daughter of a well-to-do merchant and ship-owner of Irish descent from Baltimore, of which city her brother was mayor. But Elizabeth Patterson was far from being the kind of wife, a member of a European patrician family or, preferably, of a European reigning dynasty, whom Napoleon would have preferred and considered he now had a right to expect his brother to choose.

The Bonapartes were quite prepared to welcome the attractive young American into their family. Lucien assured Mr Patterson – a man as ambitious for her future as she was herself – that 'the entire family, fully and unanimously approved of Jérôme's marriage': they were all 'highly pleased and proud of the union'; Napoleon's was the 'only dissenting voice'.

Napoleon did not merely dissent: he ordered his brother to return home immediately in a frigate which was being sent to New York for that purpose. He was not to bring his wife with him. She would not be permitted to set foot in France. If he came back alone his error would be overlooked. In the meantime, the *Moniteur* was instructed to inform its readers that no marriage had been contracted, although it was conceded that Jérôme Bonaparte might have taken a mistress.

Jérôme took no notice of his brother's orders and, towards the end of October 1804, he set sail for France accompanied by his wife and taking all their wedding presents and a great deal of other luggage with them. All these were lost when their ship was sunk; and they were lucky to escape with their lives. They set off again, but on this occasion their brig was intercepted by a ship of the Royal Navy and they were obliged to return to Baltimore.

Meanwhile, Napoleon had issued decrees instructing the civil officers of the Empire not to take notice of the so-called marriage nor to take any part in a future ceremony which might, illegally, take place in France.

Jérôme and his wife, by then pregnant, returned to Europe, in a fast clipper hired by her father, in the spring of 1805. Refused entry into Lisbon, Elizabeth went on to Amsterdam, while Jérôme set out for Milan to confront his brother.

Jérôme found Napoleon angry and obdurate; and was peremptorily told that unless he agreed to abandon Miss Patterson he would receive no help in settling his immense debts; he would, moreover, forfeit the rank and titles which had been bestowed upon him in the past; he would be banished from France; and any child he might have fathered or would father in the future would be excluded from the succession to the imperial throne.

Faced by this ultimatum, Jérôme, who had recently told his wife to have faith in him – he would 'never desert' her: the worst that could happen to them would be to have to live in a foreign country – now gave way to Napoleon on the assurance that he would be presented with a kingdom somewhere in his brother's Empire and have no cause for further concern about money. He accordingly agreed to abandon

'Miss Patterson' who was told that she must never assume the name of Bonaparte, an injunction which she ignored.

Denied entry at Amsterdam, as she had been at Lisbon, she sailed for England where her son, Jérôme-Napoleon Bonaparte, was born. She then returned to Baltimore with this child who grew up there to bear a marked resemblance to his uncle, the Emperor.

Having failed to persuade the Pope to have Jérôme's marriage declared invalid, the Emperor found a lesser cleric prepared to do so. Jérôme, enriched and ennobled, was then found another wife in the more acceptable person of the stout, amiable and, by her philandering husband, ill-used Princess Catherine Sophia Dorothea, daughter of the King of Württemberg. Soon afterwards, Jérôme was himself named King of Westphalia.

As it was with Jérôme, so it was with Lucien who, having angered his brother by marrying the illiterate, shy and kindly Catherine Boyer, gave further offence by marrying another unsuitable woman after his first wife's death. This second wife, Alexandrine Jouberthon, *née* de Bleschamps, the daughter of a minor tax official, was admittedly extremely handsome; but that was all Napoleon could find to say in her favour: a disreputable member of the Parisian *demi-monde*, she claimed to be the widow of Hippolyte Jouberthon, a bankrupt *spéculateur* who had escaped to the West Indies to avoid arrest for fraud and had subsequently disappeared. His deserted wife had then become the mistress of comte Alexandre de Laborde.

Lucien's connection with this woman, ignored at first, could no longer be tolerated after Napoleon had made up his mind to marry into one of Europe's most distinguished dynasties; and the Emperor, wanting his brother to marry the Spanish infanta, Maria Luisa, widow of the King of Etruria, persuaded his mother – who had initially been prepared to accept Alexandrine Jouberthon as her daughter-in-law – to write to tell Lucien that he must divorce the woman Jouberthon, a person of by no means impeccable behaviour. This slight on his wife prompted Lucien to respond with the insulting remarks that Napoleon's own wife had a far from unblemished past herself, that Mme Jouberthon was not, like her, 'old and smelly'; and that 'it was better at least to marry one's own mistress rather than someone else's'.

'I cannot,' Lucien protested, 'without dishonouring myself, divorce a woman who has given me four children ... I shall instead go to America if forced to do so.'

His wife added her pleas to Lucien's. 'Sire,' she wrote to Napoleon, 'I throw myself at your feet. It is as impossible for me to separate myself from Lucien, if only secretly, as it is for him to leave me publicly. We belong to each other till death do us part ... Sire, we ask only that you allow us to live peacefully together in some quiet corner of your Empire.'

Napoleon was adamant: there must be a divorce before there could be any reconciliation. So his brother decided to go to America; but, having obtained the necessary passports and, having set sail for Massachusetts with his wife and children, their ship was intercepted by the Royal Navy and they were taken to Plymouth instead.

Welcomed in England in December 1810 as a wronged exile from Napoleon's so-called empire, Lucien was offered a refuge in Shropshire by Lord Powis; but, having prudently banked part of his large fortune in London, he was able to buy a country estate, Thorngrove, in Worcestershire, where he was to live as a country squire for the next four years.

Having struck Lucien's name from the lists of the French Senate and of the Legion of Honour, Napoleon exclaimed in exasperation, 'My family did much more harm to me than the good I did for them.'

This could not be said, however, of his eldest sister, Elisa. It was not so much because he was fond of her – as very few people were – but because he was only too willing to accede to her request to be given a principality where she could exercise a penchant for government – a principality a good distance from Paris. So Napoleon created Elisa Princess of Piombino, a seaport of Tuscany, and later granted her also the former republic of Lucca. He himself confessed that he had elevated Elisa in this way 'not from fraternal tenderness but out of political prudence'. Even so, his other sisters were deeply envious and very cross.

> On the day we learned of Elisa's nomination to the principality of Lucca [Hortense recalled] my husband and I called on his other sisters. We began with Caroline who, with a very forced laugh, said to us, 'Well! So Elisa is now a sovereign princess. She is going to have an army of four men and a corporal. It really is

a fine thing!' Despite her flippancy it was obvious that she was much vexed. Princess Pauline made not the least attempt to hide her feelings. 'My brother only cared for Elisa and is not interested in the rest of us,' she said most unjustly. 'As for me [she added, disregarding her well known dislike of her other sister], I don't want anything since I am an invalid, but it's not fair to Caroline.'

Princess Elisa made her state entrance to her new capital on 14 July 1805, the sixteenth anniversary of the storming of the Bastille.

She was by now a plain, masculine woman who spoke French very quickly without the slight Italian accent which her sisters never entirely lost. She was capable of exercising a certain charm, but she rarely troubled to do so. Laure d'Abrantès considered her 'the most disagreeable woman' she had ever known. She was never nice to her mother, the duchesse d'Abrantès added. 'But whom was she ever nice to? I have never met anyone with a sharper tongue.' However, she governed her territories with undoubted efficiency, ruling them as she ruled her dense, dull husband, Felice Pasquale Bacciochi, now Prince Felice, with a firm hand, leaving him to perform various ceremonial duties while she settled down to display the authority, the intermittent charm and occasional flashes of anger, real and assumed, characteristic of the Emperor whose example as a sovereign, so she assured him, she would endeavour to emulate. She proudly signed documents with an E as he did with an N, subscribing herself in letters to her brother as 'Your most devoted and submissive sister.'

At her instigation, roads and bridges were built, tanneries and factories modernized, marshes drained, alum deposits developed, tunny fishing established as a state monopoly, fortifications strengthened, pirates driven from the coasts and the quarries of snow-white marble near Carrara, where Michelangelo had supervised the cutting of blocks for his masterpieces, were revived and rendered highly profitable, producing all manner of fireplaces, altars, tombs, architectural features, clocks, statues and busts, many hundreds of these of Napoleon, whose birthday and military victories were celebrated with appropriate festivities.

Elisa found time also to supervise the establishment of all kinds of cultural and educational foundations, libraries, schools – one of them modelled on Mme Campan's – university chairs, an Académie Napoléon, an Istituto Elisa, as well as the restoration and furnishing of several of her own country villas. The Istituto Elisa was far from the only place in Lucca to bear her own name. There was a Via Elisa as well as a Porta Elisa and a Quartiere Elisa. There was also a Banca Elisa and, for good measure, a Piazza Napoleone and a Collegio Felice.

Derided as '*précieuse ridicule*' by Laure d'Abrantès, she had literary and artistic pretensions, having made a reputation in Paris at the Hôtel Maurepas as the ambitious hostess of a salon in the manner of Mme Récamier and Mme de Staël. Here the painters David and Isabey had often been seen. So had the *academicien* Louis de Fontanes, *Grand Maître* of the University, and so had Elisa's favourite brother, Lucien, with whom she had appeared in theatricals, notably in the title role of Voltaire's *Alzire ou Les Américains* displaying herself in pink silk tights, 'almost naked', as Napoleon put it, 'on a mountebank stage'. Her *soirées* at Piombino and Lucca were also attended by men of letters, most of them much older than herself, including that 'sublime *poseur*', Chateaubriand, to whose readings from their works she would listen, lying like Mme Récamier on a chaise-long while being fanned by a page.

Her court also became, with much encouragement from her husband, who was a most enthusiastic violinist, a renowned musical centre at which various members of the Puccini family were employed as *maestri di cappella* and as organists at San Martino. Giovanni Paisiello, so extravagantly admired by Napoleon, dedicated *Proserpina*, one of his more than seventy-five operas, to her; Gaspare Spontini also dedicated an opera to her, his *tragédie lyrique La Vestale* of 1807. The virtuoso violinist and composer, the Mephistophelean Niccolò Paganini, became her occasional lover.

Paganini, five years younger than herself, sometimes accompanied her to Bagni di Lucca where she once met Prince Borghese's friend, the diplomatist Angiolini, who described her as being cleverer and wittier than he had expected. 'Her manner is much like that of the Emperor,' he thought. 'And I should be very surprised if her character were not much like his. Since her confinement [her daughter, Napoleone-Elisa, grew up to be as pretty as she herself was plain] she has put on weight. Her complexion is excellent.'

It was not only that Elisa's manner resembled Napoleon's, as Angiolini said, but her deference to his wishes was just as the Emperor desired, while her contributions to his expenses were as highly gratifying to him as they were awkward for her, since they entailed the dissolution of various religious communities at his insistence. However, despite the discontent which this aroused, she made no complaint nor did she make the unreasonable demands upon her brother which were made by other members of their family. When Tuscany and Parma were incorporated into the French Empire in 1808 she showed no open resentment, hoping that, by hiding her disappointment and continuing to govern Lucca and Piombino as he wished and in his interests, she would be considered worthy of a greater prize. She was.

In May 1809 she was created Grand Duchess of Tuscany and, to the relief of the Lucchesi who, while respecting her, shared the general dislike of her, she and her husband 'scrambled' into the Pitti Palace in Florence. She was not at all pleased with her official reception in Florence, however. As she told her friend, Joseph Fouché, there was no guard of honour to welcome her and but a few courtiers and those so 'indecently dressed' that she dismissed them. At a ball that evening, 'except for the household, the guests consisted of prostitutes and people of the lower middle class whose names nobody knew. I stayed for less than half an hour.'

Around Florence, Elisa acquired various houses in the country, most notably the Villa of Poggio Imperiale which the Medici Grand Duke Cosimo I had confiscated from the Salviati and upon which large sums were lavished by Elisa for improvements, redecoration and furniture. Almost as much was spent on entertainments, concerts, dinners and theatrical performances by both French and Italian companies. Determined to exercise her authority as she had done in earlier days at Lucca, she was at the same time anxious to behave as her brother's representative in Tuscany, his Governor-General in appearance as in fact. She continued to write to him as his 'most devoted and submissive sister'; she saw to it that the Bonaparte arms were quartered on the duchy's new flag; and she arranged for his birthday and his military victories to be celebrated with appropriate rejoicings.

She also saw to it, though, that her own grand-ducal state was sufficiently impressive. On a visit to Paris in 1810, her entourage occupied a long parade of carriages containing no fewer than five chamberlains and six ladies-in-waiting as well as pages and many lesser servants.

While not as lascivious as her sisters, she nevertheless had many lovers apart from Paganini who, giving due cause for the widespread belief that he had sold his soul to the Devil, had gone off to give a series of concerts in other parts of Italy and, soon, to begin his long affair with the dancer, Antonia Bianchi.

Among the lovers who briefly took Paganini's place in the Grand Duchess's affections were a merchant from Genoa by the name of Eynard, baron Capelle, the Prefect of Leghorn, and Bartolommeo Cerami with whom she frolicked in the vineyards of the Tuscan countryside.

Her husband was no less promiscuous, entertaining at the Palazzo della Crocetta, now the Museo Archaeologico, a series of ladies of inde-terminate age and provenance who were said to be assigned to the duty of entertaining him by the Duchess herself.

Despite their disparate liaisons, they seemed in public to have a perfectly satisfactory relationship, often appearing together in the grand-ducal box at the theatre with their young daughter, Napoleone-Elisa, and on the Cascine where they inspected parades of their soldiers, the Grand Duchess dressed in a costume of a distinctly military cut.

30

SEPARATION

'God alone knows what this resolve
has cost my heart.'

JOSEPHINE, DEPRESSED AND RESIGNED to her fate, returned to Malmaison from Strasbourg, staying first for a few days at Plombières, though she had now accepted that the waters of the spa could not cure her sterility. 'I, who have never been envious,' she said to Laure d'Abrantès who visited her at Malmaison that autumn, bringing her little daughter with her, 'have really suffered when children are brought by their parents to see me. I know I will be shamefully dismissed from the bed of the man who crowned me. God is my witness when I say I love him more than life itself, and far more than the throne.'

As Josephine wandered mournfully past the aviaries and through the gardens and hothouses at Malmaison, Napoleon eagerly set about finding a bride, comforting himself, when his thoughts turned to Josephine, with the belief that his 'star', his 'destiny', demanded that he sacrifice her. He must sacrifice Marie Walewska too; and when she asked him for permission to go to Paris for the birth of their child, he told her instead to return to her husband, from whom she was now divorced, and to give birth in his house.

Obediently she obeyed the man with whom she was now deeply in love; and Alexandre Florian Joseph Collona Walewski, her child, was born at Walewice near Warsaw on 4 May 1810. Napoleon sent her a present of Brussels lace, but thereafter for three months she heard nothing from him; and then the letter which did arrive was not encouraging:

Madame . . . assuming you are now completely recovered, I desire you to come to Paris in late autumn where I should very much like to see you. Never doubt my interest and the affectionate feelings I have for you, of which you must be fully aware – Napoleon.

As though in compensation for their changed relationship, Napoleon was, however, generous in his treatment of her, if partly, at least, for their son's sake. He had her house in the rue de la Houssaye redecorated and refurnished; he bought her a pleasant house at Boulogne; he asked Duroc and the physician, Corvisart, whom she liked, to keep an eye on her and her child. He provided her with free tickets to the Paris theatres and with passes to enter all Paris's museums and galleries, as well as with a monthly allowance of ten thousand francs.

Her behaviour as a discarded mistress was beyond reproach:

> During her stay in Paris, Madame Walewska has become an accomplished woman of the world [wrote Anna Potocka]. She possesses rare tact . . . she has acquired self-assurance but has remained discreet, a combination not easily achieved in her delicate situation.

In his search for a bride, Napoleon again had approaches made to the Tsar, asking his ambassador in St Petersburg to find out if Alexander's younger sister was now ready to bear children, though she was only fifteen. He was quite prepared, he said, disregarding all the promises he had once made to Marie Walewska, to agree with the Tsar that Poland should be obliterated.

Before his remarriage, however, there was the divorce to be arranged. Declaring that he was 'impatient to see her again', he sent for Josephine to meet him at Fontainebleau.

When she arrived, she was immediately made to realize that she was not to be received in the affectionate manner which his recent letters had led her to expect. She found him seated at his desk, pen in hand. He glanced up at her and murmured without enthusiasm, 'Ah, here at last.' She soon discovered that the door linking his rooms with hers could no longer be opened. Worse than this: various members of Napoleon's family were also staying at Fontainebleau and were clearly determined to make her time there as unhappy as possible. Her sister-in-law Pauline gave regular dinner-parties for her brother to which his wife was not invited, a pretty young Italian being asked instead.

Josephine was not provoked. She behaved with her usual grace and tact, seeming to take no notice when ladies sat down without leave in her presence, hiding her distress when Napoleon took energetic part in a brutal hunt in which almost a hundred wild boar were slaughtered in an enclosure, maintaining her dignity even when her husband, relieving feelings of uncertainty and guilt, stormed at her on what Constant called 'the slightest pretext'.

He could not bring himself to broach the subject of divorce. He asked Hortense to do so, and, when she declined, he asked Eugène, then he approached Régis Cambacérès, the former Second Consul, now Archchancellor of the empire. He, too, asked to be spared the unpleasant duty. Joseph Fouché, however, undertook the unwanted task, telling Josephine that 'the cohesion of the dynasty' demanded that the Emperor should have legitimate children.

The longer Napoleon delayed, the more tense the atmosphere at Fontainebleau became. When Napoleon's family and Josephine and her daughter had a meal together, they did not speak to each other and, after a quarter of an hour, Napoleon would suddenly stand up and leave the room. 'They barely touched the dishes offered them,' the comte de Bausset, the Prefect of the Palace, reported. 'The only words spoken were when Napoleon asked me, "What's the time?"'

Bausset recorded the painful events of an evening when Josephine followed Napoleon out of the room, a handkerchief pressed to her mouth. In the adjoining drawing room coffee was, as usual, offered to her on a tray so that she could pour it out for her husband. 'But he took it himself, poured the coffee into his cup and let the sugar dissolve, staring all the while at the Empress who stood as if stupefied. He drank it and handed everything back to the page.' Then he indicated that he wished to be left alone with the Empress. So Bausset left the room and the door was closed behind him.

From the adjoining room Bausset then heard shouts of anguish. The Emperor went to the door and recalled the Prefect who found the Empress lying on the carpet. He helped to carry her down the staircase to her apartments – the Emperor, he said, being in 'an extraordinary state of agitation and with tears in his eyes'. Of the two, the Empress by now seemed to Bausset the less distraught. She whispered to him as he helped to carry her down, 'You are holding me too tight.'

When they had succeeded in getting her on to her bed, the Emperor sent for Hortense. Before telling her to look after her mother, he endeavoured to explain himself to her.

'Nothing will make me go back on the divorce,' he began, 'neither tears nor entreaties.'

'You are the master, sir,' Hortense replied, according to her own account. 'No one will oppose you. It is enough that your future requires it . . . Don't be surprised by my mother's tears. It would be remarkable if, after a marriage that has lasted for thirteen years, she did not shed them. She will submit to your will, and we will all go away, taking the memory of your kindness with us.'

'What! Are you all going to leave me?' Napoleon asked in a voice choked by sobs. 'You don't care for me any more?'

'We cannot live near you any more. It will be a sacrifice for us but we have to make it.'

When Eugène came into the room, the Emperor told him, too, that he could not bear the thought of all three of them leaving him. He would rather not have a divorce at all than bear that. It was all very well to think of that now, Eugène said: it had already gone too far. Too much had been said for the Empress to live happily with him any longer.

Now that it was all settled, Napoleon became less impatient and taciturn in Josephine's company, assuring her that she could keep Malmaison as her own home. She could also have the Elysée as her residence in Paris. She would be able to retain her rank as Empress; all her debts would be settled and she would receive an allowance of three million francs a year. She could also keep all the jewels which she had acquired, and could assume the additional title of Duchess of Navarre, the former kingdom united to the crown of France by Henri IV, founder of the Bourbon dynasty.

Within days, however, Napoleon was once more as demanding and difficult as he had been on his return from Vienna. He now insisted that Josephine should withdraw from the limelight: she was no longer to be accorded the public respect with which she had been treated in the past. The Emperor would not speak to her in public; she was to receive no special attention at official functions.

She accepted it all without complaint or demur, determined not to give way to self-pity or petulance. The evening before she was to be formally divorced, her demeanour was as gracious and serene as it had been in the days of her eminence. Étienne-Denis de Pasquier, the future Foreign Minister, thought that her behaviour on this occasion was perfect: he doubted that 'any other woman' could have acted with such perfect grace and tact. Napoleon's bearing was less distinguished than his victim's.

It was not until she had to go through the ceremony of the divorce, a public occasion held in the candle-lit Throne Room, that she at last broke down under the hostile, triumphant gaze of the assembled Bonapartes.

Her husband spoke first. 'God alone knows what this resolve has cost my heart,' he began. 'I have found the courage to go through with it only in the conviction that it will serve the best interests of France ... I have nothing but gratitude to express for the devotion and tenderness of my beloved wife. The memory of the thirteen years in which she has adorned my life will be treasured by me for ever.' He was seen to be in tears when he finished.

'With the permission of my dear husband,' Josephine replied, reading from a prepared text held in trembling fingers, 'I proudly offer him the greatest proof of devotion ever given to a husband.' Here she stopped and could not bring herself to continue. After a long silence, she passed the text to an attendant to finish for her. When they had both signed a record of the divorce, Napoleon kissed Josephine and accompanied her to her apartments.

Later, she went to his with her hair 'disordered', so Constant said, 'and her face contorted. She fell on his bed and put her arms around him ... The Emperor also began to weep. "Be brave," he said, "I will always be your friend." The Empress, overcome by sobbing, could not answer him. There was then a silence lasting for several minutes while their sobs mingled.'

It was pouring with rain when Josephine set out for Malmaison. Hortense was with her and a long procession followed with the ladies and officials of her household, her dogs, her parrot and case upon case of luggage. The next day, Napoleon, who had spent the previous night at

Versailles – where he had woken the curator to instruct him to change the furnishings and the position of all the pictures – came to see Josephine at Malmaison. It was still raining, but they were seen walking hand in hand in the grounds. He came the following day and the day after that.

On his return to Versailles he was depressed and irritable. The young Italian who had been procured for him was there, but he was seen to take little notice of her and, when he did, he was rude to her. He wrote to Josephine every day and she replied with a regularity which she had never felt able to maintain in the past.

He did all he could to make amends for the 'sacrifice' which he was imposing upon her no less than upon himself 'in his duty to maintain the dynasty'. He went through her accounts to make sure she was well provided for; he sent money for her to spend on the gardens at Malmaison; he presented her with a new Sèvres dinner service; he gave careful consideration to her rank and precedence as Empress Dowager; he offered her a principality in Italy which she declined; he later granted sufficient money to restore the dilapidated château in the duchy of Navarre in Normandy; he made sure that she was not lonely at Malmaison by asking various members of his household if they had been to see her there, so the road leading to it, Mme Rémusat said, 'became one ceaseless procession of carriages of people going to pay their respects'.

One of these visitors was the Austrian ambassador's wife to whom Josephine had remarked some time before that she hoped a marriage between Napoleon and a daughter of the Emperor would take place and that the sacrifice she was making would be worthwhile.

31

MARIE-LOUISE

'Marry a German. They are the best women in the world,
obliging, innocent and fresh as roses.'

EVER SINCE THE SIGNING of the Treaties of Tilsit in the summer
of 1807, Metternich had been aware of rumours that Napoleon intended
divorcing the Empress and taking a new wife who could provide him
with a son and heir; and he had feared that this new wife might be a
Russian grand duchess, ensuring a relationship between France and
Russia which would certainly not be to Austria's advantage. Metternich
accordingly began to press diplomatically for a marriage between
Napoleon and the Archduchess Marie-Louise, the eldest daughter of his
master, the Emperor Francis I, and a great niece of Marie-Antoinette.
He had asked General von Bubna, one of the Emperor Francis's most
trusted military advisers, to broach the subject at the French head-
quarters, while Engelbert von Floret, First Secretary at the Austrian
embassy in Paris, made guarded approaches to the French Foreign
Minister, J.B. de Champagny. Soon after taking up residence at the
Ballhausplatz, Metternich himself mentioned the possibility of the
marriage of Napoleon to Marie-Louise to a French diplomat, Count
Alexandre de Laborde, who was on the point of leaving Vienna for
Paris.

In Paris, Laborde found Talleyrand, the former Grand Chamberlain
of the Empire and still one of the Emperor's consultants, inclined to
favour the proposed match.

According to Metternich's own account, his wife Eléonore was then
invited to a masked ball given by Napoleon's legal adviser, Jean-Jacques-

Régis de Cambacérès at which Napoleon himself was also to be a guest. At this ball she was approached by a masked figure whom, of course, she knew to be Napoleon. He took her into a private room and, after some preliminary remarks, asked her if she thought the Archduchess Marie-Louise would agree to marry him and would she write to her husband about it? Countess von Metternich suggested that perhaps it would be better if he himself approached her husband by way of the Austrian Ambassador in Paris, Prince Charles Schwarzenberg.

Whether or not a meeting between Napoleon and Countess von Metternich took place in this way – and it certainly did not on the date Metternich ascribed to it – Napoleon did arrange for Schwarzenberg to be approached with a view to his sounding out the Austrian Emperor. Moreover, Countess von Metternich discussed the possibility of Napoleon marrying Marie-Louise with the Empress Josephine and her daughter, Hortense, both of whom hoped that if he were to remarry at all, he would choose an Austrian rather than a Russian bride.

Napoleon himself, however, was still waiting for the Tsar to make up his mind about an approach which he had made to Alexander concerning his youngest sister, Anna. Weeks passed and Armand de Caulaincourt, the French ambassador in St Petersburg, could get no satisfactory answer from the Russian court about his master's proposal, the mother of the girl proposed as a bride being strongly opposed to such a match, having heard stories about the French Emperor's impotence.

Impatient for marriage to what he described as 'a walking womb', Napoleon had decided by the end of the first week in February 1810 to wait no longer for a definite decision by the Tsar: he would marry the Austrian girl instead. By all accounts, she was not particularly good-looking. Nor was she graceful: her walk was particularly ungainly. Tall and fair with a clear, smooth skin and ample bosom, she had rather protuberant eyes and the ugly lip characteristic of her family; but she was said to be malleable and obedient, likely to become deeply attached to her husband, as she was to her father. She was sensible, well-read and musical: she played the piano quite well, was a competent harpist and a talented painter in both oil and watercolour. She was shy and blushed readily – her shyness was later to lead to criticism of her offhand manner on public occasions, her failure to be affable, her gaucheries and occasionally haughty demeanour. She was also said to be very innocent, being allowed only female pets in case she developed an unfortunate curiosity about sexual relations, and having illustrations which were considered unsuitable cut out of books before she was allowed to read them. Above all, she was likely to be fecund: her mother had had thirteen children, her great-grandmother twenty-six.

Although she was excited by the thought of becoming an empress in France, she nevertheless regarded her future with some apprehension: France had been her country's enemy; her great-aunt, Marie-Antoinette, had been driven through the streets of Paris to be beheaded by the guillotine; Napoleon was some twenty years older than herself; during her childhood he had been represented as an ogre, *ein Menschenfresser*.

The very thought of meeting the man had filled her with alarm, she told her friend, Victoria de Poutet. 'I assure you,' she said, 'that to see this creature would be a worse torture for me than all the martyrdoms.' And when, in January 1810, she came across a newspaper report of Napoleon's separation from his wife she wrote to 'dear Papa' to tell him how disturbed she was by the news. 'The thought that I may be counted among those from whom he will choose his future wife impels me to let you know something that I would like to lay in your fatherly heart.' He had always said that he would not force her to marry against her will; and she suggested that she might be allowed to marry someone more to her liking.

The next day, she told Victoria de Poutet, 'I pity the unfortunate woman on whom [Napoleon's] choice falls: that will undoubtedly put an end to her *beaux jours*.' However, she comforted herself with the thought that her father was 'much too kind to force' her to accept a marriage so distasteful to her.

Yet dutiful and obedient to her father, whom she hero-worshipped, she did her best to conceal her fears from him when the marriage to Napoleon seemed inevitable; and when the French Ambassador Extraordinary in Vienna, Marshal Alexandre Berthier, gave her a beautiful casket containing a portrait of Napoleon, she seemed, so Berthier thought, fascinated by it and one of her ladies described her as being much relieved. Perhaps marriage to the French Emperor would not be so bad after all. She asked about the museums in Paris, and would she be allowed to have a botanical garden, and was Napoleon musical?

Napoleon, meanwhile, had forced the pace of the negotiations, sending Eugène de Beauharnais to the Austrian embassy in Paris to make a proposal on his stepfather's behalf for the hand of the Emperor Francis's daughter. The proposal had to be accepted at once and the contract signed the following day: there would be no time for reference to Vienna. The Ambassador endeavoured to delay a decision, at least for a day or two; but, in face of Napoleon's insistence, he felt obliged to give way.

Once he had done so, Napoleon wrote to the Tsar withdrawing his offer to the Grand Duchess Anna, and occupied himself with plans for the wedding to Marie-Louise, going into every detail of the marriage rites with his master of ceremonies, neglecting other duties, supervising the unpacking of wedding presents and the making of the bride's trousseau, ordering for her an extravagant amount of jewellery, including a diamond *parure* reputed to be valued at 3,325,724 francs, as well as an enormous amount of clothes, among which were twelve dozen embroidered cambric chemises and twelve dozen pairs of stockings, thirty-six petticoats, twenty-four bed-jackets and eighty nightcaps, as well as dressing gowns, cashmere shawls, fichus, pin cushions, sixty-four dresses from Leroy and twenty-four dozen handkerchiefs.

At the Vienna Hofburg on 11 March 1810, Marie-Louise was married by proxy to the Emperor Napoleon, the bride's uncle, the Archduke Karl, standing as his deputy. Two days later, as bells pealed and cannon thundered in cacophonous farewell, Marie-Louise set out by way of Munich and Strasbourg for the fortified medieval castle of Compiègne which King Louis XV had transformed into a huge country palace and upon which large sums had been lavished for the reception of her entourage and that of Napoleon.

Followed by Metternich who left Vienna three days later, Marie-Louise was accompanied on her journey by Marshal Berthier who was in command of the escort, by comte de Laborde and by the bride's sister-in-law, Caroline Murat, Queen of Naples, who was sent to greet her on her way at the frontier town of Braunau. Here she had not only to say goodbye to her pet dog and to the ladies of her Austrian household but also to exchange her Austrian clothes for smarter Parisian ones. 'She took two hours undressing and dressing me,' she complained of Queen Caroline. 'I can assure you that I am scented like these French ladies.' She did not much like them: if she could not be with her father she would just as soon make the journey to Paris on her own.

Caroline herself had already had a most uncomfortable journey on her way to meet Marie-Louise and to accompany her to Paris. The roads were in an appalling state, the thawing of the snow, so she complained, having flooded the highway to such an extent that the horses swam while the wheels remained stuck in the mud. By the time she reached Braunau, she was covered in bruises. At Braunau, however, she met Marie-Louise and was immediately taken with her. Admittedly, her complexion was rather too fresh and she was certainly no beauty; but she had a good figure, 'charming blonde hair, hands and feet, a cultivated mind and dignified bearing; all in all she was very amiable and sweet.'

The journey to Munich was quite as difficult and tiring as the drive to Braunau. Marshal Berthier annoyed Caroline by making everyone get up and on the road by five o'clock in the morning and by keeping the carriages on the move until eleven at night: it was, she said, as though they had all been in the army and it was made infinitely worse by their not being able to get out of the carriage for hours on end, not to mention being surrounded by equerries and guards. It was 'terrible'. However, Marie-Louise 'put up with it all very well'. 'Of course,' Caroline added, 'she is very young.'

On 20 March, the increasingly weary party reached Stuttgart, capital of Frederick I, the King of Württemberg. Marie-Louise was not favourably impressed by him; nor did she like any of his family except the Queen, daughter of the English King George III, and his daughter, the Princess Royal. King Frederick was equally unimpressed by his guests. 'The Queen of Naples is very weary,' he told his daughter, Catherine, 'and surely that is not in the least unexpected. What a task they have given her! Between ourselves it is inconceivable. She is doing the best she can. But I think she is a bit fed up with her job. The Empress did not speak to anyone except me, the Queen and the Princess Royal. Your brother did not get a single word from her.'

Marie-Louise, shy in this strange company, was by now developing a cold and a sore throat; by the time her party reached Strasbourg on 23 March, she stayed in bed for most of the morning. The next day, the day before her eighteenth birthday, they reached Lunéville on the Meurthe and here Caroline was much relieved to hear that her husband had not only decided to attend the wedding, which she had feared he might have declined to do, but had already arrived in France. The relief was evident in her light-hearted letter to him from Lunéville: 'From six in the morning to ten at night I hear so much shouting of *Vive l'Impératrice* that I wake up with a start during the night and begin to shout it too. I beg you to warn the family that as soon as they see me I shall reply to the first question I am put with *Vive l'Impératrice!*'

'I hope the Emperor likes the letters I write to him,' she added the next day. 'I am afraid he may have the idea that the Empress is beautiful, since everyone who has seen her from a distance says so.'

The description which Napoleon's secretary, Claude Méneval, gave of her after meeting her for the first time was more positively favourable. He was much taken with what he described as her 'natural dignity', combined with an appealing timidity. 'Her fine, abundant and light chestnut-coloured hair framed a face to which her kindly eyes gave a charming expression.' Her nose was slightly hooked; her rather thick lips characteristic of her family; her young body plumpish. She was 'considerably taller' than Napoleon.

The other reports which Napoleon received of her were not enlightening. The answers which he received from those who had seen her were ambivalent; and he was at length driven to declare that it didn't matter whether or not she was pretty. 'So long as she is kind and gives me healthy sons,' he said, 'I will love her as if she were the most beautiful girl in the world.' He was clearly anxious, though. In her memoirs, Hortense described his restlessness, his questioning of anyone who had first-hand knowledge of her. He asked Hortense to teach him how to waltz, but he soon gave up the lessons: he was, he said, 'not intended to excel as a dancer'. He ordered new boots and then changed his bootmaker; he was measured for new clothes by Murat's tailor, Léger, but found them so stiff with embroidery that he declared them unwearable. Queen Catherine of Westphalia told her father, 'He behaves in a way neither you nor I would have imagined possible.'

Towards the end of March, Napoleon set off in the pouring rain for Compiègne. It was still raining hard when he and his brother-in-law, Joachim, King of Naples, hurried towards their calèche, footmen bustling beside them with umbrellas. Once in the coach, Napoleon called for his secretary to give him some last-minute instructions. Then, pushing the window shut in the man's wet face, he ordered the coachman to take the muddy road towards Soissons and to drive as fast as he could.

At the village of Courcelles, he was given warning of the approach of his bride and so here he and Murat alighted from the calèche and ran across to the shelter of the porch of a nearby church to await her arrival. At the approach of a long cavalcade of carriages and cavalry, Napoleon emerged from the porch to stand in the road to bring the horses to a halt. He then threw open the carriage door and, ignoring his sister Caroline, he embraced his bride who pleased him by saying, 'Your portrait does not flatter you.' If he was disappointed by his bride's appearance he did not show it. He asked her how she had been told to behave towards him. 'To obey you in every way,' she said. Napoleon, evidently pleased by the answer, got down from the carriage, slammed the door shut again and told the coachman to drive on to Compiègne.

Marie-Louise's carriage entered the *cour d'honneur* of the palace at about ten o'clock at night, splashing over the cobbles to discharge its occupants by the steps to the entrance hall where members of Napoleon's family and household had been waiting in court dress at the bottom of the grand staircase to be presented to her. Napoleon led Marie-Louise inside the hall and had her escorted to her room. Hortense thought she looked 'gentle and sweet though rather embarrassed'. Then, ignoring the programme for the evening which had been prepared, Napoleon said goodnight to the assembled company – including his current mistress, Mme de Mathis, with whom he had spent the previous night – went upstairs to his bride and, after what Louis Constant described as 'a long conversation', he went to his own room where he undressed, patted himself with eau de cologne, 'and then, wearing only a dressing gown, returned secretly to the Empress'.

The sequel, so Lord Liverpool heard, was 'more like a rape than a wooing'. But Marie-Louise seems not to have found it unpleasant. Having been told by her father to give way to her husband in everything, she evidently did not find it difficult to do so. Napoleon was to recall complacently that, after he had taken her virginity, she asked him 'to do it again'. She wrote home to say that there was certainly something 'very attractive and eager' about her husband.

The next morning he appeared later than usual in an obviously happy and satisfied mood. Encountering Méneval, he pulled the man's ear, beaming in his face. 'Marry a German. They are the best women in the world, obliging, innocent and fresh as roses.'

Marie-Louise for her part told her father shortly afterwards, 'There is something very forceful and captivating about [my husband], which it is impossible to resist.'

Napoleon also wrote to his father-in-law to say that his bride 'fulfilled all [his] expectations'. 'I have,' he continued, 'not failed to give her and receive from her proofs of the tender sentiments which bind us together. We suit each other perfectly.'

It was not long before they were seen playing blind man's buff with her ladies and game after game of billiards at which she was so much more skilled than he that he felt driven to take lessons from one of the chamberlains. He even overcame his reluctance to sit still and posed patiently while Marie-Louise sketched his portrait.

32

MARRIAGE AND HONEYMOON

'Everything was uncomfortable and dirty.'

IN THE WEEKS BEFORE the French civil marriage ceremony took place at St Cloud, Napoleon hurried about making detailed arrangements, overseeing the conversion of Josephine's apartments in the Tuileries which were to be painted a 'virginal white', ordering miniature uniforms and weapons for the son he felt sure he was now to have, going through the lists of silk dresses, stockings, hats and shoes which were to be provided for this child's mother whose measurements he had had sent to him from Vienna, closely inspecting pieces of jewellery, humming to himself abstractedly (and, as usual, out of tune), and irritably brushing aside questions about military and political affairs.

On 1 April 1810, the civil marriage ceremony took place. The next day, in a long procession of carriages, Napoleon and his bride entered Paris, passing the Arc de Triomphe which, begun in 1806 and not to be finished until 1836, was covered in canvas, rolling in the clear sunshine down the Champs-Élysées and through the gardens of the Tuileries.

The religious ceremony of marriage was performed in a specially created chapel in the Louvre, Napoleon appearing before his bride in the most flamboyant white-and-gold embroidered costume, his satin cloak covered with golden bees, his black velvet cap surrounded by white feathers and encrusted with diamonds, one of them from the Bourbon crown jewels.

The ceremony was attended by four hundred guests and by three queens, Joseph Bonaparte's wife, Queen Julie of Spain; Queen Hortense, whose husband, Louis Bonaparte, had been proclaimed King of Holland on 6 June 1806; and Jérôme's Queen, Catherine of Westphalia. Also in attendance on the bride were the bridegroom's sisters, the Princess Elisa, now the Grand Duchess of Tuscany, and a reluctant and grumpy Princess Pauline, who had unsuccessfully pleaded that the bride's train was too heavy for her to carry in view of her delicate state of health. Napoleon's other sister, Queen Caroline, had also been invited to be a trainbearer, but she had haughtily declined. Eugène's wife, the Vicereine of Italy was in attendance, bearing candles. So was Stéphanie de Beauharnais, Josephine's first husband's lively kinswoman, the Grand Duchess of Baden.

The ceremony was performed by Cardinal Fesch; but, although thirty other cardinals had been asked to attend, only eleven did so, the seats reserved for the rest remaining tellingly unoccupied, much to the annoyance of Napoleon who later had them all summoned to the Tuileries where they were kept waiting for two hours in their full ceremonial dress. 'The eyes of every onlooker were turned on the cardinals who were hustled out publicly in front of everyone and in shameful ignominy,' Cardinal Consalvi was to report. 'They were made to cross reception rooms and the grand hall in great confusion. Outside, their carriages had disappeared.'

Napoleon had endeavoured to ensure that the marriage was a popular event with the people of Paris: chickens and geese and joints of meat had been distributed in their thousands throughout the sections; barrels of wine had been set up in the city's squares; the bells of the churches pealed as cannon thundered at the Invalides; prisoners were released; thousands of old soldiers were rewarded with extra pensions; medallions stamped with portraits of the Emperor and the new Empress were distributed with the utmost liberality. Hundreds upon hundreds of soldiers of the Imperial Guard marched through the courtyard beneath the balcony of the Pavillon de l'Horloge where the bride and bridegroom stood to accept their homage.

At the Château de Neuilly, which Napoleon had made over to her, Pauline gave a grand reception for her brother. The evening, planned with the help of her versatile financial administrator, J. P. L. Michelot, began with a musical play after which the guests sauntered down into the park.

Fairy lights twinkled on every side as motionless statues suddenly leapt into life from their pedestals to act as guides to a Temple of Hymen and a miniature reproduction of the palace of Schönbrunn. Fireworks twinkled and blazed in the sky as an orchestra played for dancing. Napoleon asked his sister to repeat the splendid entertainment a week later. He appeared to be in the very best of spirits, pinching his wife's cheeks, slapping her bottom. 'He is so much in love with her,' Metternich reported to Vienna, 'that he cannot hide the fact even in public.'

Pauline's fête was followed by a ball given by the Minister of War, General Henri Clarke, then by another fête presented by the Imperial Guard, then by yet another given by Prince Schwarzenberg. This was not a success, and ended in tragedy when the specially constructed wooden ballroom caught fire. Marie-Louise was led out by Napoleon who returned to direct the fire-fighting operations. Several guests were burned to death; others, including Princess Schwarzenberg, were scarred for life; Marie-Louise's uncle, the Grand Duke Ferdinand of Würzburg, seized the opportunity of lifting up Napoleon's sister Caroline and carrying her unconscious, pregnant form to safety: she afterwards miscarried.

On his return to Compiègne with his bride, Napoleon was seen to be in an uncharacteristically gracious mood at a reception given in the Salon de Jeu for a party of French and foreign nobles, senior officers and their ladies, diplomatists and high-ranking officers. Napoleon strolled between the tables, where guests had settled down to play cards, greeting the guests with a few unusually condescending words.

> When he reached the end of the room [General Thiébault recalled] he walked through the open doors into the next. Immediately, nearly everyone stood up, and formed a long procession behind him. Walking slowly, he suddenly stopped when he reached the middle of the room, crossed his arms across his chest, stared down at the floor and remained motionless.

The guest following him naturally stopped, too; while those nearest to him nervously formed a circle around him. As Napoleon remained motionless in what was evidently an epileptic trance, they were at first embarrassed, then puzzled.

> No one spoke a word [Thiébault continued]. The French in particular were obviously embarrassed by Napoleon's strange, inexplicable behaviour. At first I thought that he had suddenly

remembered something and had stopped to think about it. But all the time he seemed transfixed; five, six, seven, eight minutes passed and no one could make the least sense of his extraordinary behaviour . . . They watched as though spellbound.

After what seemed like as long as a quarter of an hour, Marshal Masséna approached Napoleon and addressed a few words to him in a quiet voice. Without raising his eyes, or making the least movement, he suddenly shouted at Masséna, 'Why are you pestering me?' A minute or so later he raised his head, uncrossed his arms, looked about him and, without another word or change of expression, walked slowly to the Salon de Jeu. At his approach, Marie-Louise put down her cards as she stood up from the table. 'Let us go, Madame,' he said to her; and she followed him obediently out of the room.

Submissive as she appeared to be, however, Marie-Louise was not as pliable as her husband had expected. She was often timid in public and inclined, as she said herself, to say 'many foolish things'. But she was not shy with him. While he had hoped that the Empress Josephine might return to court, Marie-Louise was determined that she should not. Nor should she be permitted to reside in her accustomed luxury at Malmaison.

'You promised that you would never abandon me,' Josephine wrote to her former husband in evident distress. 'I need advice. You are the only friend I have left . . . I have been completely banished from Your Majesty's memory.'

'You will need courage,' Napoleon replied coolly. 'If you are concerned for my well-being, you must control yourself. You can never doubt my friendship for you, and must, indeed, know very little about my regard for you if you think I could possibly be happy knowing you are not. *Adieu, mon amie*, good night.'

Such letters did nothing to comfort her. She was so often in tears that, in Claire de Rémusat's words, it was 'painful to see her'. 'Sometimes,' so Josephine herself said, 'it seems as though I were already dead.'

Well aware of Marie-Louise's jealousy, as well as his family's antagonism and dislike of her, Josephine decided to leave France: she set out for Switzerland by way of Aix and Savoy.

* * *

At the end of April 1810, Napoleon also left France, taking Marie-Louise on a honeymoon through the Low Countries. The expedition was not, however, a pleasant experience for her. She had been looking forward to it: it would be a really enjoyable journey since she 'loved travelling'. But she had not long been on the road in a caravan of rattling carriages before she was bitterly disappointed: when she arrived at St Quentin, so she wrote in her diary, she was shown up to rooms in the Prefecture 'where everything was uncomfortable and dirty'. When she went to bed she was suffering from what she described as lumbago and 'the next morning the Emperor made [her] get up at four o'clock to go to see a cotton-mill'. Moreover, her ladies were grumpy, constantly complaining of the horrid *estaminets* and the uncomfortable travelling, the awful food and the unpleasant, windy weather, the need to stand up for so long at civic receptions, and the dreary countryside through which they had to pass – in particular, the dismal, desolate plain that stretched on both sides of the bumpy road to Breda.

There were, admittedly, amusing incidents to be recorded in Marie-Louise's diary from time to time: the duc de Bassano falling into a pond, having climbed down from his carriage to thrash his coachman; the prince de Neuchâtel blundering into her bedroom under the impression that it was his own; and her strait-laced, outspoken and tactless *dame d'honneur*, the duchesse de Montebello, being driven out in her carriage to buy contraband goods at a warehouse and being set down by her coachman at a brothel.

But these were rare episodes in a diary much of which was given over to descriptions of wearisome travelling, humdrum statistics, stomach cramps and the ministrations of the doctor whom she tried to fluster by pretending to faint: 'He hurried in, felt my pulse, which he declared he could not find, so rubbed my nose with vinegar. After five minutes I pretended to return to consciousness, as he was by this time talking of bleeding me.'

To make matters worse, her husband was not in the best of moods either. When, in defiance of his order that she should not eat while travelling in a coach, she asked for food, he told her sharply that a lady ought never to be hungry. More than once he protested that she ate too much. He treated her and her ladies like grenadiers, she complained; and in revenge she fell into a doleful silence, declining to answer him, complaining of a painful headache. Irritated by her petulant mood, he opened the carriage window, which had been rattling in the wind, and allowed a blast of rain to spatter her clothes. By then she had decided that, if she had her life to live over again, she would certainly not get married.

To add to her disgruntlement, her sister-in-law, Queen Caroline and Count Metternich were both of the party and Caroline soon made it clear that she wished she had stayed behind. As on the journey from Württemberg, she had been obliged to get up before dawn to be rattled along over bumpy, muddy roads, and, on more than one occasion, to cross a river on foot because the bridges were too narrow for carriages to pass over them. She was by now in such an ill temper, so Marie-Louise confided to her diary, that 'one could not speak to her'. Making the excuse that she believed herself to be pregnant again, she returned to Paris, taking Count Metternich with her. Marie-Louise was not in the least sorry to see either of them go, having fallen out with Caroline and never having liked Metternich. But she was annoyed that her uncle, the Grand Duke Ferdinand, had also gone with them, still clearly much taken by the charms of the sly Queen Caroline.

In Paris, where she returned to the Pavillon de Flore, it was now widely rumoured that Caroline was having an affair with Metternich. Marshal d'Abrantès's wife, Laure, who had had an affair with him herself, liked to suppose that Metternich did not care for Caroline, alleging that he had once told her that she disgusted him physically. But there were others who felt sure that they were lovers.

Certainly Stendhal told Balzac that he had seen Metternich at St Cloud wearing a locket containing strands of Caroline Murat's hair as a bracelet round his wrist; and Charlotte Bonaparte, Lucien's daughter, wrote: 'Queen Caroline is behaving in a very odd way. Her husband has gone back to Naples, and she has not gone with him, which Grandmama thinks very wrong; but what is worse is that she spends every moment of every day with a man called Metternick, an ambassador who is quite young [actually nine years older than Caroline]. There is a lot of gossip about it. [She causes] Grandmama a great deal of sorrow by [her] conduct.'

Caroline's letters to her husband were as exceptionally affectionate at this time as they had been when conducting Marie-Louise to Paris, assuring him how much she missed him, how dear he was to her, how much she hated being parted for a single moment from the father of her children. 'Think of me often,' she wrote. 'I am most miserable at your leaving . . . very bored and very sad. My God! How miserable I am! . . . We went to a ball at Princess Pauline's yesterday, and hunting today. It was very wet. The Emperor said to me, "Well! The *Lazzarone* [Neapolitan beggar] has forgotten you. He doesn't think about you any more" . . . When we are together again we must never in future be apart . . . Kiss the children for me and keep telling them that their mother can never know perfect happiness far from them or far from you.'

She was experiencing difficulty in obtaining her brother's permission to return to Naples. When she asked him if she might go he merely expressed surprise that she should wish to do so since the summer in Naples was so hot. Eventually he agreed that she might leave but withdrew his permission within a few days; and then, towards the end of July, she was invited to Rambouillet where she found the Emperor in an unusually happy, almost playful mood. He had reason to believe that Marie-Louise was pregnant; and now, at last, his sister was given permission to go home. She left before he had an opportunity to change his mind and was back in Naples by 5 August 1810.

33

THE KING OF ROME

'I have a son. I am at the height of happiness.'

WHEN HIS HONEYMOON WAS OVER, Napoleon had seen to it that his wife was as isolated as a begum in a zenana. Surrounded by her ladies, she was rarely to be seen in the outside world and, when she was, it was noticed how ill at ease she appeared to be, how gauche, how unlike her charming predecessor, how haughty she sometimes still appeared when she was shy. She spent many hours at her lessons, her music lessons, her drawing and painting lessons, her lessons in needlework, arranging her collections of engravings, medals and coins, choosing presents for her family, reading one of her many books – she read eighteen novels by that prolific author of popular romances, Mme de Genlis in a single year. Men were kept at a distance: tradesmen, who might by chance come across her, were forbidden to speak to her; her dressmakers were obliged to use models for trying out costumes made for her. On one exceptional occasion, Metternich was permitted to see her on her own; but it was understood that this interview was allowed so that he could report to her father that he had had an intimate conversation with her and that she was happy in her marriage.

And, indeed, now that their travels were over, Napoleon did try to please her. He spent his evenings with her; he arranged entertainments for her and her ladies; he had traces of his former wife removed from the Tuileries, her monogram obliterated, her likeness in David's *Distribution des Aigles* was painted out. Indeed, so anxious did he appear to please his wife, provided she obeyed the rules he laid down for her, that she once remarked to Metternich, 'I am not afraid of the Emperor, but I am beginning to think that he is afraid of me.'

He was certainly, as Hortense said, 'gentler and more complaisant' with his new wife than he had been of late with Josephine. When, for instance, she kept him waiting for dinner, he would remark without rancour, 'Ah, here she is. I see why you are late: you have been making yourself beautiful.' When she became pregnant, he was clearly delighted with her. One day, he said to Hortense, displaying her as a couturier might point proudly to one of his creations on a favourite model, 'Look, how her figure is swelling!'

He had, indeed, grown fond of her. She was innocent and pliable, still rather gauche, clearly enthralled by him, admiring him. 'You can imagine we are never short of amusements in Paris,' she told a friend, 'but the most satisfying are the moments I spend with the Emperor.' He had come to regard her as both sensible and intuitive, well worth talking to; he mused aloud in her company; he told her of his plans; he behaved towards her with a consideration he rarely showed to others.

As her pregnancy progressed, the more nervous the expectant mother became. Looking out of a window at Fontainebleau, Louis Constant saw her, supported by her ladies, being sick in the garden.

Her husband was persuaded to suppose that there would be less chance of a miscarriage if her mind was distracted from apprehension by her being entertained by plays and masques; and, since riding in a carriage made her feel sick, and walking to the terrace at the Tuileries entailed her being troubled by people calling out to wish her well, Napoleon ordered that a tunnel be specially dug for her.

The mother's pains began on the evening of 19 March 1811. Ministers and officials, whose presence would be required at the birth, were told to hold themselves ready to attend at the Tuileries and to wear the appropriate dress. Eugène de Beauharnais was summoned; so, too, was his sister Hortense who described how agitated Napoleon became when Marie-Louise suffered 'long-drawn-out birth pangs'. 'He would ask us,' Hortense said, 'whether, as a result, there might be bad consequences for mother or child.' 'He dared no longer rely on the hope for a son,' she added. 'One could see he was trying to prepare himself for the contrary; and announced that if the baby were to be a girl she would be known as the Princess of Venice. He was anxious to find out if there were any indications by which the sex of a child could be ascertained in advance. He showed by his questioning how anxious he was.' Constant described him as being 'quite shaken'.

As the mother's labour continued, Hortense decided to try to rest, fully dressed, on one of the ladies' beds. Others went to sleep on chairs. 'It was a strange scene,' wrote the comte de Saint-Aulaire. 'Drowsy men, ministers with nothing to do, the Emperor deeply moved – all jumbled up together round the tables on which wine and chocolate etc. were being served.'

Napoleon walked in and out of his wife's room; and, from time to time, he supported her as she paced up and down in an attempt to relieve the pain. At about five o'clock, her suffering became less intense and she fell into a troubled sleep. Napoleon took the opportunity, as he so often did when worried or restless, to take a very hot bath. He was still in the bath when the *accoucheur* came into the room to warn him that he might well be unable to save both mother and child. 'Well, then,' Napoleon said without hesitation, as he stood up to get out of the bath, 'save the mother, think only of the mother.'

'He stepped out of the bath in a great hurry,' Constant recorded. 'Hardly giving me time to dry him, he put on his dressing gown and hurried downstairs to comfort his wife. Overcome by emotion as he held her hand and kissed her, he went into the next room.' While he was there the struggle continued. The *accoucheur* said that he would be obliged to use instruments. At this Marie-Louise protested weakly, 'Must I be sacrificed because I'm Empress?'

Soon after this the child was born and, when Napoleon rushed back into the room, it had been placed on the floor as though it were presumed to be dead. Picked up from there, it was swung about and slapped and dosed with drops of brandy, as Napoleon left the room, meeting Hortense as she hurried downstairs.

'It's all over,' he told her.

'He looked so dejected that I asked him apprehensively, "Is it a boy?"'

'Yes,' he said, looking little comforted by the thought. She kissed him and was greatly surprised to hear him add, 'I can't feel the happiness of it. The poor woman suffered so.'

He then went into the Empress's room, crossing to the window to look down upon the crowds that had gathered below to listen to the roar of the cannon which began firing at about nine o'clock. It had been announced that there would be twenty-one salutes for a girl, a hundred and one for a boy. After the boom of the twenty-first had died away, the people below the windows of the Tuileries fell into apprehensive silence. Then, as the twenty-second announced the birth of the prince, it was greeted with cheers, and with shouts of 'Vive l'Empereur!' People threw their hats in the air and hugged each other. 'We heard the cheers in the streets,' wrote Stendhal in his journal. 'My wigmaker informs me that in the rue Saint-Honoré people cheered just as they would a famous actor coming on to the stage.' Constant looked across to his master and saw the tears running down his cheeks. Below him the people in the streets were chanting:

> Et bon, bon, bon,
> C'est un garcon
> Vive Napoléon

'Dear Josephine,' Napoleon later wrote, 'I have a son. I am at the height of happiness.' Now that she was out of danger, Marie-Louise was, too. 'Never could I believe I could be so happy,' she wrote home. 'My love for my husband grows all the time, and when I remember his tenderness I can hardly help crying. Even had I not loved him before, nothing could stop me from loving him now.'

'How happy Napoleon was,' wrote Laure d'Abrantès, recently returned from Spain. 'How he enjoyed his good fortune!' She described him, standing beside the baby's elaborate silver gilt and mother-of-pearl cradle, designed for him by Pierre-Paul Prud'hon, holding the child in his arms, kissing his head. Others later wrote of him playing with the child as with a toy, going to his study door to take him in his arms. 'Many times I have watched him holding his son closely to him as if he were impatient to teach him the arts of government,' wrote Baron de Méneval. 'Even when, seated on his sofa near the mantelpiece, on which stood bronze busts of Scipio and Hannibal, he was concentrating on some important document, or when he was working at his desk signing a dispatch, he liked to have his son sitting on his knee or pressed to his chest.' He was constantly picking him up and hugging him, something Marie-Louise was nervous of doing for fear of dropping him.

'My son is plump and well,' he reported complacently to Josephine. 'He has my chest, my mouth and my eyes ... I hope he will fulfil his destiny.'

Nothing was to be spared in the upbringing of this heir to the Empire, this child who was to be known as the King of Rome. His governess, Countess de Montesquiou, assisted by four assistant governesses, had her own steward and secretary. His household also included various ladies who were provided with a special blue merino uniform to which, in winter, was added a blue cashmere shawl. There were also cradle-rockers and valets, nurses who wore black silk aprons to distinguish them from the chambermaids whose aprons were white, ushers and cooks, as well as a physician, a surgeon and a lady entrusted with the duty of supervising the activities of the wet-nurse who was to be confined within the walls of the Tuileries except when riding abroad in a carriage with a chaperone.

The child's own little coach, provided with coachmen, equerries and outriders, was decorated with the imperial arms and drawn by two patient, well-disciplined sheep, a present from the baby's aunt Caroline.

As he grew older, the child was indulged in countless other ways: he was allowed to sit on the floor beside his father and nudge the coloured bricks with which Napoleon was in the habit of simulating military manoeuvres and planning battles; he was provided with miniature military uniforms and a Sèvres dinner service specially made for him with historical subjects pictured beneath the glaze; he was presented with a specially printed library of instructive and inspiring books as well as with conventional toys such as a set of ninepins; he was given charts which demonstrated the distinction of his descent from royal forbears, a most important factor in Napoleon's pride in having fathered him. This was evident in his behaviour towards his son which was witnessed one day by François-Joseph Talma of the Comédie-Française.

'Talma,' he said to him as he took his son on his knee and tapped him once or twice on the bottom, 'tell me what I'm doing.' Talma had no idea what to say, so Napoleon enlightened him. 'You really don't see what I'm doing? ... I'm beating a king.'

The child himself was frequently reminded of his royal birth. When his father indulged in one of those displays of petty bullying in which he would pinch the arms of young women rather too hard to be considered playful, he would offer the boy a bonbon only to snatch it out of reach when he tried to take it, or he would lift the child up to look at his reflection in a mirror, then suddenly thrust his own frighteningly distorted features up to be reflected beside his son's face in the glass. 'Why are you crying?' he would ask. 'A king should not cry, a king should not be frightened.'

The delight and pride of his father, the centre of so numerous a household, precocious and captivating in the eyes of the ladies of his protective court, the boy grew up to regard his mother almost as a stranger, certainly as a presence far more remote than that of his governesses. She, in turn, as one of these ladies observed, was obviously nervous when playing with him or lifting him up, seeming to be afraid of hurting or upsetting him. It is clear from her letters that she felt excluded from the circle that surrounded and protected the boy and that, while he responded readily to his father's evident love for him and all that he represented, the child was ill at ease with her.

> When Mme de Montesquiou brought him to his luncheon [according to the son of one of his nurses], the Emperor would take him on his knees and have him taste his watered wine – although he was still being breastfed – or he would place to his lips a little gravy or sauce that he found at hand. Countess de Montesquiou complained about this mixture: the Emperor would burst out laughing, and the royal child shared in his father's laughter. The Empress, when present at these scenes, did not know how to initiate them, either out of shyness or out of fear of hurting her son. One did not find the spontaneous signs of affection that mothers have for their children in her. She was even ill at ease carrying him, and that gave birth to the rumour that she did not like her son. My mother always told me the opposite: she had much affection for the King of Rome. It is true that she seldom took him in her arms, but if she did not show all her affection for him, it was because he was always accompanied by Madame de Montesquiou. She had been made to feel uncomfortable in the presence of this lady.

Mme de Montesquiou was devoted to Napoleon; but the same certainly could not be said of Marie-Louise's principal lady-in-waiting, the young duchesse de Montebello, widow of the blunt and outspoken Marshal Jean Lannes, a former dyer's apprentice and son of a livery stables keeper, who had been mortally wounded at the battle of Aspern-Essling. The handsome, virtuous duchesse detested Napoleon and the Bonapartes, and did her devious best to persuade Marie-Louise to share her views of them. At the same time, the Bonapartes were in agreement as to their dislike of Marie-Louise. 'She is,' said Mme Mère, 'not one of us.'

34

DISASTER IN RUSSIA

*'You cannot imagine my feelings when I pass by
your room and see windows and shutters closed.'*

THE EMPRESS JOSEPHINE had been obliged to leave Paris before
the wedding of the Emperor and Marie-Louise and to establish herself
in Normandy at the Château de Navarre.

Here in this vast castle, Josephine had been uncomfortable and
deeply unhappy. Her household had resented their having to remain
here while Paris was *en fête*; and several of both her ladies and her
gentlemen-in-waiting had asked to be recommended for posts in the
capital. Good-naturedly she obliged them, longing to be back in Paris
herself rather than exiled in this gloomy Norman château where what
passed for entertainment in the evenings were games of backgammon
with the local bishop, unending games of patience and billiards and the
telling of fortunes by the turn of cards.

Occasionally, dinners were given for the leading citizens of Evreux;
sometimes there were concerts; but most evenings were spent more
quietly as the Empress bent over her needlework while one of her
chamberlains read aloud from books to which she paid scant attention.
'Tranquillity is such a sweet thing,' she wrote resignedly to Eugène.
'Ambition is the only thing that can spoil it, and thank God I do not
suffer from the disease of ambition.'

Yet she was often in tears and this, so her doctor told her, was
responsible for her failing sight. However, she assured Hortense that
she had cried 'only occasionally for some time past. I hope that the

quiet life I lead here, far from intrigue and gossip, will strengthen me and that my eyes will get well.'

She wrote to Napoleon asking to be allowed to return to Malmaison, a move which she heard Marie-Louise had opposed on the grounds that it was too near Paris. Napoleon gave his consent but did so in a markedly reluctant manner which elicited from his former wife a letter of gratitude mingled with sad reproach: 'You promised never to abandon me ... I was afraid you had banished me from your memory ... While I am at Malmaison Your Majesty may be sure that I will live as though I were a thousand miles from Paris and, in his great happiness, Your Majesty need not fear of being troubled by my own regrets.'

Josephine had not been allowed, however, to remain at Malmaison when Marie-Louise became pregnant, and it had been suggested that the former Empress might travel for a time in Italy. Marie-Louise was clearly very jealous of her predecessor. When she and Napoleon were driving near Malmaison one day and he suggested that they should go to see it, she began to cry. 'How can he want to see that old lady?' she is reported to have said. 'A woman of low birth at that.' And when Josephine herself expressed a wish to see the new Empress, Napoleon dissuaded her. 'No,' he said, 'she thinks you are very old. If she sees how charming you are, she would ask me to send you away and I would have to do so.'

As it happened, Josephine was away for a year, travelling in Savoy and Switzerland; and when she returned to Malmaison, she was subjected to a series of renewed instructions as to her conduct, affectionately but firmly conveyed: she must guard against extravagance; she must not give so much to charity; she must take a leaf out of Marie-Louise's book, by being moderate in her donations and keeping accurate accounts as she did; she should be more strict about protocol and, when driving about, she must ensure that she had an escort befitting her rank. Napoleon sent the Secretary of the Treasury to emphasize the need for economy and accurate accounting; and, as a woman frustrated by the very idea of economy and accounts, she began to cry, as she so often did now, more even than in the past. When he heard about this, Napoleon reprimanded the Secretary and wrote to Josephine a comforting and reassuring letter.

He had little cause to impress upon Josephine the need to live in some state at Malmaison. There were still no fewer than thirty footmen in attendance in the entrance hall and, when she went out for a drive, as well as equerries on either side of the coach, there were fourteen cuirassiers riding behind it. Guests at her table were highly impressed by the extravagant concoctions of her Italian chef and the pyramids of rare fruits from her greenhouses.

She seemed by now to have quite resigned herself to her new status. She drew as much enjoyment as ever from her animals, her swans and ostriches, her chamois, her sheep and her Swiss cows. She relished her food and was growing rather stout. Indeed, Laure d'Abrantès said that 'one special feature of her figure assumed really incredible proportions, and she was persuaded to agree, with the utmost reluctance, to wear boned corsets like other ladies.'

It was rumoured that she was not abstemious in other ways: on her way to Aix for a holiday in the summer of 1810, she travelled incognito with a single equerry, one female companion and her unmarried young chamberlain, Lancelot de Turpin Crissé.

Contented as Josephine appeared to be at Malmaison, the country beyond its gates was far less so. Bread had doubled in price; the cost of the war in Spain was at least partly responsible for a serious financial crisis; conscription was now extended to apply to men between the ages of twenty and sixty; and, although he was presumed to be unaware of it, the Emperor was losing much of his former popularity. Yet he was planning a new campaign, this time against Russia where the Tsar had been showing increasing disinclination to treat Napoleon as a trusted partner and must, so Napoleon decided, be intimidated. No fewer than 675,000 men, from all over his vast dominions, were accordingly to be raised for this purpose.

Before leaving in the summer of 1812, he went to say goodbye to Josephine and remained talking to her for two hours. She herself went to see Constant to ask him to look after his master. Constant was surprised by her 'care for the man who had abandoned her. It was as though she were still his most beloved wife.'

Soon afterwards, he set out for Dresden, taking his new wife with him, surrounding her with large and unnecessary numbers of attendants and seeing to it that she was dressed most expensively, glittering with jewels so as to impress the allied leaders gathered there.

Marie-Louise was still devoted to him and not long before, when he had gone to Boulogne to inspect the fleet and review the troops still stationed there for the long-threatened assault upon England, she assured him how much she missed him during this the first time they had been apart in the seventeen months since their marriage. 'You cannot imagine my feelings,' she told him, 'when I pass by your room and see windows and shutters closed.'

The Russian campaign was a disaster and a tragedy. Well over half a million men were lost in the desolate, snowbound wastes, as the bedraggled survivors struggled home from the charred and deserted ruins of Moscow.

> The ravages of cold were equalled by those of hunger [wrote an officer in the Württemberg contingent]. No food was so rotten or disgusting as not to find someone to relish it. No fallen horse or cattle remained uneaten, no dog, no cat, no carrion, nor, indeed, the corpses of those that died of cold or hunger. It was not unknown for men to gnaw at their own famished bodies. But not only men's bodies suffered unspeakably, their minds, too, became deeply affected by the combined assault of extreme cold and hunger. All human compassion vanished, each thought and cared only for himself and be damned to his comrade. With complete indifference he watched him lie down and die, without emotion he seated himself on his corpse by the fireside. Dull despair or raving madness had taken possession of many and they died muttering, with their last breath, the most horrible imprecations against God and man.

Napoleon had remained too long there. But this was the only mistake to which he would admit as he abandoned the remains of his army and set out for France in a sleigh. Not long before he had shown symptoms of *folie de grandeur*, referring to Louis XVI as his 'poor Uncle' and declaring that the elevation of Marshal Bernadotte to the throne of Sweden, the placing of a commoner on a throne, was 'an injustice to crowned heads'. Now he spoke as though the destruction of an army more powerful than any previously known was a temporary misfortune: his return to France would soon put things right again.

Throughout the campaign his letters home to Marie-Louise had struck an optimistic note. 'My health is good,' he had assured her in the middle of July 1812, 'my affairs progress very well.' 'My health is fine,' he had written later from Vitebsk. 'It is very hot. I love you very much. Kiss my son.' She had been little comforted by the letter. 'I am endlessly tormenting myself and am always uneasy,' she told a friend. 'For a day to pass without a letter from him is enough to throw me into the deepest depression; and, when one does arrive, it comforts me only for an hour or so.'

Caulaincourt, Napoleon's companion on the sad journey back to France, described him as having lost all sense of reality, refusing to accept the fact of the *Grande Armée*'s disaster, making light of its dreadful losses, pinching Caulaincourt's cheek when he endeavoured to bring the Emperor down to earth, joking that it would be a fine thing if the Prussians took Napoleon Bonaparte prisoner and handed him over to the English who would exhibit him in London like a wild animal in a cage.

To Constant, he seemed quite unconcerned by the Russian disaster. As he was himself to observe, 'A man such as I does not concern himself much about the lives of a million men.' 'I have three hundred thousand men to spend,' he had once told the Tsar; while General Kléber referred to him as 'a General who consumes six thousand men a day'. 'Small change,' he once commented, turning over the corpses of his soldiers with his foot; and, in contemplating his men drowning in the Beresina in 1812, he was quoted as having commented, 'Look at those toads!'

Murat, who was left in command of the army, deserted his post, ostensibly on the grounds of ill health but in fact, in order to save his kingdom of Naples, much to the fury of Napoleon who wrote to Caroline: 'Your husband deserted the army on the 16th [January 1813, leaving Eugène de Beauharnais in command]. He is a brave man on the battlefield but weaker than a woman or a monk when the enemy is out of sight. He has no moral courage whatever. I leave it to you to make him aware just how displeased I am by his disgraceful behaviour.'

Napoleon had by then arrived in Paris and, having gone to Malmaison to see Josephine, soon afterwards set about organizing a series of balls and galas as if in celebration of a victory and in defiance of the dispatch sent to him by General Berthier, 'Sir, your army exists no more.' 'The stories told by officers who had survived the retreat were such that the diversions of the carnival stopped,' wrote Major Raymond de Montesquiou, duc de Fezensac. 'Everyone stayed at home, preoccupied with present misfortunes and anxiety for the future. In the midst of the general consternation, people were shocked to see the Emperor entertaining at the Tuileries. This was an insult to private grief, and revealed a cruel insensitivity to the host of victims. I shall always remember one of those dismal balls, at which I felt I was dancing on graves.' Marie-Louise told a friend, 'I don't like dancing any more.'

It was, wrote Constant, 'the first time that Napoleon had returned from a campaign without bringing with him a new peace which the glory of his arms had won. On this occasion, everyone who looked on Josephine as the Emperor's talisman and guardian of his fortunes could not but reflect upon the fact that the Russian campaign was the first which had been undertaken by the Emperor since his marriage to Marie-Louise.'

35

FUGITIVES

'They were watching the funeral of the Empire.'

THE EMPEROR SEEMED to be quite unaware of the extent of the humiliating disaster of the Russian campaign, and of the effect that the calamity had upon his reputation. 'The Emperor was invincible no longer,' as the duc de Fezensac said. 'While we were dying in Russia, another army was perishing in Spain . . . The defection of Prussia was no longer in doubt; the Austrian alliance was at the very least shaky; and the exhaustion in France increased in proportion as the list of her enemies grew longer.'

Indeed, at the beginning of 1813, having signed a treaty with Russia, the King of Prussia broke with Napoleon while Austria joined the Allies. Napoleon ordered that Marie-Louise should not be told of her father's defection and, having rejoined his reconstituted army, he wrote her loving letters every day, giving her encouraging reports of his army's progress, by no means justified by its situation. In July 1813, he allowed himself a week's leave at Mainz and asked Marie-Louise to join him there. He arrived late at night when she was in bed, so she recorded in her journal. 'He crossed all the rooms where my page and my women were asleep without anyone hearing him. I will not attempt to write down all the joy I felt at seeing him [for the first time in almost four months]. That is not for putting down on paper. It can only be felt.'

As well as writing affectionate letters to Marie-Louise during this summer of 1813, Napoleon wrote also to Josephine and, on his return to Paris, he asked Méneval to go to Malmaison to give her the same reassurance that he had given Marie-Louise.

Josephine was not comforted, though. She could not sleep; she suffered from agonizing migraines; she had premonitions of disaster; and when she heard in October 1813 that Napoleon's army had been defeated at Leipzig, she wrote to comfort him: 'Sire, although I can no longer share in your joys, your grief will always be mine, too. I cannot resist the need to tell you that I love you with all my heart.'

Napoleon set out for Paris again, hoping to raise yet more men and more money for a war that most of his marshals now believed could not possibly be won. He himself spoke of the possibility of defeat, of his fear that his luck was running out, that, as Eugène put it, his 'star' was no longer bright.

On Sunday 23 January 1814, after Mass, he addressed several hundred officers of the National Guard of Paris drawn up on parade in the Salon of the Marshals at the Tuileries:

'I entrust to the courage of the National Guard the Empress and the King of Rome, my wife and my son, whom, after France, I hold most dear in this world. You will protect them, won't you? You will protect them?'

Cries of 'Vive l'Empereur!' filled the air.

The next day, he left Paris to join the army in an effort to halt the allied advance, angrily assuring Queen Hortense, who had come to the Tuileries at his request, and had unwisely commented on the odds against him, that his presence on the battlefield was worth a hundred thousand men. Marie-Louise, so Hortense said, could not stop crying at her husband's departure. 'Embracing her, the Emperor murmured "Have confidence in me. Do you think I've forgotten my trade?"'

'When will you come back again?' Marie-Louise asked him.

'That, my dearest,' he replied, 'is a secret known only to God.'

Already many of his troops had deserted, while many of those that remained were ill-trained conscripts; yet, with the remarkable skill he had displayed in earlier campaigns, he defeated his enemies at Champaubert, at Montmirail, then at Vauchamps, then at Monterau, and, having gained these four victories in little more than a week, he wrote confidently to Marie-Louise that he expected to secure peace within a few days, a peace worthy of himself and 'worthy of France'. But now that

ABOVE Charles Maurice de Talleyrand-Périgord, a portrait by Pierre-Paul Prud'hon.

LEFT Napoleon, standing in characteristic pose, in front of the château de Malmaison in 1804, by François-Pascal-Simon, Baron Gérard.

The Empress Josephine at Malmaison, also by Baron Gérard.

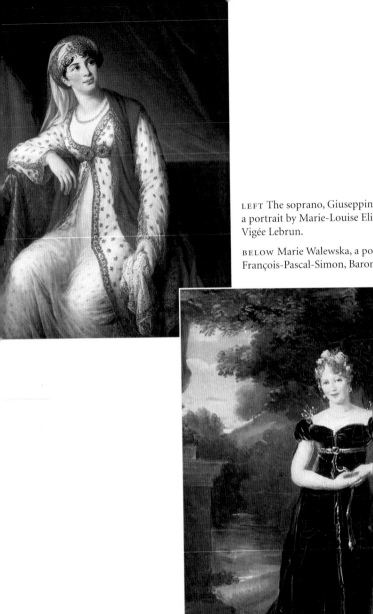

LEFT The soprano, Giuseppina Grassini, a portrait by Marie-Louise Elisabeth Vigée Lebrun.

BELOW Marie Walewska, a portrait by François-Pascal-Simon, Baron Gérard.

ABOVE Marie Walewska, a portrait by Robert Lefevre.

RIGHT Marguerite-Joséphine Weimer (the actress Mlle George).

BELOW Jeanne-Françoise, Mme Récamier, the portrait by Jacques-Louis David.

The ceremony of the coronation of the Emperor Napoleon in the presence of Pope
Pius VII on 2 December 1804 by Jacques-Louis David.

'The Plumb-Pudding in danger – or – State Epicures Taking un Petit Souper.' Pitt, with a carving-knife and three-pronged fork, looks wearily at Napoleon as he cuts a deep gash to the west of Britain. Napoleon greedily helps himself to a large slice of Europe. (Caricature by James Gillray, BM catalogue, 10371, 26 February 1805)

OPPOSITE Napoleon receiving Queen Louisa of Prussia at Tilsit on 6 July 1807. A detail of a painting by Nicolas Louis François Gosse.

Napoleon with his nephews and nieces on the terrace at Saint-Cloud in 1810, by Louis Ducis.

The ceremony of the divorce of the Empress Josephine by Henri-Frederic Schopin.

Prussia and Britain, Russia and Austria were all ranged against him, and all bound by the Treaty of Chaumont to continue the war until Napoleon was overthrown, it could not be long before his dwindling empire was destroyed.

As the sound of artillery fire could be heard in Paris, the Regency Council appointed by Napoleon, comprising Marie-Louise – who, he said, was 'wiser than any of my ministers' – Joseph Bonaparte, now returned from Spain, Talleyrand and Cambacérès, all agreed that the Empress and the King of Rome should remain in Paris since their departure would spread despondency and alarm. But Joseph then produced letters from Napoleon who had decreed that, should there be danger of their being taken, they must leave Paris for Rambouillet with the Senate, the Council of State and the Treasury. He would rather have his throat cut, he wrote, than see his son brought up as an Austrian prince in Vienna. So, in obedience to the Emperor's orders, preparations were made for an immediate departure from Paris.

Before leaving, Marie-Louise wrote to Napoleon: 'They insist on my going. I would have been quite brave enough to stay and I am very angry that they wouldn't let me, especially when the Parisians are showing such readiness to defend themselves. But they pointed out to me that my son would be running into danger . . . I believe in a few days' time you will agree I should have remained, but I have no choice. Joseph has shown me your letters.'

So the Empress and her son, together with numerous members of their households, as well as of the Bonaparte family, followed by a caravan of carriages piled high with luggage, set out from Paris on roads filled with refugees, carts and animals. A silent crowd watched them leave. 'They were,' wrote Méneval, 'watching the funeral of the Empire.'

Josephine was also on the road, having left Malmaison for the Château de Navarre. So were Hortense and her two children. Soon after their arrival, Josephine received a letter informing her that Paris had been occupied by the enemy and that Napoleon, unable to reach the capital, was at Fontainebleau, forty miles to the south. On learning that Joseph had agreed to the surrender of the city, he spoke of a new campaign; but when his generals told him that the situation was hopeless, he was forced to accept that his empire was lost. 'His spirits went up and down,' Constant reported. 'On one day he would be desperately gloomy, and the next whistling.' Most of the time, though, he 'appeared tired and lethargic'. 'I no longer know him,' Lazare Carnot, the military engineer, commented. 'He used to be so thin and silent. Now he is fat and garrulous. He is sleepy and his mind wanders. He the man of quick decisions, who resented offers of advice, now talks instead of acting and asks for men's opinions.'

He agreed to abdicate in favour of his son; but Talleyrand, who had contrived to have himself appointed President of the provisional government and who was working for the restoration of the Bourbons in the unwieldy shape of King Louis XVIII, the executed Louis XVI's brother, protested that Napoleon's proposal would necessarily entail a regency. So, on 11 April, he abdicated without this condition. He betrayed no emotion when obliged to do so, Caulaincourt said, and merely observed that Talleyrand was like a cat, always managing to land on his feet.

At the Tsar's suggestion, Napoleon was named sovereign of the island of Elba, a pleasant enough place with a temperate climate, most of the inhabitants of which spoke Italian. At the same time, it was agreed that the Emperor, and the various members of his family, were to be treated with financial liberality. It was also proposed later that on Elba, as well as court officials and household servants, the Emperor should have a little army comprising seven hundred men of the Old Guard, eight hundred Elban militiamen and thirty Polish cavalrymen.

'I would be braver and calmer if I were sharing your fate and consoling you for all your reverses,' Marie-Louise wrote to Napoleon. 'You really must send someone to tell me what to do ... No one loves you as much as your faithful Louise.' 'I have been thinking so much about you today,' she had written to him on their son's third birthday. 'Three years ago you gave me such moving proof of your love that tears come to my eyes whenever I recall it. So this is an especially precious day to me.'

She would like to see her father again first, she said, then go to her husband on Elba. But she did not manage to do so; a troop of cavalry, sent by Napoleon to fetch her from Blois, found that she had already left. 'They have made me leave,' she explained. 'Orders have been given to prevent me from joining you and even to resort to force if necessary ... I am desperately worried about you.' 'I shall,' she added, 'take a firm line with my father. I shall tell him that I absolutely insist on joining you, and that I shall not let myself be talked into doing anything else ... I am truly miserable ... I should be perfectly content to die, but I want to live so as to try to bring you some consolation and to be of use to you.'

Her father, however, was implacable: 'He will not allow me to see you now or go with you to Elba ... He insisted I spend the next two months in Austria, then I must go to Parma' – of which she had been created Duchess by the Treaty of Fontainebleau.

She was taken to the palace at Compiègne where the Tsar and the King of Prussia, who had come to see her there, found her in tears. She was still determined to go to Elba when she could get away.

'You will know by now that orders have been given to prevent my joining you, and to use force if necessary,' Marie-Louise wrote when it seemed that she might not be able to get to Elba after all. 'Be on your guard, my darling. We are being duped. I am in the utmost anxiety about you.'

36

THE AUSTRIAN EQUERRY

'I am ready to bet that within six
months she'll be my mistress.'

DESPAIRING OF THE FUTURE, Napoleon now, according to Caulaincourt, decided to poison himself. Having written to Marie-Louise assuring her of his love for her in a letter which he placed under his pillow,
he opened his dressing-case, removed a vial which he had taken to
wearing on a ribbon around his neck, emptied the contents of bella-
donna, opium and white hellebore into a glass of water, swallowed the
mixture, sent for Caulaincourt and got into bed.

'Come and sit down,' he said. 'They are going to take the Empress
and my son away from me ... Give me your hand. I hope you'll be
happy, my dear Caulaincourt. You deserve it.'

The effects of the poison began to take effect: he became icy cold
then hot; his limbs became rigid; his stomach heaved; he gritted his
teeth trying vainly not to be sick. 'The Emperor suffered atrociously,'
Caulaincourt said. 'I cannot begin to express the great pain this scene
caused me. "How difficult it is to die," Napoleon cried out. "Tell
Josephine I have been thinking of her. Give me your hand. Kiss me."
He pulled me down towards him, breathing heavily. I choked and could
not hide my tears.'

He begged Caulaincourt to help him die; he was in dreadful pain
and thirsty beyond measure. But early in the morning he began to
recover, the poison evidently having lost its potency; and by the afternoon of the following day he was able to read a letter from Marie-Louise:

Please, darling, don't be angry with me [for going to Rambouillet].
I really couldn't help it. I love you so much that it breaks my
heart in two. I am so afraid that you might think it a plot which
my father and I have made against you ... I really long to share
your misfortunes. I long to look after you and comfort you, be
of some use to you ... Your son is the only one happy here ...
You and he alone make life worth living.

Her father had been 'most kind and affectionate' but it was 'all contradicted by the most dreadful blow he could possibly have dealt me. He
forbids me to join you or see you, or to accompany you on your journey.
It was no good my telling him that it was my duty to follow you. He
said he would not allow it.'

This letter to Napoleon was soon followed by one written by Metternich and signed by her father: 'I have decided to propose to [Marie-
Louise] that she should come to Vienna for a few months' rest with
her family.' Marie-Louise's wish to share Napoleon's exile was beyond
her father's comprehension. 'Personally,' so he declared, he could 'not
stomach the creature': he was such a 'fearful snob'.

Slowly, Marie-Louise's feelings for Napoleon began to change and she
became increasingly reluctant to share his exile. There were in her
household both men and women who were anxious to dissuade her
from trying to join him on Elba, who warned her of what they suggested
to be the unhealthiness of the island's climate, who hinted that he had
married her for purely selfish and dynastic reasons, and that, while she
was a most faithful and dutiful wife, the Emperor was not likely to be
a faithful husband: it was known that both Mlle George and Mme
Walewska had been to see him at Fontainebleau and had offered to
share his exile with him. Besides, there was her son to think about. In
the negotiations which were to lead to the Treaty of Fontainebleau being
signed on 11 April 1814 and to Napoleon's 'renunciation of the thrones
of France and Italy for himself and his heirs', it was proposed that
Marie-Louise and her son be awarded the duchies of Piacenza and
Guastalla as well as Parma; and she must not endanger the boy's in-
heritance. There was yet a further matter to consider: her marriage to
Napoleon was deemed by the Vatican to be invalid on the grounds that
his former marriage to the Empress Josephine had been annulled not

on the authority of the Holy See as required by canonical law, but merely by the Archbishop of Paris. She was, accordingly, in the eyes of the Church, Napoleon's mistress rather than his wife and their son was, therefore, illegitimate. This thought weighed heavily on her conscience.

So the hope that his wife and son would accompany him into exile was finally dashed; and on 29 April he bade farewell to the soldiers of the Old Guard before sailing for Elba in the British frigate *Undaunted*. It was a moving ceremony. 'Goodbye, my children,' he was reported as having said. 'I have sacrificed all my rights and am ready to sacrifice my life, for my one aim has been the happiness and glory of France . . . I have chosen to go on living so that I can write about the great things we have done together and tell posterity of our great deeds . . . I should like to press you to my heart. But at least I shall kiss your flag.' As he did so, the soldiers wept. Tears came also to the eyes of the British, Prussian and Austrian commissioners. Only the Russian commissioner appeared unmoved. Napoleon lifted his hand in a gesture of farewell. 'Adieu,' he said. 'Keep your memory of me in your hearts.'

Some two months after the signing of the Treaty of Fontainebleau, an officer, dispatched by the Austrian Emperor to act as an equerry, introduced himself to the Emperor's daughter who had by then, having returned to Austria, set out to take the waters at Aix. This new equerry was Adam Adalbert, Graf von Neipperg, a general in the Austrian army who had served as his country's ambassador in Stockholm. Thirty-nine years old, he was a man of great charm and cultivated tastes whose features were rendered romantically mysterious by the black cloth he wore to conceal a wound which had cost him the sight of an eye. Having obtained a divorce from his wife, and having recently married his mistress, he was, as Mme de Staël observed, notoriously attractive to women. With the approval of Metternich, he had been chosen for his task as Marie-Louise's equerry by the Austrian Emperor who had asked Prince Schwarzenberg to recommend a personable man who could be trusted to provide reliable reports upon his daughter's movements and intentions and give her suitable advice. He was to ensure that she not only never reached Elba but also that she was persuaded, in Baron de Méneval's words, to 'forget France and consequently the Emperor'.

If she succumbed to Neipperg's charms, so much the better. His instructions from Metternich made this quite clear:

> Graf von Neipperg must dissuade the Duchess of Colorno [Marie-Louise's incognito] with all possible tact and delicacy from any idea of going to Elba, a journey which would deeply pain her father's heart. His Majesty harbours the tenderest wishes for his beloved daughter's happiness. Graf von Neipperg must not fail, therefore, in dissuading her from doing so, by any means whatsoever.

At first Marie-Louise did not take to him. She did not care for the way he looked sidelong when he spoke to her, turning his face away as though to divert attention from the black cloth over the socket of his eye. But, as the English demagogue, John Wilkes, remarked of his own deformity, it took only half an hour to talk his face away; and it was not long before Neipperg had captivated Marie-Louise by his insinuating charm of manner. According to his grandson, before embarking on his mission, he had remarked, 'I am ready to bet that within six months she'll be my mistress.'

Marie-Louise trusted him, and was evidently persuaded to believe that her husband's insistence that she should join him on Elba was dictated less by his desire to have her company there than by the damage her not doing so was having upon his reputation in the world. She was also led to the view that Napoleon's notorious affairs with other women, his 'levity' in such matters, his '*inconséquence*', were intolerable. When she received a peremptory order from her husband to set out immediately for Genoa and from there proceed in the brig *Inconstant* to Elba, she described the tone of the letter and its contents as 'thoughtless'.

Neipperg undertook his mission with characteristic tact, accompanying Marie-Louise on her walks, sitting with her in the evenings, playing the piano with skill and sensitivity as she worked on tapestries for the chairs in her husband's study or wrote him letters.

Few of these letters reached him, however; and one that was intercepted was sent on to Vienna where the authorities required Marie-Louise to give a strict undertaking that she would not sail to Elba without her father's consent. She was also required to return to Vienna by the beginning of October: her presence there was essential, she was told, if she were to be granted full sovereignty of the duchies of Parma and Piacenza as had been proposed.

Before returning to Vienna, however, she decided to spend the month of September travelling in Switzerland with the attractive, amusing and obliging General Neipperg acting as courier. She found his company increasingly appealing, his conversation instructive, his knowledge remarkable, his taste for music so agreeable and so comforting in comparison to the tone-deafness of her husband whose habit of singing and humming tunelessly to himself was on occasions so exasperating. Before the month was out, Marie-Louise had fallen in love with Neipperg and, on the 24th of the month, so it appears, a storm having forced them to take shelter for the night at an inn, *zur Goldenner Sonne*, she became his mistress.

Her tour of Switzerland at an end, Marie-Louise returned with Neipperg to Vienna, where she was installed in the Palace of Schönbrunn under the watchful eyes of her father and Metternich, as the future of Europe was discussed at the meetings of the Congress. With her lover attentive at her side, she spent her days contentedly listening to and playing music, painting and learning to speak Italian in preparation for her new role as Duchess of Parma. All thoughts of joining her husband in his exile long since abandoned, she dutifully handed over the letters she received from him unopened to her father.

Supremely content with her lover – who was rewarded for so successfully helping to estrange her from her husband by being appointed her *maréchal de cour* – Marie-Louise declared that she would never set foot again in France, that 'horrible country', for 'anything in the world'. She would rather enter a convent.

'I hope that we shall have a lasting peace now that the Emperor will no longer be able to disturb it,' she was to write to her father. 'I hope he will be treated with kindness and I beg you, dearest Papa, to ensure that this is so. It is the only request I feel I can make and it is the last time I shall concern myself with his fate. I owe him a debt of gratitude for the calm unconcern in which he allowed me to spend my days with him instead of making me unhappy.'

And to her friend, Victoria de Poutet, she was to write after Napoleon's death:

Although I never felt strong sentiments of any kind for him, I cannot forget that he is the father of my son, and far from treating me badly as most people suppose he did, he always showed the deepest regard for me, the only thing one can hope for in a political marriage, so I am very affected, and although I ought to be thankful that his miserable existence is over, I could have wished him many years of a contented life – provided it could have been spent far away from me.

Napoleon did not hold her behaviour against her. Towards the end of his life he made excuses for her, rebutting suggestions that she should have made more exertion on his behalf. 'I believe that Marie-Louise is just as much a state prisoner as I am myself . . . I have always had occasion to praise the conduct of my good Louise, and I believe it is totally out of her power to assist me. Moreover she is young and timorous.'

37

THE DEATH OF JOSEPHINE

'Never forget one who has never forgotten you
and never will.'

JOSEPHINE HAD STILL BEEN AT NAVARRE where she received a
letter from Napoleon written on 16 April: 'An enormous burden has
been removed. My fall has been great, but at least it is useful. When I
go into retreat, I shall take up a pen instead of a sword. The history of
my reign will prove to be most curious, for in the past I have been seen
only in profile, but I shall now reveal the whole ... I have heaped
benefits on thousands of ungrateful wretches; but what have they done
for me in return, at the end? They have betrayed me. Yes, all of them
except dear Eugène, so worthy of us ... Adieu, my dear Josephine.
Resign yourself as I am doing and never forget one who has never
forgotten you and never will ... I am in very poor health.'

'We are broken-hearted,' Josephine had written to Talleyrand. 'I
place my situation and that of my children in your hands ... I shall
follow your advice with confidence.'

Talleyrand had been sympathetic, having regard to the probability
that the goodwill of the former Empress might be useful to the returning
King, an obese figure crippled by gout, who arrived in Paris to a muted
welcome on 4 May 1814.

Meanwhile, Josephine and Hortense followed the advice of the Tsar
– whose troops now occupied the capital – and returned to Malmaison
where Alexander visited them every day. He was clearly much taken
with them both, offering Josephine a palace in St Petersburg, though
warning her that the cold climate might well not suit her, and persuading

Louis XVIII to create Hortense duchesse de Saint Leu, to increase her income and to confirm her in possession of her château.

The Tsar was far from the only visitor entertained by Josephine and her daughter at Malmaison. Grand Duke after Grand Duke came, so did the King of Prussia and Prince Frederick of Mecklenburg-Strelitz who had asked Josephine to marry him after her divorce, as well as King Maximilian I of Bavaria and Prince Leopold of Austria, all of whom were conducted around her greenhouses, her aviaries, her picture gallery and shown the black cygnets on the lake.

She did not, however, attempt to disguise her continuing love for her visitors' defeated enemy, Napoleon. She told her doctor that, had she still been Empress, she would have driven straight to him to share his fate; and, when Mme de Staël, with characteristic inquisitiveness, asked her, among many other impertinent questions, if she still loved him, she declined to answer her and walked away, later protesting that since she had loved him in his days of good fortune, how could she love him any the less now?

She had much changed of late: she had become painfully thin and lined, coughing convulsively, her voice hoarse, her skin discoloured. Wearing one of her numerous flimsy white muslin dresses, she went out driving with the Tsar and Hortense one cold day in the middle of May. She caught a cold and soon became feverish. The Tsar offered to send his personal physician to see her; but she refused the offer, unwilling to hurt the feelings of her own doctor who had not considered her condition at all serious. She herself also made light of her illness and on 24 May, ignoring Hortense's pleas that she should stay in her room, insisted on coming down as hostess to a dinner she was giving for the Tsar and the King of Prussia. Not only did she come down for the dinner, she later opened the dancing with the Tsar and then went for a walk with him in the garden. That night her fever increased; her doctor applied mustard plasters in an attempt to relieve her sore and congested throat. The next morning her condition worsened, and she was obliged to stay in bed: an autopsy was later to reveal symptoms of pneumonia and what was described as a 'gangrenous angina'. Two days later, she became delirious, and that night she was heard to murmur, 'Bonaparte . . . Elba . . . the King of Rome.' She died, as her children wept, on the morning of 29 May. Her son said that she passed away 'as gently and as sweetly to meet death as she had met life'.

'Why did they let my poor Josephine die?' Napoleon later asked his own doctor. 'Sire,' said Dr Corvisart, 'I believe she died of a broken heart.' The reply clearly pleased Napoleon. 'That *bonne* Josephine,' he said. 'She really loved me, didn't she?'

38

EXILE ON ELBA

'Welcome to my palace.'

NAPOLEON HAD LANDED at Portoferraio on the north coast of the island of Elba, where he had been welcomed by a large number of its thirteen thousand inhabitants of Tuscan, Spanish and Neapolitan descent, who greeted him with shouts of *'Evviva il Imperatore!'*

From the beginning, he showed himself determined to do all that he could to improve their poor lot, to give them due cause to be grateful to their master, whose flag, based on the emblem of the Medici, rulers of the island in the sixteenth century, with the addition of his own three golden bees, fluttered from the forts above Portoferraio. At the same time, he was also determined to work hard so that thoughts of his misfortune should, as far as possible, be dispelled. His valet, Louis Marchand, said that he 'rarely slept for more than six hours' and could be found very early in the morning 'with the labourers, masons and carpenters, listening to and laughing at their comments'.

He had mulberry trees planted to provide food for silk worms as well as olive trees and chestnuts to check erosion on the mountain slopes above the open-cast iron mines. He supervised the growing of vegetables and of wheat on the nearby small island of Pianosa on which he envisaged settling a hundred or so families from Elba. He set about establishing a body of refuse collectors to cleanse the rubbish-choked and fly-ridden streets of Portoferraio; and the establishment of a market for the bottled mineral water from the sparkling *acqua minerale* of a spring at Poggio. Colonel Neil Campbell, the British Commissioner on

Elba, said that he had never seen 'in any walk of life a man with so much activity and restless perseverance'. He even found time to record, in his meticulous way, the amount of lettuces and grapes eaten in his household.

He inspected the salt ponds and water supply, paid particular attention to the island's fortifications, went out with the men who fished for tunny and anchovy and tried his hand – not very successfully – at ploughing. He dug over the gardens of the Palazzina dei Mulini – the house he occupied overlooking the Tyrrhenian Sea near Portoferraio – and he worked in the grounds of the smaller Villa San Martino in the hills four miles to the south-west.

In these and other houses on the island, his large entourage occupied cramped quarters, made all the more so by the amount of furniture in them, much of it appropriated from Elisa's palace at Piombino and from a boat transporting the effects of Princess Pauline's husband from Turin. 'In this way,' Napoleon commented sardonically, 'it doesn't leave the family.'

As well as the officers of his little army of guardsmen and lancers, his entourage included no fewer than thirty-five men working in the stables, eight chefs, two valets, eight footmen, two ushers, a porter, two equerries, a butler, a doctor, a chemist, two secretaries, a military governor, a treasurer, four chamberlains and General Henri Bertrand, Duroc's successor as Grand Master of the Palace, as well as the British Commissioner. His valet, Louis Marchand, said that the ceremonial on the island was as it had been at the Tuileries, but, not surprisingly, 'on a lesser scale'.

From time to time, Napoleon spoke to his staff of Marie-Louise and of their son, both of whom, he still hoped, might even yet come to join him on the island. Rooms were prepared for their reception, the ceiling of one of which he employed an artist to paint with an allegory of marital fidelity, two doves separated by clouds but attached to each other by ribbons, the knots of which were tightened as the birds flew apart.

He thought also, and often, of Josephine to whom he wrote asking her to write to him: he had never forgotten her, he said not for the first time, and never would. Nor had she been able to forget him. His rooms at Malmaison were kept just as he had left them, the clothes on a chair, the book he had been reading left open on a table.

On learning of Josephine's death, according to Louis Marchand, he had locked himself in his study for three days. 'I have not passed a day without loving you,' he wrote as though in a letter to her. 'I have not passed a night without clasping you in my arms ... No woman was ever loved with more devotion, passion and tenderness.'

He often spoke of her to Marchand, who wrote:

> She had the elegance of a Creole together with infinite grace and charm, and an evenness of temper that never failed. All her clothes were elegant and once worn by her immediately set the fashion ... He conceded that she was extravagant and that on several occasions he had had to settle her debts, but these debts were frequently incurred through her generosity in giving presents and she exceeded everyone else by the grace of her manner as she gave them ... With her kind nature and sensitivity she would pity other people's misfortunes and weep with those who came to tell her of their troubles which, the Emperor said, often made her the prey of those who took advantage of her generosity.

Three weeks after Josephine's death, Napoleon was comforted by the arrival on the island of Marie Walewska.

Like Josephine, Countess Walewska had protested that she could never forget him. She had assured him so in a message inscribed in a locket which contained a lock of her fair hair: 'When you have ceased to love me, remember that I love you still.'

Her husband had died, and she had written to Napoleon asking him if she might now come to him, bringing their son with her. He replied that she could, but, concerned that Marie-Louise might hear of her visit, he told her that she must do so secretly. She arrived on 1 September accompanied by Alexandre, now four years old, her sister, Emilie Leczinska, and her brother, Colonel Theodor Leczinski. They were met in the harbour by the Grand Marshal, General Bertrand, who conducted them up the mountains on the west side of the island, at first in Napoleon's carriage and then on saddle horses, by way of steep and rocky paths, shadowed by pine trees, to a small isolated cottage on Monte Giove.

'Welcome to my palace,' Napoleon said, taking them into one of the cottage's four rooms. The next morning, with Alexandre sitting on his shoulders, and holding Marie's hand, he took them for a walk in the mountains. On their return, he played hide and seek with the boy and rolled about with him in the grass. 'I hear you don't mention my name in your prayers,' he said to him. The boy admitted he didn't say Napoleon; but he did remember to say '*Papa Empereur*'. Pleased by this, Napoleon said to the child's mother, 'He'll be a great social success, this boy: he's got wit.'

He was clearly much taken with him. He asked Marie if the boy might have dinner with them; but Mme Walewska replied that he was far too unruly. His father maintained that he was quite used to this: he himself had been unruly and stubborn at that age.

So the child was allowed to join the grown-ups at dinner and, while quite well-behaved at first, soon became as obstreperous as his mother had predicted. She scolded him and his father said, 'Aren't you afraid of being whipped? I think you should be. I was whipped only once; but I have never forgotten it.' He told the story of how this had happened, of the day when he and Pauline had been beaten for having mocked the crippled walk of their aged grandmother.

'Well, what do you think of that?' he asked the boy who had listened to the story with close attention.

'But,' Alexandre protested, 'I don't make fun of Mama.'

The reply pleased Napoleon who kissed the boy and said, 'That's a good answer.'

That night Marie's sister and her brother, Colonel Leczinski, sang Polish songs and danced the *krakoviak*, a lively complicated dance in which Napoleon was induced to take part but could not master the convoluted movements required. He joined in their laughter.

Marie Walewska offered to remain on the island 'in a small house somewhere'. But Napoleon was unwilling to allow it, for fear lest her continued presence on the island became known not only to Marie-Louise but also to its inhabitants who, so he said, would strongly disapprove of it. So, after two nights in the cottage on Monte Giove, Marie was spirited away from the island on a brig.

39

MADAME MÈRE

'The Emperor is always thinking of ways to make
my stay at Porto-Ferrajo an enjoyable one.'

ANOTHER REASON for dismissing Mme Walewska was the presence
on the island of Napoleon's mother who had by now arrived from
Leghorn in the British brig, the *Grasshopper*, under the name of Mme
du Pont.

The announcement of the official title bestowed upon Mme Mère
had appeared in the *Moniteur* on 23 March 1805. It had also been decreed
at that time that Mme Mère should take precedence immediately after
the Emperor. Her state allowance had at the same time been increased
from a hundred and eighty thousand francs a year to three hundred
thousand, and had later been increased again, much to her satisfaction.
'Napoleon's mother cared for nothing but money,' Metternich had been
assured. 'Neither her turn of mind nor her tastes inclined her towards
social elevation. She had an immense income but without her son's
explicit instructions would have done nothing but invest it.' In obedience
to her son's wishes, her household was much enlarged. Its members
were now to include a grand chaplain and two chaplains-in-ordinary, a
grand chamberlain, the duc de Cossé Brissac (an ill-favoured hunchback
whom Madame Mère did not like), and an under-chamberlain, two
equerries, a physician-in-chief, assistant physicians and surgeons-in-
ordinary, two *dames d'honneur*, several ladies-in-waiting, including
Laure d'Abrantès, a lady reader and a private secretary.

Mme Mère had strongly protested against this pomp and extravagance. So had her old down-to-earth servant, Severia, who had

accompanied her mistress from Corsica and acted as an unofficial house-keeper, a reminder of far simpler days in Ajaccio.

Mme Mère had never entirely thrown off the manners of those days. Although most generously helped by Napoleon financially and, in her early days in France when she had been enabled by him to live in the Sallé château, the large country house near Antibes which he had rented for her, she had still behaved in a Corsican manner. After all as she, the most parsimonious of women, was so often to say in the future, who could tell how long the family's present good fortune would last?

Now, at the age of fifty-six, although more elegantly and expensively dressed than she had been in her homeland, she had not lost, and never entirely did lose, her Corsican accent and was inclined to use Italian rather than French words and to speak as little as possible in the company of people she did not know well. Nor could she ever bring herself to spend money in the way Napoleon urged her to do: her household had strongly complained of her bourgeois tastes and parsimony. They had also complained of the tedium of their lives.

Laure d'Abrantès, so much younger than most of them, wrote of the boredom she had had to endure and of the tiresome nature of several of the other ladies-in-waiting, in particular Madame de Fleurieu:

> I don't think I've ever known a person so devoid of grace as Madame de Fleurieu. She dances with so grave an air that one might suppose she was taking the collection in church, holding out her skirt with outstretched arm and looking like an espaliered fruit tree. She is always chattering away about nothing in particular, like tepid water from a dripping tap.

Another tiresome lady, often to be seen in Madame Mère's company, was Mme de Brissac, the fifty-two-year-old wife of her chamberlain, who was extremely deaf and concerned that, on being presented to Napoleon, she would be unable to hear what he might say to her. She was assured that the presentation was a mere, short formality and that the Emperor was in the habit of asking only two questions: where the lady being presented to him lived and, with characteristic lack of tact, how old she was. Unfortunately, when it came to her turn to be presented, having made the prescribed curtseys, she was not faced with the questions she had been led to expect; and when Napoleon, instead of asking how old she was, enquired how many children she had, she astonished the other ladies present by replying, 'Fifty-two.'

Mme Mère's household had been settled in Paris in the Hôtel de Brienne, a splendid mansion set back from the rue St Dominique in the faubourg St Germain which she had bought from her son Lucien for six hundred thousand francs. Her private apartments were on the first floor and here she had spent most of her time, appearing as infrequently as she could in the reception rooms on the ground floor to receive her guests, but going every day to her private chapel to hear Mass celebrated by one of her chaplains.

The Hôtel de Brienne was not Mme Mère's only property. In May 1805, her son had assigned to her the Grand Trianon at Versailles so that she could be near to her daughter, Pauline, who had been given the Petit Trianon; and in that same month Mme Mère had received a letter from the Emperor informing her of another gift, a fine seventeenth-century château between Provins and Troyes in the Aube which he had bought for two hundred thousand francs:

> Madame, I have purchased the Château du Pont for you. Send your Steward to see it and take possession of it. I am going to spend 60,000 francs on furnishing it. It is one of the finest country houses in France, much more beautiful than Brienne. I hope you will see this as fresh proof of my desire to please you. Your loving son, Napoleon.

His mother had thanked him gracefully for this generous present; but, with that ever alert concern to keep a close watch on her expenditure, she had wondered whether the sixty thousand francs would be enough to cover the cost of necessary repairs as well as furniture: eventually Napoleon had had to increase his grant by over one hundred thousand francs.

He had not begrudged the money. Indeed, he had told his mother more than once that she was too careful: she should spend more; she ought to spend a million a year. She would quite like to do so, she had said, provided he gave her two million. She was by then already receiving an allowance from the state of four hundred and eighty thousand francs a year, but she had solicited and received an extremely large increase.

'I'm richer than my children,' she had told the comte de Girardin.

'I have a million a year. I don't spend it all, though. I save more than half.' Always concerned to accumulate more and more capital while the good fortune of her family lasted, she is reported to have said more than once, '*pourvu que ça doure*' – 'if only it lasts'. 'Who knows,' she also said, 'whether or not all these kings Napoleon has created won't one day come to me begging for bread.'

Life at the Château du Pont had been quite as tedious, so Laure d'Abrantès found, as life in Paris at the Hôtel de Brienne. 'One got up at whatever time one wanted,' she wrote. 'Luncheon was at half past eleven for midday. Everyone who was staying at the Château congregated then. After luncheon, we settled down to embroidery; and very often Madame played cards ... Then we went up to our rooms or visited each other's rooms. Then we went down for dinner. In the summer, we drove out along the banks of the Seine or to the woods near Paraclet.' In the evenings, Madame had played game after game of *reversi*.

One evening, when Napoleon was of the company, he had gone over to Mme d'Abrantès and asked if she were happy acting as one of his mother's ladies-in-waiting. 'She's a good child,' Mme Mère had said. 'I'll try and see that she doesn't find life here too dull with me.' 'Yes,' the Emperor had replied, pinching Mme d'Abrantès's ear, 'and take special care that she doesn't fall asleep watching you play your endless games of *reversi*.'

Immediately after Napoleon's exile to Elba, Mme Mère had moved back into the Palazzo Falconieri in Rome with a severely attenuated household, including the faithful Severia, and here she had arranged for the sale of the Hôtel de Brienne for eight hundred thousand francs, while waiting for a reply to her letter asking permission to go to stay with her son on Elba. At the end of June 1814, she heard from General Bertrand that the Emperor would be delighted to see her on the island where accommodation was being prepared for her.

When she arrived, Napoleon was not to be found and when it was suggested that a message should be sent to the Grand Marshal for instructions, so Colonel Campbell recorded, she 'gave her assent with great violence, turning round quite pale and huffed'. When her son at last appeared, according to Marchand, he kissed her 'several times to comfort her because she was in tears, being so disappointed that he had not been on the quay to welcome her'. 'One would have to imagine an ardent young man who, after a cruel separation, finds himself in the presence of his beloved, to form an idea of the ineffable joy his mother's arrival aroused in the Emperor,' yet another onlooker said. 'He gave orders, contradicted them, said yes, then no, without knowing what he was doing.'

Napoleon took her to a spacious house, the Casa Vantini, near the Palazzina dei Mulini which had been prepared for her. She struck Marchand as 'still showing great beauty. She had kept her figure and appeared to be ten years less than her age.' Colonel Campbell agreed with Marchand. The 'fine old lady' was still 'very handsome', he thought. 'She is of middle size with a good figure and fresh colour.' Campbell described how he had been shown into her room before she sailed in the *Grasshopper* and how she had 'got up from her chair painfully'. 'I addressed her as 'Madame' and 'Altesse'. She was very pleasant and unaffected ... She spoke much of the Empress Marie-Louise, of her being at the baths of Aix, of her bad health and with many sighs and expressions of great regard, as if her separation from Napoleon was not voluntary on her part ... Captain Battersby and I dined on deck with Madame. She had been given a sofa from which she did not move the whole voyage, except once to see the house which had been pointed out to her as Napoleon's. Then she mounted upon the top of a gun with great alacrity.'

She was accompanied by her chamberlain, two ladies and her household staff, including two maids, her cook, four other servants and Severia who came to see Napoleon one day and spoke to him in Italian. 'Well, Severia,' he said to her in that bantering way of his, 'are you still as miserly as ever?' 'It's not miserliness,' she protested, as her mistress might well have done. 'It's prudence.'

Mme Mère was by now a very rich woman, having by careful and astute management of the large income which her son allowed her, accumulated a most handsome fortune with investments not only in France and Corsica but also in Spain and Italy, and even in England, the value of which – indeed the existence of many – remained a secret from the rest of her family. Having always taken care, following Cardinal Fesch's advice, to invest safely, and having always been so fearful, as she often said, that the family's good fortune might not last, she had also acquired a valuable collection of precious stones as well as landed property which would ensure that she would be able to live in comfort in an unforseeable future. She offered her son some of her jewels; but he declined to accept them, agreeing, however, that she should pay her own household expenses, as she herself had required of guests staying with her in the past, even her own son Louis, who had been told to do so when spending a few weeks in her house.

She went to the Palazzina dei Mulini for dinner every Sunday night and after the meal she sat down to play cards or chess with her son who cheated with her as he did with everyone else. One evening she accused him of this. 'Madame,' he replied, only too conscious of the fact that the Bourbon government was probably not going to pay the annual allowance which had been agreed for him. 'You are rich: you can afford to lose money. But I am poor and so must win.' Little did cheating profit him, however: his mother, as careful not to spend money unnecessarily as she was eager to acquire it, did not settle her gambling debts.

She clearly felt quite at home on Elba. Napoleon had taken care to make the house where she was living, the Casa Vantini, as comfortable as possible, having a large terrace built over the sea. 'The Emperor,' she wrote, 'is always thinking of ways to make my stay at Porto-Ferrajo an enjoyable one.' She did, indeed, seem to enjoy it. She held receptions in her drawing room; on fine days she went for rides across the island in an open carriage; she felt at ease speaking Italian to the islanders; she had Severia with her to attend to her wants in the old way.

Madame Mère was so contented, indeed, that she brought herself to contribute large sums to Napoleon's expenses when the handsome subsidy granted to him by the Treaty of Fontainebleau did not, in fact, materialize, despite Colonel Campbell's advice 'that if Napoleon receives the sums stipulated by the treaties he will remain perfectly contented [on Elba], barring any unforseen events in Italy or France'. Mme Mère even offered him her diamonds which one of her ladies was sent to Rome to collect. Her contentment was enhanced when her son's favourite sister, Pauline, came to join her on the island.

40

PAULINE BORGHESE

'He lived in a state of undisguised concubinage
with two of his sisters.'

NOT LONG AFTER HER RETURN to Paris from Saint-Domingue, Pauline had accepted an offer of marriage from a man whose birth and riches were a compensation for his rather nondescript character. This was a member of one of Rome's most ancient and respected families, Prince Camillo Borghese. He was twenty-eight years old in August 1803 at the time of his marriage to Pauline who was still no more than twenty-two. Her brother Napoleon urged her not to marry so soon after the death of her first husband; but the lure of the Prince's name and rank, his marvellous collection of diamonds, some of which she wore ostentatiously for a surprise visit to Josephine at St Cloud, and the prospect of living in Rome at the magnificent Palazzo Borghese all overcame her own reluctance to marry a man of supposed homosexual tendencies and transvestite tastes.

Yet, from the beginning, tempted as she had been by her husband's name and possessions, she was far from satisfied by his person. When wished a happy honeymoon, she expostulated, 'What, a honeymoon, with that idiot?' He was 'such a eunuch' she later complained: she wished she had remained a widow, even though that would have meant contriving to live on twenty thousand francs a year. On meeting him in later life, Fürst von Metternich's mistress, Princess de Lieven, while acknowledging that his palazzo was 'beautiful and decorated with taste', found that he himself could 'scarcely breathe for fat, diamonds and stupidity'.

'I shall never forget,' wrote the Countess Potocka, 'how, when the conversation took a slightly serious turn for a few, very brief moments, Borghese went off to look for chairs, arranged them two by two right in the middle of the drawing room, and amused himself by humming a tune as he danced about with these dumb partners, practising his steps. He was mad on dancing.'

Not only did Pauline find her husband exasperating as a companion and useless as a lover, she felt bored to distraction in the company of those members of the Roman aristocracy in which he moved. Within months of her arrival there, she decided that she could not bear to spend the rest of her life in Rome. Before returning to Paris, she went to stay for a time in Florence, maintaining that the Roman climate and air did not suit her; and it was in Florence that she sought out the sculptor, Antonio Canova, whom she commissioned to create the statue of her which, now in the Borghese Gallery, portrays her as Venus Victrix reclining on a couch with an apple in her hand. This pose and the nakedness of her breasts were her own idea and embarrassed the sculptor who had not wanted to reveal so much of his distinguished model. When she was asked how she could have brought herself to pose almost in the nude, she replied characteristically that it had not worried her at all: there was a stove in the studio.

Her husband was much displeased when he saw the statue and had it locked up in the attic of the Borghese Palace. Her brother was angry, too, when he was given reports of the scandalous behaviour with other men of this, his favourite sister; and he let it be known that she would no longer be received at the Tuileries without the Prince.

Napoleon had had further cause to be cross with Pauline at his coronation when she and her sisters, 'all sparkling with innumerable precious stones', had made it so obvious that they resented having to carry Josephine's train. 'When the moment came for [the newly crowned Empress] to proceed to the altar from her throne,' the comtesse de Rémusat had recorded, 'there was a sharp exchange with her sisters-in-law who were carrying her train so reluctantly that I thought [she] would be brought to a complete halt.' The Emperor had turned to them angrily and had told them to behave themselves. Pauline took no notice.

As beautiful as ever with a seemingly ageless body – whose charms, so General Baron Thiébault said, she was not exactly ungenerous in displaying – she carried on in her extravagant, sybaritic way, giving regular balls at the Hôtel de Charost, receiving visitors in baths of milk to which she was carried by a black servant of massive proportions who rinsed the milk from her smooth skin from a hole in the ceiling above. When admonished for allowing the man such intimacies she replied, 'A negro is not a man.'

Living for pleasure, she seems to have taken in her stride the death of her eight-year-old son, Dermide Leclerc, after a period of passionate mourning during which she cut off locks of her hair to cast in the boy's coffin; and she was clearly delighted when her husband was appointed Governor of Piedmont and went off to Italy, leaving her to enjoy the pleasures offered her by her life in Paris and at the Petit Trianon at Versailles, that delightful little *pavillon* of honey-coloured stone which had been designed for Madame de Pompadour, King Louis XV's entertaining mistress. Napoleon ordered Pauline to join her husband in Turin; but she, pleading that she was too ill to go, simulated alarming fits and set off for a cure at Aix-les-Bains. Her brother, exasperated though he was, continued to indulge her, increasing her allowance and enabling her to add to her ever-growing collection of jewels. In return she persuaded one of her ladies-in-waiting, a reluctant, tubby little ingénue, Cristina Ghilini, to become his mistress, an office which she filled for a time with a *gaucherie* which amused both Napoleon and his sister.

In Prince Camillo's absence, Pauline's chamberlain, comte Auguste de Forbin, a portrait painter of slender talents but a handsome and most charming man of exceptional sexual vigour and intriguing physique, became her own favourite lover for two years. Known to have other lovers besides the comte, it was rumoured maliciously that one of these was her own brother, the Emperor, a rumour later spread abroad by King Louis XVIII's Minister of Police and by various publications in England. One characteristic example of these was *The Secret History of the Cabinet of Bonaparte* by Lewis Goldsmith, a journalist of Jewish-Portuguese extraction who proposed the establishment of a subscription for setting a price on Napoleon's head and who claimed that he had been offered two hundred thousand pounds by the Emperor to discontinue his attacks in such newspapers as *The Anti-Gallican Monitor* and *Anti-Corsican Chronicle*.

Napoleon has much immoral intercourse with women [Goldsmith wrote in his *Secret History*]. But he has shewn himself addicted to that vice with which Socrates is accused, perhaps falsely, with respect to Alcibiades. I should not wonder if he should, like his prototype, Nero, marry a boy ... he has been guilty of the most nefarious transgressions of decency; he lived in a state of undisguised concubinage with two of his sisters, Mesdames Murat and Borghese; the former made a public boast of it.

This was patently untrue; but it was certain that Pauline's sexual appetite remained voracious, and, exhausted by it at last, Forbin approached Napoleon asking to be sent abroad in some military capacity.

While Forbin was still living with Pauline in 1806 she was pleased to be told that her brother was to create her Princess and Duchess of Guastalla; but when she learned that Guastalla was an insignificant small town in the province of Reggio with a much-restored cathedral and few inhabitants, she wrote to Napoleon to complain that, while her sister Caroline had been made Grand Duchess of Berg and Cleves, all she had been given was a 'miserable village with a few beastly pigs'. She told him that if he didn't give her 'a proper state, a bit bigger than a pocket handkerchief and with subjects who don't have four feet and wiggly tails', she would scratch his eyes out. She needed such a state, she said, for herself and her husband. Why her husband? her brother asked. 'He's a fool.' No one knew that better than she did, she told him. But what had that to do with ruling a country? She accepted Guastalla, however, kept the title and sold the duchy for six million francs.

When Pauline had pleaded to be excused from the duty of carrying Josephine's train at her coronation, she was not pretending to be ill: she was suffering from salpingitis, a painful inflammation of the Fallopian tubes, which perhaps had been induced by the venereal disease from which she had suffered in earlier times and which induces in its victims urgent sexual desires. These her doctor had advised her to leave unsatisfied, advice she was disinclined to take; and, having rented a villa on the Riviera where she began to feel better in the warm and sunny air, she sent for her Italian music master, Felice Blangini, the prolific and versatile composer of some thirty operas as well as church music, vocal nocturnes and canzonets, who, soon after his arrival in Nice, was deeply embarrassed by the sight of the black servant, Paul, carrying his naked employer to her bath.

As the days passed, however, Blangini seems to have felt more at ease with Pauline. They spent hours together, singing songs of his own composition and setting her own indifferent, not to say infantile, verses to music. She grew so attached to him that she could not bear to have him out of her sight for long: when he did go out alone, she sent a servant to fetch him back if he remained abroad for more than two hours. When they drove out together along the Baie des Anges, he was in a constant state of alarm, afraid that his intimacy with her would be reported to Napoleon who might well take steps to punish him, as he had punished a previous lover, Achille de Septeuil, who not long before had been sent to fight against the English in Spain where he had been badly wounded.

Blangini had become even more apprehensive when his eccentric, indiscreet and demanding mistress insisted on his accompanying her to Turin, the future capital of an Italy united under the House of Savoy, where, on orders from her brother, she had been required to rejoin her husband who had been appointed Governor-General of what was then known as the Department-beyond-the-Alps. She had not remained long in Turin, however, claiming that the climate would be the end of her. Her brother Joseph had tried to help her. 'I have found Paulette in a deplorable state,' he had written to Napoleon after a visit to Turin. 'She has not eaten for eight days and cannot keep even the slightest bouillon down. The doctors say she ought to leave this humid climate and go to Aix.'

'I am sorry to learn your health is bad,' Napoleon had written unsympathetically to Pauline. 'I hope you are behaving yourself and that none of this is your own fault. Make yourself liked. Be more affable with everybody. Try to keep the Prince happy.' A fortnight later he had sent her another letter: 'You are merely suffering from the effects of spring weather. I see no objection to your going to the waters at Saint-Didier since that is nearby ... But you are not to leave the region without my permission.'

She had taken no notice. She left Piedmont for Aix-les-Bains and, after five weeks there, taking the waters of the spa's hot springs, she had gone back to Paris where she had become once more an endless source of gossip and surmise.

Helped financially by Napoleon, whose exasperation with his sister alternated with fond indulgence, she had moved back into the Hôtel de Charost from which she could be seen emerging, her dress ablaze with the jewels that she bought in such quantities, on her way to the Tuileries in a sedan chair carried by two sturdy footmen in green liveries. As a reward for her brother's having increased her allowance, she urged one of her ladies, the plump and pretty Mme de Mathis, to go to bed with him, telling her that one must never say no to the Emperor and, according to Laure d'Abrantès, adding, 'Were he to tell me that he desired me, I would forget that I was his sister and reply, "Your Majesty, I am yours to command."'

Shortly after her return to Paris, Pauline, now thirty years old, had taken a new lover, another soldier this time, Captain Armand-Jüles-Elisabeth de Canouville, five years younger than herself, aide-de-camp to Louis-Alexandre Berthier, prince de Wagram, the chief of staff of the Grande Armée. Canouville appeared to be devoted to her: it was said that to persuade her to have a rotten tooth extracted, he followed the example of the Bishop of London who, faced by the reluctance of Queen Elizabeth I, had one of his own pulled out in her presence to show that the operation was quite a simple one.

This relationship, like so many of its predecessors, had not, however, lasted long.

One day Canouville's horse had bolted on parade and crashed into Napoleon who noticed upon the impact that the aide-de-camp's uniform jacket was lined with a valuable fur which, part of a set presented by the Tsar to Napoleon, had been given by him to Pauline. Like Achille de Septeuil, Captain de Canouville had been sent to fight in Spain; but, unlike him, he returned unscathed, only to be sent back on three occasions and then to Russia and eventually to his death.

Pauline remained exceptionally good-looking and, indeed, having recovered from salpingitis, healthy – despite her hypochondriacal lamentations of recurring illnesses. In February 1812, during a ball at the Tuileries, she and Caroline and various ladies of the court had performed a mimed allegory in the palace theatre. The subject was France and Rome which had recently been annexed into the French Empire. The duchesse d'Abrantès was not much impressed by Caroline's looks and performance; whereas Pauline, playing the part of Rome, was 'like an angel descending from heaven on a sunbeam'.

She had soon found admirers to replace the dashing, energetic Canouville. One of these was Colonel Augustin Duchand, at thirty-two her own age, who had gone to Aix in 1812 to recover from wounds received at the siege of Valencia and who, after distinguishing himself at Leipzig, was created a Baron of the Empire. Also at Aix that year was the celebrated actor, François-Joseph Talma, who had fallen deeply in love with her, writing her passionate letters, protesting that she could not possibly conceive the depth of his love for her or the grave wounds which she had inflicted on his heart:

> Ah, tell me [one of his several scarcely coherent letters began] do you not recall those moments of passion and delirium into which you plunged me before [my departure from Aix for Switzerland]? Alas, I must one day renounce possessing you, if my destiny demands that I should never again find you as you were for me, then let providence allow me to die – dear one, never never in this world has anyone loved you or will love you more than I.

Flattered as she may well have been by such outpourings of the great man who had won the admiration and patronage of her brother Napoleon, she did not answer his letters. The man was 'rather fat and nearly fifty years old'; she preferred the ardent vigour of Colonel Duchand.

After his defeat at Leipzig in October 1813, Napoleon's route to the coast at Saint-Raphael had taken him through Bouillidou in Provence where Pauline had been living in a country house, brooding on the fall of the Bonapartes though comforted by the thought of the three hundred thousand francs which the terms of the peace had allowed her, and by the possession of a cabinet which Michelot had had made to contain the jewels which she had acquired by selling state bonds. Her brother had appeared at Pauline's door wearing an Austrian uniform lent to him by an officer of his escort so as to escape the attention of the menacing royalist crowds beside the road. Napoleon was not at his best. Brave as he was on the battlefield, he was intimidated when faced by hostile crowds. 'It was evident that he entertained great apprehension of attacks upon his life,' reported Colonel Neil Campbell who had not been favourably impressed by the appearance of the Emperor when he met him for the first time a few days before. He was 'rapidly pacing the length of his apartment like some wild animal in his cell. He was dressed in an old green uniform with gold epaulets, blue pantaloons and red top-boots, unshaven, uncombed with fallen particles of snuff scattered profusely on his upper lip and breast.' Now, on his journey to the coast, Campbell thought that he 'certainly exhibited more timidity than one would have expected from a man of his calibre'. He had insisted on sailing to Elba in a British ship, talking of the danger of capture by Algerian pirates and believing he would be safer in the hands of the Royal Navy than in those of French naval officers, many of whom shared a dislike and distrust of him. This, too, had surprised Campbell, as had his praise of the British people. '*Votre nation*,' he declared, '*est la plus grande de toutes*.' 'I esteem it more than any other. I have been your greatest enemy; but now I am so no longer. I have wished likewise to raise the French nation. But my plans have not succeeded. It is all destiny.'

Pauline had greeted her brother warmly at Bouillidou but had declined to embrace him until he had taken off the Austrian uniform and put on a French one instead. In tears she told him that as soon as she was well enough to travel again, she would join him on Elba. And so she did. 'We must not leave the Emperor alone,' she wrote to her mother. 'Now that he is so unhappy we must show our love for him.' Rumours that she and her brother enjoyed an incestuous relationship continued to be spread abroad; and she herself once remarked that it would be a good idea if they reigned together in Egypt. 'We would do as the Ptolemies did,' she said. 'I would divorce my husband and marry my brother.'

In her anxiety to be with Napoleon she had demonstrated a business-like decisiveness which astonished those who had known only her *prodigalité* and *libertinage* in the past. She had sold her house in Paris, the Hôtel Charost, 39 rue du Faubourg St Honoré (now known as the Hôtel Borghese), and its contents to the Duke of Wellington, the English Ambassador in Paris, for 861,500 francs, over twice what she had given for it in 1803. The Duke had referred to her as 'a heartless little devil'; but there was no doubt he was attracted by her, went to see her several times while the negotiations for the sale of the Hôtel Charost were in progress, called her by her Christian name, and was clearly much taken by the portrait of her hanging in his room.

Pauline's château at Neuilly had also been sold. So had some of her jewels, enabling her to give Napoleon three hundred thousand francs before his defeat at Leipzig; and on 1 November 1814, escorted by four officers sent to accompany her, she arrived at Portoferraio in the brig *Inconstant* – the one naval vessel allowed to Napoleon by the Treaty of Fontainebleau – to be greeted by salvos of gunfire from the port's batteries.

Her brother went out in a gig to welcome her, to bring her ashore and to take her to see their mother before escorting her to her own apartments which had been constructed for her on the first floor of the Palazzina dei Mulini. Marchand was distressed to relate that the Emperor, while supervising the arrangement of the furniture in these apartments, had inadvertently dipped his finger into a small dish in which aloes had been left burning. 'As an inkwell was handy, the Emperor plunged his finger into it, without complaining of the slightest pain.' Marchand was 'the more saddened by the accident' as it was he who had placed the burner there, and the Emperor had moved it to look at a marble statue of himself by Canova, a statue which displeased him, so he had told the sculptor, because of the athletic physique he had been given, 'as though it had been the arm that had won his battles and not the use of his head'.

Princess Pauline had brought two friends with her, Mme Colombani, the good-looking and good-natured wife of an Italian army major who was already serving on Elba, and Mme Bellini, the Spanish wife of a Polish major, an attractive woman renowned for the verve and grace of her fandango dancing. A third member of her entourage was Mlle Lebel, the charming daughter of Antoine Lebel, an army officer who was to enlist in King Louis XVIII's service in 1815.

With the help of these three lively young women, Princess Pauline initiated what Marchand described as 'a new way of life in Porto-Ferrajo. Parties, balls and concerts were given at her apartments; evening receptions were held at the Emperor's and at his mother's.' Pauline did her best to please him, wearing dresses which she knew he liked, taking care not to outshine the Elban ladies by refraining from wearing her diamonds, and curtseying to her brother as though they were still at the Tuileries.

Napoleon remained very fond of her; but he had to concede that she was not the easiest person to have in the house, alternating between moods of extreme – on occasions hectic – cheerfulness and of gloom and hypochondria. On her happy days she flirted with the officers of her brother's military household, organized masked balls, and staged plays in a makeshift theatre which had been constructed for her, acting in them herself in décolleté dresses which revealed much of her voluptuous body.

By now, however, Napoleon felt incapable of sharing her intermittent enthusiasms. Not long after Mme Walewska's departure, Colonel Campbell described him on 20 September as having fallen into 'a state of inactivity never known before'. 'He has of late,' Campbell continued, 'retired to his bedroom for repose during several hours of the day. If he takes exercise, it is in a carriage and not on horseback as before.'

Instead of the active pursuits of his earlier days on Elba, he now took to lying in salt-water baths, reading in a desultory manner while eating liquorice and biscuits dipped in Malaga wine, and wandering about his stables, patting the horses which he had brought over to the island with him, reminding himself of the adventures they had shared with him in the past, feeding lumps of sugar to one of his favourites, an Arab he had ridden at Wagram. He was also now given to outbursts of petty irritation: once when Pauline appeared in a black dress covered with pink flowers in an effort to please her brother, he told her that it was quite unsuitable and that she must go away and change it; and when he was presented with a modest bill of 62 francs and 30 centimes for sunblinds for the windows of her apartments, he wrote pettishly: 'As this bill was not authorized, the Princess must settle it herself.' He also relieved his boredom by tiresome practical jokes such as inserting a fish into Bertrand's pocket, then asking to borrow his handkerchief.

He was watched not only by Campbell but also by a succession of agents who were sent over from France for this purpose and who prepared a series of misleading reports which repeated such canards as that Napoleon was having an incestuous affair with his sister. What these agents did not report, however, was that Napoleon was planning to leave the island and return in triumph to France. Shortly before her death, Josephine had said to her friend, Georgette Ducrest, 'Sometimes

The Empress Marie-Louise, a portrait by François-Pascal-Simon, Baron Gérard.

OVERLEAF The entry of Napoleon and Marie-Louise into the Tuileries Gardens on the day of their wedding, 2 April 1810, by Etienne-Barthelemy Garnier.

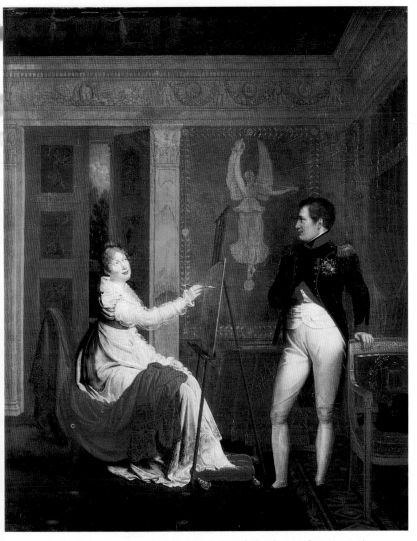

OPPOSITE ABOVE The marriage ceremony of Napoleon and Marie-Louise in the Salon Carré du Louvre by Georges Rouget.

OPPOSITE BELOW Napoleon and Marie-Louise disembarking at Antwerp during their travels in 1810, by Louis Philippe Crepin.

ABOVE Marie-Louise painting a portrait of Napoleon, by Alexandre Menjaud.

ABOVE Marie-Louise with her baby son, the King of Rome, in 1812,
by Joseph Franque.

OPPOSITE ABOVE Napoleon and the King of Rome 'swearing Eternal Enmity
to England'. A caricature by George Cruikshank.

OPPOSITE BELOW Napoleon, Marie-Louise and the King of Rome.
A painting by Alexandre Menjaud.

ABOVE Sir Hudson Lowe, Governor of St Helena, after the pastel by Abraham Wivell.

RIGHT Napoleon towards the end of his life, a portrait by James Sant.

Longwood Old House, a lithograph by W. Gauci. The verandah and front door are to the left; next to this is the room with shuttered windows which contained the billiard table.

I feel so sad I could die of despair. I cannot be reconciled to Bonaparte's fate.' Nor could Bonaparte himself.

One evening in February 1815, he was playing cards with Pauline and his mother when he abruptly stood up and went out into the garden where their mother, who had followed him outside, found him leaning against an olive tree. She asked him what was the matter. 'I am going to leave Elba,' he said; but she must not tell anyone, not even Pauline. She said nothing; so he leaned forward to kiss her and asked her what she thought of his going to Paris. 'Paris! *Per San Cristino!*' she exclaimed; and then, after a moment's pause, 'You're doing the right thing. Better to die sword in hand than in unworthy retirement like this.'

The following evening he said goodbye to her and to Pauline who, though she had more than once urged him to return to France, was now in tears. At the last moment, he seemed reluctant to leave them. At length, he said, 'I must go now or I shall never go.' He then drove down to the harbour in Pauline's pony carriage.

'The street was full of people wishing to say a last goodbye to the Emperor,' Louis Marchand wrote. 'All those who were going with him were allowed to kiss the ladies' hands ... Countess Bertrand [the wife of the Grand Marshal], impatient to get back to France, and not doubting the expedition's success for a moment, sailed a few days after the Emperor, in spite of Madame Mère's advice, and landed on the coast of Antibes.'

After Napoleon had driven down to the harbour, where the crew of the brig which was to take him back to France were singing the *Marseillaise*, Marchand found Madame Mère in tears. 'I am putting my son in your hands,' she said to him. 'Here,' pressing into his hands a small bonbon box with a portrait of herself on the lid, 'give him this in place of the one he now uses.'

Princess Pauline was again also in tears. 'She came up to me, holding a diamond necklace worth five hundred thousand francs,' Marchand wrote. 'She wanted to speak but sobs choked her voice ... At length she said, "Here, the Emperor sent me to hand you this necklace, as he may need it if he is in trouble. Take good care of him."

'"Your Highness, I am hopeful this is but au revoir."

'"This is not what I think." Some secret premonition seemed to tell her that she would never see the Emperor again.'

On 1 March the *Inconstant*, having in the night passed a ship taking Colonel Campbell back to Elba after a short visit to the mainland, sailed into Antibes and Napoleon's invasion force of scarcely more than a thousand men, forty horses and two cannon began to disembark. 'I am the sovereign of the island of Elba,' he announced, 'and I have come with six hundred men to attack the King of France and all his six hundred thousand soldiers. I shall conquer this kingdom.' He would, he promised with confidence, be in Paris three weeks later on the King of Rome's birthday.

On his way north at Lyon, he sent Marchand to see Mme Pellapra, 'a ravishing beauty' whom he had first met, and to whom he had made love, on his visit to Normandy in 1812. She was staying at Lyon with her family and Napoleon was anxious to talk to her about the attitude of the people of Lyon to his arrival there. 'He was unable to grant her an audience until a late hour,' Marchand said, 'because of all the bustle around him and the orders he was sending out in all directions.'

In Paris on 20 March, Napoleon was greeted by a cheering crowd at the Tuileries from which King Louis had hurriedly fled.

Hortense came to him there. So did the Countess Walewska, followed by two of his other mistresses, Mlle George and Adèle Duchâtel. He told Hortense that he was shortly going to visit Malmaison. She went with him and later described how he climbed the stairs and entered the room where Josephine had died. When he came down there were tears in his eyes. He seemed, Hortense thought, 'no longer to care for his former mistresses'.

He still, however, cared for his wife and their son; and, hoping even now that they might come to join him, he wrote to tell Marie-Louise to bring the King of Rome to Strasbourg where Hortense offered to meet them. His letter never reached Marie-Louise, who certainly would not have obeyed the instructions contained in it had it done so.

Upon hearing of Napoleon's escape from Elba, several members of her household had clapped their hands in delight while she burst into tears. She had written to her 'very dear father' to assure him that, relying upon his 'parental affection', she and her son would not 'seek any instructions other than' his.

41

QUEEN CAROLINE

'I should be quite happy to be utterly destitute
if that were the price to pay to spare him.'

HAVING RETURNED TO NAPLES after enduring the rigours and dangers of the Russian campaign, Joachim Murat, accompanied by his wife, had attended a service of thanksgiving in the cathedral of San Gennaro. Here, traditionally on the first Sunday in May, was held the ancient ceremony of the liquefaction of the dried blood of San Gennaro, the fourth-century martyr and Bishop of Benevento. Some years before, the exiled English politician, John Wilkes, had witnessed the miracle which had at first been delayed, much to the consternation of the congregation since the failure of the blood to liquefy was taken to be the presage of fearful calamities. As the officiating cardinal agitated the glass phial, in which the dried blood was contained, 'the people grew quite outrageous. The women shriek'd hideously, beat their breasts and tore their hair. The men seemed equally frantic. They began the most frightful yelling, and several were cutting themselves with knives.'

On this occasion, however, the blood liquefied obediently; and the King and Queen took their children to the cathedral to kiss the phial containing it.

The Queen had not been well of late. She had grown 'thin as a cuckoo', had lost her appetite and was often sick. She spent much of the day in bed, dictating letters when she felt up to it, while her ladies-in-waiting, dressed in yellow silk with white, plumed caps, sat by the window intent upon their embroidery.

In his apartments nearby, her husband rose early and, having plunged his head into a basin of cold water, offered his long, black locks of hair to the attention of his valet who twisted them round his fingers to keep the curls in place. Having walked for a few minutes up and down the terrace between the potted lemon trees, the King liked to go upstairs to play with his children before settling down to work. Indeed, according to the children's English nursemaid, Catherine Davies, 'his greatest delight was in the company of the children. He spent many hours playing with them and amusing them.' 'He was our friend, I would almost say our playmate,' wrote his daughter, Louise, in later life. 'We even went so far as to *tutoyer* him ... but only when we were alone together. Custom did not permit such familiarity in those days, as it does now. We would never have dared do such a thing in the presence of our mother.'

Caroline was strict with her children, as her own mother had been with hers; and their routine, Catherine Davies recalled, was conducted with the utmost regularity, supervised by one of the two assistant governesses under the direction of the head of the nursery, Mme de Roquemont. Early-morning school was followed by breakfast at eight o'clock; lessons were then continued until luncheon at eleven, and then from half past twelve to six. As well as the usual subjects, such as mathematics and geography, the children were taught German and English as well as French and Italian. They had piano and singing lessons, and were instructed in religion and scripture by the Archbishop. They were also taught the rules of whist so that they could play this game in the evening with their mother.

They all wore a kind of uniform: the girls white dresses with black taffeta pinafores, Achille a miniature version of the uniform of a colonel in the Lancers, Lucien that of a colonel in the royal bodyguard. They had their meals in their own dining room supervised by one of the governesses or a tutor who did not sit down with them. When, once a week or so, they dined with their parents, pages in livery of red and gold stood deferentially behind their chairs.

Their father seemed to delight in the opportunities for show, for *faire parade* which his royal status gave him. He would drive to the cathedral on Corpus Domini day in a carriage drawn by eight magnificently caparisoned horses in a splendid uniform and then walk back to his palace in another uniform equally magnificent. The *lazzaroni* delighted in imitating him, describing with their fingers the waving of his plumes and his gait on horseback. But, as with their former King, the Bourbon Ferdinand IV, who might well in different guise have passed for one of them, they admired his braggadocio and warmed to his genial, responsive nature. His queen, however, less approachable, more reserved, was regarded with a kind of respectful circumspection, and by many with active dislike. The artist, Mme Vigée-Le Brun, who was commissioned to paint her portrait, found her insupportable. For her first sitting she swept into the room accompanied by two maids to attend to her hair; and, for subsequent sittings, she presented herself with different styles of coiffeur so that constant repainting was required. Nor was this all: she frequently failed to appear at the time appointed for her sittings, so that the exasperated artist was heard to murmur, 'I have painted real princesses [she is believed to have painted Marie-Antoinette twenty-five times] who never caused me so much trouble nor ever kept me waiting.' 'The truth of the matter is,' she commented later, 'that Madame Murat was completely ignorant of the fact that punctuality is the politeness of kings as Louis XIV so truly said, and indeed he was no parvenu . . . It would be impossible for me to describe all the torments and annoyances which I had to endure while I was painting this portrait' of the Queen of Naples.

Queen Caroline's hauteur was remarked upon by others. So was the grandeur of her court which was presided over by a Grand Marshal of the Palace and a Master of Ceremonies and included numerous equerries, pages, chamberlains, twenty-eight ladies-in-waiting, twelve of them princesses, eleven duchesses, and several *dames d'annonce* in uniform dresses of yellow and white who were stationed at the entrance to all the rooms of state. 'Everything was conducted in an admirable manner and with perfect regularity,' Catherine Davies recorded. 'Moments passed without employment were irksome to the Queen. Nor did she allow others to spend time unoccupied.' Determined to demonstrate that she was perfectly capable of wearing the crown in her own right should her husband not survive her, and of governing the state quite as efficiently as Elisa governed hers, she assumed a dictatorial manner which was much resented – not least by her husband whose thoughts turned increasingly towards a united Italy while hers were drawn to a Naples subordinated to the interests of France.

Yet, resented as Queen Caroline's imperious manner was at the Neapolitan court, foreign visitors found her quite charming if inclined to talk to them *de haut en bas*. In the opinion of the writer, Thomas Baring, for example, the Queen was 'elegant in her person and in her manners'; indeed, she was 'fitter to be a queen than any woman in Europe', whereas her husband, Baring continued, was 'a stout middle-sized man, with strong black hair and whiskers, dark complexion and black eyes'. 'He is fond of parade,' Baring added, 'and generally dresses in a showy manner.'

Baring's fellow-Englishman, the poet Samuel Rogers, thought Queen Caroline was 'still beautiful, tho' *un peu maigre*, very graceful and wreathed with diamonds from head to foot'. 'She danced,' Rogers added, 'like a gentlewoman' whereas her husband 'danced like a dancing master, perfect in his steps and affecting an ease not natural to him.'

It was at a court ball such as this one attended by Samuel Rogers that news had arrived in Naples of Napoleon's escape from Elba.

According to Count Mier, the Austrian ambassador in Naples, Murat had been 'extremely agitated' by this news, 'not able to make up his mind what he wanted'. Caroline had also been deeply upset. She had felt sure her brother was 'heading for disaster'; and assured Mier that she would do everything she could to persuade her husband not to break with Austria. As the days passed, however, it had become clear that Murat was determined not to remain inactive while history was being made in the north; and, on 7 March 1815, in conversation with the Neapolitan General Angelo d'Ambrosio, he had expressed his determination to march north and fulfil his destiny by driving the Austrians back towards the Alps and uniting Italy in one kingdom with himself as their liberator and monarch.

Caroline had done all she could to dissuade him; but, ten days after his conversation with d'Ambrosio, he left her in tears as he set out for Ancona. Driving from there to Rimini he had issued a dramatic proclamation:

> The hour has come for the accomplishment of the great destinies of Italy. All Italians are summoned to belong to an independent nation . . . 80,000 Italians from the Kingdom of Naples will march north, commanded by their King, swearing they will not rest until

Italy is free ... I call upon you, brave, unhappy Italians to join
me in this fight.

The time for a united Italy had, however, not yet come. Murat's
army, having occupied Rome, Bologna and Florence was routed by the
Austrians at Tolentino on 2 May 1815 and the former Bourbon King
Ferdinand IV prepared to return to his capital under the protection of
the victorious army.

Queen Caroline had left Naples for Portici when her husband had
set out on his foolhardy mission; but she had since returned to act as
Regent and, in an effort to restore confidence, on 13 April she had shown
herself in the royal box at the San Carlo theatre, together with her
mother, who had arrived in Naples ten days before and her brother-in-
law, Jérôme, who had fled from Trieste disguised as a sailor. Soon after
her appearance at the theatre, the Duke of Bedford, who was in Naples
on his tour of Italy, had a long audience of the Queen, whom he
'liked very much', and was greatly impressed by her apparent calm, the
'firmness, moderation and propriety which [governed] her conduct in
the very critical situation in which she [was] placed'.

On learning of the disaster which had overtaken her husband at
Tolentino, she had persuaded the editor of the Neapolitan newspaper,
the *Monitore*, to publish the news of a great victory to allay the city's
fears. She had then made plans for her children to leave Naples for the
fortress of Gaeta and for her mother and brother and her uncle, Cardinal
Fesch, who had also arrived in Naples, to sail in a French ship back to
France.

While the children's nurse, Catherine Davies, was hastily packing
her trunk, the eleven-year-old, Lucien, came into the room, clothed as
usual in the uniform of the royal bodyguard. 'Are you afraid of the
enemy, Davies?' he asked, taking her hand. 'No, your Highness,' she
told him. 'And you need not be,' he said, 'so long as I have this sword
by my side.'

Caroline was also in uniform when, two days after the departure
of the others, she reviewed the few remaining loyal troops in the garden
of the villa Reale. In the city beyond its gates the fickle *lazzaroni* were
marching through the streets, threatening to march on the palace. The
Queen remained calm; so did her husband when he returned to Naples

on 18 May 1815, a fortnight after his defeat at Tolentino, declaring to his wife in his most grandiose manner, 'All is lost except honour. There is nothing left for me but death.'

Soon after making this announcement, he left Naples for Gaeta, intending, so it was supposed, to bid farewell to his children before making for France to offer his services to Napoleon. Caroline also prepared to leave for France aboard the *Tremendous*, a British ship placed at her disposal in accordance with an agreement signed with the captain, Robert Campbell, under the terms of which all Neapolitan warships and arsenals were to be handed over to him to be disposed of 'as the respective governments may hereafter decide'.

While she was waiting to sail aboard the *Tremendous*, the Bourbon Prince Leopold arrived in the city with the vanguard of the Austrian army to claim the throne in the name of his father, King Ferdinand IV. He was greeted with the utmost enthusiasm, flowers were showered on his head as he marched through the streets, while parties of people in boats were rowed around the *Tremendous*, jeering and shouting insults at their former Queen who now found herself a virtual prisoner aboard the ship, since Captain Campbell's agreement with her had been repudiated by Admiral Lord Exmouth, Officer-in-Command of the British Mediterranean fleet, on the advice of Lord Burghersh, British envoy extraordinary in Florence, who had arrived in Naples with the Austrian army.

Depressed by the delay of her departure, and feeling seasick in the swaying *Tremendous* as it lay at anchor in the Bay, Caroline sent a message to Lieutenant-General Count von Neipperg, who had commanded the advance guard of the Austrian army. He was neither helpful nor encouraging. He told her that in the eyes of the occupying power she was no longer Queen and, she would not be allowed to return to France without the permission of his government in Vienna. In the meantime, she would be taken to Trieste to await a decision as to her future.

On 25 May the *Tremendous* set sail for Gaeta where her children were taken aboard together with their two English nurses and two *valets de chambre*, all of whom had agreed to go with the family wherever they might be taken.

Upon their arrival at Trieste, Caroline presented Captain Campbell with a gold snuff box for his wife, in acknowledgement of the kindness he had shown her during the six-week voyage and his patience with the children who had amused themselves by jumping down on him from the rigging. He in turn ordered a twenty-one-gun salute in her honour and accompanied her to shore in his launch.

His offer to serve under Napoleon again having been spurned, Joachim Murat once more turned his thoughts to Italian liberation and to his own return to power as the ruler of a united kingdom. With this in view, he sailed to Corsica where he enlisted a pitiably small army of three hundred officers and men. He landed in Calabria in the bay of Santa Eufemia at the beginning of October, but was soon taken prisoner and summoned to appear before a court whose jurisdiction he declined to recognize. While the court was sitting he was brought a meal of bread and pigeon. The bread had been cut into small pieces and the bones had been removed from the pigeon. He was given a spoon but no knife. 'Even if I were not sure of dying already,' he said, 'this would be proof enough.' He was being denied the opportunity of suicide so that he could be sentenced to death and executed.

'My dear Caroline,' he wrote in a farewell letter to his wife, 'My last hour has come. In a few moments I shall have ceased to exist. You will no longer have a husband, and my children will have no father ... Goodbye, my Achille! Goodbye, my Letitia! Goodbye, my Lucien! Goodbye, my Louise! Show yourselves worthy of me in the world ... Remain united always. Show yourselves always superior to misfortune, and always think more of what you are than what you have been ... My greatest sorrow in the last moments of my life is to die far away from my children. Receive my tears and my kisses. Never forget your unhappy father. God bless you.'

He gave the letter to one of his captors, together with a lock of his curly, black hair and a watch which had a portrait of Caroline inside the case.

Soon afterwards, on 13 October 1815, he was brought before a firing squad. He declined the blindfold which was offered him and refused to sit down in the chair. He asked the soldiers not to shoot at his face, opening his shirt and pointing to his chest. He gave the order to fire himself. The roughly made coffin containing his body, riddled by bullets, was pushed into a common grave.

Murat, Napoleon eventually decided, had done him 'more mischief than any other person in the world'.

No longer Queen of Naples, now calling herself the contessa di Lipona, an anagram of Napoli, Caroline had accepted the Emperor Francis's invitation to come to Austria. She had arrived on 24 August 1815 at the Schloss Hainburg, near Vienna, where she had been told that she must consider herself and her children only as temporary visitors. Forbidden to live in France – an interdict which applied to the other members of her family – she had been obliged to remain at the Schloss Hainburg while anxiously awaiting news of her husband.

> I am extremely anxious as to what can have happened to him
> [she had written to her sister, Elisa], and I shan't be able to rest
> until I see him again ... I should be quite happy to be utterly
> destitute if that were the price to pay to spare him.

'The children are very anxious,' she had told him. 'We need to see you, to look after you. We talk about it all the time. All our thoughts are of you ... Write to me and do not forget the least detail ... Your ever loving Caroline.'

The news of her husband's execution was kept from her for as long as possible by her companion, General Francesco Macdonald; and when at last she was shown a newspaper which contained a report of it, she burst into tears and cried intermittently all night long.

Her future seemed bleak. At thirty-three, she was still a very good-looking woman, graceful and vivacious. But she had little money; she struggled to meet the demands of those who had real or pretended claims upon Murat's fortune; she was obliged to sell several of her favourite works of art, including two Corregios which Murat had acquired in Spain, to the Marquess of Londonderry. Her applications to repossess her properties in France were ineffective; her elder daughter, Letitia, was to leave her when she married the marchese Pepoli and went to live in Bologna; the younger daughter, Louise, was also to leave her when she married conte Giulio Rasponi.

Unable to return to France, Caroline went to live in Trieste in a villa on the Campo Marzio. She arrived in Trieste in June, bringing with her several pieces of furniture and jewellery, a few pictures and other works of art, but very little money.

A lonely woman, she received rare visits from people she had known in the past. Mme Récamier came and so did Countess Potocka, who thought that she 'needed to be loved by everyone who came near her'. Anna Potocka who, like everyone else, had heard rumours that Caroline was secretly married to the faithful General Macdonald, detected nothing in his deferential manner towards her to indicate that this was so. It was he, rather than Caroline, who took Countess Potocka into a large room in the villa which was devoted to family memorabilia and to the memory of Joachim Murat, an enormous equestrian portrait of whom almost entirely covered one wall.

To Countess Potocka, Caroline spoke fondly and admiringly of her brother Napoleon, and disdainfully of Marie-Louise, whose Austrian accent she mimicked derisively.

Soon after her arrival in Trieste, a decree issued from Paris deprived all members of the Bonaparte family of their possessions and rights, and forbade them to move from one habitation to another without permission. Caroline had recently entered into negotiations for the renting of a castle at Hainburg; but this was considered too near Vienna and Metternich suggested she might move to Prague. She declined to do so and was able to offer a temporary home to her brother Jérôme and his wife, Catherine, while they were themselves looking for somewhere to live. Eventually, Jérôme and Catherine, no longer King and Queen of Westphalia but now known as Prince and Princess de Montfort, settled near Frohsdorf, while Caroline also found a suitable property, a mere two post-stages distant.

Such propinquity did not suit any of them; and after a time visits between the two families ceased. 'We have good reason to believe that Caroline is well disposed to this situation, because she did not come to see him when Jérôme was ill,' Catherine wrote to her sister-in-law, Elisa, 'and when I was ill myself twice recently, she did not even bother to send to ask how I was ... Of course Caroline is not her own mistress to behave as she would like since she is dominated and overruled' by the unnamed General Macdonald.

Despite the presence in her life of Francesco Macdonald, Caroline was not happy at Frohsdorf. Constantly worried about money and often ill, she found it a 'very sad place', she told Louis-Frédéric Bourgeois de Mercey, who had once been her secretary and now acted as her business adviser in Paris. 'Everything is getting me down ... You know how much the General would like to help me, but he doesn't understand this kind of thing.' She felt the need of a female companion: would Mercey find her one, healthy, able to accompany her out walking and not too young. If she were young 'there would be love affairs and intrigues', and she needed peace. 'I feel,' she added, 'that I am getting old and my responsibilities are becoming too much for me to bear.'

She wanted a change of air, she said, and sought unsuccessfully for permission to go to Rome to see her mother. Still desperately in need of money and owing Jérôme tens of thousands of francs, she hoped, vainly, that her mother would come to her help. She felt obliged to sell some of her pictures to finance her son Achille's journey to America where her brother, Joseph, was now living in grand style as the comte de Survilliers at Point Breeze on the banks of the Delaware. When at last Achille received leave to go to America, on condition that he did not return to Europe without permission, Caroline was miserable to see him go, but she conceded that it was probably best that he should start a new life and, after all, she still had Achille's brother Lucien, the 'living portrait of his father', to comfort her.

42

DEFEAT AND EXILE

'Others may suppose his career finished,
but I am sure he does not.'

AT ABOUT EIGHT O'CLOCK on the morning of 18 June 1815, the day
of his final defeat at Waterloo, Napoleon ordered breakfast to be served
to him in the farmhouse where he had spent the night. He had been
up since dawn; but not until he had finished his meal did he trouble
to talk to the generals who came to his makeshift headquarters for
advice, and even then he was dismissive of their concerns, displaying a
confidence which they could not share.

'The people are running to me in droves,' he had told Marie-Louise
not long before. 'Entire regiments are quitting and joining me. Come
and rejoin me with my son. I hope to embrace you before the month
is out.'

'We have ninety chances in our favour,' he now told one of his
generals, determined to dispel their anxious, cautious mood, 'and not
ten against us.' 'Because you have been beaten by Wellington, you think
him a great general,' he said to Marshal Soult, his Chief of Staff. 'I tell
you, Wellington is a bad general, the English are bad troops, and this
affair is a mere picnic.' Soult replied, 'I sincerely hope so.' His own
opinion was that English infantry '*en duel c'est le diable*'.

To another officer, who suggested that British infantry could not
be defeated by a frontal attack, Napoleon made an irritable gesture of
dismissal. There was no need for complex manoeuvring, he insisted;
and when General Reille referred to the tenacity and steady aim of
English infantry, he turned his back on him and marched off. It was

absurd to have such a high regard for this Wellington, a Sepoy general after all: a frontal assault would settle the matter. 'If my orders are carried out,' he said, '*nous coucherons ce soir à Bruxelles*.' He had decided upon a frontal attack and that was that: what was the use of advocating a more subtle manoeuvre, one general said to another outside the farm-house, the Emperor would not listen. 'The Napoleon we knew,' another officer said, 'does not exist any more.'

Having ordered a shoulder of mutton for his dinner, he left the table upon which he had spread his maps, called for his horses and, riding in that clumsy way of his, sliding about in the saddle 'like a butcher', as a German had once observed, he set off to inspect the dispositions of the enemy. Two Belgians had been brought to him to give advice about the local terrain. One of them was so overawed by this responsibility that he was quite unable to speak. Sent away, he later explained his trepidation: 'If his face was the face of a clock, you would not dare even to look at it to tell the time.'

Napoleon did not complain; but there seems little doubt that he was ill and intermittently in great pain from piles, an ailment from which, according to his brother Jérôme, he had been suffering increas-ingly for two years. He may also, so it seems, have been undergoing an attack of cystitis, an inflammation of the bladder and urinary tract which, as had been the case with him at the battle of Borodino, made urination distressingly frequent as well as painful.

Certainly, throughout the subsequent battle, Napoleon appeared to his staff to be weary and withdrawn, occasionally impatient and irritable, quite without that incisiveness which had brought such impressive vic-tory at Austerlitz; and no longer given to those outbursts of temper, real or assumed, in which he would strike men who had offended him with his riding crop, swear at them furiously, even kick them in the testicles, and, as he once vented his rage on Marshal Berthier, seize them by the throat and hammer their heads against a wall.

A staff officer, Colonel August-Louis Pétiet, was shocked by the change in his appearance:

> During his stay on Elba, Napoleon's stoutness had increased rapidly. His head had become enlarged and more deeply set between his shoulders. His pot-belly was unusually pronounced for a man of forty-five. Furthermore it was noticeable during this

campaign that he remained on horseback much less than in the past. When he dismounted, either to study maps or else to send messages and receive reports, members of his staff would set before him a small deal table and a rough chair made of the same wood, and on this he would remain seated for long periods at a time . . .

His stoutness, his dull white complexion, his heavy walk [with his arms crossed or, more often, with the thumbs in the pockets of his slate-coloured greatcoat from which he would from time to time extract his watch or his snuff box] made him appear very different from the General Bonaparte I had seen at the start of my career during the campaign of 1800 in Italy, when he was so alarmingly thin that no soldier in his army could understand how, with so frail a body and looking as ill as he did, he could stand such fatigue.

Now he looked far older than his years; his breathing was laboured; he was obliged from time to time to lick the saliva from his lips. General Thiébault remarked upon his awkward gait, his hesitant gestures. 'Everything about him seemed twisted, shrivelled. The normal pallor of his skin had been replaced by a noticeably greenish tinge.'

Having reviewed his troops he rode to a small inn from which an armchair and a table were brought out for him and set upon rising ground beside the road. For a long time he sat there, his head in his hands, his elbows on his knees as though stupefied while his staff awaited his orders. Now and again he aroused himself, stood up, brought his telescope to his eye, peered through the glass from side to side, then slumped back in his chair.

At about three o'clock, so Jérôme said, he went back to the farmhouse where he had spent the night in order to put leeches on his piles. He then rode forward to see what he could through the dense gunsmoke of the battle in progress.

Up till now he had left the tactical handling of the battle largely to Marshal Ney whose infantry columns had been repulsed and scattered. Ney had then sent in his cavalry unsupported, only to see them broken after two hours of gruelling fighting. Napoleon, more alert now and taking control of the battle, then decided to throw into the conflict fourteen thousand men of his reserve; and, later, a further five battalions of the Guard were launched into a final assault. But by then it was too late: Napoleon had insisted that Wellington's allies, the Prussians, could not possibly join him for at least two days. But the Prussian commander, Gebhard Leberecht, Fürst Blücher von Wahlstatt, urging his hungry men forward through the rain-soaked countryside as their guns sank ankle-deep in the mud, and telling them repeatedly, 'I have promised Wellington. You must not have me break my word', succeeded in reaching the field of Waterloo in time.

That night, a young French infantry officer retreating down the road to Charleroi beyond the crossroads known as Quatre Bras, where the corpses of soldiers, stripped naked by Belgian peasants, lay thick upon the ground, came upon a wood where men who had survived the battle were throwing sticks upon a fire. Advancing towards it for warmth, he saw a figure, standing apart from the rest, silent, his arms crossed over his chest. Recognizing the Emperor, he turned away.

Napoleon had climbed into his campaign carriage at Genappe; but, before the horses could be harnessed, he had heard the shouts of enemy soldiers and had stepped down in haste to mount his horse and gallop off across the bridge. The soldiers then clambered over the carriage, finding numerous toilet articles, silver chamber pots, pistols, medals, a dinner service, an *éscritoire*, a uniform with two million francs sewn into the lining, and a folding camp bed.

Napoleon was now so tired that he had to be held on to his horse as he escaped to Charleroi, his pale face wet with tears.

He returned to the Elysée with his brother Joseph whom he had appointed president of the Regency Council during his absence with the army. Joseph handed him a large quantity of diamonds, which Marchand later learned 'amounted in value to eight hundred thousand francs'. 'They were each wrapped separately,' Marchand said. 'Giving them to me, the Emperor told me to lock them in the secret compartment of his travelling luggage . . . He also handed me two thick packages sealed with his crest, telling me to take one to Countess Walewska and the other to Madame Pellapra. Later, at his request, Mme Walewska came to see him at the Elysée, bringing her five-year-old son, Alexandre, with her. Also there was his thirteen-year-old son by Eléonore Denuelle, Charles Léon, and Louis-Napoleon, Hortense's son, the future Napoleon

III, then seven. The children played together while the crowds beneath the windows could be heard shouting, '*Vive l'Empereur!*'

A fortnight later, soon after midnight, Napoleon left the Elysée, having announced his abdication in favour of his son, the King of Rome, whom he proclaimed Napoleon II, *Empereur des Français*. He climbed into his carriage which stood waiting at the garden gate on the Champs-Élysées and made for Malmaison, sending a message to his mother and Hortense to join him there, although he was upset that Hortense had accepted favours from the Tsar and had remained in Paris with his enemies while he had been on Elba. 'I never would have thought that you would forsake my cause,' he said to her. 'If one shares in a family's success, one ought to share in its misfortunes.' 'You haven't a single excuse,' he added when she began to cry. 'But you know that I am a very good father. There, I forgive you; and we'll say no more about it.'

Soon after Napoleon's arrival at Malmaison, his valet, Marchand, joined him there, bringing various objects which he thought his master would like to have with him, including pictures of Marie-Louise and a superb silver washstand by Martin-Guillaume Biennais, into which the Emperor was in the habit of 'plunging his face after shaving'.

> That evening as he was going to bed [Marchand recalled], I told the Emperor of the state of ferment in which I had left the people of Paris, and about my visits to Mme Pellapra and Mme de Walewska. The latter proposed to come to Malmaison the next day with her son. Mme de Pellapra asked me to say how sorry she was about not daring to come without his instructions.

Mme de Pellapra accordingly received his instructions and she also went to Malmaison where, in Marchand's discreet words, she brought 'consolations of the heart which were much appreciated by the Emperor'. Also there was Adèle Dûchatel, the woman whose presence at St Cloud had caused such uproar when Josephine had demanded to be let into the room just as her husband and his mistress were about to make love.

The death of Josephine still deeply affected him. 'That poor Josephine,' he said. 'I cannot get used to being here without her. I keep expecting to see her appearing on a path, gathering the flowers she loved so much . . . We never had any quarrels except those about her debts

... She was the most graceful woman ever known,' he added later, 'a real woman, spirited and volatile and the kindest person in the world.' He spent hours at Malmaison, absently turning over the pages of the early volumes of Alexander von Humboldt's monumental book about the New World, *Voyage de Humboldt et Bonpland aux Régions Equinoxiales du nouveau Continent*. He was thinking of going to America himself to start a new life there. He seemed, so Hortense said, to be the only person at Malmaison to be quite indifferent to all that was going on about him, as though he were already living in another world.

While there was still time to do so, he settled down to dispose of his wealth, giving his brothers Joseph, Lucien and Jérome one million and fifty thousand francs between them; his stepdaughter Hortense, a million francs in shares; and entrusting his banker, Jacques Lafitte, with eight hundred thousand francs and another three million in gold.

Having now made up his mind to go to America, he asked the authorities in Paris – to which King Louis XVIII was shortly to return – to provide the necessary papers for him to proceed to the coast at Rochefort.

While he was waiting for these papers to reach him, the Prussian commander, Marshal Blücher, was at Compiègne writing a letter to his wife which suggested that Napoleon would be well advised to leave for the coast as soon as possible:

> Here I sit in a room where Marie-Louise celebrated her wedding night. Nothing could be more beautiful, more agreeable than Compiègne. The only sad thing is I have to leave here early tomorrow, as I must reach Paris in three days. It is highly likely that Bonaparte will be handed over to me and to Lord Wellington. I shall probably not be able to do better than to have him shot, which would be a service to mankind. In Paris everyone has deserted him and he is hated and scorned. I believe the whole affair will soon be ended, and I shall then hurry home. Farewell, the orderly wants to leave.

Two days after this letter was written, on 27 June, the necessary documents enabling Napoleon to reach the coast arrived at Malmaison; and, soon afterwards, Mme Mère, who had come there to wish him well, said goodbye to her son for the last time. François-Joseph Talma, then serving in the National Guard, was a witness to the scene and afterwards described Napoleon kissing his mother's hand before hurrying from the room. 'My life,' she said years later, 'came to an end with the downfall of the Emperor.'

Before stepping into the calèche which was to take him from Malmaison, never to return, Napoleon gave Hortense a diamond necklace worth two hundred thousand francs. 'How beautiful Malmaison is, isn't it, Hortense?' he said to her. 'It would be wonderful if I could stay here.' Mme Walewska asked if she might go with him into exile but he refused her offer. The door of the coach was closed and he was driven fast for the coast at Rochefort. Here he delayed several days while ships of the Royal Navy gathered to blockade the port. So it was decided that, instead of attempting to break out of Rochefort and cross the Atlantic, an appeal should be made to the Prince Regent for asylum in England:

> Your Royal Highness [Napoleon accordingly wrote on 13 July], Exposed to the factions which distract my country and to the enmity of the greatest powers of Europe, I have ended my political career and I come, like Themistocles, to throw myself on the hospitality of the English people. I put myself under the protection of their laws, which I claim from Your Royal Highness as the most powerful; the most constant and the most generous of my enemies.

'Upon my word!' the Regent exclaimed on receipt of this appeal. 'A very proper letter – much more so, I must say, than any I received from Louis XVIII.' But the Regent agreed with the government that there could be no question of Napoleon living in England. So the request was refused with the agreement of the other allied powers and England was made responsible for selecting his place of confinement.

When the Royal Navy's ship, the *Bellerophon*, in which Napoleon had been taken across the Channel to what he had hoped, and had been led to believe, might be asylum in England, people on holiday in Torbay crowded into boats to catch sight of Boney, the defeated ogre, whose image had been conjured up by nurses to frighten children into good behaviour.

From Torbay Napoleon was taken further along the coast to Plymouth where Lord Keith, Commander-in-Chief of the Channel Fleet, came aboard to inform 'General Bonaparte' that he was not to land in England but to sail into exile far away in the South Atlantic on the remote island of St Helena, a place well suited to this purpose, as the Prime Minister, Lord Liverpool, explained in a letter to the Foreign Secretary:

> We are all very decidedly of the opinion that it would not answer to confine him in this country. Very nice legal questions might arise on the subject, which would be particularly embarrassing. But, independent of these considerations, you know enough of the feelings of people in this country not to doubt he would become the object of curiosity immediately, and possibly of compassion, in the course of a few months: and the circumstances of his being here, or indeed anywhere in Europe, would contribute to keep up a certain degree of ferment in France ... St Helena is the place in the world best calculated for the confinement of such a person. There is a very fine Citadel there in which he might reside. The situation is particularly healthy. There is only one place in the circuit of the island where ships can anchor, and we have the power of excluding neutral ships altogether, if we should think it necessary. At such a distance and in such a place, all intrigue would be impossible; and, being withdrawn so far from the European world, he would very soon be forgotten.

Napoleon was, accordingly, transferred from the *Bellerophon* to the *Northumberland*, an ancient, uncomfortable ship in which the smell of fresh paint made him feel sick.

Lady Charlotte Fitzgerald, daughter of the Earl of Moira, described in a letter to General Sir Charles Hastings, how she had 'witnessed the whole business of Napoleon's transfer off the Devon coast from one ship to another!!!'

> Believe me, the most unwise step our government ever took was showing John Bull that Bonaparte had neither horns nor hoofs! One used to hear the epithets 'Monster', 'Rascal' or 'Roast him alive' tacked to his name, but that time is gone by, and he is now mentioned as 'Poor fellow, well do I pity him' or 'What an air of grandeur he has tho' he is so dejected.' Such are the remarks amongst the common people and in not one instance has a severe opinion been passed upon him ...
>
> During his stay at Plymouth the popular tide in his favour ran alarmingly high, and one evening the mob, won by his smiles, cheered him with enthusiasm; after that all visitors were enjoined to preserve silence and neither to rise up in their boats or to touch their hats when he came forward. How the appearance of

Napoleon could thus soften their hearts rather surprises me, as
his effect on mine was so different. I went to see him, admiring
him through all his crimes, compassionating him as a prisoner,
and one whom I thought had been harshly treated since he gave
himself up to the British clemency, but I came away with my
heart considerably steeled against him and with many fears lest
the lion should again escape from his cage! ... He was scrupu-
lously neat ... He is growing full though not quite fat ... He
has *pale* brown hair. He is bald at the back of his head ... He is
very dark but his complexion is so *clear* an olive that it gives the
effect of a fairer man ... His eyes are dark and round. He is not
handsome but he is not plain. He resembles no human being I
have ever seen ... He is *apart* from the rest of mankind ... I
never saw so *immovable* a countenance. There sits in it solemn
composure blended with stern determination. Not in the least of
a military air nor yet of a royal one, but *a something* greater than
either, more imposing, more extraordinary than any creature I
have ever seen ... I never saw a man look less hopeless ... Others
may suppose his career finished but I am sure he does not. He
appears most to resemble a bust of marble or bronze as *cold* and
as fixed. He seems quite inaccessible to human tenderness or
human distress – still he is wonderful ...

Napoleon was received on board the *Northumberland* only
as a lieutenant-general! He touched his hat to the sentry as he
passed the gangway. He desired Lord Keith to introduce the
officers of the *Northumberland* to him, and if he felt his situation
he concealed it ... During the removal of Napoleon the most
awful silence prevailed. You could have heard a pin drop in the
sea.

The captain of the *Bellerophon*, Frederick Maitland, a grandson
of the Earl of Lauderdale, also described Napoleon's appearance and
demeanour:

Bonaparte's dress was an olive-coloured great coat over a green
uniform, with scarlet cape and cuffs ... the uniform of the Chasseur à Cheval of the Imperial Guard ... He had on a small hat
with a tri-coloured cockade, plain gold-hilted sword, military
boots, white waistcoat and breeches. The following day he
appeared in shoes, with gold buckles, and silk stockings – the
dress he always wore while with me ... He had a fine ancle and
very small foot of which he seemed rather vain ... He came on
the quarterdeck, pulled off his hat and, addressing me in a firm

tone of voice, said, 'I have come to throw myself on the protection of your Prince and laws.'

His eyes were light grey, his teeth good; and when he smiled the expression of his countenance was highly pleasing; when under the influence of disappointment, however, it assumed a dark gloomy cast. His hair was of a very dark brown and, though a little thin on top, had not a grey hair amongst it. His complexion was a very uncommon one, being of a light sallow colour, differing from almost any other I ever met with. From his having become corpulent, he had lost much of his personal activity ... It is certain that his habits were very lethargic while he was on board the *Bellerophon*; for though he went to bed between eight and nine o'clock in the evening and did not rise until about the same hour in the morning, he frequently fell asleep on the sofa in the cabin in the course of the day.

Rear-Admiral Sir George Cockburn, who was instructed to convey 'General Bonaparte' to St Helena in the *Northumberland*, also described the prisoner's behaviour on board: 'On reaching the deck he said to me, "Here I am, Admiral, at your orders!"'

At dinner he ate heartily of almost every dish [Cockburn recorded]. He praised everything and seemed most perfectly contented and reconciled to his fate ... although his manner was not very polished ... He talked with me during dinner much on his Russian campaign ... He said nothing could have been more horrible than was that campaign. For several days together it appeared to him as if he was marching through a sea of fire owing to the constant succession of villages in flames in every direction as far as his eye could reach ... Many soldiers lost their lives by endeavouring to pillage in the midst of the flames. He spoke much of the cold during their disastrous retreat and stated that an entire half of his guard were frozen to death.

'He seemed to be as much at his ease as if he had belonged to the ship all his life.' That evening, and on several subsequent evenings, he 'proposed a round game at cards and played at vingt-et-un until about half past ten', regularly losing money. He also played chess, which he did 'but badly'.

He gets up late (between ten and eleven) [Cockburn continued]. He then has his breakfast of meat and wine in his bedroom and continues there in his *déshabillé* until he dresses for dinner, generally between three and four in the afternoon. He then comes out of his bed-cabin and either takes a short walk on deck or plays a game of chess until the dinner hour (which is at five o'clock). At dinner he generally eats and drinks a great deal and talks but little. He prefers meats of all kinds, highly dressed and never touches vegetables. After dinner he generally walks for about an hour and a half and it is generally during these walks that I usually have the most free and pleasant conversations with him. About eight he quits the deck and we then make up a game of cards for him, in which he seems to engage with considerable pleasure and interest until about ten, when he retires and, I believe, goes immediately to bed. Such a life of inactivity, with the quantity and description of the food, makes me fear he will not retain his health.

43

ST HELENA

'He seated himself on one of our chairs and,
after scanning our apartment with his eagle glance,
he complimented Mama on the pretty situation of The Briars.'

'IT'S NOT AN ATTRACTIVE PLACE,' Napoleon decided as he stood on the deck of the ancient, creaking *Northumberland* looking at the dark shape of the island of St Helena which was to be the place of his exile and, some five years later, of his death, at the age of fifty-one. He would have done better, he thought, 'to have remained in Egypt'. The black rocks, menacing with cannon, rose steeply to a gloomy sky, towering over the cramped and huddled buildings of Jamestown, the island's only settlement, which had been named after the Duke of York, later King James II, when the British East India Company appropriated the island in 1673 after the ejection of the Dutch. By the time of Napoleon's arrival, there were some seven hundred white inhabitants, a thousand or so soldiers, fourteen hundred slaves, several Chinese and four hundred and fifty 'free people of colour'.

Among those aboard the *Northumberland* and the ships of her escort when anchor was dropped in Jamestown Bay on the morning of 15 October 1815 were Rear-Admiral Sir George Cockburn, who had been appointed Governor of the island and Commander-in-Chief of the station and of the frigates which were on constant patrol off the coast; the small, reliable former naval officer, the comte de Las Cases, who, helped by his fifteen-year-old son, was to act as Napoleon's secretary and amanuensis; the impertinent and sulky General Gaspard Gourgaud, his jealous, quarrelsome aide-de-camp, whose petulant outbursts and vituperative comments on his colleagues in exile were tolerated by

Naploeon with extraordinary patience; the very small, loyal and decent General Henri Bertrand, who in happier days had been his Grand Marshal of the Court; and the thirty-two-year-old Charles Tristan de Montholon, a devious man with a largely invented past, who had been at school with Eugène de Beauharnais, had been Chamberlain to the Empress Josephine, and in 1814 had been accused of embezzling military funds. Both he and Bertrand were accompanied by their wives and the Bertrands by their good-looking children.

Fanny Bertrand was an imposing, smartly dressed, intelligent young woman with a patrician nose, royalist sympathies, a rather haughty air, and what the valet, Marchand, described as 'charming feet'. She was the granddaughter of the Irish peer, the eleventh Viscount Dillon, and daughter of General Arthur Richard Dillon, who was born in England in 1750 and, after serving in the French army, then as Governor of St Kitts and subsequently of Tobago, was chosen as deputy for Martinique in the National Assembly. Having fallen foul of the revolutionary authorities after his return to France, he was guillotined in 1794. Mme Bertrand's mother was Laure Girardon de Montgerald, a cousin of the Empress Josephine.

According to an English lady who became acquainted with her on St Helena, Fanny Bertrand was 'a most engaging, fascinating woman'. 'She spoke our language with perfect fluency, but with a slight French accent. Her figure was extremely tall and commanding; a slight elegant bend took from her height and added to her interesting appearance. Her eyes were black and sparkling, soft and animated; her deportment that of a young Queen, accustomed to *command* admiration.'

She had dreaded the idea of going with her husband into exile, having enjoyed life as she had done in France as the wife of the Grand Marshal of the Court, an ornament to imperial society. Indeed, on learning that the Emperor was to be sent to an island in the South Atlantic and that her beloved husband was to go with him, her passionate nature got the better of her and, after making a scene in Napoleon's cabin aboard the *Northumberland*, she attempted to throw herself into the sea. Her husband managed to grab her before she fell through the port-hole, and he struggled to pull her back, much to the amusement of her *bête noire*, General Jean-Marie-René Savary, who had sailed with the Emperor to Plymouth in the *Bellerophon* but had not been permitted to accompany him to St Helena. 'Let her go!' shouted Savary, laughing uncontrollably, 'Let her go!'

Not only General Savary had found her tiresome: Captain Maitland of the *Bellerophon* had had constant difficulties with her, until the 'little self-possession that still remained to him gave way', and, calling her a 'very foolish woman', he told her not to speak to him again.

Soon afterwards, however, she came up to him to apologize, held out her hand, and said that she was unwilling to leave his ship while there was this cloud between them, since 'God knows' if they would ever meet again. Maitland immediately succumbed to her capricious charm, deciding that, after all, she was a very good sort of woman, even though, perhaps, 'a little warm'. She was certainly a fond, considerate and affectionate wife and a kind mother to the children she was taking to St Helena with her. Her husband was devoted to her.

On the island she made the best of a way of life which she had been so reluctant to adopt and was to prove an effective peacemaker in many of the petty squabbles which were so frequently to erupt. Her good humour was never failing: when she had given birth on the island to her third child, she went to present it to the Emperor, telling him that little Arthur was the first French visitor to call upon him on the island without the permission of Lord Bathurst, His Britannic Majesty's Secretary for War and the Colonies.

Napoleon's relationship with her was not to be of the easiest, although it started well enough; she went for drives with him in his carriage and he often went to see her in the house, Hutt's Gate, which she and her husband occupied. When she came to dinner with him she was repeatedly late and was once rebuked so harshly and publicly that, as the valet, Marchand, heard from his colleague, Saint-Denis, a former Mameluke known as 'Ali', she was 'quite taken aback, and the handkerchief she used attested to the tears in her eyes'. The rebuke did not, however, premanently cure her of her unpunctuality; and on at least one occasion she compounded her offence by leaving the table early to go to see some English friends. It was to be rumoured that the Emperor was particularly annoyed with the woman because he had made advances to her and had been rebuffed. Thereafter, it was said, he referred to Mme Bertrand in the most derogatory terms, describing her as a 'whore who slept with all the English officers who passed her house ... the most degraded of women'. He went so far as to tell her husband that he should put her on the streets as a common prostitute. He said something as insulting to Mme Bertrand herself who once more left the room in tears. In a calmer mood towards the end of his life he said that he held it against her for not having become his mistress.

Napoleon's relationship with General de Montholon's wife was also to end unhappily.

Albine Hélène de Montholon was an amenable and cheerful woman, tall and graceful, three years older than her husband, gifted and attractive, determined, as Mme Bertrand was, to make the life of exile to which she was now destined as agreeable as possible. A member of a family ennobled by King Louis XVI, she had been married twice before, the second time to a Swiss financier, Baron Roger, whom she hurriedly divorced to marry de Montholon. She had a pleasant singing voice and played the piano with more than average competence. She had rather a coquettish manner; and it was not long before she was rumoured to be having an affair with a handsome young lieutenant in the Staff Corps, Basil Jackson, who was certainly often to be seen in her company and who was described by her as 'a nice young man but very simple-minded and unintelligent'. It was evident that the Emperor was strongly attracted to her. This enraged the jealous General Gourgaud who, so Napoleon said, 'every day wanted to bugger me against my will' and 'loved me as a lover his mistress ... He was impossible.' After listening to one of Gourgaud's diatribes against Mme de Montholon, Napoleon burst out in exasperation, 'And if I should sleep with her what is wrong with that?'

'Nothing, Sire. I do not imagine Your Majesty has such depraved tastes.'

Soon after their arrival on the island, so Gourgaud said, 'the Emperor wanted to know how all the people with him were settling in, so he left his room after dressing and went straight to the lodgings of Mme de Montholon which were separated from his own only by the small adjoining room. He knocked lightly and the Countess opened the door. She and the General expressed their embarrassment at being surprised in their disarray while moving in. "Sire," said the Countess, "this is both my drawing room and my bedroom." The Emperor thanked them both for being satisfied with so little in order to be near him.'

This proximity became a bone of contention for Mme de Montholon who had to endure the inconvenience of it while Mme Bertrand and her family had their own house just over a mile away. After a time, the two women were scarcely on speaking terms, Mme Bertrand referring to Albine de Montholon as 'that woman', and both of them dreading those evenings when they were required to play card games with Napoleon, whose brazen and habitual cheating exasperated them.

The Emperor's first uncomfortable rooms on St Helena were at Porteous House, Jamestown, a bug-ridden building facing directly on to the street without a garden or a courtyard, where Arthur Wellesley, the future Duke of Wellington, had stayed on his way back from India, ten years before. As the Emperor was escorted there a large, silent crowd of islanders, their black slaves and Chinese workmen gathered to catch a sight of him by the light of the bobbing lanterns. Among them was Betsy Balcombe, the pert and lively, hoydenish fourteen-year-old daughter of William Balcombe, an agent and purveyor of the East India Company, and – so it was improbably said of him, as it was of numerous others – an illegitimate son of the Prince Regent. 'The earliest idea I had of Napoleon,' Betsy wrote, 'was that of a huge ogre or giant, associated in my mind with everything that was bad and horrible.'

'It was nearly dark,' she wrote, 'when we arrived at the landing place and, shortly after, a boat from the *Northumberland* approached, and we saw a figure step from it on to the shore, which we were told was the Emperor, but it was far too dark to distinguish his features. He walked up the lines between the Admiral and General Bertrand and, enveloped as he was in his surcoat, I could see little but the occasional gleam of a diamond star which he wore on his heart.'

Upon leaving Porteous House, the Emperor was taken to Betsy's family's house, The Briars, while Longwood House, the house where he was to spend the rest of his exile, was prepared and enlarged for his reception. Looking down from a hillock at his party approaching her house on horseback, and hoping to identify a figure in a 'grey surtout and small cocked hat', Betsy Balcombe could not at first distinguish the Emperor amongst the riders. But on his nearer approach she was able to recognize his shorter figure beside the 'noble height and aristocratic bearing' of Sir George Cockburn. 'He was deadly pale, and I thought his features, though cold and immovable, and somewhat stern, were exceedingly beautiful. He seated himself on one of our cottage chairs and, after scanning our little apartment with his eagle glance, he complimented Mamma on the pretty situation of The Briars. When once he began to speak, his fascinating smile and kind manner removed every vestige of the fear with which I had hitherto regarded him.' 'I studied his face,' she continued. 'I have never seen a more remarkable one. Many portraits give quite a good likeness of Napoleon, but what none of them has been able to reproduce precisely is his smile and the expression of his eyes. That is what made him so charming.'

Betsy Balcombe's four-year-old brother, Alexander, was also captivated by the visitor whom he thought was a 'nice man'. In later years, he recalled sitting on his knee and playing with his fobs and seals, a star that scratched him, his green coat and fat tummy, the man's pinching of his cheek.

Napoleon remained at The Briars for almost two months, sleeping in a summer-house with big windows which the children used as a playroom, with Las Cases and his son occupying a tiny attic, and his valets, Marchand and Saint-Denis, sleeping by the door on a mattress brought from the *Northumberland*.

Here at The Briars, Napoleon spent much of his time dictating an account of his past life to Las Cases, living in the past, as Las Cases said, drawing upon the resources of an astonishing memory, endeavouring to create a legend, while pacing up and down in a marquee which had been erected for him on the lawn. Las Cases also gave him English lessons; but these were not successful. He was no linguist: a fragment of his attempt at the language has survived: 'Count Las Casses. Since sixt wek, y Learnt the english and y do not any progress. Sixt wek do fourty and two day. If might have learn fivty word, for day, i could known it two thousands and two hundreds.' One of the *Northumberland*'s officers said that Napoleon, after week upon week aboard the ship, could not even pronounce their names correctly.

In the evenings, Napoleon would ask Las Cases to find out if the Balcombes were alone; and, if they were, he would join them, thankful not to have to spend another evening in the company of Las Cases whose grave demeanour once provoked him into playing upon him one of those practical jokes which appeal to those with scant sense of humour, leaping upon him, clutching at his throat and crying, 'Your money or your life, aristocrat!'

Sometimes in the evenings at The Briars, Betsy sang and he himself once sang *Vive Henri Quatre* in his most unmusical voice, then declared emphatically that English music was the worst in the world: it was the Italians and only the Italians who understood how to compose an opera. Giovanni Paisiello, who had been Catherine II's *maestro di cappella* in St Petersburg and had subsequently directed the music in Napoleon's chapel, was, he said, as he had often maintained before, his favourite composer.

He was clearly intrigued by Betsy, who was asked to entertain him because she spoke better French than the others, having had a French nurse and having learned the language while at school in England.

He questioned her closely about this English education:

'What is the capital of France?'

'Paris.'

'Of Italy?'

'Rome.'

'Russia?'

'Petersburg now, Moscow formerly.'

'*Qui l'a brûlée?*'

She did not answer immediately. She knew about the burning of Moscow but could not remember who had been responsible for it.

He asked the question again.

'I don't know, sir.'

'*Qui, qui,*' he said, laughing at her confusion. '*Vous savez très bien. C'est moi qui l'a brûlée.*'

'I believe, sir, the Russians burned it to get rid of the French.'

He gave another of those false, high-pitched laughs like the mirth of a ventriloquist's dummy, rose from his chair, ended the conversation with a dismissive gesture, and asked the girl to show him the garden. Later that day he pinched her ear as a sign of affection.

As the days passed at The Briars, Napoleon and Betsy became increasingly friendly. She called him 'Boney', a nickname he could not understand, protesting in a puzzled tone that he was not thin when, having asked Las Cases what the word meant, he was told it meant 'a bony person'.

Napoleon's staff were astonished and appalled by the liberties the frisky girl took with him, holding his hands in hers to examine them more closely, studying the skin of his face which a Scottish naval officer, who saw him a few months later, described as being like marble 'without a single wrinkle or trace of a furrow', feeling his hair which she described as 'dark brown and as fine and silky as a child's, rather more so, indeed, for a man, as its very softness caused it to look thin'.

'The children call His Majesty "*Monsieur*", and behave most shockingly,' Gourgaud commented. 'Betsy was today quite amazing in her behaviour towards the Emperor. But he did not seem to mind.' Indeed, he not only tolerated it, he seemed to enjoy it. He also clearly enjoyed the rowdy games he played with Betsy and her sister, chasing them across the garden in games of blind-man's-buff, running after them in what Betsy described as 'something between a strut and a waddle', out of breath and puffing, pouncing upon their hiding places in games of hide-and-seek, racing away with them and jumping over a low wall when chased by one of Mr Balcombe's cows, hiding Betsy's dress when she was going to a ball and reducing her to tears, provoking her to pounce upon him when he cheated brazenly at games of whist.

He also enjoyed the company of the amiable Mrs Balcombe at whom he would stare in that disconcerting way of his, telling her how strongly she reminded him of his dear Josephine. He came across her once while on one of his regular morning rides. She was with a pretty woman, a Mrs Stuart, who was on her way home to Scotland from India. He stopped to talk to them, and plied Mrs Stuart – as he often did with people he met for the first time – with a succession of personal questions and complimenting her on her pleasing looks and clear complexion. He enquired about the reasons for her presence on the island, dilated upon the inconvenience to women of long voyages by sea, discussed the customs of the Indian subcontinent and, since she was Scottish, quoted her passages from Macpherson's *Ossian* for which his enthusiasm was undimmed. While they were talking in the road, a procession of slaves carrying heavy burdens approached them. Mrs Balcombe gestured to the slaves, indicating that they were to walk round them on the verge. 'Consider their loads, Madame,' Napoleon said, drawing his horse aside for them to pass. 'Heavens,' exclaimed Mrs Stuart when he had ridden off. 'What a character! And what an expressive countenance! How different he is from the idea I had formed of him!'

44

LONGWOOD HOUSE

'It possessed neither running water
nor shade.'

EVERY MORNING, while Napoleon was staying at The Briars, a large
party of sailors marched up from Jamestown to carry out the necessary
work on Longwood House to make it suitable for the reception of his
suite, comprising the quarrelsome General Gourgaud, comte de Las Cases
and his son, General de Montholon and his wife and their female servant,
five valets, a butler, a chef, a steward and an usher as well as ten other
servants, two of them Chinese, ten soldiers and a British officer who
was to satisfy himself twice a day that General Bonaparte was still there.

His valets did not find Napoleon an easy master to serve until they
had grown accustomed to his demanding ways. For example, Louis
Marchand, who had been so 'taken aback' when his master hurled a
cup and saucer against the wall because they were of the wrong set,
admitted to being afraid of him at first. But he eventually decided that
there were 'always good reasons for Napoleon's anger', and that, while
unpredictable, he was generally a considerate master.

Admittedly, the Emperor 'was not in the habit of saying he was
satisfied. He even seemed to pay little attention to efforts made to please
him, or he greeted them with indifference. But, if after scolding someone
and noticing that he seemed hurt, he would go up to him and either
pinch his ear hard or tug at it. This implied all was forgiven.' Yet he
could not resist maliciously teasing servants when the mood to do so
took hold of him. When the wife of his valet Saint-Denis, the governess
of the Bertrand children, became pregnant, he suggested that Saint-Denis

was not the father. 'You think the child will be yours,' he said, pretending to believe that an 'ugly Chinese' had been making love to Mme Saint-Denis when the valet's back was turned. 'You'll be well caught, won't you, when she brings forth an ugly, dirty little Chinaman?' Napoleon then gave one of his hooting, false laughs.

While most of the members of Napoleon's suite occupied small, dark rooms, nearly all on upper floors, Napoleon was provided with a relatively large, though by no means unduly commodious, apartment with a study, dining room, drawing room, bedroom, bathroom and a billiard room in which the table occupied almost the entire space and in which there was scarcely room to hold a cue without hitting the wall, a disadvantage of no consequence to Napoleon who massaged the balls continuously as he peered at the maps spread over the table, throwing them across the baize and buffeting them so violently that before long they were quite misshapen.

Although he had far more room than any member of his suite, Napoleon had no reason to be satisfied with the accommodation provided for him at Longwood, nor with the exposed position of the house, nor with its damp and clammy atmosphere, nor yet with its smell, a mixture of paint and mildew which, like the smell of the *Northumberland*, made him feel sick. In his palaces in France he had suppressed unpleasant smells with aloe burning in silver gilt bowls in his bedroom. The smell of Longwood – which at least did not reek of burning coal, a smell he particularly detested – was, however, not its principal fault: as his valet, Marchand, said, 'it possessed neither running water, nor shade' and was 'exposed to the prevailing south-east wind'. Moreover, the severe and extremely changeable climate of the island was far from healthy: as Barry O'Meara, the *Bellerophon*'s Irish ship's doctor, who took over as Napoleon's physician, reported, 'The most prevalent complaints are dysentery, inflammation of the bowels, liver infections and fevers, all of them generally of a violent form . . . During the first twelve or thirteen months after its arrival at St Helena, the second battalion of the 66th Regiment [a unit of the large guard stationed on the island to prevent the prisoner's escape] lost, by these diseases, 56 men out of a strength of 630, being one in eleven.'

Nor was Longwood House itself conducive to healthy living, being cramped as well as damp and infested with rats that scampered about across the floors and over the feet of guests at Napoleon's table, nipping the exposed limbs of servants in their beds and once biting deeply into the Emperor's hand. 'They came out at night through holes they had made and were so thick on the floor it appeared black,' Marchand said. 'They climbed up the walls and then jumped on to pieces of meat suspended from the ceiling on iron hooks.' They even dived into a saucepan which Saint-Denis was heating on a stove and 'carried the contents off including the spoon'. Pieces of tin were nailed over the holes, but the swarming rodents soon found other ways into the rooms. Competitions were held to see how many could be killed in a single evening.

Fleas as well as rats were a pest on the island. 'There were such horrible quantities of Fleas that my Life has been nigh tormented away,' wrote Mrs Younghusband, whose husband, an army officer, was serving on the island. 'If I take a walk on the Grass I come home literally covered from head to foot, and am obliged to pull off my clothes and throw them outside the tent.'

At Longwood House, bedbugs hid in the mosquito nets and Mme de Montholon complained of a 'horrid insect' that hovered about in the gum trees in the garden and attacked anyone walking or riding in the vicinity.

Daily life at Longwood House soon began to assume a fairly regular pattern. Napoleon awoke early in the iron bedstead in his austere room on the walls of which hung miniatures of Marie-Louise and her son, the King of Rome. There was also later to be a portrait of the Empress Josephine painted by Marchand who related in his memoirs how it came to be done:

> Among his snuffboxes, the Emperor had a portrait of Empress Josephine which he did not consider a good likeness. Countess Bertrand had one decorated with pearls that the Empress had given her: it had been painted by Saint and was a very good likeness. The Emperor asked her for it and told me to make a copy. I thought this was a joke and protested, but the Emperor insisted. I painted a little but even so, I was not capable of under-taking the copy of a portrait by Saint! I tried my best and when

I showed it to him, the Emperor found it a very good likeness.
He had me frame it and then hung it on one side of his mantelpiece, where it remained until his death.

As soon as he was awake, Napoleon called for his valet to open the
window and bring his coffee; then he shaved before a mirror held for
him by the valet, and washed at the silver Biennais washstand basin
brought by Marchand from Paris. He brushed his teeth thoroughly and
had his body rubbed down vigorously with eau de Cologne, urging the
valet to 'rub harder', rub as though 'he were scrubbing a donkey'. In
fair weather, before going out, he would dress in white breeches and a
coat with silver buttons under which he wore the ribbon of the Legion
of Honour. If he were to do a little gardening he put on a nankeen
shirt and trousers and a straw hat with a wide brim such as planters
wore.

His morning ride might take him to Fisher's Valley where there was
a cottage occupied by a strange old Englishwoman, Miss Mason, who
saddled and rode a bullock and, when encountering the Emperor, treated
him with the utmost deference. There was another cottage nearby in
the Valley of Silence occupied by a family named Robinson. There were
two daughters, Marchand recorded: 'The elder was fifteen or sixteen
and both of them, whenever the Emperor rode that way, approached
and offered him flowers. They were not pretty; but they were pleasant
enough . . . and the Emperor would greet them with kindness . . . The
two young ladies thus acquired a certain fame that soon reached
Jamestown. This fame led the naval captain of a merchant ship belonging
to the East India Company to seek out the older daughter for his wife
when he came through Saint Helena, and he married her. Before leaving
the island, the couple came to see the Emperor who congratulated the
husband on his choice and hoped that the young woman would become
the mother of a fine numerous family.'

Her name was Mary Anne and, although Marchand's description
of her appearance was not very flattering, others described her as 'very
pretty'. Certainly she was known as 'the Nymph' and Napoleon referred
to the valley where they lived as the 'Valley of the Nymph'. The French
Commissioner on the island maintained that Napoleon had been greatly
attracted to her before her marriage to Captain Edwards, that he had
'made her a declaration' and that she was in the habit of going for 'early

and solitary walks' in the hope of meeting and, presumably, seducing him.

When she came with Captain Edwards to say goodbye to him, Napoleon observed in that teasingly embarrassing way of his that she had the air of a nun while her husband resembled his stepson, Eugène de Beauharnais. 'Napoleon, as is his wont, asks him some crude and tactless questions; the mariner blushes, the Emperor pledges him in a toast and, after an hour and a half of this sort of thing, the couple take their leave. After a while, Napoleon follows them, and insists on embracing, not "the Nymph" but her husband' on the grounds that he is so like Eugène de Beauharnais.

One day in October, accompanied by Bertrand and de Montholon, Napoleon called upon Sir William Doveton, a former Governor of St Helena, who lived in a house called Mount Pleasant. Doveton invited them into the house where they were introduced to his daughter, Mrs Greentree, who had with her a baby and two little girls. Sitting down on a sofa in the drawing room, Napoleon beckoned to one of these girls and, taking out a small lump of liquorice from the box which he almost invariably carried with him, he popped it into her mouth, squeezing her nose with his other hand. Her sister was treated in the same way.

Sir William invited his visitors to stay for breakfast; but Bertrand, who, despite his poor English, acted as interpreter, said that they had brought provisions with them and, since it was a fine day, would very much like to eat in the garden. Supposing that his guests would prefer to have breakfast in the house, Doveton took Napoleon into the dining room where he indicated a big plate of butter on the table. By way of a response, and with what was presumably intended to be a grateful gesture, Napoleon surprised Doveton by tweaking his ear.

It was decided, as a compromise, that Doveton's family and their visitors should share their breakfast and all eat together on the lawn. It was an excellent meal: they had potted meat, pies and turkey, curried chicken, salad, a joint of some unidentified meat which the Frenchmen had brought with them and which Doveton thought was either ham or pork, oranges, dates and nuts. There was champagne as well as coffee.

After the meal they all returned to the drawing room where

Napoleon, with Bertrand acting as a none-too-efficient interpreter, interrogated his host and Mrs Greentree by means of a series of disconcerting questions: Did Sir William ever get drunk? He enjoyed a glass of wine on occasions. How often did Mrs Greentree's husband get drunk? Once a week? No. Once a fortnight? No. Once a month, perhaps? No. It was some years since Mrs Greentree had seen her husband drunk at all. 'Bah!' Having thus satisfied himself as to the drinking habits of his host's family and expressed disapproval of their sobriety, Napoleon took his leave.

When he returned from his ride, the Emperor's midday meal would be served to him either in the room where he had changed his clothes – as usual throwing the discarded shirts and trousers on to the backs of chairs or the floor – or, weather permitting, in the garden. The simple meal of soup, a main course perhaps of chicken or mutton and beans, and a glass of red wine mixed with a generous amount of water, would last no longer than ten minutes or a quarter of an hour at the most.

After the meal and a cup of very hot coffee, Napoleon settled down to sleep or to dictation, displaying his still astonishingly retentive memory for facts and figures. He would then have a bath almost as hot as the coffee, talking to one or other of the generals or reading a book as he lay immersed in the water. Books were littered about the bath as they were about his bed. As one of the doctors said, 'As long as the Emperor holds a book in his hand he will not suffer anyone to interrupt him. Good books are allowed to slide down on to the floor, indifferent ones are disdainfully pushed aside, and bad ones thrown against the wall.'

As in the past in Europe, he would often linger in the bath for an hour or more, once at least having a valet top it up for four and a half hours. After this, Marchand or St-Denis having helped him to dress, he might receive a visitor before dinner.

Clementina, Lady Malcolm, wife of Cockburn's successor as Commander-in-Chief on the St Helena station, was one of those guests whose company he seemed to enjoy. She was the eldest daughter of the Hon. William Fullerton Elphinstone, a director of the East India Company, and a niece of Lord Keith. In her *Diary of St Helena* she gave a description of Napoleon's appearance at this time:

His hair is ... brown-black, thin on the forehead, cropped ... rather a dirty look; light blue or grey eyes; a capacious forehead; high nose, short upper lip; good even teeth, but small (he rarely showed them) ... pale complexion, particularly short neck. Otherwise his figure appeared well proportioned, but had become too fat; a thick short hand with taper fingers and beautiful nails, and a well-shaped leg and foot.

He was dressed 'in an old threadbare green coat, with green velvet collar and cuffs, silver buttons ... a silver star of the Legion of Honour. White waistcoat; white silk stockings and shoes with oval gold buckles.'

She was struck with the 'kindness of his expression' so 'contrary to the fierceness' that she had expected. She 'saw no trace of great ability'.

Her husband remarked upon the extreme smallness of his feet and the plumpness of his pale hands ('like a woman's'). His breasts were also plump, so one of his doctors was later to record, and they, too, might almost have been a woman's, and he had scant if any pubic hair.

'The Emperor displayed a kind of plumpness that was not typical of our sex,' Las Cases observed. 'He occasionally remarked upon this quite cheerfully himself.' To the doctor, Francesco Antommarchi, he also drew attention to the feminine appearance of his body with pride rather than embarrassment: 'As you can see, Doctor, beautiful arms, rounded breasts, soft white skin, not a hair ... More than one beautiful lady would glory in a chest like mine.'

'His complexion was a very uncommon one,' Admiral Malcolm continued, 'being of a light sallow colour, differing from almost any other' Malcolm had 'ever met with ... His manners were extremely pleasing and affable ... He possessed, to a wonderful degree, a facility in making a favourable impression upon those with whom he entered into conversation; this appeared to me to be accomplished by turning the subject to matters he supposed the person he was addressing was well acquainted with, and on which he could show himself to advantage.' The Admiral and his wife much enjoyed their conversations with him which the Malcolms conscientiously recorded, noting down Napoleon's opinions and dissertations upon all manner of subjects from Ossian's poems to the benefits of income tax.

Often in the afternoon he would go for a ride in a carriage drawn by six horses, sitting beside Mme de Montholon and Mme Bertrand with Las Cases and Bertrand in front and Gourgaud, who was Napoleon's 'master of the horse', riding alongside. Galloping fast up and down the rough roads, rattling along and shaking the ladies this way and that, the horses might be pulled up at Hutt's Gate where Napoleon would get out to play with the Bertrand children of whom he was fond and of whose company, like that of most children, he enjoyed for short periods. The valet, Saint-Denis, described a day when Napoleon had gone to the Bertrands' house for a meal. 'The luncheon had gone very well,' he said, 'but towards the end the children started throwing balls of bread at each other. The Emperor had taken the youngest child on his knees and was kissing and teasing him as he pulled at his ears.'

Sometimes he would come to Hutt's Gate to see the parades and horse races organized by the soldiers of the British garrison, peering at them through the holes he had had cut in the shutters, as he had in the shutters at Longwood, so that he could watch without being seen. And sometimes he would go for a walk down from Hutt's Gate beneath the trees towards a spring where, so he told Bertrand, he would like to be buried 'if his body was left in the hands of his enemies when he died'.

On occasions, Mmes Bertrand and de Montholon would be amongst those accompanying him on these walks, growing increasingly exhausted as Napoleon rambled on and on about the past and any other subject that might catch his fancy. 'If we got too tired,' Mme de Montholon recorded, 'we tried to slip down a side path, but, however surreptitiously this was done, it never escaped the Emperor's notice, even when he was absorbed in his conversation. He might be several paces ahead of us but he always saw that we had vanished and he never failed to comment, "there's Madame de Montholon (or someone else) creeping away."'

After the walk the members of his suite would meet in the drawing room before dinner, the men in full uniform, the women in décolleté dresses which they had brought with them from Paris. The atmosphere was formal. No one sat down in the Emperor's presence without permission; no one spoke to him until a conversation had been opened. Mme de Montholon once saw Gourgaud almost faint with exhaustion as he leant against the door watching a game of chess. No servant was permitted to address him with even a hint of familiarity. When Saint-

Denis once addressed him as 'you' instead of 'Your Majesty', Napoleon kicked him as a punishment for this 'impertinence and lack of respect', berating him 'in the harshest and most humiliating terms'.

Upon the Emperor's appearance in the drawing room, everyone stood up and remained standing unless permitted to sit down for a game of cards or chess which he played impatiently and, now as ever, with an unexpected lack of skill, cheating without compunction. 'He would insist that a piece touched was a piece played,' Mme de Montholon said. 'But this applied only to his opponent, never to himself. He always had a good reason for this. If anyone commented on it he just laughed.'

At the appointed time, Francesco Cipriani, the major-domo, appeared in the green and silver livery, which all the servants wore, to announce that his Majesty's dinner was served.

Napoleon would then lead the way into the dining room, sit down with his back to the fireplace and to the two servants, Saint-Denis and Marchand, standing behind his chair. He then indicated a seat for Mme Bertrand, if she were present, on his right and for Mme de Montholon on his left, both elegantly dressed, though it amused Napoleon to say, in that teasing, needling way of his, that they looked like washerwomen. One evening, when Mrs Younghusband was a guest, 'During the whole of Dinner,' so she said, 'no one uttered a syllable above their breath ... and for the greater part of the time a dead silence prevailed among the party.'

The meal cooked by Napoleon's expert chef, La Page, was 'most superb' in the words of an occasional guest, Brigadier-General Sir George Bingham, commanding officer of the garrison, and 'most formally served'. 'The people who [lived] with Napoleon, however, scarcely spoke above a whisper, and he was so much engaged in eating that he scarcely said a word to anyone. He had so filled the room with candles that it was as hot as an oven.'

'The [Sèvres] coffee cups were the most beautiful I ever saw,' Bingham continued in his account of the evening after the diners had returned to the drawing room. 'On each cup was an Egyptian view [by Dominique Vivant Denon], and on the saucer a portrait of some Bey or other distinguished character. In France, they would have cost twenty-five guineas a cup and saucer.'

After dinner there were more card games in the drawing room, piquet being the most commonly played, or Mme de Montholon would sing at the piano, or, to the evident boredom of his guests, Napoleon would launch into a monologue about the past or upon some subject which was of far greater interest to him than to them, or, worst of all – with his still faintly foreign accent and mistakes of pronunciation – he would read aloud, from Corneille or Voltaire, Racine, Molière, Ossian or Homer, or from a translation of Hume's *History of England* which confirmed him in the belief that the English were 'a ferocious race' whose men treated their women disgracefully. He read on and on monotonously until, as Gourgaud said, 'we were all dropping with fatigue or boredom'.

'He had no ear for rhythm,' Mme de Montholon said, 'and would often add one or two syllables to a line without realising it. During these readings the ladies would stifle their yawns, but if he noticed one of them doing so, out of spite he would hand the volume to the culprit and ask her to continue. He would then immediately fall asleep.'

Once Mme de Montholon was brave enough to help Gourgaud hide the book from which Napoleon was at that time reading; and once Mme Bertrand had to be rebuked for dropping off. 'Madame, you're asleep,' he said crossly.

'No, sire.'

'What time is it? Oh! What does it matter? Let's go to bed.'

By then it was generally almost midnight. Sometimes he had talked for three hours at a stretch. His guests thankfully left the room. Marchand would help him undress; then Montholon or Gourgaud would come in to read to him before he went to sleep. It was not long before he woke up, called his valet, began to talk again and sometimes got up to pace about the room, like a tiger in its cage. 'He often treats night as day, or day as night,' Saint-Denis said. 'In fact, he acts like someone overcome by *ennui* who does all he can to make time pass more quickly.'

45

'MACH' AND 'SULTANA'

'What a damned stupid fool the fellow was,
damned idiot.'

ON 4 APRIL 1816, a new Governor, the humourless and pedantic Sir
Hudson Lowe, arrived on St Helena. The son of an army officer, Lowe
was then thirty-five years old. The Duke of Wellington dismissed him
as 'a damned fool' and considered his appointment 'a very bad choice
since he was a man wanting in education and judgement, a stupid man
who knew nothing of the world and, like all men who know nothing
of the world, he was suspicious and jealous'. He had a reddish complexion and reddish hair grew out of his nostrils and ears. His face
turned very pale when he was angry. Napoleon was to say that he looked
like a debt collector.

His career so far had not been undistinguished, but his manner,
abrupt and reserved, was certainly, to say the least, unprepossessing;
while his lack of tact, suspicious interference, paranoiac distrust and
insistence on the observance of rules which the exiles deemed quite
unnecessary, were to them exasperating. The Russian Commissioner on
the island thought that he was 'not quite right in the head'.

It had to be said, though, that Lowe, upright and conscientious to a
fault, had much to put up with from Napoleon and his entourage who
contrived to send letters to England making complaints and accusations
which were often spurious and which made no acknowledgement of the
favours accorded them, such as the use of the Governor's library and his
rejection of a demand from London that the eight thousand pounds a year
spent on the maintenance of the Longwood household should be reduced.

'Make your protests,' Napoleon told his staff, declining to make them himself. 'I command,' he said, 'or I remain silent.' 'Make Europe learn how badly we are being treated here, so that they become indignant . . . Our situation here may even have its advantages. Everyone in Europe is looking at us. We are the martyrs of an immortal cause.'

Lowe had but five interviews with Napoleon at which he seems generally to have behaved with frigid correctness in the face of the Emperor's rude hostility, a hostility increased by the knowledge that Lowe had once commanded the Corsican Rangers, a regiment of Napoleon's countrymen who were in arms against France and were declared enemies of Bonaparte.

Speaking to each other in Italian, at one of these interviews Napoleon said, 'If Lord Castlereagh [the Foreign Secretary] has ordered you to poison or kill us all, get it over with as soon as possible.' 'Sir,' replied Lowe, 'I have not come here to be insulted.'

Sir Hudson's military secretary, Major Gideon Gorrequer, a much put-upon and touchy young man, recorded in a diary – elaborating countless petty squabbles at the Governor's residence, Plantation House – numerous occasions when he was accused of losing documents which the Governor then found among his own papers without a word of apology, and just as numerous examples of Lowe's fussy, difficult and, on occasions, 'outrageous' temperament – his 'furious gusts of rage and passion', his 'most brutal rage', 'revolting tone and manner', 'moroseness and sulky manner', his 'furious (foam at the mouth) manners and billingsgate expressions', his 'detestable habit of muttering and cursing thro' his teeth', his 'affectation', 'strutting' and 'preening':

> At pranzo [lunch] one day Mach's [Lowe's] ridiculous vain way of going on with his new paraphernalia from London [Gorrequer wrote, giving an example of this irritating preening], his strutting about like a peacock, admiring and looking at himself in the [looking glass] buttoning and unbuttoning [his coat] . . . and for 2 or 3 days doing nothing else at dinner than admiring the aigulettes and asking Donna [Lady Lowe] what she thought of it.

Sir Hudson, so Gorrequer said, had scarcely a good word to say of any of his staff or colleagues. Barry O'Meara, Napoleon's doctor, was a 'damned rascal', 'the greatest rascal that ever existed', Count Balmain, the Russian Commissioner, was 'a complete blackguard', a 'mean dirty

fellow', 'a damned little snapper, a rascal', a 'popinjay', a 'jackanapes'.
William Balcombe was also 'a damned rascal'. Lowe was disgusted with
both Bertrand and de Montholon. As for Admiral Malcolm, he was the
'cause' of 'all his difficulties' and of the trouble he had had with 'our
Neighbour' [Napoleon]. Had Malcolm not left the island, Lowe would
not, he said, have remained himself to act with such a devil. The very
thought of Colonel Charles Nicol, commanding officer of the 66th,
drove him to a furious rage: 'What a damned stupid fool the fellow
was, damned idiot.'

Caustic and intolerant as he appears in Gorrequer's journal, however, there are times, unmentioned in it, when Lowe appears in a less
unpleasant light: he abolished slavery on the island, for instance; and,
when Napoleon, protesting absurdly that he had insufficient food to
put on it, sent his silver plate to Plantation House to be sold in
Jamestown, Lowe put it into store and sent its value, £250, to Longwood
without explaining where the money had come from.

On meeting Lowe's wife one day while walking in Sandy Bay, Napoleon
was surprised to find her both pretty and agreeable; he was also taken
with the appearance of Suzanne Johnson, Lady Lowe's daughter by her
first husband. On being shown round the garden at Longwood by de
Montholon, Suzanne Johnson came 'face to face with the Emperor under
a long bower covered with passion leaves where he was strolling'. 'Her
first reaction,' according to Marchand, 'was one of great embarrassment
but it soon ceased because of the gracious way in which the Emperor
received her. Sweets were served to her and he offered her a rose as a
memento of her pilgrimage.'

The Austrian Commissioner, Baron von Stürmer, also spoke well
of Suzanne Johnson, as he did of her sister and of their mother. After
attending one of her balls at Plantation House, he described Lady Lowe
as 'a born hostess'. 'She loves entertaining,' he said, 'and she does it
gracefully. She receives officers, civil servants and any notable visitors
to the island and is the life and soul of its society.' Las Cases tended to
agree with von Stürmer. 'Amiable and beautiful', Lady Lowe had 'something of the actress about her'. A different portrait of her emerges,
however, from the pages of the diary of the highly critical and obviously
rather tiresome Major Gorrequer who, as her husband's military

secretary, saw her almost every day and found her scarcely less difficult than he did her husband, alternating rudeness with charm, expressing affection for some and having numerous *bêtes noires*, most fickle in her friendships and enmities. Once in January 1818, 'on looking at a picture of Napoleon's son' – which had been confiscated by her husband – 'and upon [Gorrequer's] saying how delighted General Bonaparte would be to see it, she exclaimed as for me she would not allow him to have anything that could afford him pleasure or delight. That (meaning the picture) would only add to his pride and vanity.' Four months later, however, she was 'pitying the situation of B. and saying he really was to be pitied, contrasting his former situation with his present, and Sir H. [Lowe] saying he deserved more contempt than pity which gave rise to a lengthy reasoning between them. Both looked at me alternately, as they spoke, and as if engaging me in conversation. I observed that something must be allowed for the personal feelings of a man who (as he said, trusting to the generosity of the British nation and expecting a refuge in England) had delivered himself into the hands of the English and instead of an abode in England had found himself fixed at St Helena.'

As with Napoleon, so with General de Montholon, Lady Lowe's opinion was inconsistent: 'Sultana [Lady Lowe] was quite in rapture at Veritas's [de Montholon's] politeness. He was so pleasant so amiable, so clever and gentlemanly; and this after all the abuse she had so frequently lavished upon him.'

In the same way she changed her mind about the chaplain, the Revd Bowater Vernon, upon whom and particularly upon whose wife she was at first particularly severe; but then she underwent a period of what Gorrequer called 'religious affectation and church going' in which she delivered tirades upon 'the whole society of the Island' for not going to church as regularly as she did herself, having previously gone 'not much more than a dozen times in 3 years'. She later developed 'a high enthusiasm' for Vernon and his 'admirable delivery (a short time before so monotonous), his evident goodness – in fact, a demi-god'.

Among other people on the island towards whom her feelings ranged from the affectionate to the contemptuous was Mrs Wynyard, the wife of Gorrequer's colleague, Edward Buckley Wynyard:

> Donna [Lady Lowe] ridiculed in the most indecent way the appearance of Mrs Vignoble [Wynyard] . . . She mentioned her

dress, her looks, the manner in which her clothes and the flowers on her head were huddled upon her as if thrown at her, and as if she really had been endeavouring to make herself look as ridiculous as she possibly could. She wondered how she could make herself so absurd and appealed to me if I had observed her. I answered I never could recollect the dress but that I thought she looked very well. 'I wonder how you can think so. For my part I never saw anything so strange as her appearance altogether, for I am sure I never saw her look worse.'

As for Mrs Wynyard's husband, his manners were 'extremely unpleasant'; Lady Lowe had never been 'treated with so much rudeness' in her life. 'He has often, as you were both coming up from the office for tiffin, passed so close to me, looking at me full in the face without taking the least notice, bowing or speaking to me. Frequently at dinner he has looked as sulky as possible without scarcely deigning to notice or even answer when I spoke to him. I have heard a number of people speak in the same way of him.'

'Sultana's' abuse of E. E. Vidal, secretary to Admiral Robert Lambert, was even more outspoken. 'I can't bear that nasty, disagreeable fellow,' she said. 'I detest him. Is that fellow coming to dinner here on Monday? How could Mach [Lowe] continue asking people to his table so disagreeable to him?' She did not think she ever would dine at the same table again with those two impertinent fellows [Vidal and Flag Captain Thomas Brown] who had 'behaved' with so much rudeness and who took pleasure in irritating her. Complaining of her 'constant railing and exclamations against people's rudeness and want of attention to her', Colonel Thomas Lyster, the Orderly Officer at Longwood House, observed to one of his junior officers that it was 'very well that she was in the first place here, otherwise she would not be suffered to abuse and run down every body, as she did, with impunity. Pick Axe [Lyster] himself inveighed strongly against her.'

The trouble was that her tirades and extravagant encomia were often fuelled by alcohol. Gorrequer was told that she would drink a bottle of brandy every two or three days, and that she got through a whole bottle of sherry every day or a bottle of cagnini every two days or so. Colonel Wynyard thought that her behaviour must often have been due to drink, since, whereas when sober she appeared to be quite strait-laced, when she had had a few drinks she was quite capable of 'talking bawdy' to Mrs Wynyard or of offending Gorrequer's sensibilities by referring to Napoleon's habit of pinching people's noses and observing, with what he called a 'dirty simile', that 'that would be very dangerous in England where colds in the head are so frequent'.

Liquor also played its part, no doubt, in her flagrant flirtation with Captain Den Taafe, one of her husband's aides-de-camp, who appears frequently in Gorrequer's diary:

> Her rudeness again, all at once at Dinner, shunning speaking to me, and her caresses to Yam [Den Taafe], who did nothing in return but breathe like a porpoise, following his usual grunt . . . Sultana asking Yam languishingly at Tiffin to biberete [drink] with her; and her rudeness to Ego then and at pranzo same day . . . Sultana, great caressing and petting of Yam, looking quite languishingly at him even whilst speaking to Ego . . . When Yam, who was late for dinner sat down she immediately began addressing him in the most friendly way and from that moment never gave Ego an opportunity of entering into the conversation . . . At pranzo when Sultana came in she scarcely acknowledged Ego's low bow. Went in to dinner enquiring, 'Where is Yam?' in a soft tone . . . and the moment Yam came in simpered so prettily and kindly in his face. At table her constant rating of servants quite annoying with her cross noisy manner going on for hours at a time. Treated Ego with marked slight. She received Yam with all the simpering smiling ways possible who came in when soup was almost over, a thing which he frequently did, and which would have been high treason with Ego.

Flirtatious as was her manner with Den Taafe, it was equally so with Sir Thomas Reade, the Deputy Adjutant General on St Helena, referred to in the diary as 'Ninny', next to whom she sat one evening when the wife of Dr John Thomas Short was entertaining the company with some Tuscan songs. 'I heard Sultana enquiring of Ninny with whom she was flirting and had been all day, "What language were they singing in?" Ninny said "Chinese" whereat she got in a furious gust.'

Lady Lowe's daughter, Charlotte was married to Count Balmain, the Russian Commissioner on St Helena, who, before his marriage, had shocked the other Commissioners by proposing bringing over from

Paris a young seamstress to comfort him in his exile. 'Not that such a proceeding would have conspicuously jarred with the morals of St Helena,' Lord Rosebery commented in his *Napoleon: The Last Phase*, 'for, if we may credit our French chroniclers, the naval chiefs there lived with mistresses; and the loves of Gourgaud himself were neither limited nor refined.'

Lady Lowe, to give her her due, apparently did what she could to modify Sir Hudson's tactlessness. She seems to have vainly pointed out the indelicacy of his inviting 'General Bonaparte' to a party to celebrate the Prince Regent's birthday, an invitation which followed one – also referring to the Emperor Napoleon as 'General Bonaparte' – asking him to come 'to meet' the Countess of Moira, wife of the Governor-General of India. Napoleon, commenting that the last he had heard of 'General Bonaparte' was in Egypt, instructed Bertrand to make no reply to the 'silly' invitation. Lady Lowe's comment on all this was: 'He would not come to my house, and I thought him perfectly right not to do so.'

46

SEXUAL ADVENTURES

*'If I should sleep with her,
what is that to you?'*

IT WAS ONLY TO BE EXPECTED that in the frustrating boredom of life on St Helena men turned to illicit love affairs. Las Cases contrived to find opportunities in his son's absence to indulge a taste for black women. Lieutenant Basil Jackson of the Staff Corps, who was rumoured to be Mme de Montholon's lover, was described by Gideon Gorrequer as 'shagging Negra Kate', a black servant at Plantation House; while General Gourgaud's sexual adventures were notorious and the subject of numerous entries in his journal: 'I came across a pretty slave girl and asked her to come to see me and she said she would . . . I got a woman from the town to come to me. I took her to bed and gave her six pounds . . . I picked up a pretty mulatto girl . . . I asked in the town for a negress.'

Having such tastes, Gourgaud predictably found the balls at Plantation House a 'dreadful bore'. 'One dances twice running with the same partner,' he complained. 'I was told to take Mme Defontaine, wife of one of the councillors, to supper. After the second dance we went into the dining room . . . I sat down beside an old lady in a different place from the one assigned to me, and I did well, for with the insolent one must be insolent . . . Because of my six quadrilles I could not escape and get away until five o'clock in the morning. One of the rosy young ladies let off a fearful fart as she was dancing.'

Several of these young ladies of St Helena, so a resident on the island maintained, were 'extremely pretty'. One of them was Laura

Wilks, daughter of Lieutenant-Colonel Mark Wilks, a former governor of the island, once private secretary to Lord Clive and author of a highly praised history of Mysore. Laura Wilks was 'then in the first bloom of youth,' wrote a lady who accompanied her when she first paid a visit to Napoleon at Longwood, 'and her whole demeanour, affability and elegant, modest appearance conspired to render her the most charming and admirable young person I ever beheld, or have since met with in all my peregrinations in Europe, Asia and Africa for the space of thirty years.'

The susceptible Gourgaud was much taken with her. 'There is a woman!' he exclaimed after meeting her for the first time. Napoleon also greatly admired her and gave her a bracelet to remember him by when she came to say goodbye. She told him she was sorry to be leaving the island for England, where she was to marry Major-General Sir John Buchan. He replied sadly, 'Ah! Mademoiselle, I only wish I could change places with you.'

Laura Wilks was far from being the only white woman on the island to attract the attention of the cantankerous, morose, quarrelsome and lascivious Gourgaud. He had his eye upon Mme de Montholon whose husband he challenged to a duel; he pursued a Miss Kneipps, known as 'Rosebud', as well as two sisters, the daughters of a Mrs Churchill. He responded willingly to the flirtatious overtures of the pretty Parisienne wife of Baron von Stürmer, the Austrian Commissioner. She, coveting a diamond-headed pin, said to him coquettishly, 'You ought to give me a present in token of our friendship – a pin, for instance – sharp you know, but it fastens things, too.'

Baron von Stürmer's colleague, the French Commissioner, the marquis de Montchenu, was, or at least claimed to be, quite as much of a gallant as General Gourgaud. A persistent prowler around Longwood House, in conscientious fulfilment of his orders to 'assure himself of General Bonaparte's continued presence on St Helena' – a duty which he and his colleagues found difficult to perform, since the invisible prisoner threatened to shoot anyone who presumed to enter his room without permission – Montchenu was known to his colleagues as M. de Monter-chez-nous because of his readiness to accept and his reluctance to return hospitality. He was generally considered to be a buffoon, and certainly his behaviour on St Helena seemed to confirm the verdict of Napoleon, who had known him in the past, that he was an 'old fool' as well as a satyr. He spread the ridiculous canard that Napoleon was having an affair with Betsy Balcombe; he himself pounced upon one Mrs Martin, an alarmed islander who indignantly rebuffed him; he boasted of having enjoyed the favours of no fewer than four hundred English ladies; and he wrote a letter extending to eight pages declaring his undying love for Lady Lowe. When Napoleon heard of his attempt upon the virtuous Mrs Martin, he commented, 'I suppose the old ram wanted to violate her.'

The sexual adventures and escapades of Napoleon's servants were matters of great interest to their master who liked to be told about them, relishing the details of them and enjoying the opportunities of teasing those involved by pretending to have evidence of their girlfriends' promiscuity. His devoted, faithful valet, Marchand, had an affair with a mulatto girl, Esther Vesey, an English sergeant's daughter, and had fathered a child, James Octave Vesey, by her. Marchand's fellow valet, Saint-Denis, slept with and eventually married the Bertrand children's governess, Mary Hall; another valet, the Swiss Novarra, married Mme de Montholon's maid; one of the two Archambault brothers who worked in the stables, had a mistress, Mary Foss; Gentilini, a handsome footman from Elba, seduced several soldiers' wives and, according to Major Gideon Gorrequer, was known to go to the house previously occupied by Gorrequer's colleague, Lieutenant-Colonel Wynyard, 'for the avowed purpose of fornicating with Mrs Snell, living there with her husband'.

Gorrequer himself evinced a taste for the young black women who worked as domestic servants at Plantation House and were constantly propositioned by the soldiers whose duties brought them there, much to the annoyance of Lady Lowe.

The noise made at Longwood by fornicating servants, soldiers and sailors was so obtrusive that de Montholon complained of it to Sir Hudson Lowe, who consequently doubled the number of sentries at the house, greatly annoying Napoleon who crossly upbraided de Montholon, 'You say whores are being brought in. If that's a scandal, you could easily have stopped it yourself without appealing to the English. You don't suppose this house is a convent, do you?'

Napoleon became irritated also with Gourgaud, an entry in whose journal runs: 'His Majesty is angry. So am I. He is calming down. I am not speaking.' 'Boredom is wearing you down,' Napoleon told him after one of these fits of petulance. 'You need a pretty little woman.' 'That,' Gourgaud commented, 'is what I feel myself.'

Napoleon complained to Lowe about the obtrusive sentries posted around Longwood House as well as about the prying Commissioners, one of whom, the ludicrous marquis de Montchenu, kept an eye on Longwood through a telescope while concealed in a hole in the ground. If he had a mistress, Napoleon said, he would not be able to receive her in the house, being so relentlessly watched. Lowe was immediately curious. Did General Bonaparte have a mistress then? he asked him. 'I might have,' Napoleon replied teasingly.

'Oh! I shall inform my government.'

It appears that on one occasion at least a young woman was brought to Napoleon who sent her away because she was too young; just as, in 1805, he had, in his former valet, Louis Constant's, words, 'respected the innocence' of a 'charming young girl' who had come to Schönbrunn and been taken back from there to her parents.

> One evening [recalled his valet, Saint-Denis, of the later occasion at Longwood] contrary to the usual practice, a light meal was served consisting of a few rather delicate dishes . . . These unaccustomed preparations made me ask M [de Montholon] why they were being done. He did not reply, but later I had heard that a woman or girl was to be entertained. When this woman came, however, the Emperor considered her too young and innocent and consequently he gave instructions for her to be paid and sent away.

Whether or not Napoleon had a mistress on the island was a question constantly discussed not only on St Helena but also in London. There were rumours on the island, eagerly promoted not only by Gourgaud, but also by Balmain, Montchenu and Baron von Stürmer, the Russian, French and Austrian commissioners, of affairs with the Balcombe girl, with Mary Ann Robinson, the 'Nymph of the Valley', with Miss Kneipps, 'the Rosebud', and, of course, with Mme Bertrand and Mme de Montholon, whose flirtatious manner in the Emperor's presence Gourgaud deprecated.

'What right have you to complain of Mme de Montholon coming to see me,' Napoleon angrily expostulated one day when Gourgaud made some sulky remark about the woman's visits to Longwood House, annoying him by repeating rumours which might be 'published in the gazettes and do some damage' to his reputation. 'You said the other day that every Jack had his Jill . . . Did you mean Mme de Montholon? . . . If I should sleep with her,' he demanded, not for the first time, 'what business is that of yours?'

'Well, Mme de Montholon certainly did her best to dote on his Majesty with her melting eyes, her dress so tightly nipped in at the waist, her ridiculous attempts to attempt the impossible by trying to be beautiful. And he encouraged her, allowing her to make such remarks as "some men of forty-eight still behave like young men". He teased her; he pinched her.'

'So long as I am on St Helena,' Gourgaud told Napoleon one day, 'I will never consent to give precedence to M. de Montholon and even less to his wife. She can be a whore if she wishes to, but I despise a man who lets himself be overborne by a woman, particularly by a scheming, ugly one.'

Alexander Balmain, in his reports to the Tsar, also described Mme de Montholon unjustly as ugly, as well as 'old' and 'dissipated'. 'She is now the great man's mistress,' Balmain continued with a malice designed to please his master. 'She used to be merely his confidante and act as his procuress. Persevering and simpering, she contrived to get there herself and she acquitted herself very well when she did get there. He is mad about her and gives her expensive presents of dresses and jewels. Luncheon, dinner, the times of getting up and going to bed are all dictated by her. In fact all Longwood is at her mercy.'

Anxious to get more reliable information than the gossip disseminated by Gourgaud and the flights of fancy dispatched to Russia by Balmain, the British government seized every opportunity of questioning those who returned from St Helena with accounts likely to be reasonably accurate. Thus, for instance, when in May 1819 Dr Baxter, the chief medical officer, returned to England after three years' service on the island, he was summoned to the Colonial Office by Lord Bathurst.

'On entering the room His Lordship came up to me and took me by the hand familiarly, desiring me to be seated. His first question was how

Bonaparte was. I said that as far as could be ascertained he was well at least. He asked whether he went out or took any exercise. I replied that he had been out in the evenings lately and that it was believed he took a great deal of exercise in the billiard-room [where, in fact, there was scarcely room to take any exercise at all]. He was anxious to know whether Bonaparte had access to women and whether it was thought Mesdames Bertrand and Montholon were condescending. I said I was not aware that anything of the kind took place, but it was not unlikely that either of these ladies would feel proud of any attention he might pay to them.'

Whether or not either or both of these women were 'condescending' during Napoleon's earlier time on the island, it seems certain that, as the months went by, while still intrigued by the sexual behaviour of various members of his entourage, he himself became increasingly disinclined to take a mistress. When Mme de Montholon made her provocative remark about forty-eight-year-old men behaving like young ones, he replied resignedly, 'Yes, but they don't have so many sorrows to bear as I do.' At that age, he said on another occasion, women had no longer cause to be afraid of him: he could not woo them successfully any more.

In July 1819, Mme de Montholon – suffering from severe depression and a liver complaint since the birth of a child believed to be Napoleon's and acknowledged by him as such – received permission to leave the island with her children and a nurse. Her husband was to remain with Napoleon who undertook to pay a large sum of money to his wife when she reached France and to bequeathe an even larger sum to de Montholon himself in his will.

> The day chosen for the departure having arrived [Marchand recorded], the Emperor went into the drawing room to receive Madame de Montholon and her children. He thanked her for the sacrifice she was making in letting her husband remain with him, and he gave her a valuable gold box with his portrait surrounded by very large diamonds, assuring her of his wishes for her happiness and that of her family. He gave her various instructions for Europe and his family which the Countess received in tears. The poor children shared their mother's sorrow. It soon became such a sad scene that the Emperor, too moved himself, did not wish to prolong it. He embraced them one after the other and went back into his apartment.

Concealed behind a curtain, he watched Mme de Montholon's departure and, for the first time on the island, so Gourgaud said, he wept. If they all left, Gourgaud thought, he would have to kill himself. 'You will return to Europe,' he said self-pityingly to Marchand that evening in his bath. 'You will see your family again. Your friends will surround you. You will want to know every detail of my existence on this miserable rock ... Montholon will find his wife and his children. You will find your mother. I will be dead, abandoned in this sad, solitary place.'

Mme Bertrand had also hoped to leave the 'abominable' island which, she said in a moment of vulgarity, the Devil must have 'shat as he flew from one world to the next'. She had, indeed, packed her trunks in readiness to depart with her children whose education, she felt, could no longer be entrusted to their present tutors – a British sergeant, a Corsican priest and Mme Bertrand's English maid who was married to the Emperor's valet, Saint-Denis. It was understood that General Bertrand would follow his wife in a year's time; but, at the last moment, Napoleon refused to agree to the departure of her husband, so Mme Bertrand remained also and, having for some time declined to dine at Napoleon's table any more, she refused to have anything more to do with him until a few hours before his death, never having forgiven him for his rude and insulting remarks, or for shooting her pet kids and any other vagrant animals that strayed into the garden when he was indulging a brief but enthusiastic taste for horticulture.

47

DREAMS AND MEMORIES

'Bah! Women! When you don't think of them,
you don't need them.'

IN THE EVENINGS AT LONGWOOD when he settled down to talk,
Napoleon often spoke of the women in his past life. As de Caulaincourt
had observed some years before, 'He enjoyed talking about his success
with women. If there was a weak side to the gifts of this great and
wonderful man it was vanity about the past.' He told Bertrand of his
taking Marie-Louise's virginity and of her 'asking for more', and it was
to Bertrand also that he had said that Josephine had 'the prettiest little
cunt in the world', comparing it to Les Trois-Îlets, the three small islands
in the wide bay in Martinique. He wondered if he had ever really
loved any of the women in his past life except Josephine and she not
unreservedly: she was such a dreadful liar, a skilful liar too, except with
regard to her age: and over this she would 'get into such a tangle that
her statements could only be reconciled on the hypothesis that her son
Eugène was twelve years old when he was born'. Besides, Napoleon said,
she was very jealous, except of Marie-Louise, who was, by contrast,
extremely jealous of her and who burst into tears when he tried to take
her to see the woman she took to be a rival for his affections.

He had been fond of Marie-Louise and extolled her good qualities,
her discretion, her truthfulness, her courtesy, her innocence, her love
for him. She would have followed him to Elba if she had not been
dissuaded by Mme de Montebello, her lady-in-waiting, who hated him,
and by her doctor, Jean Courvisart; and then her father, whom alone
of all the members of her family she truly loved, placed that 'scamp',

General Adam Albrecht von Neipperg by her side and she now had no inclination to return to her husband. One night he had a vivid dream of her. 'She looked as young as she was when I saw her at Compiègne,' he said. 'I took her in my arms but try as hard as I could to hold her tight, I felt her slipping away from me, and when I tried to embrace her again, everything had disappeared and I woke up.'

Should Marie-Louise die he would not marry again, he said, as though forgetting for the moment that the likelihood of finding a suitable bride on St Helena was very remote. Marie-Louise had given him the child for which he had left Josephine, from whom he would never have parted had she been able to do so herself. He had loved Josephine more than he had loved Marie-Louise, he said, returning to a favourite theme. He had chosen Josephine for no other reason than desire and affection. They had risen in the world together. He should never have married Marie-Louise: it was the 'greatest mistake' of his life; he should have married a Russian.

He spoke also of his sisters, principally of Caroline, working himself up into a fury whenever he mentioned her supposed second marriage within little more than a year of the death of her first husband, and choosing, of all people, Francesco Macdonald, the Italian-born General of Scottish and Irish descent. When he first heard of this misalliance his anger was unrestrained. Montholon said that he had never seen him in such a rage. At dinner that evening he complained with shocking violence that the pastry was gritty. The cook responsible must immediately be beaten and dismissed.

He also talked of his mistresses, counting them up on his fingers and, underestimating their number, announced that there had been seven of them. He mentioned the 'seventeen-year-old' Mme Fourès, though not by name, and Mlle George and Mme Grassini and Mme Duchâtel and Mme Pellapra and Eléonore Denuelle. There was also a Mme Mathis 'who accepted presents' and an Austrian woman, an 'agreeable person' whom he mentioned on another occasion. 'She wore no perfume,' he said. 'When day came she woke me up and I have never seen her since. In 1809, however, the Chief of the Vienna police told me she was a Judith, a Jewess.' And he talked as well about Countess Walewska. 'She is rich,' he commented, 'and must have saved money, and I settled a great deal on the two children.'

'Your Majesty,' said Gourgaud, 'paid Madame Walewska ten thousand francs a month.'

Gourgaud maintained improbably that at this tactless interposition Napoleon blushed and asked him how he had come to know this.

'Good Lord!' Gourgaud said. 'As if I were not so close to your Majesty not to know this sort of thing. Your household knew everything.'

After hearing 'with complacency' of her remarriage, Napoleon soon lost interest in Mme Walewska; and he learned of her death with apparent indifference. Indeed, by then, while obviously appreciative of an attractive woman, he was beginning to lose his libido. He maintained that ever since being crowned Emperor, while still 'naturally susceptible' to the attractions of women, he had tended to avoid them for fear of becoming dominated by them. This was a great blunder, he went on to say. If he were still on the throne he would spend at least two hours a day with a woman: 'one could learn so much from them'. He enjoyed talking about them to the end. 'Let's discuss women,' he would say to his male companions when the conversation had taken a gloomy turn; and then he would wonder why he preferred fair women to dark or whether a woman who was fairly fat was to be preferred to one who was thin. He himself preferred them 'well covered'. 'I will soon be with you,' he had once written to Josephine. 'May I find you plump and rosy.'

He was certainly plumper than ever now himself. As early as 1817, on seeing him for the first time, the surgeon of the 66th Regiment said that 'his general look was more that of an obese Spanish or Portuguese friar than the hero of modern times'. Some time later he was described as being 'as fat as a Chinese pig'.

Occasionally, he displayed homosexual tendencies. He said one day, so de Caulaincourt related in his *Mémoires*, that his friendship with handsome men generally started with a physical attraction 'in the loins and in another place which shall be nameless'. Talleyrand believed that he and Bourrienne had once been lovers. Certainly he liked to surround himself and promote the interests of handsome young men such as Roustam Raza, Saint-Denis, Louis Constant – who, as a young man in Josephine's service, had been the object of one of Napoleon's intense stares before being taken into the Emperor's own service – Louis Marchand, 'Mamzelle Marchand', as his master often called him, General

Duroc, whose death affected him so grievously, and the effeminate Chevalier de Sainte Croix, whose advancement, as Constant said, was 'both brilliant and rapid'. 'Enlisting at the age of twenty-two,' Constant wrote, 'Sainte Croix was already a general of division when he was killed in Spain. I often saw him at the Emperor's headquarters – a slightly built, dapper little fellow, with a pretty, smooth face more like a girl's than that of a brave soldier, which he certainly was.'

After the departure from St Helena of Mme de Montholon, Napoleon no longer desired a mistress. Gradually, he became confirmed in an ever-increasing misogyny and lost interest in the gossip which had previously intrigued him. No longer did he relish hearing about what André Pons de l'Hérault, manager of Elba's iron mines, had called 'the salacious details of married lives'.

'I don't like women very much,' he confessed, 'nor games of any kind. I am, I suppose, a purely political animal.' 'Bah!' he once exclaimed to Gourgaud. 'Women! When you don't think of them, you don't need them.' 'You spend your time enjoying everything,' he had said years before to his brother, Joseph. 'I spend mine in thought and never in enjoyment. You love women, I scarcely ever think of them.' After all, sexual love was harmful 'both to society and to the individual happiness of men'.

When he did think of women and speak of them he was rarely complimentary. He told the surgeon, Barry O'Meara, that too many of them were allowed to accompany his armies. 'Women,' he said, 'when they are bad, they are worse than men, and more ready to commit crime.' When degraded 'they fall lower' than men. 'Witness the *tricoteuses de Paris* during the Revolution.' Women, after all, as he said more than once, were 'mere machines for making children'.

'Women!' he declared on another occasion. 'They belong to the highest bidder. Power is what they like. It is the greatest of aphrodisiacs. They are fascinated by it ... As for me, I take them and forget them.'

'For every woman who inspires us to do good things,' he said one evening, no doubt to rile Mme Montholon and Mme Bertrand, 'there are hundreds who bring us to folly ... Really we Westerners do not understand women at all. We have spoiled everything by treating them far too well. It was utterly wrong to lift women up almost to our own level. The orientals managed these things much better. They maintained that woman was man's property; and in very truth nature made woman to be the slave of man.'

48

DEATH OF THE EMPEROR

'My death is premature. I have been assassinated
by the English oligarchy and their hired murderer.'

BY THE END OF 1819, it was already clear that Napoleon's health was failing. Although he himself claimed that he had 'never needed any doctors', that his constitution was 'made of steel', he had, in fact, throughout his adult life suffered intermittently from an extraordinary variety of complaints – these included insomnia, headaches, persistent coughing, pain while urinating (which he believed was relieved by his very hot baths), scabies, chronic dermatitis which drove him to scratch his skin until it bled, fits of shivering, profuse sweating, nausea, acute pain in his side, vomiting, a high temperature, swelling of the gums, loosening of the teeth, a much-distended stomach, a slow heart beat, syphilis possibly, possibly also from acromegaly, which induces both torpor and over-optimism, and certainly from epileptic fits, experiencing another severe one in October 1805 during the stressful days before the victory at Ulm. During this fit he had fallen to the ground in convulsions, fighting for breath, vomiting, his lips covered in foam. Recovering after a quarter of an hour, he had instructed those who had witnessed his distress, the comte de Rémusat, his chamberlain, and the alarmed Talley-rand, not to breathe a word of it to anyone.

After O'Meara's departure from the island, Napoleon was treated by a succession of doctors, one of whom, a British army surgeon, was, as others were, submitted to a succession of often unrelated questions on trivial subjects:

'What do your sailors drink?'

'Beer.'

'But when they get their pay I suppose they drink wine?'

'No, they drink brandy or beer.'

'What sort of brandy? French?'

'Usually English brandy, grain alcohol.'

'Does it taste very different?'

'Yes, very.'

'Have you been to Paris?'

'Yes.'

'How long did you stay?'

'Five weeks.'

'Did you visit Lord Wentworth?'

'Yes.'

'Did you see Lady Dorset?'

'Yes.'

'Did you have dinner with them?'

'No.'

'Where did you stay?'

'At the Hôtel Saint-Thomas.'

'Where did you eat?'

'At various restaurants.'

'How much did it cost? ... Would it have cost twice as much in London?'

'Yes.'

'How much does land in England yield?'

'Three to four per cent.'

And so the cross-examinations would proceed, persistently and tiresomely, minute after minute.

Another of Napoleon's doctors, Francesco Antommarchi, was also submitted to them. This doctor, a Corsican dissection-room assistant, had been recommended by Cardinal Fesch. He and Madame Mère, who addressed several unavailing letters to the Prince Regent on her son's behalf, also sent two servants to replace men who had departed as well as two Corsican priests, one of whom was very young and so ill-educated that he wrote with difficulty, the other an old man who could scarcely speak coherently because of a recent stroke. In one of the trunks brought to the island by these Corsican priests was a miniature of the King of

Rome. 'The Emperor smiled with great pleasure at the sight of this miniature of his son,' Marchand recalled. 'Tears came into his eyes. "Poor child," he said. "What a destiny!" Then, handing it to me, he said, "Here, place it open on my desk so that I can see it every day."'

By the middle of April 1821 it was obvious that Napoleon was dying, the huge doses of calamel administered to him, as well as tartar emetic, merely hastening his death.

It was difficult by now to persuade him to get out of bed in the morning; and, when he did so, he walked, or rather waddled unsteadily for short distances in a dirty dressing gown, breathing hard. 'I am dying,' he said one day. 'I can feel it. My hour has come ... There is nothing left of me ... My strength and faculties are deserting me.' It was a rare outburst: he spoke little now and would remain silent in his room, with Bertrand for company, for hours on end. He was only occasionally seen outside the house. Indeed, he had been increasingly reluctant to go for walks or rides since Lowe had limited his excursions – to be undertaken only in sight of a British officer – to within eight miles of the house. On one of these rare excursions he was observed by an English officer who wrote that his face was 'as white as a sheet of paper. He seems weak and staggers when he walks. His body is bent. He is as fat as ever. He goes muffled up in a greatcoat and wears long pantaloons.'

He often felt dizzy and complained of deafness and such lassitude that it was an effort, so he said, to open his eyes. In the night when he awoke from a troubled sleep and saw someone sitting in his room he asked to be left alone; and, when he was left alone, he called out for someone to come to keep him company.

'My death is premature,' he wrote in a final version of his will in which he left 'ten thousand francs to the sub-officer [Marie-André-Nicolas] Cantillon' who had 'attempted to assassinate Lord Wellington'. 'I have been assassinated by the English oligarchy and their hired murderer.' At the end of the month, after he had refused to see Antommarchi or any of the other doctors who had been called in to attend to him, his condition grew worse as he shivered and hiccupped on his iron bed. Bertrand, who was standing beside it, was reduced to tears as the dying man asked repeatedly and vainly for a cup of coffee, 'always without success and always without any display of bad temper ... He, who had been so feared and had so confidently commanded, was as docile as a little child.'

On 2 May, the younger of the two Corsican priests administered extreme unction, despite Bertrand's protests that Napoleon as a free-thinker would not have wanted it but was too weak to resist. He lingered on for three more days. The room filled with servants and members of his suite. Mme Bertrand was there. She called for her children who were brought into the room only to be taken out when the eldest fainted. Her maid, Mary Hall, also came and asked if her child, though barely one year old, might be allowed to kiss the dying man's hand. So Marchand lifted the little girl up and, kneeling down, he 'brought the Emperor's hand close to her so that her lips could touch it without causing undue fear'.

On the afternoon of 6 May 1821, at the age of fifty-one, Napoleon died with a sigh. Among the last words he was heard to murmur was 'Josephine'.

49

ELISA AND CAROLINE

'She speaks with much agitation of
the Allies' persecution of her.'

THE DAY AFTER Joachim Murat's troops had entered Florence, Elisa
Bacciochi had left it. The Florentines had not been sorry to see her go.
She had done her best to establish good relations with them, in so far
as the directives transmitted to her by her imperial brother would allow.
She had given grand levees at the redecorated Pitti Palace; she had saved
various religious houses from extinction, and had given valuable aid to
a number of charitable institutions. But she had none of the alluring
charm of her sister-in-law, Josephine, and her stolid, unimaginative,
placid husband, Felice Bacciochi, had even less.

She settled in Trieste in a house on the Campo Marzio, later also
owning a villa by the sea, calling herself the contessa di Compignano.
Trieste was a dull city; but at least Jérôme, the Prince de Montfort, her
favourite brother since she had fallen out with Lucien, also came to live
there with his family. Joseph Fouché, duc d'Otrante, also settled in
Trieste, having acquired a fortune; and he and Elisa enjoyed reminiscing
about the days of the Empire while her husband went for walks by the
sea. Their daughter, Napoléone-Elisa became increasingly masculine,
wearing men's clothes and driving her carriage. She married an Italian
count whom she bullied and soon deserted.

Napoléone-Elisa's father had become quite an imposing figure; but
his wife, embittered and often grumpy, was now immensely fat and
almost bald, bearing an extraordinary resemblance to her brother, Napoleon, who had never overcome his dislike of her. She was not in good

health and in July 1820, at the age of forty-three, while inspecting the excavations which she had initiated at the site of Aquileia, she caught a fever from which she did not recover. Jérôme was with her when she died: her last wish was that he should look after Felice Bacciochi who, in fact, lived on in apparent contentment for several more years.

In 1823, for the sake of her health, Metternich granted permission for Caroline Murat to go to take a course of the waters from the warm saline springs at Battaglia in Venetia, and from there to go on to Venice. She was delighted to be able to get away, she told her former secretary, Louis Frédéric de Mercey, and to talk Italian again. 'I talk to everyone I meet,' she said. 'I have been almost deaf and dumb for eight years, for you know I don't speak German.'

She would have liked to remain in Italy or go to Holland to stay with Joseph's wife, Julie, or to Switzerland. But, for one reason or another, all these places were considered unsuitable, so she was obliged to return to Trieste with a view to going to America with her son, Lucien, who had decided to emigrate like his brother and who eventually joined him there without his mother.

'My patience is exhausted,' Caroline expostulated to Metternich. 'They are compelling me to leave every country where I might find peace and shutting me out of every town other than those which suit neither my health nor my means.' She said as much to Julie Récamier who called at Trieste on her way back from Naples to Paris. 'Why do they refuse me what they readily allow to other members of my family? . . . They are left alone, free to travel. I'm the only one who is persecuted.'

She was still plagued by money troubles: there was difficulty in selling her property at Frohsdorf and both her sons, 'completely mistaken' about her financial position, were constantly asking her to send them money, even though she had 'not a penny in income'.

When her mother, aged seventy-nine, stumbled and fell while walking in the gardens of the Villa Borghese in April 1830, Caroline did, at last, obtain permission to go to Rome to see her for the first time in fifteen years. But no sooner had she arrived than complaints were made by King Ferdinand in Naples and by the authorities in Paris who demanded her expulsion.

When Henry Edward Fox, later fourth Baron Holland, called upon her at the Palazzo Raspoli, he found her servants packing up in readiness for her enforced departure. He thought she was still beautiful, though stout and stumpy. 'However, notwithstanding that, she is very graceful and dignified,' he wrote. 'Her complexion, which I had heard was blotched and bad, was very clear and her features are regular. Her mouth has a very peculiar expression of firmness and decision, which, when it relaxes into a smile, is uncommonly pretty and playful . . . Her voice is very sweet. She speaks French with a very strong Italian accent but with great fluency . . . She speaks with much agitation of the Allies' persecution of her. However, her vanity is considerably flattered by the importance all the foreign courts seem to attach to her movements . . . All ideas of being still an object of admiration to men she has not yet relinquished.'

She was, however, on this occasion extremely annoyed and in a very bad temper, having been told she must leave the Papal States immediately. She spoke angrily of her ill treatment and the persecution to which she was subjected. She said that she would refuse to go: the papal authorities would have to remove her by force. She did not, in the end, put them or herself to this embarrassment. Having gained an extra day's grace, she left Rome for Trieste, calling on the way to see her daughter, Letitia, who had not long since married the conte di Castiglione.

In Trieste there were further trials for her to face: her son, Achille, had returned from America and had gone to England with wild ideas of fulfilling his father's dream of liberating and uniting Italy. His career in America had not led anyone to suppose that it was remotely probable that he would succeed in this ambition. Thirty years old, fat and bald, with a finger partially severed in a duel, he was married to a woman distantly related to George Washington. She had brought him little in the way of a dowry apart from a house in Virginia and ten black slaves. He had been a planter, a lawyer, a colonel in the militia, and was remarkable for certain eccentricities of which he seemed unaccountably proud, such as declining to wash, sleeping in his boots, and, while chewing tobacco, expectorating on to a long-haired dog in the absence of a spitoon. He let it be known that he had eaten every kind of food that the New World had to offer, including crocodiles and buzzards, and claimed to be not averse to Indians if well fried. He had had ludicrous plans of placing Napoleon's son, the King of Rome, known since 1818 as the Duke of Reichstadt, on the throne of France with himself as Regent.

Caroline heard of Achille's activities in England with alarm, as she did those of his brother, Lucien, who was reported to have dashed home naked from a tavern in a thunderstorm with his clothes tied up in a bundle and to have been brought to court for repeatedly kicking a stableboy. She was even more alarmed when she learned that Achille had gone to Belgium with the intention of seeking King Leopold's help in creating a foreign legion. Having failed, of course, in this endeavour, he left for Portugal where he was as unsuccessful as he had been elsewhere in arousing enthusiasm for his Italian dream. He returned to London and thence back to America.

Weakened by worry and sleepless nights, Caroline contracted cholera in the European epidemic of 1831, and was kept in bed, feverish and in pain, for several weeks, nursed attentively by her two kind daughters. Having at last, with Metternich's help, received permission to live in Italy, she settled in Florence where her brother Jérôme and his family were then living. For a time she lived in the apartments of her other peripatetic brother, Louis, then in Casa Capponi in the via del Mandorlo and finally in Palazzo Grifoni, now Palazzo Riccardi-Manelli, in Piazza Santissima Annunziata.

Here in Palazzo Grifoni, Caroline established a kind of salon such as those her sister-in-law Josephine had known in Paris:

> There are normally four or five rooms open [wrote one of her guests, the American sculptor, Horatio Greenough]. In one there are card tables; in another billiards; in a third tea is served throughout the evening ... It is very pleasant.

The poet, journalist and novelist, François-Joseph Méry, thought so, too.

> In her house [Méry wrote] no one asks the political opinions of her guests. On the threshold one says, 'I am French', and the doors are thrown open and one is given a cordial welcome. The whole universe is represented in the salon of the comtesse de Lipona ... Sorrow and years have passed over her without the brilliant *éclat* of her youth being dimmed by the tears she has shed. If a stranger went into her salon for the first time and saw

a room filled with the most beautiful women in Florence he would not hesitate in picking out the one who is the comtesse de Lipona.

'About midnight,' wrote another of her guests, 'we gathered to talk, often until morning. There was inexpressible charm in those vigils. The room would still be in disarray after a concert or a ball: although the musicians had disappeared, the sheets of music were still scattered on the stands, the lamps extinguished on the card tables and the four chairs around each of them unoccupied. The conversation continued until morning, with tea and delicious biscuits stamped with the arms of the Queen of Naples.'

Her guests were amazed by her vitality. She would stay up until the early morning, listening to music, talking, protesting that she needed no more than three hours' sleep. 'It's a good habit,' she claimed. 'I owe it to my brother, the Emperor.' But she was not happy.

She saw little of Louis while she was living in Florence, and she quarrelled with Jérôme whose daughter, Mathilde de Montfort, said that, when she saw her approaching in the Cascine park, 'we had to turn back and look the other way so that we did not have to greet her. I must say we did not feel very friendly towards her ... She was never nice to us ... She never failed to make some rude remark such as "Mathilde is growing too fat" or "Napoleon has not grown an inch." '

Caroline became increasingly unhappy and contentious as the months went by. She was suffering from cancer of the stomach and was often in severe pain; yet in the summer of 1836 she brought herself to seek permission to travel to Paris to seek payment of the money due to her under the terms of the Treaty of Fontainebleau. She received permission to do so on the understanding that she would stay no longer than a month and, while there, behave with the utmost circumspection. The longed-for *permis* so excited her that she became ill and felt so weak that she was unable to move or make any plans. At the beginning of September, however, although still feeling wretched, she set sail from Leghorn to Marseilles and, within a few days, was staying in the rue Royale in Paris in the house of Napoleon's former secretary, Claude-François de Méneval. From there she moved to apartments in the rue de la Ville-l'Exchêque where she received calls from former friends, one of whom described her as little changed after more than twenty years' absence from France and still in possession of her 'delightful smile'.

She managed to extract a pension of a hundred thousand francs a year before returning to Florence; but the money brought her little contentment. Nor, after General Macdonald's death in 1837, did the offhand attentions of her French secretary and lover, a handsome, grasping wastrel named Chavel.

In the winter of 1837, Josephine's daughter Hortense died in Switzerland in a ramshackle villa on the shores of Lake Constance; Cardinal Fesch died in Rome on 13 May 1839; and Caroline herself, at fifty-seven, had little time left.

At the beginning of March 1839, her niece Charlotte, Joseph's and Julie's daughter, died unexpectedly. Caroline visited the bereaved mother regularly thereafter, endeavouring to comfort her. But the house was so cold and the atmosphere so miserable that she felt unable to continue her visits into the spring and she took to her bed again. The cancer in her stomach in an advanced stage by now, she died on 18 May.

50

PAULINE AND MADAME MÈRE

'People peer at me from behind curtains.'

STROLLING THROUGH THE BORGHESE GARDENS in Rome, the young poet, Alphonse de Lamartine, was often intrigued by the sight of a beautiful woman driving by in the shade of the umbrella pines.

> It was during the last years of her short life [he recalled]. She was still resplendent like the head of a Greek Venus . . . I do not know by what whim, in a woman who was capricious all her days, that she usually had a poor monk by her side in the carriage. The contrast between his coarse brown cowl and that face of beauty dying now after so much brilliance, made one either smile or brought the tears to one's eyes.

Pauline Borghese was also to be seen from time to time walking on the Palatine Hill or in the grass-covered ruins of the Colosseum, a thin figure often wearing 'a severe black merino dress and an Empire-style turban'. She was still married to Prince Borghese and, thanks to the intervention of Pope Pius VII, she was still enjoying the use of the Palazzo Borghese, despite the attempts of her husband – who was openly living with the beautiful duchessa Lante delle Rovere – to get the marriage annulled. As well as the Villa Paolina by the Porta Pia in Rome, the Princess owned another Villa Paolina at Viareggio; and, having sold her house in Paris (the Hôtel de Charost) so satisfactorily, she did not have the financial worries that beset so many of the other members of her family.

In her houses in Rome she entertained a stream of visitors, many of them English noblemen now free to travel in a continent at peace, among them the Duke of Devonshire, the Marquess of Hamilton, Lord Kensington and Lord Holland. It was, so a French writer observed, their recognized meeting-place: they were 'always there in great numbers, most of them . . . very rich.'

Lady Morgan, the Irish novelist, described one of these gatherings at Princess Pauline's house:

> The day before we left Rome, we breakfasted at the Villa Paolina, with a circle composed of British nobility, of Roman princes and princesses, German Grandees and American merchants – a singular congress. The collation was of sweetmeats, ices, light wines, coffee; and the principal amusement, looking at the elegant apartments of the Villa, sauntering in the gardens, and visiting some antiquities within their walls . . . It is the most hospitable house in Rome . . . No lady was ever so attended by Cardinals as the beautiful Pauline.

She was still beautiful, certainly, but ever conscious of that beauty slowly fading. When the duchesse d'Abrantès came to see her in 1817 she said to her, 'You find me very much changed, don't you?' She sent her to see Canova's statue which was still held in a locked room at the Palazzo Borghese. But only too well aware that her thin body no longer resembled the enticing one that the sculptor had seen and had portrayed in what Laure d'Abrantès described as 'all its voluptuous perfection', she wrote to Prince Borghese a few months later, 'I know that you sometimes allow my statue in marble to be seen. I shall be glad if that were no longer the case: because of the nudity of the figure which borders on indecency. It was made only to give you pleasure. Since that is no longer the case, it is only right that it should be removed from view.'

Often to be seen in Pauline's company was her lover, the composer, Giovanni Pacini. Such pleasure as he brought to her, however, was overwhelmed when she heard that Napoleon was dying on St Helena. She wrote to Lord Liverpool, the Prime Minister, on 11 July 1821 to 'demand, in the name of every member of his family', a change of climate. 'If a request so just is refused, then it will be his death warrant,' she continued, 'and so I ask permission to go to join the Emperor and to be with him in his last moments.'

She wrote numerous similar letters to other ministers and heads of state, to which she received no reply. Her brother had already died two months before the last of these letters was written. For days thereafter, Pauline shut herself up in her room, refusing to see anyone.

When she emerged she set out for Lucca with Pacini who had been appointed *maestro di cappella* there. They passed through Pisa where Lord Holland called on her.

> Her manner and reception could not have been more royal if Napoleon was still upon the throne [he wrote]. She has been very ill. Her face is very beautiful but angular. The expression of her countenance is very *vif* and full of talent. Her voice was affected by a cold but very harmonious and I was far from disappointed. Her manner is very royal, and with that well-bred indifference which persons in such exalted stations must assume, and which makes them, while engaged in one conversation, say a civil word in another ... She was amazingly civil to me and talked a good deal.

It was true that she had been very ill; and, well aware of this, her husband was persuaded by Pope Pius VII's successor, Leo XII, to abandon the duchessa Lante delle Rovere and come to live with her again at the Palazzo Borghese.

Their reunion was brief. Suffering from pulmonary tuberculosis, she did 'nothing but vomit and suffer', she told her brother Louis on 13 May 1825.

'I am reduced to a shadow,' she added. 'They are mending the street and I can't bear the terrible noise. The Prince is going to take a villa in the suburbs here where we intend to spend the rest of the month. It is impossible to consider going to the Villa Paolina at Lucca ... Embrace Mamma. I send a thousand good wishes to the family.' Less than a month later she died at the Villa Strozzi, concerned, even at the end, that she would look 'such a fright' when dead.

The house at Lucca she bequeathed to her husband in recognition, so she said, 'of the sincere care he has shown me in my long last illness ... and because he always behaved towards the Emperor, my brother, with the greatest loyalty.'

Among her last requests was a wish 'not to be exposed in the apartments as is the custom'. 'I desire to be embalmed and taken to Rome,' she wrote. 'That is my domicile . . . I wish to be placed in the church of Santa Maria Maggiore in the Borghese chapel. I die a prey to the cruel and horrible pains of a long illness . . . I die without feelings of hatred or animosity towards anyone.'

Far away on St Helena, her brother had spoken of Pauline with affection: 'Pauline was probably the most beautiful woman of her time and . . . the best creature in the world . . . But she was too prodigal, too wild. She could have been immensely rich considering the sums I gave her, but she gave it all away, though her mother often lectured her [Mme Mère told Joseph "she amuses herself with drawing up budgets but she never keeps to them for more than a month"]. She warned Pauline that she would die in the workhouse.'

Mme Mère had long since returned to Rome and was now living in her well-furnished apartment on the first floor of the Palazzo Falconieri. Cardinal Fesch, whose apartment was on the floor above, had covered her walls as well as his own with part of his enormous collection of paintings, hundreds upon hundreds of them overflowing into rooms rented in nearby houses and stacked up in piles against the walls, so many of them, indeed, that Fesch once remarked that there was only one government which could afford to purchase them.

'We often visited Mme Letizia,' wrote Lady Morgan who was then living in Rome, 'and always found a number of fires burning in the rooms. Their servants were in gorgeous livery; Madame's was green and gold. There were carpets everywhere.'

Comfortable in Rome though she was, she had written to her son on St Helena, offering to go there to live with him. Las Cases described his response when he received the letter:

> He read it through at once, sighed, read it again, tore it up and threw it under the table. It had arrived opened. He took up a newspaper again, then, after a few minutes, looked up and said, 'It's from poor Madame. She's well and wants to join me.' Then he went on reading the paper.

She wrote again, more than once; but, receiving no reply, she complained to Lord Holland who approached Lord Bathurst on her behalf but, did not find him sympathetic. As well as letters she sent money, much of which did not arrive.

Receiving no replies from her son, she appealed to the Pope who, in turn, wrote to the Prince Regent of the 'deadly climate' of the island to which the 'poor exile' had been confined. If the Regent received this letter he did not reply to it.

Mme Mère wrote also to Lord Liverpool as well as to Lord Holland:

> The account sent to me by the surgeon Antommarchi, of the condition of my son Napoleon, which is confirmed by an eye-witness, removes all hope of seeing my son again if he continues to be detained on St Helena . . . Oh! has not the might of England the means of keeping him in a European climate, where he could recover his health and be aided by medical care and a good climate, and have the consolation of being looked after by one of his family? The feelings of a sorrowing mother could say much, but I would rather your humanity and your own feelings were the means . . .

Towards the end of 1818, Mme Mère moved to the Palazzo Rinuccini, afterwards known as Palazzo Bonaparte and now Palazzo Misciatelli, on the corner of the Corso and the Piazza Venezia. Her apartments, filled with busts and portraits of her family, were on the first floor, and Canova's statue of Napoleon stood at the foot of the grand staircase. One day her reader came across a report in the *Gazette de Rome* which announced Napoleon's death. 'It surely isn't possible,' she said, 'that Napoleon's mother should have been left to learn of his death through a newspaper.'

She had turned so pale when the report had been read to her that it seemed she was on the verge of fainting; but she insisted it could not be true and wrote to complain to the papal authorities of their allowing such a report to be published without checking its reliability. Having protested to the papal Secretary of State, she vainly appealed to the allied sovereigns, then in conference at Aix-la-Chapelle, begging them to put an end to her sick son's anguish and to set him free.

*   *   *

Despite her concern for Napoleon's well-being on St Helena, although her sight was becoming appreciably poorer by the month, Mme Mère still took pleasure in looking down upon the carriages and people passing through the piazza below her windows, and in the visits of Cardinal Fesch, who came to see her almost every day, making an occasional comment, falling asleep in his chair, and, when awakened, soon nodding off again, his constitution weakened by the strictness of his penitential fasting and the rigidity of other forms of self-denial and punishment.

Mme Mère also took pleasure in listening to extracts from books and plays about Napoleon which were now appearing in Paris and, in particular, she enjoyed *Napoleon Bonaparte*, a play by Alexandre Dumas, the son of the general, which she asked to be read to her more than once, although its last act, set on St Helena, made her cry.

Both the Cardinal and Mme Mère had become convinced that Napoleon was no longer on St Helena, a conviction impressed upon them by an Austrian clairvoyante, Frau Kleinmüller, who persuaded them to believe that the English had taken him elsewhere.

> You must have gathered from our letters [Fesch wrote to Las Cases] how certain we are of the deliverance ... Although the gazettes and the English still maintain that he is at St Helena, we have good reason to believe he is no longer there and, although we do not still know where he is or when he will reappear we have enough proof for persisting in our beliefs ... There can be no doubt that the gaoler of St Helena is making Count Bertrand write to you as though he still held Napoleon in his clutches.

Pauline had been appalled by her mother and uncle 'letting themselves be deluded by this scheming Austrian woman, "who said she was in touch with the Holy Virgin and persuaded them to believe the wildest nonsense".'

'Louis and I have done all we could to overcome the effects of this witch but to no purpose,' Pauline had continued. 'Mama is very devout and gives a lot to her. It's all a horrible intrigue and Colonna, her Chamberlain, abets it all. He is in church from morning to night ... The Cardinal has almost gone mad, for he openly says the Emperor is no longer at St Helena and that he has had revelations as to where he is ... he hid the letters and news he received from St Helena and told us that this silence ought to be enough to convince us ... I won't dwell on the scenes and quarrels, and the coolness that has naturally come between us as a result . . . I quarrelled so bitterly with the Cardinal that I never want to see him again.'

So persuaded was Mme Mère that her son had escaped from St Helena that she urged Joseph's wife Julie not to go to America to join her husband since Napoleon would shortly reappear and they would all, once again, be able to go where they liked.

It was on 22 July that Mme Mère was at last convinced that her son had died almost two and a half months before. The news, which had been received in Rome on 16 July, had been kept from her for six days. When eventually she was told she fainted; and for over a fortnight she remained inconsolable, refusing to see visitors, even Cardinal Fesch, and leaving letters of condolence unanswered and unacknowledged.

Surrounded by portraits and busts of her family, Mme Mère lived on at the Palazzo Rinuccini in her mourning clothes of a black merino gown with a black or white apron year after year, rarely emerging from it except to go to Mass, receiving few visitors other than members of her family, listening to the voice of her reader as she gazed all but sightlessly out of the window, her eyes grey and cloudy with cataracts. From time to time she could be seen running her fingers over the sculpted features of a bust of her grandson, the former King of Rome.

One of her other grandsons, Jérôme Bonaparte's youngest son, wrote of the 'extraordinary atmosphere of laurels and snuff' in the Palazzo Rinuccini where one was always 'aware of mighty shadows passing. A singular solemnity dominated an atmosphere that was at the same time domestic and epic. It was extraordinary to hear [my grandmother's] voice sometimes saying things strangely at variance with the majesty of the setting.'

'My children gave me a lot of trouble,' she said one day. 'But at least I spanked them soundly.' Speaking of a later time, she said, 'Twenty years ago, whenever I entered the Tuileries, drums were beaten, soldiers presented arms, and crowds flocked around my carriage. Now people peer at me from behind curtains and are afraid to display indiscreet curiosity.'

One day, while walking in the gardens of the Vigna Palatina, Lady

Blessington came upon her. She was attended by her chaplain and others of her suite; and, 'having heard that Mme Mère disliked meeting strangers', Lady Blessington 'retired to a distant part of the garden'.

> But the ex-King of Westphalia [Jérôme Bonaparte], having recognised my carriage in the courtyard sent to request us to join them and presented us to his mother. Madame Letitia Bonaparte is tall and slight, her figure gently bowed by age, but nevertheless dignified ... Her manner is graceful and gentle ... Her face is, even still, remarkably handsome, bearing proof of the accuracy of Canova's remarkable statue of her ... She is pale, and the expression of her countenance is pensive, unless when occasionally lighted up by some observations, when her dark eye glances for a moment with animation, but quickly resumes its melancholy character again ... Her feet are small and her hands admirable. Her voice is low and sweet ... she spoke of the Emperor Napoleon; and her lips quivered and her eyes filled with tears. 'I shall soon join him in that better world where no tears are shed,' she said, wiping away those that chased each other down her cheeks. 'I should have done so long ago, but God sees what is best for me.' ...
>
> Madame Mère invited us to visit her, and in parting touched my forehead with her lips, and shook hands with Lord Blessington, saying kind and flattering things to us both.

In 1830, the year of revolution in France, Mme Mère fell and fractured her thigh. She was over eighty years old by now and was not expected to survive. As many of her children and grandchildren as could reach her, together with their wives and husbands, came to the Palazzo Rinuccini to see her, to receive her blessing before she died. But she went on living, pushed from room to room in an invalid chair, attended by a household much reduced, though still numerous, comprising her chamberlain, her lady-companion and reader, her black-clothed secretary, her door-keeper and footman, her coachman, her cook and her maids. Advised to do so by her doctor, she went out on most days for a drive, attention drawn to her carriage by the brightly painted coat-of-arms on its doors. This carriage and its pale, black-clothed occupant were by then one of the sights of Rome. Tourists' guides could be heard announcing to their followers, '*Ecco, signori e signore: la madre di Napoleone.*' The wife of the French painter, Louis Boulanger, thought that the most memorable sights in Italy were Vesuvius in eruption, the carnival in Venice and the mother of Napoleon.

Her eyesight quite gone, Mme Mère lived in the past. When her son Jérôme came to see her one day, he told her that Napoleon's statue was to be replaced on the column in the Place Vendôme. Since she made no comment, Jérôme thought that she had not heard what he had said; so he repeated it. She had heard him the first time but, overcome by emotion, she could not bring herself to reply. At last she squeezed his hand and repeated the words he had spoken, 'The Emperor's statue, the Emperor's statue.'

She was close to death now; and did not long survive the shock and grief she endured upon learning of the death of her grandson, the Duke of Reichstadt, whose friend, Anton Prokesch von Osten, had been to see her while, unknown to them, the Duke was dying at Schönbrunn. She rose with great difficulty to greet her visitor and plied him with questions about his friend, asking about his illness and treatment and if he ever spoke of his grandmother. Assured that he did, tears came to her eyes and fell on her dress. Prokesch told her of the young man's intelligence and great qualities, remarking also that his mind worked slowly sometimes. 'His father was like that as a child,' she said. 'That was why I was less hopeful for him than for any of my other children when he first started at school. It was a long time before he had any success; but, when he did get his first good report he hurried to show it to me, and then put it on a chair and sat on it with all the pride of victory.' The Duke's hour will also come, she said, 'and he will sit on his father's throne'.

Keat's biographer, Lord Houghton, told Augustus Hare that she was 'a very long time dying'. 'It was a kind of lying in state,' Houghton said, 'and for a *scudo* the porter used to let people in behind a screen which was at the foot of the bed, and they looked at her through the joinings. I was only a boy then, and I thought there was plenty of time; but one day [2 February 1836], as the church bells were ringing for evensong, she died.' Soon after her death the Danish sculptor Bertel Thorvaldsen, was called upon to take a cast of her composed and still distinguished features.

A few days later, a French visitor called at the palazzo and found all the doors open and no one to take his *scudo* entrance fee. Mme

Mère was lying in state on a bed covered with silver-fringed black velvet, its canopy topped by four silver eagles. He thought the dead woman's face was the most beautiful he had ever seen.

Not long before his own death, Napoleon had paid tribute to her influence over him. 'My excellent mother,' he had said, 'is a woman of courage and great talent, more of a masculine than feminine nature, proud and high-minded ... To the manner in which she formed me at an early age, I principally owe my subsequent elevation. My opinion is that the conduct of a child entirely depends upon the mother.'

THE RETURN TO PARIS

'Now, let's go home to die.'

NAPOLEON WAS BURIED on the island near the spring from which water had been carried twice a day to Longwood House. After the July revolution of 1830, however, and the establishment of the bourgeois monarchy of King Louis-Philippe, there was a recrudescence of the Napoleonic legend and demands were made for the return of the Emperor's remains to the banks of the Seine where he had asked to be buried. Accordingly, in 1840, the King's son, François, prince de Joinville, was sent to recover the body from its grave in St Helena. The Abbé Coquereau, who was present at the disinterment and sprinkled the body with holy water, said that it was 'covered with light foam', caused by putrefaction.

> His cheeks were swollen [Coquereau wrote], his mouth, which was half open, revealed three remarkably white teeth. On his chin the traces of his beard were perfectly clear. His two hands seemed to belong to someone still alive, they were so fresh in colouring. His nails were long and white. One of his boots had come unsewn and revealed four dull-white toes.

These remains were escorted back to Paris by Bertrand, Gourgaud, Louis Marchand and Emmanuel Las Cases; and in December a grand funeral was held in Paris. The Emperor's body was taken through the Arc de Triomphe, the memorial to his victorious armies, to its entomb-ment under the dome of Les Invalides, where, waiting to sing the requiem, was the mezzo-soprano, Giuditta Grisi, niece of the Emperor's former mistress, Giuseppina Grassini.

Waiting there also were three of the Emperor's former marshals, and the ailing, eighty-six-year-old Bon Adrien Jennot de Moncey, Governor of Les Invalides, who had asked his doctor to keep him alive for this day so that he 'could receive the Emperor'. Having watched General Bertrand place Napoleon's sword on the coffin and General Gourgaud put his cocked hat beside it, and having heard the Archbishop of Paris and four bishops read the prayer of intercession, and endured the two hours of the Communion followed by the choir's singing of Mozart's *Requiem*, Moncey asked the soldiers who had carried him in to take him out. 'Now,' he said to them, 'let's go home to die.'

Fifteen years later, in August 1855, Queen Victoria and Prince Albert arrived in Paris on a state visit to the France of Napoleon III, Louis-Philippe's successor as monarch, the son of Napoleon's brother, Louis, and of Josephine's daughter, Hortense. Accompanying his parents was the thirteen-year-old Prince of Wales who was taken with them to pay his respects to the memory of the great Napoleon, his country's former enemy, at Les Invalides.

Never afterwards did he forget kneeling down in his Highland dress at his mother's prompting to say a prayer by the Emperor's tomb as the thunder rolled above them in the stormy sky and the attendant French generals wept.

APPENDIX

POST MORTEM

BLAMING THE 'ABOMINABLE CLIMATE' of St Helena for the destruction of his health, Napoleon complained from time to time of abdominal pain in the region of his liver which was later diagnosed as hepatitis. He also experienced pain in his right shoulder, and was subject to what Marchand described as 'severe vomiting' and to headaches, a swollen stomach, perpetually cold feet, occasional constipation for which he was in the habit of applying leeches, and cystitis. It has been suggested that a fall from Josephine's carriage before his exile may have brought about Fröhlich's disease, a condition usually afflicting children, the result of disturbed pituitary function, and characterized by obesity, somnolence and lack of libido.

On 25 April 1821, he was violently sick and felt sure that he was dying of cancer of the stomach as his father had done. Two days later the violent sickness returned; and, although he always objected to taking medication, he was dosed with tartar emetic and orgeat, a syrup of orange-flower water and oil of bitter almonds. On 3 May, he was given an extremely strong dose of calomel as a purgative which resulted in difficulty in breathing and loss of consciousness. He died two days later.

An autopsy was performed the following day by Dr Francesco Antommarchi in the presence of two British surgeons. It was noticed that the liver was much enlarged, and that the stomach was ulcerated and perforated, and that the liver was sealing a large perforated gastric ulcer, while one of the doctors, Walter Henry, reported that the body was hairless and feminized with white, delicate skin, well-defined breasts and a mons Veneris, and that the genitalia were exceptionally small. It has since been suggested by leading oncologists that the symptoms from which Napoleon complained and suffered were those not of cancer of the stomach as had originally been supposed but of arsenical poisoning, arsenic being a toxic metaloid element which would have been readily available on the island as a rat poison. Had cancer been the cause of death the body would have been wasted and shrunken, without the fat which was described as 'abundant'. There would also, very likely, have been a secondary growth in the liver.

In recent years, samples of Napoleon's hair have been examined and have been found to contain, as well as antimony, very large quantities of arsenic, the levels of which indicated that the poison had been ingested in different quantities at different times. It was, therefore, proposed that Napoleon had been poisoned by a member of his entourage who was able to place the poison, from time to time, in the wine which, mixed with water, was reserved for his exclusive use, the food he ate being eaten by everyone else. Dr Sten Forshufvud, a Swedish dentist and authority on poisons, and Ben Weider, the International President of La Société Napoléonienne Internationale, concluded, that Napoleon 'died of chronic arsenical intoxication combined with acute cyanide poisoning'. It was pointed out that, of the thirty-one known symptoms of arsenical poisoning, he had suffered from twenty-eight.

It has, however, been suggested that the arsenic found in Napoleon's hair came, not from poison intentionally administered, but from Schalers Green, a colouring in wallpaper widely used in his day and containing copper arsenite. Examination of the wall paper at Longwood proved it to be arsenical and capable of giving off poisonous vapours which, combined with the mould found in the damp atmosphere of the house, may also, so it was proposed, have been responsible for the frequent illnesses of Napoleon's staff and servants who were treated for complaints with similar symptoms. The fact that Napoleon was much improved in health when he spent days outside Longwood working in the garden, was seen as a significant indication that the fumes inside the house were having a deleterious effect.

Moreover, those who doubted that poison was intentionally administered to Napoleon point out that arsenic was widely used in his time to treat various complaints from which he suffered or may have suffered, including epilepsy and skin diseases, and that various notable signs of arsenical poisoning, such as a leathery texture of palms of the hands and soles of the feet, were not recorded in the autopsy report. It was, however, emphasized that the body of Napoleon, when exhumed in 1840, was exceptionally well preserved as well as hairless, indications of poisoning by arsenic. The dose of calomel administered to him shortly before his death may have combined with arsenic to produce a fatal dose of strychnine.

Forshufvud and Weider identify the poisoner as Charles, comte de Montholon whose stepfather was a friend of Louis XVIII and who was himself, it seems, a Bourbon agent and may have been blackmailed into murder by the Count of Artois, later King Charles X, who was concerned that Napoleon might return to France and stage another *coup d'état*. Deeply in debt, de Montholon was being badgered by creditors in France and hoped, having shared Napoleon's exile, to inherit a part of his fortune. As Chamberlain of Napoleon's household, he had ready access to his wine, as well as to the arsenic which was used as a rat poison.

Two recent biographers of Napoleon, whose books were published in 1998, Frank McLynn and Alan Schom, both agree that Napoleon was poisoned by de Montholon. So does the historian and Special Historical Consultant of the International Napoleonic Society, David Chandler.

In their *L'énigme Napoléon résolue*, published in 2001, René Maury and François de Condé-Montholon, a descendant of Napoleon's companion in exile, proposed that Charles de Montholon did, indeed, give the Emperor low doses of arsenic in the hope that he would become ill enough for the English to agree that he should be allowed to return to France. The arsenic, however, reacted violently with the calomel which he was taking and so killed him. The authors maintain that Charles de Montholon was devoted to Napoleon and quote a letter which he wrote to his wife assuring her of his 'tender' love for the Emperor and assuring her that he would always be 'his faithful friend'.

René Maury and François de Condé-Montholon also say that de Montholon, who had the reputation of a skilful and virile lover, willingly shared his wife with Napoleon who was, by then, 'half-impotent'. But, on returning home in 1821, he discovered that his wife had fallen in love with the Emperor and they separated soon afterwards.

THE FATE OF CHARACTERS WHOSE
END IS NOT RECORDED IN THE TEXT

ABRANTÈS, DUC and DUCHESSE D', *see* JUNOT

ANTOMMARCHI, FRANCESCO

After Napoleon's burial in Geranium Valley on St Helena, Antommarchi appeared in Parma with, so it was alleged, the Emperor's heart which had been bequeathed to Marie-Louise together with a bracelet and some strands of his hair. Evidently hoping to be granted a pension by Napoleon's widow, he was denied an interview with her and was received by Neipperg instead. Rather than accede to Antommarchi's request and his offer of the heart, thus making Parma a likely shrine for Bonapartist pilgrims, the Parmesan authorities advised him to leave their country. He was last heard of practising medicine in Cuba where he died in 1838.

AUGEREAU, PIERRE-FRANÇOIS-CHARLES, DUC DE CASTIGLIONE

An avowed royalist by 1814 when he welcomed the return of Louis XVIII, Augereau nevertheless offered his services to Napoleon in 1815. He was ignored; nor would the King employ him thereafter. He retired to the country and died at his estate at La Houssaye in June 1816.

BALCOMBE, BETSY

Having accompanied her family to Australia, where her father had received a government appointment, she married a man named Abell on her return to England. Widowed before long, she published her *Recollections of the Emperor Napoleon* in 1848. In recognition of her kindness to his uncle, Napoleon III granted her property in Algeria. She died in London in 1873.

BARRAS, PAUL-FRANÇOIS-JEAN-NICOLAS, VICOMTE DE

Having lost influence and power after Napoleon's coup in November 1799, he was escorted from the Luxembourg to his country estate of Grosbois. Upon the restoration of King Louis XVIII, he sought an indemnity for past anti-monarchical activities and was permitted to live undisturbed on his estate until his death there in 1829. His unreliable *Mémoires* were published in 1895–6.

BEAUHARNAIS, EUGÈNE-ROSE DE

Having been obliged to accept the armistice of Schiarino-Rizzino in April 1814, he left Italy for Munich and the court of his father-in-law, King Maximilian I, who bestowed upon him the title of Duke of Leuchtenberg and Prince of Eichstädt. He lived, contented and rich, at Eichstädt with his loving wife, Amelia Augusta, dying of cancer in 1824 at the age of forty-one, leaving two sons and three daughters. One of these daughters, Princess Josephine, married Prince Oscar, son of Bernadotte.

BEAUHARNAIS, HORTENSE-EUGÉNIE DE

Banished from France in 1815 because of her support for Napoleon, she eventually settled at Arenberg on the shores of Lake Constance in Switzerland where she died in 1837. Her memoirs, written between 1816 and 1820, were published in three volumes in 1927.

Her son by Louis Bonaparte, Charles-Louis-Napoleon, became the Emperor Napoleon III in 1852. In 1814 her lover, the sexual adventurer and diplomatist, comte Flahaut de la Billarderie, former lover of Caroline Murat and of Countess Potocka and father of Hortense's child, the future duc de Morny, asked her to marry him. But she refused, unwilling to divorce Louis Bonaparte and thus to lose her sons by him. Flahaut subsequently married the daughter of Admiral Lord Keith.

BERNADOTTE, DÉSIRÉE

Her husband, Jean Bernadotte, was elected Crown Prince of Sweden in 1810 and became King of Sweden and Norway in 1818, reigning as Charles XIV John for over twenty-five years until his death in 1844. He married Désirée Clary on 17 August 1798. She much disliked Josephine and imitated her voice and mannerisms. She asked Napoleon to be godfather to her child Oscar whose name was chosen by him. He also maintained, most improbably, 'I made Bernadotte a marshal and then a king only because I had taken Désirée's virginity at Marseilles.' Queen

Désirée spent as little time in Scandinavia as she could, protesting that she had believed that Sweden was 'just another country' of which she and her husband had 'only to take the title'. She spent more time in Paris than she did in Scandinavia and, when given an order by Napoleon to leave Paris, she ignored it. Her love for him having long since evaporated, she died in 1860.

BERTRAND, HENRI-GRATIEN, COMTE DE

Appointed Grand Marshal of the Palace in 1813, he returned to France after Napoleon's death and in 1831 was elected Deputy for Châteauroux, where he had been born and where he died in 1844. His *Cahiers de Sainte-Hélène, 1816–21* was published in three volumes in 1949–59. He returned to St Helena in 1840 to escort Napoleon's remains to Paris.

BONAPARTE, HORTENSE, *see* BEAUHARNAIS, HORTENSE-EUGÉNIE DE

BONAPARTE, JÉRÔME, KING OF WESTPHALIA

Returned to France in 1815 and commanded a division on Napoleon's left wing at Waterloo. He left France for Württemberg on his brother's second abdication, and, after his return in 1847, having lived in Trieste, in Switzerland and Italy, he was appointed Governor of Les Invalides, a marshal of France and President of the Senate. He died at Villegenis at the age of seventy-five in 1860. His devoted wife, Princess Catherine of Württemberg, had died in 1835.

BONAPARTE, JOSEPH and JULIE

Joseph left France for the United States of America after Napoleon's second abdication, and settled for some time in New Jersey as the extremely rich comte de Survilliers, the possessor of several of the Spanish crown jewels which he had appropriated before fleeing from Madrid.

Having spent a short time in England, he moved to Genoa, then to Florence where he died in 1844.

His wife, the former Julie Clary, was not a prepossessing woman: Mary Berry, for instance, described her as 'a perfectly vulgar little woman – very thin and very ugly'; but she had a good heart and was the only woman in the Bonaparte family who treated Josephine with kindness and respect. She did not accompany her husband to America, but joined him later in Italy. She died within a year of her husband.

BONAPARTE, LOUIS

Having abdicated as King of Holland in 1810, he lived in Bohemia, Austria and Switzerland as the comte de Saint-Leu, under which name he published several books of little interest. He died at Leghorn in 1846.

BONAPARTE, LUCIEN

Supported Napoleon during the Hundred Days of 1815 and, after his brother's second abdication, went to live in Italy where he died, at Viterbo, in 1840. His *Mémoires*, the first volume of which was published in 1836, were never completed.

His *La Vérité sur les Cent-Jours* appeared in 1835.

BOURRIENNE, LOUIS-ANTOINE FAUVELET DE

Having made a fortune in shady dealings in Hamburg where he was sent to discuss measures of commercial war against England, he was recalled in disgrace. He lent his support to Louis XVIII in 1815 and later served in the Chamber of Deputies. His memoirs appeared in 1829–31. He died in an asylum near Caen in February 1834, having suffered from a mental illness for two years.

CAULAINCOURT, ARMAND-AUGUSTIN-LOUIS, MARQUIS DE

Having become foreign minister after the battle of Leipzig, he resumed the appointment in 1815. Following Napoleon's defeat at Waterloo he lived in retirement, endeavouring to clear his name in the murder of the duc d'Enghien. He died in Paris in 1827. His memoirs, *Souvenirs du duc de Vicence*, were published in 1837–40.

CLARY, DÉSIRÉE, *see* BERNADOTTE, DÉSIRÉE

CLARY, JULIE, *see* BONAPARTE, JÉRÔME and JULIE

COLOMBIER, CAROLINE

She married one of Napoleon's fellow officers, Captain Garembel de Bressieux, in 1792. Napoleon later appointed her one of his mother's ladies-in-waiting, while her husband became Chief Administrator of Forests. On seeing her again on his way to be crowned in Italy, Napoleon was shocked by her appearance. She had changed '*furieusement*'.

CONSTANT, LOUIS, *see* WARY, LOUIS CONSTANT

DENUELLE, CHARLES LÉON

Having made generous provision for the boy in his lifetime, Napoleon, in a codicil to his will, left him three hundred and twenty thousand francs for the purchase of an estate. He had been fond of him, and had often sent for him when he was dressing or having breakfast and would play with him. The boy grew up to be a quarrelsome spendthrift, and was dismissed from his command of a contingent of the National Guard. His fortunes improved during the Second Empire when he received a pension of six thousand francs and his debts were paid out of the Civil List.

Although registered at birth as being the child of a spinster and unknown father, his resemblance to Napoleon became increasingly striking with the passing years, so much so, indeed, that passers-by stopped to stare at him in the street.

A mentally unbalanced wastrel, he was a habitué of gambling houses and brothels and died in poverty of stomach cancer at Pontoise on 15 April 1881.

DENUELLE, ELÉONORE

Granted an income of twenty-two thousand livres by Napoleon in February 1808 as well as the house in the rue de la Victoire. She married, firstly a lieutenant of infantry, Pierre-Philippe Augier, in 1808, and after his death, in 1814, a major in the Bavarian service, Charles-August-Emile, Count Luxburg. She died in Paris in 1868.

DUCHESNOIS, JOSEPHINE

Having acted at the Comédie Française for twenty-eight years, she was obliged to retire from the stage because of her ill health, She died in poor circumstances in 1835, leaving three children, two sons and a daughter, all of them by different men. The elder son's father was the adopted son of that inexhaustible writer, Mme de Genlis; the younger was her grandson.

ELLIOTT, GRACE DALRYMPLE

Having returned to France from England, towards the end of her life she went to live at Ville d'Avray where she died in her mid-sixties in May 1823. Her unreliable *Journal of My Life During the French Revolution* was published posthumously.

FESCH, JOSEPH

Having made a large fortune by means of rather dubious commercial ventures, Napoleon's uncle was appointed Archbishop of Lyons in 1802. A year later he became a cardinal and French ambassador in Rome. Thereafter, he grew closer to the papacy than to his nephew. Several of the works of art in his enormous collection were bequeathed to the city of Lyons. He died in Rome in May 1839.

FOUCHÉ, JOSEPH, DUC D'OTRANTE

'If only I had hanged two men, Talleyrand and Fouché,' Napoleon said, 'I would still be on the throne today.' Having helped Talleyrand restore King Louis XVIII to the throne after serving as President of the provisional government, Fouché was proscribed as a regicide by the returning royalists in 1816. Having by then accumulated great wealth, he lived in exile in Prague and Linz before moving to Trieste where he died on Christmas Day 1820. His memoirs were published in two volumes in 1824.

FRANCIS I, EMPEROR OF AUSTRIA

After the Congress of Vienna he supported Metternich's conservative, not to say repressive policies. He died in Vienna in March 1835.

GEORGE, MLLE, *see* WEIMER, MARGUERITE-JOSEPHINE

GORREQUER, GIDEON

Having returned to England after Napoleon's death, he was promoted lieutenant-colonel in 1826. He served for thirty years in the Royal Irish Regiment and then in the King's Own Regiment. He died suddenly, having collapsed in Jermyn Street, London, in July 1841.

GOURGAUD, GASPARD

Returned from St Helena to France in 1821, resumed his military career and wrote a number of historical works including a detailed refutation of Sir Walter Scott's life of Napoleon and the two-volume *Saint-Hélène: Journal inédit*. Elected to the Legislative Assembly, he became a strong supporter of the future Napoleon III. He died in Paris in 1852.

GRASSINI, GIUSEPPINA

When Napoleon had been in Milan during his first campaign in Italy, Grassini had endeavoured to seduce him; but, preoccupied as he was with thoughts of Josephine at that time, he 'remained cold'. On his way back from Marengo, however, Napoleon 'surrendered to her charms'. Known later as '*La Chanteuse de l'Empereur*', she died at the age of seventy-seven in 1850.

JUNOT, ANDOCHE, DUC D'ABRANTÈS

Sent to Spain, he was defeated by Wellington at Vimeiro in August 1808. He served without distinction in the Russian campaign; and after his appointment as Governor of the Illyrian provinces in 1813, he became deranged. In July that year he committed suicide by throwing himself out of a window.

JUNOT, LAURE, DUCHESSE D'ABRANTÈS

Napoleon's '*petite peste*' joined her husband, Andoche Junot, in Portugal after he had entered Lisbon in triumph in 1807, and displayed her characteristic prodigality there. Having had affairs with both Metternich and Maurice de Balincourt, she was told to leave Paris by Napoleon, who objected to her caustic wit and her association with former émigrés. She did not take Napoleon's side in 1815 and thereafter spent much of her time in Rome.

She wrote a six-volume history of the salons of Paris, an account of her time in the Peninsula, and eight volumes of lively, often sarcastic and malicious memoirs, the last volume of which appeared in 1835. She died in Paris three years later.

LAS CASES, EMMANUEL-AUGUSTIN-DIEU-DONNÉ-MARIN-JOSEPH, COMTE DE

Removed from St Helena after writing a letter condemning the way Napoleon was treated, and forbidden to return to France, he travelled in Germany and Belgium until allowed to re-enter France after Napoleon's death. He was chosen as deputy for St-Denis in 1831 and became a leading opponent of Louis-Philippe. Having recovered the manuscript of his *Mémorial de St Hélène*, which had been seized by the British Government, he published it in 1823. In 1840 he accompanied Napoleon's remains back from St Helena to Paris. He died at Passy in May 1842.

LOWE, SIR HUDSON

Left St Helena some three months after Napoleon's death, having handed over the governorship to Brigadier-General John Pine Coffin.

In 1823, he was appointed Governor of Antigua and later served in Ceylon, returning to England in 1831, having been promoted lieutenant-general the year before. Although he was quite rich when he left St Helena, legal expenses incurred by his proceedings against Barry O'Meara and Sir Walter Scott, both of whom had written hostile accounts of his governorship of St Helena, much diminished his fortune. When a play about Napoleon on St Helena was put on in Paris, the actor playing the part of Lowe was insulted and stoned as he left the theatre and had to be provided with a bodyguard every night on his way home. He died at his house in Chelsea in January 1844. His wife had predeceased him in 1832.

MARCHAND, LOUIS

Louis Constant Wary's successor as Napoleon's principal valet. He was appointed an executor of his master's will in which he was enjoined to 'marry a widow, sister or daughter of an officer or soldier of my old Guard'. He obeyed this instruction two years after his return to France by marrying Michelle-Mathilde Brayer, the daughter of a general of the Guard. 'His services to me,' Napoleon wrote, 'were those of a friend.' He was left sufficient money to live in comfort for the rest of his life, having bequeathed a sum for the care of the child whom Esther Vesey had borne him on St Helena. He died at the age of eighty-four.

MARIE-LOUISE

Soon after learning of Napoleon's death, Marie-Louise, who had been granted the duchies of Parma, Piacenza and Guastalla, secretly married her lover, Adam Adalbert, Graf von Neipperg, having already by then given birth to two of his children, a girl, who was baptised Albertina Maria in the ducal palace, Parma, in May 1817, and a boy, Guglielmo Alberto, in August 1819. Marie-Louise could 'truthfully say that [she] had never been happier'. Hers was 'a delightful existence,' she said, 'and were I not to commit the sin of pride, I could say I deserve it, because God knows all I have suffered in life'. With the help of Neipperg she was an enlightened ruler of her duchies where she was known as the '*buona duchessa*'.

After Neipperg's death in 1829, political matters in Parma were entrusted to his principal secretary, Baron Joseph Werklein, who abandoned the city at a time of civil disturbances during which Marie-Louise felt obliged to take her children to Piacenza. She became the subject of numerous stories of sexual escapades with a succession of lovers including guards and sentries. But in February 1834, she married the Grand Master of her court, a French count, Charles de Bombelles, and settled down to a life of more settled propriety. She died at the age of fifty-six in 1847, and was buried beside her father and her son, Napoleon II, in the vault of the Kapuzinerkirche.

METTERNICH, KLEMENS FÜRST VON

Remained highly influential in the Austrian government until 1848 when, as a symbol of repression, he was forced to resign and sought refuge in England. He returned to Vienna in 1851. His first wife died in 1825, his second in 1829, his third in 1854. He died himself in 1859.

MONTHOLON, CHARLES TRISTAN, MARQUIS DE

After his return from St Helena, Montholon spent several years in Belgium. His *Mémoires pour servir à l'histoire de France sous Napoléon* (written in collaboration with General Gourgaud) was published in 1823. In 1840, he took part in Louis-Napoleon's expedition to Boulogne and was subsequently imprisoned at Ham. On his release in 1847 he moved to England and published his *Récits de la captivité de Napoléon à Ste Hélène* in two volumes in that year. Two years later, he was chosen as a deputy for the Legislative Assembly. He died in August 1853. The marquise de Montholon's *Souvenirs de Ste Hélène, 1815–16* was published in 1901.

NAPOLEON II

Excluded from the succession to Marie-Louise's possessions in Italy by the Treaty of Paris of 1817, he received the title of Duke of Reichstadt the following year but was allowed no political role in Austria. He died of tuberculosis at Schönbrunn in July 1832 at the age of twenty-one.

In 1940, on Hitler's orders, his body was taken to Paris to be buried next to his father.

NAPOLEON III

Louis-Napoleon Bonaparte, the son of Louis and Hortense, was elected President of the French Republic in 1848. He adopted the title of Napoleon III in 1852 after a *coup d'état*. Following France's defeat in the Franco-Prussian War, he died in exile at Chislehurst, Kent in 1873.

PATTERSON, ELIZABETH

Her marriage to Jérôme Bonaparte having been annulled by Napoleon, she continued to live in England where she and her two sisters, Louisa and Marianne, were said to have been 'universally admired' in London society. Marianne was believed to have had a brief affair with Wellington, either after or before marrying his licentious brother, Richard, Marquess Wellesley. Her sister, Louisa, married Colonel Felton Harvey, one of Wellington's aides-de-camp and, after Harvey's death, the Marquess of Carmarthen. Elizabeth returned to Baltimore and died in 1879, extremely grumpy and extremely rich, at the age of ninety-four. Her grandson, Charles J. Bonaparte-Patterson, became attorney-general in the presidency of Theodore Roosevelt.

PELLAPRA, EMILIE DE

Although tacitly acknowledged by Napoleon as his daughter by Mme Pellapra, Emilie's claim to be so seems to have been largely based on her fancied resemblance to him. She became the princesse de Chimay. Her memoirs, *A Daughter of Napoleon: Memoirs of Emilie de Pellapra, comtesse de Brigode, princesse de Chimay*, appeared in 1922. Her correspondence was published by Princess Bibesco in 1950.

RÉCAMIER, JEANNE-FRANÇOISE-JULIE-ADELAIDE

Married when she was fifteen to the rich and elderly banker, Jacques Récamier, she was both beautiful and virtuous. She rejected Napoleon's advances, as she had rejected Lucien's; and, when her husband, in financial difficulties, approached the Bank of France for a loan, Napoleon saw to it that his request was refused. Récamier's bank was consequently ruined.

Upon Mme Récamier subsequently going to stay with her friend, Mme de Staël, in Switzerland, Napoleon gave orders that she should be banished to a distance of at least forty leagues from Paris. She returned to Paris after Napoleon's exile to St Helena and, although in straitened circumstances, she presided over a salon established at the Abbaye-aux-Boix. Here her friend, François Chateaubriand, was a prominent figure. She appears as a character in Mme de Staël's novel, *Corinne*. She died in Paris in 1849.

REICHSTADT, DUKE OF, FRANÇOIS-CHARLES-JOSEPH BONAPARTE, *see* NAPOLEON II

RÉMUSAT, CLAIRE

Née Claire-Elisabeth-Jeanne Gravier de Vergennes, she was married at the age of sixteen to Auguste Laurent, comte de Rémusat, Napoleon's chamberlain. She was appointed Josephine's *dame du palais* in 1802. She died in 1821. Her *Mémoires* were published in three volumes in 1879–80 by Paul de Rémusat, her grandson, the journalist. Her letters, covering the years 1804–14, were published in 1881.

STAËL, ANNE-LOUISE-GERMAINE, MADAME DE

On the Bourbon Restoration in 1814, she returned to Paris, but went back to Coppet, her family house in Switzerland, during the Hundred Days and in September went to Italy, going back again to Coppet the next year. When she went back to Paris for the last time, she was in poor health and died there in July 1817. 'That whore', as Napoleon referred to her, had continued to preside over her salon to the end, 'receiving all day and all night'.

TALLEYRAND, CHARLES-MAURICE DE TALLEYRAND-PERIGORD, PRINCE DE BÉNÉVENT

Appointed Foreign Minister by King Louis XVIII in 1814, he was the country's highly effective representative at the Congress of Vienna. From 1830 to 1834 he was French Ambassador at the Court of St James. He died in Paris in 1838.

TALLIEN, JEAN-LAMBERT

Distrusted by all parties, Tallien supported the First Restoration, then Napoleon during the Hundred Days. Under the Second Restoration he failed in his endeavours to obtain a pension and died in poverty in Paris in November 1820, having sold his books to buy food. He had by then become disfigured by scabs and the loss of an eye from yellow fever, and had divorced his wife who had by then deserted him.

TALLIEN, THÉRÉSIA

The divorced wife of the comte de Fontenay, and daughter of the Spanish banker, François Cabarrus, she became Jean-Lambert Tallien's mistress and later his wife. She was known as 'Our Lady of Thermidor' in recognition of the lives she saved by her entreaties to her husband. Eventually she became the mistress of the banker Ouvrard and deserted her husband who divorced her. She then married the comte de Cara-man, later prince de Chimay. When he was appointed chamberlain at the court in Brussels she accompanied him there; but, because of her licentious past, she was excluded from court functions. Her reputation, indeed, was such that, when she visited the Louvre with a collection of her children by four different fathers, a threatening crowd surrounded her and forced her to leave. She died in 1835.

WALEWSKA, MARIE

Her husband, the aged Count Walewski, having died in 1814, she married Count d'Ornano, a former officer in the Imperial Guard, at Liège in 1816. She bore him a child the following year, but did not recover from her confinement and died in her house in the rue de la Victoire on 15 December 1817. Napoleon heard of her second marriage 'with some displeasure'. It was 'not in his nature to suffer anyone he loved to love any but himself.'

WALEWSKI, ALEXANDRE FLORIAN JOSEPH COLONNA

Napoleon's son by Marie Walewska, he took out letters of naturalization in France and entered the French army. Resigning his commission in 1837, he thereafter became a journalist and playwright.

After the accession to power of Louis-Napoleon, he was sent as envoy to Florence, Naples and London. In London the diarist, Charles Greville, described him as being 'popular in society', 'wonderfully handsome and agreeable'. He became Minister of Foreign Affairs in 1855 and subsequently a senator and President of the Chamber. He died at Strasburg in 1868.

Lord Palmerston said that his only fault was a complete lack of a sense of humour. He had a son by the tragic actress, Rachel (stage-name of Elisabeth Félix). In December 1831, he married the second daughter of the sixth Earl of Sandwich, Lady Catherine Montagu, who died in 1834.

WARY, LOUIS CONSTANT

The son of a Belgian innkeeper, Louis Constant, as he was generally known, served as Bonaparte's valet from 1800 until the First Abdication, when he was succeeded by Louis Marchand. He then retired to Picardy where ghost writers induced him to provide materials for his *Mémoires*, published in 1830.

WEIMER, MARGUERITE-JOSEPHINE (MADEMOISELLE GEORGE)

Discarded as his mistress by Napoleon, Mlle George went to

St Petersburg on the mistaken understanding that she was to marry Count Maurice Benckendorf. She remained in St Petersburg for five years until Napoleon's invasion of Russia, when she left the country by way of Sweden. On her return to Paris she was, at Napoleon's request, reinstated at the Comédie Française from which she was dismissed in 1817 because of her tyrannical and capricious behaviour. Having found a new lover in Jean Charles Harel, who had had a child by Mlle Duchesnois, she joined the company at the Odéon where she enjoyed a new success.

In her middle age she grew to such an immense size that she was known as 'the whale'.

Driven to touring the provinces and acting abroad, she found occasional work on her return to Paris at the Porte-Saint-Martin and the Théâtre-Italien; but by then her obesity, according to Victorien Sardou, had 'reached the point of the ridiculous'.

Various attempts were made to help her financially but her improvidence led to the poverty in which she died a few weeks before her eightieth birthday in 1867.

CHRONOLOGY

1763	23 January	Jean Bernadotte (later Charles XIV John of Sweden and Norway) born at Pau
	23 June	Marie-Josèphe-Rose Tascher de la Pagerie, later Empress Josephine, born at Trois-Îlets, Martinique
1767	25 March	Birth of Joachim Murat at La Bastide-Fortunière
1768	7 January	Giuseppe (Joseph) Buonaparte born at Corte, Corsica
		The Republic of Genoa cedes Corsica to King Louis XV of France
1769	15 August	Napoleone Buonaparte born at Ajaccio, Corsica
1774	10 May	Louis XVI ascends throne of France
1775	21 May	Luciano (Lucien) Buonaparte born at Ajaccio
1777	3 January	Maria Anna (Elisa) Buonaparte born at Ajaccio
1778	2 September	Luigi (Louis) Buonaparte born at Ajaccio
1779	13 May	Napoleon enters École Militaire at Brienne
1780	20 October	Maria Paola (Pauline) Buonaparte born at Ajaccio

1781	3 September	Eugène de Beauharnais born
1782	25 March	Maria Annunziata (Caroline) Buonaparte born at Ajaccio
1783	10 April	Hortense de Beauharnais born in Paris
1784		Napoleon moves to École Militaire in Paris
	6 November	Laure Permon, later duchesse d'Abrantès, born at Montpellier
	15 November	Girolamo (Jérôme) Buonaparte born
1785		Napoleon's father, Carlo Buonaparte, dies of stomach cancer
		Napoleon posted to the Regiment of La Fère
1786		Marie Walewska born
1787		Eléonore Denuelle de la Plaigne born
1789	5 May	States-General meet at Versailles
	14 July	Fall of the Bastille
		Napoleon returns to Corsica on leave
1790		Napoleon politically active on Corsica
1791		Napoleon rejoins his regiment
	20 June	Flight of royal family to Varennes
	October	Napoleon returns to Corsica
	December	The Empress Marie-Louise born in Vienna
1792	20 April	France declares war on Austria
	8 July	France declares war on Prussia
	August	Prussian and Austrian troops invade France
	10 August	The storming of the Tuileries and massacre of Swiss Guard
	13 August	Royal family imprisoned
	22 September	French Republic proclaimed
1793	21 January	Louis XVI guillotined

	1 February	France declares war on Britain and Holland
	7 March	France declares war on Spain
	11 June	The Buonapartes sail from Corsica to France
	Sept–Dec	Napoleon makes a name for himself as an artillery officer at the siege of Toulon
	22 December	Napoleon promoted brigadier-general
1794	February	Napoleon appointed commander of the artillery in the Army of Italy
	22 April	Josephine arrested and imprisoned in Les Carmes
	23 July	Alexandre de Beauharnais guillotined
	28 July	Robespierre guillotined in the Thermidorian reaction
	1 August	Joseph Bonaparte marries Julie Clary
	8 August	Napoleon arrested
1795	5 October	Napoleon fires cannon on insurgents besieging the National Convention in Paris and this 'whiff of grapeshot' puts down insurrection on the 'Day of the Sections'
1796	9 March	Napoleon marries Josephine de Beauharnais
	11 March	Napoleon appointed Commander-in-Chief of the Army of Italy
	July	Talleyrand appointed Foreign Minister under the Directory
	15–17 November	Napoleon defeats Austrians at Arcola
1797	4 January	Austrians defeated at Rivoli
	2 February	Mantua surrenders
	5 May	Elisa Bonaparte marries Felice Bacchiochi and Pauline Bonaparte marries General Leclerc
	1 June	Napoleon welcomes his mother at gates of Milan
	9 July	Cisalpine republic proclaimed
	4 September	The successful coup d'état of 18 Fructidor
	17 October	Treaty of Campo Formio ends the first Italian campaign

Napoleon appointed to command forces for invasion of England

Napoleon encounters Giuseppina Grassini

1798	3 January	Josephine returns to Paris from Italy
	19 May	Napoleon sets sail for Egypt
	10–12 June	Malta is occupied
	1 July	Alexandria is taken by storm
	19 July	Junot tells Napoleon of Josephine's affair with Captain Charles
	1 August	Nelson destroys French fleet in the Battle of the Nile
	17 August	Jean Bernadotte (later Charles XIV John of Sweden and Norway) marries Désirée Clary
1799	February	Napoleon marches into Syria
	21 April	Malmaison purchased
	10 May	Napoleon's assault on Acre repulsed
	25 July	Turks defeated at Aboukir
	22 August	Napoleon sets sail for Alexandria
	14 October	Napoleon returns to Paris
	9–10 November	A coup d'état overthrows the Directory and establishes the Consulate
	10 November	Barras is escorted from the Luxembourg to his estate at Grosbois
1800		Andoche Junot marries Laure Permon
	19 February	Napoleon as First Consul establishes himself at the Tuileries
	May–June	Napoleon's second Italian campaign
	14 June	Austrians defeated at Marengo
	24 December	Napoleon escapes assassination in Paris
1801	9 February	Treaty of Lunéville with Austria signed
	16 July	Concordat concluded with Pope Pius VII
1802	4 January	Louis Bonaparte marries Hortense de Beauharnais
	25 March	Treaty of Amiens signed with Great Britain
	2 August	Napoleon appointed First Consul for life

	November	death of Victor Emmanuel Leclerc
1803		Pauline Bonaparte, latterly Leclerc, marries Prince Camillo Borghese
	18 May	England declares war
		Napoleon plans invasion of England
		Napoleon encounters Marguerite-Joséphine Weimer (Mlle George)
1804	20–21 March	The duc d'Enghien kidnapped and executed
	21 March	The Civil Code is promulgated
	28 May	Napoleon becomes Emperor
	2 December	Napoleon crowns himself and Josephine in Notre Dame
1805		Jèrôme Bonaparte brings his American wife, Elizabeth Patterson, to England
	23 March	The official title, Mme Mère, bestowed on Napoleon's mother
	26 May	Napoleon crowned King of Italy in Milan Cathedral
	July–Aug	Britain, Austria, Sweden and Russia form anti-French coalition
	20 October	Austrians defeated at Ulm
	21 October	French Fleet defeated by Nelson at Trafalgar
	13 November	Napoleon enters Vienna
	2 December	Napoleon triumphs at Austerlitz
1806	30 March	Joseph Bonaparte becomes King of Naples
	5 June	Louis Bonaparte becomes King of Holland
	12 July	The states of southern Germany formed into the Confederation of the Rhine under French protection
	14 October	Prussia and Saxony defeated by Napoleon at Jena and Auerstädt
	13 December	Charles Léon Denuelle, Napoleon's natural son, born
	15 December	Napoleon enters Warsaw
1807	1 January	Marie Walewska meets Napoleon at Bronie

	8 February	The indecisive battle of Eylau fought between France and a combined Russo-Prussian army
	14 June	France defeats combined Russian and Prussian army at Friedland
	7 July	Napoleon, having met Tsar Alexander and Frederick William III on the river Niemen, signs the Treaty of Tilsit by which Russia agrees to the establishment of the Duchy of Warsaw and recognizes the Confederation of the Rhine
	August	Jérôme Bonaparte is created King of Westphalia
	2–5 September	British bombard Copenhagen to prevent Napoleon's use of the Danish fleet
	27 October	By Treaty of Fontainebleau, Spain and France agree to conquer Portugal
	19 November	French army invades Portugal
	29 November	Portuguese royal family flees to Brazil
1808	16 February	France invades Spain
	March	Joseph Bonaparte appointed King of Spain
	20 April	Charles-Louis-Napoleon Bonaparte, later Napoleon III, born in Paris
	May	Mlle George leaves Paris for Russia
	19 July	General Dupont surrenders at Bailén
	21 August	French defeated by Wellesley at Vimeiro
	4 December	Napoleon enters Madrid to restore Joseph to Spanish throne
1809	22 April	Napoleon defeats Austrians at Eckmühl
	May	Elisa Bonaparte created Grand Duchess of Tuscany
	5–6 July	Austrians defeated at Wagram
	28 July	Wellesley defeats French at Talavera
	8 October	Metternich appointed Foreign Minister by Francis I
	14 December	Napoleon signs preliminary statement of divorce from Josephine
1810	1–2 April	Napoleon marries Marie-Louise of Austria

	4 May	Napoleon's natural son, Alexandre Walewski, born at Walewice near Warsaw
	27 September	Wellington defeats French at Bussaco
1811	20 March	Napoleon's son, the King of Rome, born in Paris
1812	24 June	Napoleon crosses the Niemen and enters Russia
	12 August	Wellington enters Madrid
	7 September	After their defeat at Borodino, Russians abandon Moscow
	14 September	Napoleon enters Moscow which burns until 19th
	19 October	Retreat from Moscow begins
	5 December	Napoleon leaves army under command of Murat and returns to Paris
1813	2 May	Napoleon defeats Prussians and Russians at Lützen
	22 May	Napoleon's close friend, General Duroc, mortally wounded
	21 June	Wellington defeats French at Vitoria
	16–19 October	Napoleon defeated at the battle of Leipzig
1814	1 January	The Allies invade France
	11 January	Murat deserts Napoleon
	30–31 March	The Allies enter Paris
	11 April	Napoleon abdicates at Fontainebleau
	13 April	Napoleon attempts suicide
	20 April	Napoleon sails for Elba
	3 May	King Louis XVIII arrives in Paris
	29 May	The Empress Josephine dies at Malmaison
	1 November	Congress of Vienna opens
1815	26 February	Napoleon escapes from Elba
	1 March	Napoleon lands at Golfe Juan
	20 March	Napoleon returns to Paris and Louis XVIII flees to Ghent
	3 May	Murat defeated by the Austrians at

		Talentino
	18 June	Napoleon defeated at Waterloo
	22 June	Napoleon abdicates for the second time
	8 July	Louis XVIII returns to the Tuileries
	25 July	Napoleon surrenders to the British and boards the *Bellerophon*
	7 August	Napoleon departs for St Helena in the *Northumberland*
	13 October	Murat shot after failing to regain Naples
	15 October	Napoleon disembarks on St Helena
1816	4 April	Sir Hudson Lowe arrives on St Helena
1817	15 September	Marie Walewska dies in Paris
1818		Napoleon II receives title of Duke of Reichstadt
1819	July	Mme de Montholon receives permission to leave St Helena
1820	6 August	Elisa Bonaparte dies
1821	5 May	Napoleon dies on St Helena
	7 September	Marie Louise marries Count von Neipperg
1825		Pauline Bonaparte dies of cancer
1829		Adam, Count von Neipperg suffers fatal heart attack
1830	2 August	Abdication of Charles X
1832	22 July	Napoleon II, Duke of Reichstadt, dies from tuberculosis at Schönbrunn
1834	February	Marie-Louise marries Charles de Bombelles
1835		Josephine Duchesnois dies

1836	2 February	Mme Mère dies in Rome
1837		Hortense, née de Beauharnais, dies at Areneberg, Switzerland
1838	7 June	Laure, duchesse d'Abrantès, dies in Paris
1839	13 May 18 May	Cardinal Fesch dies Caroline Murat dies
1840	29 June	Lucien Bonaparte dies in Rome
1844	28 July	Joseph Bonaparte dies in Rome
1846	25 July	Louis Bonaparte dies
1847	17 December	The Empress Marie-Louise dies at Parma
1850		Giuseppina Grassini dies
1852		Louis-Napoleon adopts the title of Napoleon III
1860	24 June	Jérôme Bonaparte dies
1867		Mlle George, Napoleon's former mistress, dies
1868	27 October	Alexandre Walewski dies Eléonore Denuelle de la Plaigne, Napoleon's former mistress, dies
1869		Pauline Ranchoup, Napoleon's 'Cleopatra', dies at the age of ninety
1873	9 January	Napoleon III dies in exile at Chislehurst in England
1881	15 April	Napoleon's natural son, Charles Léon Denuelle, dies at Pontoise of stomach cancer

BIBLIOGRAPHY

NOTES ON SOURCES

Books about Napoleon are numbered in their thousands. The most recent lengthy biographies in English are those of Alan Schom and Frank McLynn, both published in 1997. Also published that year was Geoffrey Ellis's *Napoleon*. Andrew Roberts's *Napoleon and Wellington* was published in 2001. Among the most rewarding of earlier works are Michael Broers's *Europe Under Napoleon* (1996); Vincent Cronin's *Napoleon* (1971); Charles Esdaile's *The Wars of Napoleon* (1995); Peter Geyl's *Napoleon, For and Against* (1949); Martyn Lyon's *Napoleon Bonaparte and the Legacy of the French Revolution* (1994); Felix Markham's *Napoleon* (1963); J. M. Thompson's *Napoleon Bonaparte: His Rise and Fall* (1952); and Jean Tulard's *Napoleon: The Myth of the Saviour* (1984) in which there is a comprehensive bibliography.

Previous biographies of Josephine – those of Theo Aronson (1990); André Castelot (1964); Bernard Chevallier and Christophe Pincemaille (1988); Carolly Erickson (1999); André Gavoty (1961); Jacques Janssens (1963); Ernest John Knapton (1964); Charles Kuntsler (1939); Frédéric Masson (1907); Frances Mossiker (1964) and Jean Savant (1955) – have been superseded to a large extent by Evangeline Bruce's *Napoleon and Josephine: An Improbable Marriage* (1995). Nina Epton's *Josephine: The Empress and Her Children* was published in 1975. Napoleon's letters to Josephine have been edited by Jacques Bourgeat (1941), Leon Cerf (1929) and Jean Tulard (1981). Louis Hastier's *Le Grand Amour de Josephine* appeared in 1955.

Biographies of Marie-Louise are naturally not so numerous. The most recent is Alan Palmer's *Napoleon and Marie-Louise, the Second Empress* (2001). Others are by Geneviève Chastenet (1983); Leonardo Farinelle (1983); Alexandre Mahan (1933); Gilbert Martineau (1985) and Angelo Solmi (1985). Selections from her correspondence and diaries have been edited by Louis Madelin (1935); Frédéric Masson (1922); C. F. Palmstierna (1955) and C. de la Roncière (n.d.).

There are several biographies of Mme Mère. Among them are those by Marthe Arrighi de Casanova (1954); Alain Decaux (1983); François

Duhourcau (1921); Gilbert Martineau (1980); Frédéric Masson (n.d.); Lydia Péretti (1922); Clement Shaw (1928); Monica Stirling (1961); and Clara Tschudi (1900). Dorothy Carrington's *Napoleon and his Parents: On the Threshold of History* was published in 1988.

Of the several books about Napoleon's family, some of the most worthwhile are Theo Aronson's *The Story of the Bonapartes* (1990); Walter Geer's *Napoleon and His Family* (1929); Frédéric Masson's *Napoléon et sa famille* (13 vols, 1919); and Desmond Seward's *Napoleon's Family* (1986).

Books about Napoleon's sisters include Harrison Brent's *Pauline Bonaparte: A Woman of Affairs* (1946); Hubert Cole's *The Betrayers: Joachim and Caroline Murat* (1972); Piers Dixon's *Pauline: Napoleon's Favourite Sister* (1964); Paul Fleuriot de Langle's *Elisa: soeur de Napoléon* (1947); Marcel Gobineau's *Pauline Borghese, soeur fidèle* (1958); Michel Lacout-Gayet's *Marie Caroline, reine de Naples: une adversaire de Napoléon* (1990); Bernard Narbonne's *Pauline Bonaparte: La Venus Impériale* (1963); Len Ortzen's *Imperial Venus: The Story of Pauline Bonaparte Borghese* (1974); François-Joseph Talma's *Lettres inédites à la Princesse Pauline Bonaparte* (1911); Joseph Turquan's *Caroline Murat* (1899) and *The Sisters of Napoleon* (1908); and Margery Weiner's *The Parvenu Princesses* (1964).

Books on Napoleon's mistresses include Gertrude Aretz's *Napoleon and his Women Friends* (1927); Guy Breton's *Histoires d'amour de l'histoire de France*, vol. VII, (1955); Léonce Deschamp's *Pauline Fourès, Notre Dame de l'orient* (n.d.); Frédéric Masson's *Napoléon et les femmes* (3 vols, 1893–1902); Arthur Pougin's *Giuseppina Grassini* (1923); Edith Saunders's *Napoleon and Mademoiselle George* (1958); Christine Sutherland's *Marie Walewska: Napoleon's Great Love* (1979), and Joseph Turquan's *The Love Affairs of Napoleon* (1909). There is also General Frank Richardson's *Napoleon: Bisexual Emperor* (1972). Napoleon's affair with Mme Fourès is recounted in J. Christopher Herold's *Bonaparte in Egypt* (1963).

Interesting biographies of other women – friends and enemies of Napoleon – and collections of their letters, diary entries and memoirs are *Mémoires de Mme. la duchesse d'Abrantès* (10 vols, 1893); Gabriel Girod de l'Ain's *Désirée Clary d'après sa correspondance inédite avec Bonaparte, Bernadotte et sa famille* (1959); Hortense de Beauharnais's *Mémoires de la reine Hortense* (3 vols., 1927); Jacques Castelnau's *Madame Tallien* (1967); Princess de Chimay's *Madame Tallien* (1936); André Gayot's *Fortunée Hamelin*; Henri Guillemin's *Madame de Staël, Benjamin Constant et Napoléon* (1959); Peter Gunn's *Napoleon's Little Pest* (1983); J. Christopher Herold's *Mistress to an Age: A Life of Madame de Staël* (1958); Baron Hochschild's *Désirée, reine de Suède et de Norvège* (1888); Countess Anna Potocka's

Mémoires de la comtesse Potocka (1897); Claire de Rémusat's *Lettres de Mme de Rémusat* (1881) and *Mémoires* (1880); Germaine de Staël's *Mémoires* (1818) and Françoise Wagener's *Madame Récamier* (1986).

Revealing memoirs of Napoleon's servants and members of his staff include Louis A. F. de Bourrienne's *Mémoires* (10 vols, 1829); Louis Constant's *Mémoires de Constant, premier valet de chambre de l'Empereur* (6 vols, 1830); Baron Agathon Fain's *Mémoires* (1908); Louis-Joseph Marchand's *Mémoires* (2 vols, 1952), recently translated under the title *In Napoleon's Shadow* (1996), and Louis Etienne Saint-Denis's *From the Tuileries to St Helena* (1902).

Books about Napoleon, Pauline and Mme Mère on Elba, and his life in exile on St Helena, include Mrs L. E. Abell's *Recollections of the Emperor Napoleon* (1848); Fernand Beaucourt's *Napoleon à l'île d'Elba* (1991); Julia Blackburn's *The Emperor's Last Island* (1991); Dame Mabel Brookes's *St Helena Story* (1960); General Baron Gaspard Gourgaud's *Sainte-Hélène: Journal inédit de 1815 à 1818* (1899); Jean-Paul Kauffmann's *The Dark Room at Longwood* (1999); James Kemble's *St Helena During Napoleon's Exile: Correquer's Diary* (1969); Emmanuel, comte de Las Cases' *Mémorial de Sainte-Hélène*; Lady Malcolm's *A Diary of St Helena* (1846); Gilbert Martineau's *Napoleon's Last Journey* (1976) and *Napoleon's St Helena* (1968); comtesse de Montholon's *Souvenirs de Sainte-Hélène*; Général comte de Montholon's *Récite de la captivité de l'Empereur à Sainte-Hélène* (1846); Barry Edward O'Meara's *Napoleon in Exile* (1822), and Julian Park's (ed.), *The Reports of Count Balmain, Russian Commissioner on the Island of St Helena* (1928).

There are good accounts of Napoleon's son, the King of Rome, in Dormer Creston's *In Search of Two Characters* (1947), and of Napoleon's court in Philip Mansell's *The Eagle in Splendour: Napoleon I and his Court* (1952).

Abell, Mrs L. E., *Recollections of the Emperor Napoleon* (London, 1848)

Abrantès, la Duchesse d', *Mémoires de Madame la duchesse d'Abrantès* (10 vols, Paris, 1893)

Ain, Gabriel Girod del', *Désirée Clary d'après sa correspondance inédite avec Bonaparte, Bernadotte et sa famille* (Paris, 1959)

Aldington, Richard, *Wellington* (London, 1946)

Alméras, Henri d', *Barras et son temps* (Paris, 1930)

—— *La vie parisienne sous le Consulat et l'Empire* (Paris, n.d.)

—— *La vie perisienne sous la Révolution et la Directoire* (Paris, n.d.)

Antommarchi, François, *Les Derniers Moments de Napoléon, 1819–21* (Paris, 1898)

Aretz, Gertrude, *Napoleon and his Women Friends* (trs. Eden and Cedar Paul, London, 1927)

Arnault, Antoine, *Souvenirs d'un sexagènaire* (Paris, 1833)

Arnott, Archibald, *An Account of the Last Illness, Disease and Post-Mortem Examination of Napoleon Bonaparte* (London, 1822)

Aronson, Theo, *The Golden Bees* (London, 1964)

—— *Napoleon and Josephine* (London, 1990)

Atteridge, A. H., *Joachim Murat: Marshal of France and King of Naples* (London, 1911)

Aubenas, Joseph, *Histoire de l'Impératrice Joséphine* (2 vols, Paris, 1859)

Aubry, Octave, *St Helena* (trs. Arthur Livingston, London, 1937)

Avrillon, Marie-Jeanne, *Mémoires* (Paris, 1833)

Bainville, Jacques, *Le 18 Brumaire* (Paris, 1925)

Barnett, Correlli, *Bonaparte* (London, 1978)

Barras, Paul, *Mémoires de Barras, membre du Directoire* (ed. G. Drury, 3 vols, Paris, 1829)

Bartel, P., *La jeunesse inédite de Napoléon* (Paris, 1961)

Bausset, Baron Louis-F-J de, *Mémoires anecdotiques* (4 vols, Paris, 1827–9)

Beaucourt, Fernand, *Napoléon à l'isle d'Elba* (Paris, 1991)

Beauharnais, Hortense de, *Mémoires de la reine Hortense, publiés par le prince Napoléon* (3 vols, Paris, 1927)

Beauharnais, prince Eugène de, *Mémoires et correspondance politiquese et militaires* (Paris, 1958–60)

Bergeron, Louis, *France under Napoleon* (Princeton, 1981)

Bernardy, F. de, *Eugène de Beauharnais* (Paris, 1973)

Bertaut, Jules, *Le roi Jérôme* (Paris, 1954)

Bertrand, Général comte, *Journal de Général Bertrand, grand maréchal du palais: Cahiers de Sainte-Hélène* (Paris, 1951–59)

Bibesco, princesse, *Lettres d'une fille de Napoléon* (Paris, 1933)

Bingham, Captain D. A., *A Selection from the Letters and Despatches of the First Napoleon* (3 vols, London, 1884)

Blackburn, Julia, *The Emperor's Last Island* (London, 1991)

Boigne, comtesse de, *Mémoires* (Paris, 1971)

Bonaparte, Joseph, *Mémoires et correspondance* (Paris, 1861–5)

Bonaparte, Louis, *Documents historiques et réflexions sur le gouvernemont de la Hollande* (3 vols, Paris, 1820)

Bonaparte, Lucien, *Mémoires secrètes sur la vie privée, publique et littéraire* (2 vols, Paris, 1816)

Bonaparte, Napoléon, *Correspondance de Napoléon Ier* (32 vols, Paris, 1858–70)

—— *Lettres inédite de Napoléon Ier 1799–1815*, (3 vols, Paris 1897)

—— *Correspondance inédite de Napoléon Ier* (3 vols, Paris, 1912–13)

Bourgeat, Jacques (ed.), *Napoléon: Lettres à Joséphine* (Paris, 1941)

Bourrienne, Louis A. F. de, *Mémoires* (10 vols, Paris, 1829)

Boycott-Brown, Martin, *The Road to Rivoli: Napoleon's First Campaign* (London, 2001)

Brent, Harrison, *Pauline Bonaparte: A Woman of Affairs* (New York, 1946)

Breton, Guy, *Napoleon and his Ladies* (trs. Frederick Holt, London, 1965)

Bretonne, L. de, *Les Bonapartes et leurs alliances* (Paris, 1901)

Brett-James, Antony, *The Hundred Days: Napoleon's Last Campaign from Eye-Witness Accounts* (London, 1964)

Broglie, Victor, duc de, *Souvenirs* (Paris, 1886)

Brookes, Dame Mabel, *St Helena Story* (London, 1960)

Bruce, Evangeline, *Napoleon and Josephine: An Improbable Marriage* (London, 1995)

Campbell, Neil, *Napoleon at Fontainebleau and Elba* (London, 1869)

Carrington, Dorothy, *Napoleon and His Parents: On the Threshold of History* (London, 1988)

Casanova, Marthe Arrighi de, *Letizia Bonaparte a été calomneé* (Brussels, 1954)

Castelnau, Jacques, *Madame Tallien* (Paris, 1967)

Castelot, André, *Napoleon's Son* (London, 1960)

—— *Joséphine* (Paris, 1964)

—— *Bonaparte* (Paris, 1967)

—— *Fouché* (Paris, 1990)

Caulaincourt, Louis de, *Memoirs of General de Caulaincourt, Duke of Vicenza, 1812–13* (trs. Hamish Miles, London, 1935)

Cerf, Leon, *Lettres de Napoléon à Joséphine* (Paris, 1929)

Chandler, David, *The Campaigns of Napoleon* (London, 1967)

—— *Napoleon* (London, 1973)

—— *Waterloo: The Hundred Days* (London, 1994)

Chaptal, Baron, *Mes souvenirs de Napoléon* (Paris, 1893)

Chardigny, Louis, *L'homme Napoléon* (Paris, 1987)

Chastenay, comtesse Victorine de, *Mémoires* (Paris, 1896)

Chastenet, Geneviève, *Marie-Louise, l'Impératrice oubliée* (Paris, 1983)

Chateaubriand, vicomte François René de, *Mémoires d'outre-tombe* (Paris, 1951–2)

Chevallier, Bernard and Christophe Pincemaille, *L'Impératrice Joséphine* (Paris, 1936)

Chimay, princesse de, *Madame Tallien* (Paris, 1936)

Chuquet, Arthur, *La jeunesse de Napoléon* (3 vols, Paris, 1897–8)

Cockburn, Sir George, *Napoleon's Last Voyage* (London, 1888)

Cole, Hubert, *The Betrayers: Joachim and Caroline Murat* (London, 1972)

—— *Josephine* (New York, 1963)

Connelly, Owen, *The Gentle Bonapàrte: A Biography of Joseph, Napoleon's Elder Brother* (London, 1968)

Consalvi, Cardinal, *Mémoires* (2 vols, Paris, 1864)

Constant, Benjamin, *Mémoires sur les Cent Jours* (Paris, 1820–22)

Constant, Louis, *Mémoires de Constant, premier valet de chambre de l'Empereur* (6 vols, Paris, 1830)

Cooper, Alfred Duff, *Talleyrand* (London, 1932)

Correspondance de Napoléon Ier (32 vols, Paris, 1858–70)

Correspondance inédite de Napoléon Ier (3 vols, Paris, 1912–13)

Corti, E., *Metternich und die Frauen* (Vienna, 1948)

Creston, Dormer, *In Search of Two Characters: Some Intimate Aspects of Napoleon and his Son* (London, 1947)

Cronin, Vincent, *Napoleon* (London, 1971)

Davout, Maréchal, Louis-Nicolas, duc d'Auerstädt et prince d'Eckmühl, *Correspondance* (Paris, 1885)

De Chair, Somerset (ed.), *Napoleon's Memoirs* (London, 1986)

Decaux, Alain, *Letizia: Mère de l'Empereur* (Paris, 1983)

Deschamp, Léonce, *Pauline Fourès, Notre Dame de l'orient* (Paris, n.d.)

Dixon, Pierson, *Pauline: Napoleon's Favourite Sister* (London, 1964)

Ducrest, Georgette, *Mémoires sur l'Impératrice Joséphine* (3 vols, Paris, 1823–9)

Duhourcau, François, *La Mère de Napoléon* (Paris, 1921)

Durand, Général, *Mémoires sur Napoléon et Marie-Louise*, 1810–14 (Paris, 1886)

Ellis, Geoffrey, *Napoleon* (London, 1997)

Epton, Nina, *Josephine: The Empress and Her Children* (London, 1975)

Erickson, Carolly, *Josephine: A Life of the Empress* (London, 1999)

Fain, Baron Agathon, *Mémoires* (Paris, 1908)

Farinelle, Leonardo, *Maria Luigia: Duchesa di Parma* (Parma, 1983)

Fleuriot de Langle, Paul, *La Paolina, soeur de Napoléon* (Paris, 1944)

—— *Elisa: soeur de Napoléon* (Paris, 1947)

Forsyth, William, *History of the Captivity of Napoleon at St Helena* (3 vols, London, 1853)

Fouché, Joseph, duc d'Otrante, *Mémoires* (Paris, 1957)

Frémaux, Paul, *With Napoleon at St Helena* (London, 1902)

Frugier, Raymond, *Napoléon, essai médico-psychologique* (Paris, 1895)

Gavoty, André, *Les amoureux de l'Impératrice Joséphine* (Paris, 1961)

Geer, Walter, *Napoleon III* (London, 1921)

—— *Napoleon and his Family* (3 vols, London, 1929)

Geyl, Peter, *Napoleon For and Against* (London, 1949)

Giles, Frank, *Bonaparte: England's Prisoner: The Emperor in Exile* (London, 2001)

Girardin, Stanislas de, *Mémoires* (Paris, 1824)

Girod de l'Ain, Gabriel, *Désirée Clary* (Paris, 1959)

—— *Joseph Bonaparte, le roi malgré lui* (Paris, 1970)

Gobineau, Marcel, *Pauline Borghese, soeur fidèle* (Paris, 1958)

Goldsmith, Lewis, *Histoire secrète du cabinet de Napoléon* (Paris, 1814)

Goodspeed, Donald, *Bayonets at St Cloud* (London, 1965)

Gourgaud, General Baron Gaspard, *Sainte-Hélène: Journal inédit de 1815 à 1818* (Paris, 1899)

Granville, Castalia, Countess (ed.), *Lord Granville Leveson-Gower: Private Correspondence 1781–1812* (2 vols, London, 1911)

Gronow, R. H., *The Reminiscences and Recollections of Captain Gronow* (2 vols, London, 1889)

Guedella, Philip, *The Hundred Days* (London, 1934)

Guillemin, Henri, *Madame de Staël, Benjamin Constant, et Napoléon* (Paris, 1959)

Gunn, Peter, *Napoleon's Little Pest* (London, 1983)

Hamilton, Jill, *Marengo: The Myth of Napoleon's Horse* (London, 2000)

Hamilton-Williams, David, *The Fall of Napoleon* (London, 1994)

Hanoteau, Jean, *Le Ménage Beauharnais* (Paris, 1955)

Hapgood, *see* Weider

Hastier, Louis, *Le grand amour de Joséphine* (Paris, 1955)

Haythornthwaite, Philip J., *et al. Napoleon: The Final Verdict* (London, 1996)

Herold, J. Christopher, *Mistress to an Age: A Life of Madame de Staël* (London, 1958)

—— *Bonaparte in Egypt* (London, 1963)

Hibbert, Christopher, *Waterloo: Napoleon's Last Campaign* (New York, 1967)

Hillemand, P., *Pathologie de Napoléon* (Paris, 1970)

Hochschild, Baron, *Désirée, reine de Suède et de Norvège* (Paris, 1888)

Holland, Henry Edward Fox, Baron, *Journal 1818–30* (London, 1923)

Horne, Alistair, *Napoleon: Master of Europe, 1805–7* (London, 1979)

—— *How Far From Austerlitz? Napoleon, 1805–15* (London, 1996)

Hortense, Reine, *Mémoires* (Paris, n.d.)

Howarth, David, *A Near Run Thing: The Day of Waterloo* (London, 1968)

Jackson, Basil, *Notes and Reminiscences of a Staff Officer* (London, 1903)

Janssens, Jacques, *Joséphine de Beauharnais et son temps* (Paris, 1903)

Jones, Procter Paterson (ed.), *Napoleon: An Intimate Account of the Years of Supremacy, 1800–14* (San Francisco, 1992)

Kauffmann, Jean-Paul, *The Dark Room at Longwood: A Voyage to St Helena* (trs. Patricia Clancy, London, 1999)

Kelly, Linda, *Women of the French Revolution* (London, 1987)

Kemble, James, *Napoleon Immortal* (London, 1950)

—— *St Helena during Napoleon's Exile: Correquer's Diary* (London, 1969)

Kircheisen, F. M., *Napoléon* (Paris, 1931)

Knapton, Ernest John, *Empress Josephine* (Cambridge, Mass., 1964)

Korngold, Ralph, *The Last Years of Napoleon* (London, 1960)

Kunstsler, Charles, *La vie privée de l'Impératrice Joséphine* (Paris, 1939)

La Tour du Pin, marquise de, *Mémoires* (Paris, 1914)

Lacout-Gayet, Michel, *Marie Caroline, reine de Naples: une adversaire de Napoléon* (Paris, 1990)

Laflandre-Linden, Louise, *Napoléon et l'île d'Elba* (Paris, 1990)

Larrey, Baron, *Madame Mère* (2 vols, Paris, 1892)

Las Cases, Emmanuel, comte de, *Memorial de Sainte-Hélène: Journal de la vie privée et les conversations de l'Empereur Napoléon à Sainte-Hélène* (Paris, 1823)

Lavalette, A. D. Chamas de, *Mémoires et Souvenirs* (2 vols, Paris, 1831)

Lean, Tangye, *The Napoleonists* (Oxford, 1970)

Lefebvre, Georges, *Napoléon, 1807–1815* (2 vols, London, 1969)

Lentz, Thierry *Lettres inédites de Napoléon Ier* (3 vols, Paris, 1997)

—— *Le Grand Consulat* (Paris, 2000)

Levy, Arthur, *Napoléon et Eugène de Beauharnais* (Paris, 1926)

Leys, Simon, *The Death of Napoleon* (London, 1991)

Macdonald, Marshal E-J-J-A., duc de Tarante, *Souvenirs* (Paris, 1892)

Mackenzie, Norman, *The Escape from Elba: The Fall and Flight of Napoleon, 1814–15* (Oxford, 1982)

McLynn, Frank, *Napoleon: A Biography* (London, 1997)

Madelin, Louis (ed.), *Lettres inédites de Napoléon à Marie-Louise* (Paris, 1935)

Mahan, Alexandre, *Marie-Louise: Le nemésis de Napoléon* (Paris, 1933)

Maitland, F.L., *The Narrative of the Surrender of Bonaparte and of His Residence on Board H.M.S. Bellerophon* (London, 1826)

Malcolm, Lady, *A Diary of St Helena: The Journal of Lady Malcolm, 1816–17* (ed. Sir Arthur Wilson, 2 vols, 1846).

Mallet du Pin, *Mémoires* (2 vols, Paris, 1851)

Manceron, Claude, *Napoleon Recaptures Paris* (London, 1969)

Mansel, Philip, *The Eagle in Splendour: Napoleon I and his Court* (London, 1987)

Marchand, Louis-Joseph, *Mémoires* (2 vols, Paris, 1952)

—— *In Napoleon's Shadow: Being the First English Language Edition of the Complete Memoirs of L.-J. Marchand* (produced by Proctor Jones, San Francisco, 1996)

Markham, Felix, *Napoleon* (London, 1963)

—— *The Bonapartes* (London, 1975)

Marmont, Auguste, Marshal de, duc de Raguse, *Mémoires* (Paris, 1857)

Marmottan, P., *Elisa Bonaparte* (Paris, 1898)

Marquiset, Alfred, *Une merveilleuse: Fortunée Hamelin* (Paris, 1909)

Marshall-Cornwall, Sir James, *Massena* (London, 1965)

—— *Napoleon as Military Commander* (London, 1967)

Martin, Andy, *Napoleon the Novelist* (London, 2000)

Martineau, Gilbert, *Napoleon's St Helena* (trs. Frances Partridge, London, 1968)

—— *Napoleon Surrenders* (London, 1971)

—— *Napoleon's Last Journey* (London, 1976)

—— *Madame Mère* (Paris, 1980)

—— *Marie-Louise* (Paris, 1985)

Masson, Frédéric, *Napoléon et les femmes* (3 vols, 1893–1902)

—— *Napoléon chez lui* (2 vols, 1894)

—— *Napoléon Inconnu* (2 vols, Paris, 1895)

—— *Joséphine: Impératrice et reine* (Paris, 1907)

—— (ed.) *Private Diaries of the Empress Marie-Louise* (London, 1922)

—— *Napoleon at St Helena* (trs. L.B. Frewer, Oxford 1949)

—— *Napoleon's St Helena* (trs. Frances Partridge, London, 1968)

—— *Joséphine répudiée* (Paris, n.d.)

—— *Madame Bonaparte* (Paris, n.d.)

—— *Napoléon et sa famille* (13 vols, Paris, n.d.)

Mauguin, Georges, *L'Impératrice Joséphine: Anecdotes et curiosités* (Paris, n.d.)

Maury, René, *L'assassin de Napoléon* (Paris, 1994)

Melchior-Bonnet, Bernardine, *Jérôme Bonaparte* (Paris, 1979)

Méneval, Baron de, *Napoléon et Marie-Louise: Souvenirs historiques de Baron Méneval* (3 vols, Paris, 1844)

Metternich, Prince Klemens, *Mémoires, documents et écrits divers* (Paris, 1880–84)

Meynell, Henry, *Conversations with Napoleon at St Helena* (London, 1911)

Miot de Melito, comte A. F., *Mémoires de comte Miot de Melito* (3 vols, Paris, 1873)

Montholon, comtesse de, *Souvenirs de Sainte-Hélène* (2 vols, 1846)

Montholon, Général comte de, *Récite de la captivité de l'Empereur à Sainte-Hélène* (2 vols, 1846)

Mossiker, Frances, *Napoléon et Joséphine* (New York, 1964)

Mounier, Baron, *Souvenirs intimes* (Paris, 1896)

Narbonne, Bernard, *Pauline Bonaparte: La Venus Impériale* (Paris, 1963)

Nicolson, Nigel, *Napoleon: 1812* (London, 1985)

Ober, Frederick A., *Josephine: Empress of the French* (London, 1901)

Oddie, L. M., *Napoleon II* (London, 1952)

Oman, Carola, *Napoleon's Viceroy: Eugène de Beauharnais* (London, 1966)

O'Meara, Barry Edward, *Napoleon in Exile* (2 vols, London, 1822)

Orieux, Jean, *Talleyrand* (Paris, 1970)

Ortzen, Len, *Imperial Venus: The Story of Pauline Bonaparte Borghese* (London, 1974)

Ouvrard, G. J., *Mémoires* (Paris, 1826)

Palmer, Alan, *Napoleon in Russia* (London, 1967)

—— *An Encyclopaedia of Napoleon's Europe* (London, 1984)

—— *Bernadotte: Napoleon's Marshal, Sweden's King* (London, 1990)

—— *Napoleon and Marie Louise, the Second Empress* (London, 2001)

Palmstierna, C. F. (ed.), *Lettres de Marie-Louise à Napoléon* (Paris, 1965)

Papillard, François, *Cambacérès* (Paris, 1961)

Park, Julian (ed.), *Napoleon in Captivity: The Reports of Count Balmain, Russian Commissioner on the Island of St Helena* (London, 1928)

Péretti, Lydie, *Letizia Bonaparte* (Paris, 1922)

Piétri, François, *Lucien Bonaparte* (Paris, 1930)

Pincemaille, Christophe *see* Chevallier

Poniatowski, Michel, *Talleyrand et le Consulat* (Paris, 1954)

—— *Talleyrand et le Directoire* (Paris, 1982)

Potocka, Countess Anna *Mémoires* (Paris, 1897)

Pougin, Arthur, *Giuseppina Grassini* (Paris, 1923)

Ratcliffe, Bertram, *Prelude to Fame: An Account of the Early Life of Napoleon up to the Battle of Montenotte* (London, 1981)

Récamier, J-F-J-A, *Souvenirs et correspondance* (Paris, 1859)

Rémusat, Mme Claire de *Mémoires* (3 vols, Paris, 1880)

—— *Lettres de Madame de Rémusat* (2 vols, Paris, 1881)

Richardson, Frank, *Napoleon: Bisexual Emperor* (London, 1972)

—— *Napoleon's Death: An Inquest* (London, 1974)

Roberts, Andrew, *Napoleon and Wellington* (London, 2001)

Robiquet, J., *La vie quotidienne au temps de Napoléon* (Paris, 1943)

Roederer, comte Pierre-Louis de, *Journal* (Paris, 1909)

Roncière, C. de la (ed.), *Letters of Napoleon to Marie-Louise* (London, n.d.)

Rose, J. Holland, *The Personality of Napoleon* (London, 1912)

—— *The Life of Napoleon* (London, 1913)

Rosebery, Lord, *Napoleon: The Last Phase* (London 1900)

Saint-Armand, Imbert de, *The Memoirs of the Empress Marie-Louise* (London, 1886)

Saint-Denis, Louis Etienne, *From the Tuileries to St Helena* (trs. E. S. Stokes, London, 1902)

Saint-Elme, Ida, *Mémoires* (Paris, 1827–9)

Saunders, Edith, *Napoleon and Mademoiselle George* (London, 1958)

Savant, Jean, *Napoléon et Joséphine* (Paris, 1955)

Schom, Alan, *One Hundred Days: Napoleon's Road to Waterloo* (London, 1993)

—— *Napoleon Bonaparte* (London, 1997)

Schur, Nathan, *Napoleon in the Holy Land* (London, 1999)

Seward, Desmond, *Napoleon's Family* (London, 1986)

Shaw, Clement, *Letizia Bonaparte* (London, 1928)

Smith, Digby, *1813, Leipzig: Napoleon and the Battle of the Nations* (London, 2001)

Solmi, Angelo, *Maria Luigia, Duchessa di Parma* (Milan, 1985)

Sorokine, Dimitri, *La jeunesse de Napoléon* (Paris, 1976)

Staël, Germaine de, *Mémoires* (Paris, 1818)

Stirling, Monica, *A Pride of Lions: A Portrait of Napoleon's Mother* (London, 1961)

Stokoe, John, *With Napoleon at St Helena* (London, 1902)

Strawson, John, *The Duke and the Emperor* (London, 1994)

Sutherland, Christine, *Marie Walewska: Napoleon's Great Love* (London, 1979)

Talleyrand-Périgord, Charles-Maurice de, *Mémoires* (Paris, 1891–2)

Talma, François-Joseph, *Lettres inédites de Talma à la Princesse Pauline Bonaparte* (Paris, 1911)

Thiébault, Général Baron, *Mémoires* (1895–6)

Thiry, Jean, *Bonaparte en Egypt* (Paris, 1973)

—— *Les années de jeunesse de Napoleon Bonaparte, 1769–96* (Paris, 1975)

Thompson, J. M., *Napoleon Self-Revealed* (London, 1934)

—— *Napoleon Bonaparte: His Rise and Fall* (Oxford, 1952)

Thornton, M.J., *Napoleon After Waterloo* (Stanford, 1968)

Trotter, John Bernard, *Memoirs of the Later Years of C. J. Fox* (London, 1811)

Tschudi, Clara, *Napoleon's Mother* (London, 1900)

Tulard, Jean, (ed.) *Napoléon: Lettres d'amour à Joséphine* (Paris, 1981)

—— *Napoléon à Saint-Hélène* (Paris, 1981)

—— *Napoleon: The Myth of the Saviour* (trs. Teresa Waugh, London, 1984)

—— *La vie quotidienne des Français sous Napoléon* (Paris, 1988)

—— *Napoleon II* (Paris, 1992)

—— *Murat* (Paris, 2000)

Turquan, Joseph, *Caroline Murat* (Paris, 1899)

—— *The Sisters of Napoleon: Elisa, Pauline and Caroline* (London, 1908)

—— *The Love Affairs of Napoleon* (trs. J. Lewis May, London, 1909)

Vandal, Comte Albert, *Napoléon et Alexandre Ier* (Paris, 1891–6)

—— *L'Avènement de Bonaparte* (Paris, 1903)

Vigée-Le Brun, Marie-Louise-Elisabeth, *Souvenirs* (Paris, 1895)

Vossler, H. A., *With Napoleon in Russia: 1812 – The Diary of Lt. H. Vossler, a soldier of the Grand Army, 1812–13* (trs. Walter Wallich, London, 1998)

Wagener, Françoise, *Madame Récamier* (Paris, 1986)

Warden, William, *Letters from St Helena* (London, 1817)

Weider, Ben with Emile Gueguen, *Napoleon: The Man who Shaped Europe* (London, 2000)

Weider, Ben and David Hapgood, *The Murder of Napoleon* (New York, 1982)

Weil, Maurice-Henri, *Joachim Murat, roi de Naples* (Paris, 1909–10)

Weiner, Margery, *The Parvenu Princesses: Elisa, Pauline and Caroline Bonaparte* (London, 1964)

Wilson, R. McNair, *Josephine: The Portrait of a Woman* (London, 1929)

Wilson-Smith, Timothy, *Napoleon and his Artists* (London, 1996)

Young, Norwood, *Napoleon in Exile, Elba* (London, 1914)

—— *Napoleon in Exile, St Helena* (2 vols, London, 1915)

INDEX

In this index Napoleon's name is abbreviated to N. His brothers and sisters and Eugène and Hortense de Beauharnais are referred to by their Christian names. Josephine is referred to as Rose before her marriage to Napoleon, as Josephine thereafter.